"The Penalty Is Death"

"The Penalty Is Death"

U.S. Newspaper Coverage of Women's Executions

Marlin Shipman

University of Missouri Press
Columbia and London

Copyright © 2002 by
The Curators of the University of Missouri
University of Missouri Press, Columbia, Missouri 65201
Printed and bound in the United States of America
All rights reserved
5 4 3 2 1   06 05 04 03 02

Library of Congress Cataloging-in-Publication Data

Shipman, Marlin.
    The penalty is death : U.S. newspaper coverage of women's executions / Marlin
Shipman.
        p.   cm.
    Includes bibliographical references and index.
    ISBN 0-8262-1386-3
    1. Capital punishment—United States—History.   2. Executions and executioners—
Press coverage—United States—History.   3. Women prisoners—United States—
History.   I. Title.
HV8699.US S47 2002
364.66'082'0973—dc21

                                                                                    2002017955

⊛™ This paper meets the requirements of the
American National Standard for Permanence of Paper
for Printed Library Materials, Z39.48, 1984.

Text Design: Stephanie Foley
Jacket Design: Kristie Lee
Typesetter: The Composing Room of Michigan, Inc.
Printer and Binder: The Maple-Vail Book Manufacturing Group
Typefaces: Franklin Gothic and Palatino

Quotations from "Jury Hears of Potions Dealt by Anna Hahn," by Virginia Gardner, 16
October 1937, copyrighted 1937, Chicago Tribune Company. All rights reserved. Used
with permission.

Quotations from "Mrs. Dean Pays Death Penalty," by Sidney E. Elsner, 16 January 1954,
© 1954 The Plain Dealer. All rights reserved. Reprinted with permission.

TO DONNA, SARAH, AND MARY,
THE WONDERFUL WOMEN IN MY LIFE

Contents

Preface

THIS BOOK HAS BEEN IN THE MAKING since 1990 when I first became interested in how the newspaper press covered executions. That year, in June, Arkansas had its first executions since 1964. Two men were executed within a week. The fact that press coverage was enormous prompted me to do some research on the media and capital punishment. Although I found scattered references to media coverage in books and articles about the general topic of capital punishment, I found no book that specifically looked at newspaper coverage of capital punishment. That seemed odd to me for several reasons, one of which is that some scholars have said the media are second only to the courts for protecting the rights of defendants condemned to death.[1] That is a heavy responsibility. It also raises the question of just how the press has performed when reporting about condemned defendants. There is anecdotal evidence of the press playing an important role in preventing innocent people from being executed.[2] But if media effects can be helpful, then they can also be harmful, a prospect noted in fact as well as in fiction, such as Heinrich Böll's *Lost Honour of Katharina Blum*. Some authors have said that a benefit of ending the death penalty would be "no tasteless media coverage of executions."[3] I naively began work on what I hoped would be a book about newspapers and capital punishment in the United States, but I soon realized that any treatment of the full topic would have to be postponed for several years. However, one aspect of the larger topic interested me more than others: how newspapers covered the executions of women in the United States. Although there was a book written about women and the death penalty during the twentieth century, little research of any kind had been done on the press and executions of women.[4] That is the subject of this book.

This book is not about the economics of capital punishment, or about theological or philosophical issues relating to capital punishment, although parts of the book deal with those subjects. Nor is this book about politics and the death penalty, although that topic also is discussed. My hope is that the book will accomplish several things.

1. Shirley Dicks, ed., *Congregation of the Condemned*.
2. See, for example, John Hohenberg, ed., *The Pulitzer Prize Story II*, 46–53.
3. Franklin E. Zimring and Gordon Hawkins, *Capital Punishment and the American Agenda*, 164.
4. Kathleen A. O'Shea, *Women and the Death Penalty in the United States, 1900–1998*.

First, it will demonstrate how women have been stereotyped in the newspaper press during the past 150 years. Second, it will illustrate how the newspaper press has consistently reported on sensational cases. Third, it will show how the development of journalistic styles and techniques is evidenced in stories about the executions of women. Fourth, it will summarize some of the anecdotal ideas about how the press reports on the death penalty. On a larger scale, the book seeks to stimulate discussions of the death penalty that are more human and less abstract and statistical. I have tried to achieve this goal by using detailed descriptions of individual cases, so that readers will have an idea of who the women were and why society decided these women should die for their crimes.

Each chapter in the book will contain at least one case that serves as an illustration of a point, or points. Some of them are reconstructed stories, written as narratives. They are detailed. I have purposely chosen this approach. In his book *Voices against Death*, Philip English Mackey relates that William Styron's 1962 magazine article resulted in pleas for clemency for a Connecticut death row inmate who did receive a last-minute commutation. Mackey contends the article's effectiveness stemmed from its concentration on a real person and not on capital punishment as an abstract issue.[5] The approach I use will give readers a deeper understanding of the stories I have chosen to feature because it allows the telling of each story as it unfolded, thus achieving a measure of cohesiveness for the whole.

5. Mackey, ed., *Voices against Death: American Opposition to Capital Punishment, 1787–1975,* 247.

Acknowledgments

ANY BOOK IS THE COLLECTIVE WORK of a number of people, and this one is no exception. Although most people contributed no actual words to the book, it could never have reached fruition without their help. I have many people to thank. Librarians and historians at state historical societies were most helpful. Their passion for their work showed not only in their willingness to help, but also in their eagerness to do so.

Historical societies in Vermont, Nevada, Arkansas, and Minnesota were especially helpful, and space prevents me from naming all the librarians who led me to materials and gave me tips along the way. I will never forget their enthusiasm and help. My special thanks must go to Margarett Daniels and Patsy Spurlock, who work in Interlibrary Loan at Arkansas State University. They both filled more of my requests for microfilm than I (and I am sure they) care to remember, and did so with unfailing good humor and expertise. They showed interest in this project, and I cannot thank them enough.

I also owe a great debt of gratitude to Arkansas State University for providing me with several small grants, and especially for providing me with a leave of absence for a semester so I could wrap up the writing of the manuscript. My colleagues listened patiently to endless stories about executions, a subject that I am sure was not always palatable. My college dean and my department chair were both supportive of my efforts, and I thank them.

My wife, Donna; my daughter, Sarah; my mother, Mary; my sister, Missy; and one of my former Penn State teachers, Dan Pfaff, all supplied support and enthusiasm during the years I worked on this manuscript. I thank them all, most especially my wife, who went through the ups and downs with me and was always supportive. The editors at the University of Missouri Press, especially managing editor Jane Lago and acquisitions editor Maurice Manring, provided invaluable advice. Copy editor Annette Wenda's skill greatly improved the manuscript.

My greatest debt is owed to my former teacher Don Smith, who also is my mentor. Don, now retired from teaching journalism at Penn State, graciously consented—indeed, volunteered—to read the first draft of the manuscript. His intelligent questions and his suggestions for improving the manuscript helped me immensely. He saved me from a number of bonehead errors. If this book achieves any degree of success, a good deal of the credit goes to Don. Any faults in the book are my own.

"The Penalty Is Death"

Introduction

SOME AUTHORS CONTEND THAT SOCIOLOGISTS have ignored women criminals. Perhaps that is because, as legal historian Lawrence M. Friedman says, women criminals have been somewhat rare during U.S. history.[1] Women commit far fewer violent crimes than do men. Men are much more likely to commit murder than are women, although arrests of juvenile girls for violent crimes increased 25 percent from 1992 to 1996, whereas the rate for boys remained the same. In the ten years between 1983 and 1992, the violent-crime arrest rate for girls increased 85 percent, whereas it increased 50 percent for boys. However, the murder rate among juvenile girls stayed about the same during the same ten years.[2]

Since the death penalty was reinstated in 1976, only 7 women have been executed in the United States, whereas more than 700 men have been executed. Executions of women have been rare throughout U.S. history. The colonies first executed a woman in 1632, and since then about 560 women have been executed. Because there are far fewer women than there are men on death rows in the United States, the comparative numbers are not likely to change soon. Only about 50 women are on death rows, compared to more than 3,000 men.

Because few women have been executed, one might expect enormous news coverage when a woman is put to death. That is because unusualness is one of the traditional criteria of "things that make news." There are some well-known cases of massive press coverage, such as the execution of Ruth Snyder in New York in 1928, and of Ethel Rosenberg in New York, under federal authority, in 1953. Snyder's trial has been called one of the few trials to attract national attention.[3] It also, according to one book, brought about an increase in membership in capital punishment–reform organizations. Michael Emery and Edwin Emery state that a surreptitious photo taken at Snyder's execution drew so much public interest that the *New York Daily News* sold 250,000 extra copies, then reprinted the story and sold an additional 750,000 copies. Texas's execution of Betty Lou Beets in February 2000 illustrated how executions of women often draw na-

1. See, for example, Ann Jones, *Women Who Kill*, xv. Friedman, *Crime and Punishment in American History*, 211–13.
2. "Women Commit Many Assault Crimes," *Jonesboro (Ark.) Sun*, 6 December 1999; "More Teen-age Girls Turn to Violent Crime," *Arkansas Democrat-Gazette*, 1 June 1998.
3. See, for example, Friedman, *Crime and Punishment*, 399.

tional media interest. A leading U.S. authority on the death penalty says Beets's execution received widespread press attention only because she was a woman.[4]

However, many other executions of women received enormous amounts of local, regional, and sometimes even national press coverage, although they are less well remembered. Furthermore, reprints of newspaper articles about a woman's execution did not begin with Snyder. In 1873, when Susan Eberhart was hanged in Georgia, the *Atlanta Constitution* ran a story that covered slightly more than four full columns of text. The next day, in an editorial in the Sunday edition, the *Constitution* wrote: "There has been so much interest felt in the execution of Miss Eberhart, and such a demand for our special, lengthy and graphic account of the affair, covering over four columns, that we have been compelled to republish it in this morning's paper."[5]

The rarity of executions of women does fulfill the journalistic "news value" of unusualness. Nonetheless, the mere fact that a woman was executed does not necessarily mean that the news coverage will be extensive. Executions of women sometimes receive more news coverage because of the nature of the crimes, such as poisonings or ax murders, or killings of family members for insurance money. Sometimes the story line contains sexual intrigue in the form of love triangles. Historically, there has also been the social abhorrence associated with executing a woman, although that might be changing.

During most of U.S. history, the social stereotype has dictated that women should be more virtuous than men. Women were (and are) expected to be good wives and good mothers, and when they breached those expectations by being involved in love affairs that led to murder, or by killing children or spouses, that increased the news value.[6]

Another common belief was that society should protect women—even women who murdered. The image of women as gentle, caring, and motherly has made executions of women more difficult than executions of their male counterparts, especially when those making the decisions were male, as they usually were. Moreover, during most of the country's history, women were expected to be subservient to men and especially to their husbands. Women who killed husbands not only committed crimes but also violated deeply held norms about how women should behave.

4. Mackey, *Voices against Death*, xxxix; Emery and Emery, *The Press and America*, 281–86; Robert Anthony Phillips, "No Gender Equality on Death Row."

5. "The Execution of Miss Eberhart," *Atlanta Constitution*, 4 May 1873.

6. The idea of women as good wives and good mothers held well into the twentieth century. An editorial paragraph in the *Florence (S.C.) Morning News* said, "Television will reconcile the housewife to her job. She hates it now because she misses seeing people" (2 January 1947).

This increased news coverage. Women sometimes broke social norms in other ways. For example, when women displayed characteristics more often associated with men, such as being a desperado, it captured the press's fancy.

Stereotyping Women

Women as Virtuous

In 1859, the *St. Paul Pioneer and Democrat* criticized Ann Bilansky's infidelity to her husband, although some stories also reported his unfaithfulness, drinking, and four marriages. However, Ann Bilansky bore the brunt of criticism about her lack of marital virtue. The *Democrat* said murder is worse when a wife poisons her husband, because she pretends to love him while she "lies with the interlocked caress of simulated love upon the bosom which she stabs" and plans the murder while acting "in the domestic attentions of the wife."[7] If she murdered, then she deserved punishment, but the press held her to a higher moral standard in relation to her infidelity than it did her husband, and that seemed to make murder even worse for a woman than for a man.

New Jersey hanged Margaret Meierhoffer in 1881 for murdering her husband. The *New York Times* noted in earlier stories that she had been "intimate with three men" who visited her frequently, and had cheated on her husband when he was off fighting in the Civil War. Stories, though, also noted that her husband always had a bad temper, which became worse after the war. One story said she had him arrested twice for assault and he once threatened to cut her throat because he did not like the way she had cooked some meat.[8]

The *Atlanta Constitution* preached an editorial sermon in 1873 about Susan Eberhart, who had helped her lover murder his wife the previous year. The *Constitution* said Eberhart not only committed murder, but also committed adultery and "violated the sanctity of marriage." Press moralizing continued until at least the early 1900s. When Mary Rogers murdered her husband in Vermont and was executed in 1905, the *Burlington Daily Free Press* said in an editorial titled "The Wages of Sin" that her execution would deter other Vermont wives "tempted by illicit love" from murdering their husbands.[9] The newspaper said Rogers "had not a spark of wom-

7. "The Bilansky Poison Case," *St. Paul Pioneer and Democrat*, 9 June 1859.

8. "A Tramp Kills a Farmer," *New York Times*, 11 October 1879; "The Murder of Meierhoffer," ibid., 13 October 1879; "The West Orange Murder Case," ibid., 24 January 1880.

9. "Ought a Woman to Be Hanged!" *Atlanta Constitution*, 27 April 1873; "The Wages of Sin," *Burlington Daily Free Press*, 9 December 1905.

anliness in her." This is not to say that the women's actions in any of these cases were justified; rather, the press wrote about the defendants in such a way that their infidelity seemed almost as heinous as the murders they committed.

Gov. Martin Davey of Ohio voiced the societal perceptions of women in 1938 when he said he would not commute Anna Hahn's death sentence but that his failure to act should not be taken to mean that he accepted the idea of women's equality. Davey said, "[I]t seems to me that woman is cast in a finer mold than man. . . . I cannot believe that chivalry has become lifeless and meaningless in this modern world."[10]

Although the press at times lamented the governors' agonies, the newspapers almost always supported the decisions to execute, and sometimes the newspapers did not agree with gubernatorial soul-searching. The *New York Times,* in an editorial, said of Anna Antonio and her coconspirators, "[I]f anyone ought ever to be executed for murder, these three should have been." The *St. Louis Post-Dispatch,* three and a half years later, used almost the exact language when it editorially supported Marie Porter's execution for aiding in the murder of her brother on what was to be his wedding day. The *Post-Dispatch* wrote that "countless persons will agree that if ever a woman should have been required to pay with her life for a crime," it was Porter.[11] The *Times,* from the mid-1800s to the early 1900s, opposed hanging women because it said that was not a proper punishment for women. However, the *Times* supported all New York governors' decisions to not commute a death sentence for a woman, saying that the legislature, not the governor, should act. Both the *Times* and the *Post-Dispatch* have been strong opponents of capital punishment during the past three decades.

Women as Kind, Gentle

The press also reflected the societal belief that women should be kinder and gentler than men, especially toward their children. The *Philadelphia Inquirer* termed Sarah Whiteling, who was hanged in 1888 for killing her husband and two children, an "unnatural mother." And when Catharine Miller said good-bye to her children during a meeting the day before her 1881 execution, the *Williamsport (Pa.) Daily Banner* said she did so "with a mother's emotions" and that she "gave vent to those holy instincts that belong to her nature."[12] Such expressions of outrage and expectations of

10. "Text of Davey's Statement Dooming Anna Marie Hahn," *Cincinnati Enquirer,* 7 December 1938.

11. "A Painful Duty," *New York Times,* 11 August 1934; "The Lesson of a Criminal Case," *St. Louis Post-Dispatch,* 28 January 1938.

12. "Appalling Revelation," *Philadelphia Inquirer,* 13 June 1888; "Hanged! George Smith and Catharine Miller Executed To-Day," *Williamsport (Pa.) Daily Banner,* 4 February 1881.

"motherly instinct" were not found, for example, in coverage of Christina Riggs, executed in Arkansas in 2000 for murdering her two children.

In the late nineteenth century, the *Elko (Nev.) Weekly Independent* said of Elizabeth Potts, hanged for murder in 1890, and of women in general: "To her we look for everything that is gentle and kind and tender; and we can scarcely conceive her capable of committing the highest crime known to the law." Press expectations that women should be kinder than men continued well into the twentieth century. The *Burlington Daily Free Press* expressed such sentiments in 1905, when it said that one "instinctively thinks of the sex as the gentler in every sense," but that Mary Rogers, by murdering her husband, had "unsexed" herself. Almost fifty years later, a *Los Angeles Times* columnist, writing about Barbara Graham who was executed in California for murder, asked, what could turn "what we idealize as the gentleness of womanhood into a monster of hate and torture?"[13]

The press criticized women who broke the stereotype of being subservient. An Elko, Nevada, newspaper said of Elizabeth Potts, "[I]t is a notorious fact that she wears the pants" in the family. A rival newspaper noted her lack of femininity by saying that while she was jailed, she "put in her time swearing at everybody and everything."[14] Similarly, the press termed Emeline Meaker of Vermont a strong, violent, and muscular "virago" who ruled her household. Both Elizabeth Potts and Irene Schroeder, executed in 1930 in Pennsylvania, were depicted as rough, tough, domineering types in western newspapers in Nevada and Arizona, respectively.

By the end of the twentieth century, the press's and society's expectations had changed. A columnist wrote in 1998 that Texas should not spare Karla Faye Tucker just because she was a woman. The author said women could be just as violent and aggressive as men and said the idea that women are defenseless and need men's protection "is probably the last vestige of institutionalized sexism that needs to be rubbed out." Likewise, the *Houston Chronicle* said in an editorial that exempting women from the same punishment as men "undermines their position as equals in society."[15]

As the twentieth century progressed, the press less often criticized women who committed adultery and murder. More often, the condemnation came from others who were sources in news stories. This is not to say that opinions about women's roles do not find their way into today's

13. "The Death Sentence," *Elko (Nev.) Weekly Independent,* 24 March 1889; "Mary Rogers's Fate Sealed," *Burlington Daily Free Press,* 28 November 1905; Mary Ann Callan, "A Personal Verdict," *Los Angeles Times,* 6 June 1955.

14. "Should the Pottses Hang?" *Elko (Nev.) Weekly Independent,* 2 April 1890; "Executed," *Elko (Nev.) Free Press,* 21 June 1890.

15. Robyn Blumner, "Even in Death Chamber Sexism Is Alive and Well," *Houston Chronicle,* 18 January 1998; "Justice Demands," ibid., 18 January 1998.

press via more subtle methods, such as an editor's word choice or a reporter's selection of sources for stories.

A judge in Bonnie Brown Heady's case in 1953 noted that Heady and her cohort, Carl Austin Hall, were living in common-law marriage, but said that Missouri did not recognize such marriages; the judge apparently meant to imply that the two were living in adultery. In the 1940s, North Carolina's governor also noted that a pair of condemned defendants had been living in adultery for three years before their crime. Common-law marriages and adultery have little to do with kidnapping and murder charges, but they are examples of a society, which the press mirrored, that held women to higher standards of virtue than those expected of men.

News stories also more often portrayed condemned women as hard, unfeeling, or demonic in early stories, but as more "womanly" and gentle in stories near the execution. The Pittsburgh press termed Martha Grinder a "homicidal monomaniac," a "demon," and a "fiend" after her arrest and during her trial. However, at her hanging, she had a "sweet smile" on her face and seemed almost angelic. The press made similar shifts in its descriptions of Sarah Whiteling in 1888, who was termed a "fiend" and without "the least trace of grief" in early stories. Later stories detailed her religious faith and her prayers. The *New York Times* called Bridget Durgan a "fiend incarnate" when she was sentenced to death for murder, but depicted her in greatly different terms at her 1867 execution. The same process applies to women throughout the twentieth century, although the labels applied to them were not as harsh early in the story process.[16]

Labeling Women Defendants

The press had difficulty categorizing women who murdered in the nineteenth century. Perhaps that is why it often labeled them, but by so doing it in some cases virtually dehumanized them. Martha Place, executed in New York in 1898, was described as having a face "that reminds one of a rat's, and the bright, but changeless eyes somehow strengthen the impression." The press labeled many women murderers "fiends" or "demons" in the nineteenth century, including Mary Surratt, hanged in 1865 as a coconspirator in the assassination of President Abraham Lincoln. The press described her as "a large Amazonian class of woman, square built, masculine hands, rather full face, dark gray, lifeless eye."[17]

16. See, for example, "The Trial of Mrs. Grinder," *Pittsburgh Post*, 24–28 October 1865; "Another Hanging," ibid., 20 January 1866; "The Modern Borgia," *Philadelphia Inquirer*, 14 June 1888; "Mrs. Whiteling's Fate," ibid., 26 June 1889; "The Coriell Murder, Bridget Durgan Found Guilty of Murder in First Degree," *New York Times*, 1 June 1867; and "Execution of Bridget Durgan," ibid., 31 August 1867.

17. "Mrs. Place Convicted," *New York Times*, 9 July 1898; "The Trial of the Assassins," ibid., 15 May 1865.

By the twentieth century, descriptions of women murderers as fiends or demons had largely ceased, but other labels were applied. In the 1920s, the *New Orleans Times-Picayune* tagged Ada LeBoeuf as "Louisiana's love pirate," a "small town Cleopatra," and "the siren of the swamps," among other things. Irene Schroeder, in 1930, was the "blonde tiger," the "gun girl," "Iron Irene," "Irene of the six-shooters," and the "animal woman." Labeling defendants continued throughout the twentieth century with Karla Faye Tucker called a "drug-abusing, motorcycle-riding, hot-headed prostitute"; and Judy Buenoano and Betty Lou Beets "black widow" killers.[18]

The labels were not always so blatantly negative, especially in the twentieth century. The *Los Angeles Times* described Louise Peete, on trial in 1945, as "a plump and graying defendant," and said she appeared as calm as "a kindly, serene old lady of threescore years talking with a long-time friend" at a press conference following her conviction. Peete had been convicted on separate occasions of murdering two people. The *Houston Chronicle*, perhaps expressing the almost dual nature of some death row defendants, termed Tucker a "Bible-reading, angelic-looking woman" with "pink-tinged lips, lightly freckled face and cascading dark curls" who "smiled her way into hundreds of thousands—if not millions—of homes."[19]

The press often applied the "grandmother" label in the twentieth century. It was used in news stories in the 1930s to describe May Carey, in the 1940s for Ethel Spinnelli, in the 1950s for Dovie Dean, in the 1960s for Elizabeth Duncan, in the 1980s for Velma Barfield, and in 2000 for Betty Lou Beets. Quite often, the grandmother label was used near the time of execution, or in stories describing the execution.

The use of labels, either positive or negative, can create the kind of symbolic meanings that former journalist Walter Lippmann describes in a political context in his 1922 book, *Public Opinion*. The labels might not come close to describing a person, but they are a quick, handy way of describ-

18. "Mrs. LeBoeuf's Iron Nerve Still Refuses to Yield," *New Orleans Times-Picayune*, 31 July 1927; "LeBoeuf Murder Case Will Reach Jury Tomorrow," ibid., 4 August 1927; "Ada LeBoeuf Unafraid of Noose Judging from Courtroom Smile As Veniremen Answer Grim Quiz," ibid., 31 July 1927; "'Animal Woman' Denies Being 'Trigger Girl' Wanted As Killer," *Phoenix Gazette*, 15 January 1930; "Blond 'Tiger Woman' Left Trail of Crime across U.S.," ibid., 22 March 1930; "Gungirl on Stand in Own Defense," *Philadelphia Inquirer*, 19 March 1930; "Gungirl and Dague Calm As They Go to Death in Chair," *Philadelphia Evening Bulletin*, 23 February 1931; "Identify 'Trigger Woman,'" *Phoenix Gazette*, 16 January 1930; "Tucker Dies after Apologizing," *Houston Chronicle*, 4 February 1998; "Buenoano Goes to Chair Appearing Small, Scared," *Orlando Sentinel*, 31 March 1998; "Beets the Subject of True-Crime Novel," *Athens (Tex.) Daily Review*, 2 March 2000.

19. "'My Mind above Fear,' Mrs. Peete Tells Herself," *Los Angeles Times*, 30 May 1945; "Should Tucker Be Executed?" *Houston Chronicle*, 1 February 1998.

ing complex human beings. However, those same people might have changed much during the years between a crime and an execution, and the negative labels are more likely to be applied at the time of the crime or before or during trial, which means they can be more damaging. The more positive labeling often occurs at the time of execution. That fact is illustrated by the terms used to describe Elizabeth Duncan, executed in California in 1962. Depicted as angry and accused of perhaps threatening physical harm to a prosecutor during her trial, by the time of her execution, the *Los Angeles Times* said she was "like a proud woman who had achieved the ultimate in poise and dignity."[20] The changing labels might be absolutely correct inasmuch as some people probably do change a great deal after a crime. However, once a person is sentenced to death, it is too late to reverse the effects of labels that might have been simplistic or erroneous.

Women's Physical Appearances

The press consistently stereotyped women defendants and at times trivialized trials and executions by paying unusual attention to what women wore and to their physical features. Most of the cases show a routine, although specific, description of attire, and in almost every case involving a white defendant, there was some mention made of how she dressed. The press could be critical, as when the *Philadelphia Evening Bulletin* noted that Irene Schroeder wore to her execution "a gray artificial-silk dress, loose and poorly fitting." In some twentieth-century cases, the descriptions were woven throughout the reporting process and became important parts of the stories. The *Chicago Tribune* dwelled on Anna Hahn's clothing during her 1935 trial, and also gave detailed reports of what jurors and witnesses wore. Portions of the news stories resembled a report about a fashion show, such as when the *Tribune* reported in depth on Hahn's makeup and clothing each day during her trial or described a witness as wearing a "super fashionably short" skirt.[21]

The *New Orleans Times-Picayune* did perhaps the most detailed reporting about a defendant's clothing or makeup in its descriptions of Ada LeBoeuf, on trial in 1927 for murdering her husband. The newspaper described in detail each day what she wore, and tried to glean meaning on occasion, saying one day she wore "piroge green" and on another "virgin white" for her testimony. The newspaper also harshly criticized LeBoeuf's use of makeup.[22]

Barbara Graham, executed in California in 1955, went to her death

20. "Mrs. Duncan Dies with 2 Conspirators," *Los Angeles Times*, 9 August 1962.

21. "Gungirl and Dague Calm As They Go to Death in Chair," *Philadelphia Evening Bulletin*, 23 February 1931; "Hahn Defense Hunts Expert to Beat Chair," *Chicago Tribune*, 29 October 1937.

22. "Jury to Decide Which of Trio Has Told Truth," *New Orleans Times-Picayune*, 6 August 1927.

wearing a "skin-tight" suit that "clung to her 120-pound body" and wore "jangling, dangling earrings." The *Los Angeles Times* said: "The brashly attractive 32-year-old convicted murderess, her bleached blond hair turned to its natural brown and cut in a short bob, walked to her death as if dressed for a shopping trip."[23]

Women's weight also received close attention. The *New York Times* continually made reference to Marie Beck's weight during three years of stories between 1949 and 1951, calling her such things as a "200-pound mistress," "the corpulent Mrs. Beck," and her cohort's "200-pound sweetheart." Similarly, the *St. Louis Post-Dispatch* termed Bonnie Brown Heady, executed under federal authority in 1953, "plump" or "pudgy" on several occasions. The *Post-Dispatch* also said guards "struggled to support" Marie Porter's 250 pounds as she "shuffled" to her execution in 1937 in Illinois. The *Chicago Tribune* began its story about Porter's execution by saying, "Pudgy-faced Marie Porter. . . ."[24] In contrast, little was made about Christina Riggs's weight, which reportedly was about 270 pounds, when she was executed in Arkansas in 2000.

The first point to be made is that what the defendant wore to trial might be important, if the defendant's looks were markedly altered in an obvious attempt to present a certain image to the jury. However, in the aforementioned cases, that point was not made. The newspapers concentrated on women's dress with the apparent assumption that women should "look good" whatever the circumstances, which not only reinforced stereotypes but also made stories seem silly or frivolous in some instances.

The second point is that a defendant's weight seldom is relevant to the crime or the execution. If a defendant is so large that she cannot fit into an electric chair, then it perhaps would be a point worth mentioning, or if the execution process had to be altered in some way because of a defendant's weight. However, in almost all of the cases cited in this book, there was no evident reason for constantly reporting a woman's weight, and it more often seemed done to indicate that overweight women are somehow deficient in other ways, or to poke subtle fun at the defendants.

Women's "Girlish" Attributes

The press concentrated at times on female defendants' "girlish" qualities, depicting them as flighty. Ada LeBoeuf "entertained" guests in her

23. Gene Blake, "Barbara Graham Dies Despite Two Last Delays," *Los Angeles Times,* 5 June 1955.

24. "Michigan Delays Action in Slaying," *New York Times,* 5 March 1949; "Michigan Agrees to Shift Slayers," ibid., 9 March 1949; "Hall and Heady Are Taken to Jefferson City, Won't Appeal," *St. Louis Post-Dispatch,* 20 November 1953; "U.S. Rests Case in Kidnap Trial, Hall's Service in War Is Cited," ibid., 18 November 1953; "Mrs. Porter and Youth Executed in Electric Chair," ibid., 28 January 1938.

jail cell, and reportedly was more concerned about her hairstyle than her fate. The *Phoenix Gazette* wrote of Eva Dugan in 1930: "Eva played hostess in her cell this morning to all who might want to chat with her. She was gracious as a society woman entertaining at a tea and she was just as clever with repartee."[25] Reports just before executions often contained references to defendants' concerns about their hair. Dovie Dean reportedly said she had not slept the night before her execution because she had her hair fixed and did not want to muss it. A prison official also told the press that Bonnie Brown Heady said she was upset the day before her execution because she had no fingernail polish, could not wear fine clothes to her execution, and could not do her hair the way she wanted. These are but two of many descriptions that became more pronounced in the twentieth century, but also were evident in the nineteenth.

More serious were the nineteenth-century press descriptions of some female defendants as being almost animals, or as having physical features that identified them as criminals. The most extreme example was Bridget Durgan, hanged in New Jersey in 1867. Detailed descriptions of her physical characteristics compared her to a fox, panther, snake, and tiger, among other animals, and said her traits showed innate criminality, a belief held at that time. In 1865, Mary Surratt's features explained her nature: "A cold eye, that would quail at no scene of torture; a close, shut mouth, whence no word of sympathy with suffering would pass; a firm chin, indicative of fixedness of resolve; a square, solid figure, whose proportions were never disfigured by remorse or marred by loss of sleep."[26]

How the Press Reported Sensational Cases

Some things consistently surfaced, such as defendants' complaints about unfair, prejudicial stories prior to trial. The nineteenth-century press also routinely injected religion into stories, and, until the mid-twentieth century, expressed displeasure or concern about women's unseemly public interest in executions and trials. Many press reports extending into the mid-twentieth century resembled dramas, and in the nineteenth century, the press often published lengthy reviews of the cases, sometimes using more than a page of text to describe the crimes, arrests, trials, and executions. Important trials in the nineteenth and early twentieth centuries received near-verbatim coverage. Until the mid-twentieth century, the press consistently engaged in hyperbole when describing cases, and routinely reported defendants' confessions, a practice that still continues. In addi-

---

25. "Eva Holds Reception in Cell," *Phoenix Gazette,* 20 February 1930.
26. "End of the Assassins," *New York Times,* 8 July 1865.

tion, news reports routinely concentrated on what a defendant ate for the last meal. Until the mid-twentieth century, the press had much access to criminal defendants, and for the most part portrayed executioners as efficient, even when an obvious botch was reported in the same story.

Prejudicial Press Complaints

At least as early as the 1850s, women defendants or their attorneys complained about prejudicial newspaper reports. Charlotte Jones said in 1858 that the newspapers made her seem "hardened" and without feelings, and in 1866, Martha Grinder's attorney said press reports made it impossible for her to get a fair trial in Pittsburgh. In the 1930s, Anna Hahn's attorney complained about the prosecution "trying the case in the newspapers."[27]

Some of the complaints seem to have merit. In 1888, before a coroner's jury had even met, the *Philadelphia Inquirer* pronounced Sarah Whiteling "a deliberate, calculating woman, who killed her offspring for the sake of a few hundred dollars."[28] Moreover, the press at times published information from secret grand jury proceedings. The *New York Times* published information about Frances Creighton's grand jury hearing in 1922, leading her attorney to complain. In 1958, the *Los Angeles Times* published detailed information about a grand jury hearing for Elizabeth Duncan before the prosecuting attorney released the transcript. Her attorney claimed she could not get a fair trial in Ventura County, and the American Civil Liberties Union of southern California supported a motion for a change of venue. The trial was not moved. Pretrial publicity apparently made it difficult to seat a jury for Marie Beck's trial in 1949 in New York. Some six hundred potential jurors were called before twelve jurors and two alternates were seated. Declaring a defendant guilty before trial, and especially before indictment, raises First, Fifth, Sixth, and Fourteenth Amendment questions, as well as ethical concerns. Although newspapers certainly have the right to publish such information, whether they should is arguable.

Government officials occasionally restricted the press, such as in 1935 when an order barred the press and others from access to the Delaware prison where May Carey awaited execution. The *Wilmington Morning News* supported the decision and said that the warden would give detailed information to reporters after Carey and her sons were executed.

27. "The Execution," *Pittsburgh Gazette-Times,* 13 February 1858; "Another Hanging"; "Mrs. Hahn Asks Venue Change in Poisoning Trial," *Chicago Tribune,* 19 August 1937
28. "The Modern Borgia."

This confidence proved unfounded when the warden issued brief, sketchy details and refused additional comment. Sometimes a newspaper restrained itself, as when the *Elko (Nev.) Weekly Independent* wrote that it would not be proper to comment on preliminary court proceedings before trial, because "we do not desire to publish anything that could be construed as influencing the public either for or against the defendants."[29]

When women defendants were executed in the 1980s and 1990s, the courts more frequently issued orders to protect defendants' fair-trial rights, such as an Arkansas court's gag order barring everyone involved in Christina Riggs's case from talking to reporters. In that case, the *Little Rock Arkansas Democrat-Gazette* reported Riggs's confession just before her trial for murdering her two children, but the taped confession had been played in an open preliminary proceeding, and therefore the press had a duty to report from an open government proceeding that any citizen could have attended.

Press Access to Prisoners

An important part of reports about women condemned to death was the relatively free access the press had to condemned prisoners. This type of access continued until well into the twentieth century and no doubt contributed to defendants' complaints that they had been tried in the press before being tried in the courts. News stories make it seem that the press attended a psychological examination conducted by three doctors in Martha Grinder's cell in 1866, and that the press also witnessed Catharine Miller's last meeting with her children on the night before she was executed in 1881. The access and the *New York Times*'s criticism seemed unwarranted in 1887 when the *Times* published a personal letter that Roxalana Druse wrote to the wife of a prison warden. Druse explained how she wanted her few belongings distributed, and the *Times* not only published the letter but also said it was "extremely faulty in punctuation and spelling."[30] The press also interviewed Rhonda Belle Martin, executed in Alabama in 1957, within about three hours of her incarceration. States provided much more access to prisoners than did the federal government, which severely limited access to Ethel Rosenberg and Bonnie Brown Heady, both executed in 1953. Access to Heady seemed about the same as for other defendants until she was placed under federal authority.

29. "The Carlin Murder," *Elko (Nev.) Weekly Independent*, 3 February 1889.
30. "Roxie Druse's Last Sunday," *New York Times*, 28 February 1887.

Religion in News Stories

The nineteenth-century press was much more likely to inject religion and moral instruction into news stories than the twentieth-century press. In the most common scenario, news stories gave descriptions of nineteenth-century defendants praying before their executions. The execution process, as reported, seemed akin to a religious ceremony in stories such as the one about the hanging of Charlotte Jones in 1858. Defendants were commonly said to have asked God's forgiveness and to have admitted their guilt. The press also provided religious instruction for readers in news stories and in editorials, such as the *Williamsport (Pa.) Daily Banner's* 1881 editorial titled "The Wages of Sin Is Death" about Catharine Miller's execution. However, there were instances, such as in the case of black slave Jane Williams, when the local press declared that the defendant was going to hell because of her crime. The stories probably helped readers feel better about the death penalty by assuring them that the defendants were guilty and, more important, were going to a better place because they had confessed their sins and asked forgiveness.

By 1984, when Velma Barfield became the first woman executed in the United States in more than twenty years, religious statements by the press had all but disappeared, but that does not mean religious messages were not important parts of news stories. In stories about Barfield and especially about Karla Faye Tucker in 1998, religious conversions were important. However, the religious messages readers got were from sources within the news stories, and not in the form of editorials or "editorializing" in news stories, as was done in earlier years. The press, in Tucker's case, left it to international, national, and local religious leaders to instruct the public through their comments in news stories.

Press Reports as Dramas

The newspaper press of the nineteenth and early twentieth centuries often reported sensational stories as dramas, such as in 1866, when the *Pittsburgh Post* wrote that the "curtain has fallen on the second act of this startling drama" following Martha Grinder's conviction for murder. The newspaper said the third act would be her execution. Other stories followed a similar format, with the crime and arrest being the first act, the trial the second act, and the execution the third act. In 1873, the *Atlanta Constitution* noted that Susan Eberhart's hanging ended "the saddest scene in the strangest real tragic drama that ever was enacted in the history of crime in America."[31]

31. "Conclusion of the Trial of Martha Grinder," *Pittsburgh Post*, 29 October 1865; "Miss Eberhart Hanged," *Atlanta Constitution*, 3 May 1873.

Reporters played on the drama, such as when *New Orleans Times-Picayune* reporters noted the theatrical aspects of Ada LeBoeuf's 1927 murder trial and used words that emphasized the Shakespearean nature of the case. Character development and plot also were evident in stories about LeBoeuf. As late as 1941, the *Los Angeles Times* used a theatrical analogy in a story about Ethel Spinelli's execution: "The cue had come for the desperate drama—a grim performance that almost everyone but the Duchess herself seemed to hope would somehow be prevented before the curtain could rise." In 1953, the paper again used a similar analogy, equating Barbara Graham to a Hollywood movie queen starring in "a colossal production" at a press conference, and saying that she was "the star of the show."[32]

These stories served an entertainment purpose, much like early soap operas, only they were real-life dramas and not fiction, and the danger is that the reading public might see them more as entertainment than as real life. The *Times-Picayune* indicated as much in its coverage of LeBoeuf when it said local movie theaters suffered financially because the trial was the best entertainment in town.

A judicial change affected the "three-act drama" when the judicial process for capital cases became lengthier. At least through the 1950s, many defendants were tried and executed within one to two years, or less. The rapidity of the judicial process, coupled with the access that the press had to the defendants, made for the rapid-fire, sometimes daily reports that so resembled the three-act drama. Although story structure today still resembles a drama, there is much more time between "acts," especially between the trial and the execution. Betty Lou Beets died in 2000, fifteen years after her arrest; Karla Faye Tucker committed murders in 1983 and was executed in 1998; Judy Buenoano was executed in 1998, but was arrested in 1984; Wanda Jean Allen murdered her lover in 1988 and was executed in 2001. Only Christina Riggs, among the more recent defendants, died relatively soon after her crimes: she murdered her children in 1997 and was executed in 2000. However, her case is atypical because she refused to appeal or to seek commutation. There now might be a generation of readers who would not remember the defendant's crime or trial by the time of the execution.

Executions themselves were reported as high drama. That has also changed because of less access to death row inmates and because lethal injections do not lend themselves to the "drama" of earlier execution methods. The drama as a result of method is evident. The more public and brutal hangings produced more drama than lethal injections, which some experts say are the least physically (as opposed to psychologically) bru-

32. "'Duchess' Dies in Gas Chamber," *Los Angeles Times,* 22 November 1941; "Press Besieges Barbara Graham," ibid., 25 September 1953.

tal of execution methods. Some argue that a close-range gunshot to the brain, which the United States has never used, is the most "humane" execution method.[33] Hangings and electrocutions produced violent, dramatic, and sometimes horrible deaths, as when Eva Dugan was decapitated in Arizona, or when Frances Creighton was carried to the electric chair in New York.

More important, during many executions prior to lethal injections, the press observed and reported on the process of the execution, resulting in dramatic stories about women's last hours. Reporters gave vivid descriptions of the women's preparations in their cells, and of their reactions when death warrants were read. At times, reporters walked with the execution cortege from the cell to the death chamber, and described in detail the sights and sounds. This type of writing continued into the 1950s and 1960s, although some people who opposed capital punishment criticized the highly emotional reports. It does seem a thin line existed between voyeurism and titillation of the audience and the need for readers to know about the details of executions.

Lethal injections produced a major change. They appear more like a hospital procedure, with the defendant lying on a gurney, often sedated. In most states, witnesses and the press see nothing until after the needles are inserted and the chemicals have begun to flow. Media organizations, including the Associated Press (AP), challenged California's process and won a federal court suit requiring the state to allow witnesses to see the defendant being escorted into the death chamber, and the needles being inserted. The Associated Press in Arkansas reported that witnesses "stared at a closed curtain for 20 minutes" while prison officials worked to find a vein in Christina Riggs's arm.[34]

Occasionally, a lethal-injection execution produces drama, as when Texas inmate Ponchai Wilkerson, lying strapped on the gurney, spit out a universal key to handcuff and leg restraints—which reportedly would open all such restraints in the prison—in an act of defiance moments before he died. Where he got the key and why he did not use it are not known. His last words were "The secret, according to Wilkerson."[35]

The more common scenario is the sterile, low-key, sanitized execution, which some, such as Stephen Trombley, contend is just what the state wants. The executioners are invisible, as opposed to when sheriffs had to

33. For an example of Mississippi executions as "powerful theater," see David M. Oshinsky, *"Worse Than Slavery": Parchman Farm and the Ordeal of Jim Crow Justice,* 213–17. For comment about methods of execution, see Jacob Weisberg, "This Is Your Death," 23–27.

34. "Case Could Impact Arkansas Executions," *Jonesboro (Ark.) Sun,* 29 July 2000.

35. "Inmate Spits Out Handcuff Key before Execution in '90 Slaying," *Dallas Morning News,* 15 March 2000.

hang defendants or, even later, when executioners in some states were known to the public and named in news stories, and in some cases became celebrities. Guards now insert the needles, and the state claims harm might come to the guards if they are identified. Witnesses, even news reporters, describe the executions as almost like watching someone go to sleep. According to a *Washington Post* editorial, an Associated Press reporter described a 1994 lethal-injection execution in Maryland as "so gentle, so subtle."[36]

Such executions do not make for dramatic news copy, and the executions of women in the 1980s, '90s, and 2000 reflect the change. There has been little to report about the actual executions. More likely to produce stories are the sideshows, such as the "media circus" at Karla Faye Tucker's 1998 execution, or Velma Barfield's somewhat eccentric action of wearing pajamas and fuzzy pink house shoes to her execution, after a last meal of a soft drink and Cheez Doodles.

Some people argue that if the public could see the entire execution process, then public opinion against capital punishment would increase. Past experience indicates that is highly unlikely; more likely is a return to the "circus" of the eighteenth, nineteenth, and early-twentieth centuries.[37]

Media Trials and Verbatim Reports

Some cases resulted in what might be termed *media trials*, marked by near-verbatim reports and intense press scrutiny. Illustrations of these cases include Martha Grinder in 1866, Catharine Miller in 1880, Ada LeBoeuf in 1927, Anna Hahn in 1938, and Barbara Graham in 1955. In the last three cases, the defendants became celebrities, as evidenced by the press referring to them in headlines only by their first names. No *Chicago Tribune* reader had to ask who "Arsenic Anna" was in 1938, and New Orleans readers understood who Ada was when her name was used in a headline. The press came close to this near-verbatim trial reporting in the 1936 trial of Frances Creighton and the 1950s trial of Elizabeth Duncan. The latter part of the twentieth century produced far less of this type of reporting, although some defendants, such as Karla Faye Tucker, became media celebrities near the times of their executions.

Overstatement of Importance

The press often overstated the importance of the cases. This was common in the nineteenth century and continued at least through the 1930s.

36. Trombley, *The Execution Protocol;* "Ho Hum, Another Execution," *Washington Post,* 22 May 1994.
37. Marlin Shipman, "Ethical Guidelines for Televising or Photographing Executions," 95.

The *St. Paul Pioneer and Democrat* said in 1860 of Ann Bilansky: "Probably no jail ever contained a criminal, either male or female, under imprisonment for such a crime, who exhibited such a complete want of decency and propriety." The 1866 murder case of Martha Grinder was the "most extraordinary that ever was written down in the annals of murder" not only in the Pittsburgh area, but also in "the entire country, and perhaps in any country." Emeline Meaker's murder of her eight-year-old niece in 1883 was called "[o]ne of the most cold-blooded murders known in history or fiction." During the 1920s, newspapers in New Orleans and Memphis proclaimed Ada LeBoeuf's crime "one of the most brutal crimes in Louisiana history," and one of the most brutal murders "in the crime history of the south." The *Phoenix Gazette* in 1930 called Irene Schroeder "the most desperate feminine character ever to figure in police annals of Arizona." Louise Peete was described in the 1940s as "one of crime's most notorious fatal women," whose execution ended "a saga of murder and suicide rivaling some of the most sanguinary pages of history." The *St. Louis Post-Dispatch* said Bonnie Brown Heady's crime of kidnapping and murder was "one of the worst crimes in American history," and the *Houston Chronicle* called Karla Faye Tucker's crime "one of the grisliest crimes in Houston history."[38]

Reports of Confessions and Other "Routine" Information

Published confessions before trial are so common that they seem not to merit comment. In fact, though, they do deserve mention because some scholars and others say that publication of a pretrial confession perhaps most damages a defendant's chance for a fair trial. It does not matter if the women were nineteenth- or twentieth-century defendants; in almost all cases, their confessions were published, usually before trial and sometimes before indictment.

Sarah Whiteling's confession that she murdered her husband and two children was published in the first story about her arrest in 1888. The same was true for Ada LeBoeuf in 1927, and for Marie Beck in 1949. In Beck's case, the *New York Times* published the confession on the front page in the

---

38. "The Bilansky Murder," *St. Paul Pioneer and Democrat*, 24 March 1860; "The Sixth Day," *Pittsburgh Post*, 30 October 1865; "The Waterbury Horror," *Burlington Daily Free Press*, 11 May 1880; "Wife of Murder Victim, Trapper, Physician Jailed," *New Orleans Times-Picayune*, 8 July 1927; "Law Moves to Punish Slayers of LeBouef," *Memphis Commercial Appeal*, 11 July 1927; "Posse Expects Gun Battle," *Phoenix Gazette*, 14 January 1930; "Mrs. Louise Peete Meets Doom, Calm Till End," *Los Angeles Times*, 12 April 1947; "Hall, Mrs. Heady Appear Calm As Their Execution Draws Near," *St. Louis Post-Dispatch*, 16 December 1953; "48% in Poll Support Her Execution," *Houston Chronicle*, 29 January 1998.

first of eighty-one stories about her. The *Times* similarly published Frances Creighton's confession on the front page before her trial. Likewise, the *St. Louis Post-Dispatch* published Bonnie Brown Heady's confession in the first story about her arrest in 1953. Whether the publication does damage to fair-trial rights is arguable, but unless the confession is made in open court, there seems little reason to publish it, given the history of contrived or compelled confessions.

Another consistent feature of women's executions has been the involvement of celebrities. The press, as might be expected, picks up on celebrity protest against the death penalty or celebrity involvement in trials. In 1888, the Philadelphia press prominently included which important people attended Sarah Whiteling's trial. In the early 1900s, "the Divine" Sarah Bernhardt spoke out against the execution of Mary Rogers in Vermont. In the 1930s, Clarence Darrow sought commutation for Anna Antonio, not as her attorney but as a private citizen. In the 1990s, celebrities such as Bianca Jagger (former wife of Rolling Stones star Mick Jagger) were among those protesting Karla Faye Tucker's execution, and her views received prominent press attention. In the twentieth century, the press rushed toward celebrities such as the Reverend Jesse Jackson and placed more rather than less emphasis on celebrity.

Criticism of the Public's "Unseemly Interest"

Despite the newspaper press labeling defendants as demons, animals, or fiends; reporting confessions; and terming the crimes as perhaps the worst in the history of the world, the press regularly criticized the public, and especially women, for having a morbid or unseemly interest in the cases. In no instance did the press acknowledge its own role in creating that interest.

The Pittsburgh press disapproved of women's "morbid curiosity" at Martha Grinder's 1866 trial, and the *Williamsport (Pa.) Daily Banner* said it was "to the shame of Williamsport" that many women filled the streets after Catharine Miller's conviction in 1880. The *St. Paul Pioneer and Democrat* in 1860 wrote: "The most disgusting feature connected with [the hanging], was the eagerness and persistency with which females sought to obtain eligible places to view the dying agonies of one of their own sex."[39]

The *New Orleans Times-Picayune* had perhaps the harshest and least-deserved criticism of women at a trial in its coverage of Ada LeBoeuf. Af-

39. "Trial of Martha Grinder," *Pittsburgh Post*, 28 October 1865; "The Court," *Williamsport (Pa.) Daily Banner*, 10 May 1880; "Execution of Mrs. Bilansky," *St. Paul Pioneer and Democrat*, 24 March 1860.

ter using almost every questionable journalistic technique to hype the story, the newspaper said those who observed the trial were "perspiring and morbid fat ladies" or "sob sisters." The reporters said the attendees showed "the worst side of human nature, the slimy, crawling atavistic desire, to see a trio tortured."[40] This type of criticism largely ceased with the end of the jazz-journalism era in about 1930.

Society's Responsibility

On rare occasions, the press tried to explain why women killed, and sometimes the explanations placed some blame on society or on the community. In 1883, the *Montpelier (Vt.) Watchman* partly blamed the community for Alice Meaker's death because people knew she was being mistreated but said nothing. In 1912, the *Chicago Defender* argued that the State of Virginia should not execute seventeen-year-old Virginia Christian because the larger society had in part been responsible for her illiteracy and ignorance and because she had "had no kindly hand to guide her." A *Los Angeles Times* columnist wrote in 1955 that Barbara Graham never had a chance in life because she was put into a reform school for girls at age thirteen and learned to be a prostitute, forger, drug user, and murderer. The article said society had "discarded" her.[41]

Changes in Journalistic Style

For the most part, changes in reporting have been positive. Reports from the 1920s to the 1950s were at times unnecessarily sensational and concentrated on the trivial and the shocking, or were highly opinionated and riddled with stereotypes. The coverages of Ada LeBoeuf in the 1920s and Anna Hahn in the 1930s are examples. Coverage made Hahn's and LeBoeuf's trials seem almost side events, as the reporters showed off their literary skills and trivialized important proceedings.

Speculation and opinion were rampant in some nineteenth-century reports. Martha Grinder "could have" murdered as many as twenty people, the Pittsburgh press reported in 1866. The Philadelphia press reported in 1888 that Sarah Whiteling might have given poisoned candy to neighborhood children.

These examples, and others, mark a personal and opinionated style

---

40. "Franklin Quiet As People Avoid Talk of Trial," *New Orleans Times-Picayune*, 8 August 1927.
41. Editorial, *Montpelier (Vt.) Watchman*, as reprinted in the *Burlington Daily Free Press*, 14 May 1880; editorial, *Chicago Defender*, 17 August 1912; Anne Norman, "Must We Share Part of the Guilt?" ibid., 4 June 1955.

that permeated journalism in the nineteenth century. The jazz-journalism era of the 1920s concentrated heavily on personalities and was marked by opinion in news stories, huge screamer headlines, and speculation. Although some scholars note that such reporting began to fade in the late 1920s, that is not exactly true, because the late-1930s case of Anna Hahn showed elements of such reporting.

The Shameful Treatment of Black Women

Gubernatorial soul-searching, public outrage, and press stereotyping of women as pure and virtuous did not apply to condemned black women. Most women executed in southern states were black. A way of looking at the status difference of white and black women is to examine the executions of men for rape. Almost no men were executed for raping a black woman. Almost all executions for rape—a nearly exclusive southern phenomenon—were black men raping white women. In some southern states, the laws apparently were race specific in reference to the victim. A South Carolina jury reportedly sentenced a black defendant to death for "assault with intent to ravish a white woman."[42]

Before emancipation, black female slaves who were hanged usually got almost no mention in the white-owned press. In some instances, such as the hanging of Celia, a Florida slave, or of Eliza, a Mississippi slave, judges overruled jury requests for mercy and ordered the women hanged. A Florida newspaper supported the judge's ruling in Celia's case, and a Mississippi newspaper obviously approved of the action in Eliza's case. Neither incest nor a victim's age made any difference to the newspapers in either case, even though some in the local communities seemed to recognize that wrongs had been done. This indicates that some parts of the societies were ahead of the newspapers in their views about race. The press in these cases deserves few accolades for leading the community.

Jane Williams is one of the few slaves who received substantial news coverage, and most of it supported the status quo and failed to raise important questions. The *Richmond Dispatch* reported from a coroner's inquest that she had perjured herself, although no charges were brought, and that she and her husband were guilty. The *Dispatch* termed Williams a fiend and "more than a demon," and all but condemned her soul to hell. Her hanging was to be "a warning to the fractious portion of our negro population."[43] Not a question was raised about the state "paying" the

42. See, for example, Eric W. Rise, *The Martinsville Seven: Race, Rape, and Capital Punishment*. "Death Sentence Is Commuted to Life in Prison," *Florence (S.C.) Morning News*, 7 January 1947.
43. "Local Matters," *Richmond Daily Dispatch*, 20 July 1852; "The Execution of Jane Williams," ibid., 11 September 1852.

"owner" of "property" when Williams was executed. It was not as if these questions had not been raised in southern society, especially in Virginia. They had. A reading of early U.S. history and of biographies of some of Virginia's political leaders reveals that slavery was questioned. However, the press in these cases did not forcefully lead; instead, it followed the majority view.

During the last twenty years of the nineteenth century, black women got more coverage than during slavery. References to their look or to their dress, however, were often negative. Black defendants were referred to as "colored," "darkies," or "negroes." Physical descriptions included such things as "a black, muddy complexion," "coal black," or "very large hands and feet." At times, the press seemed to subtly question whether blacks were married. In addition, in some instances, the press stereotyped blacks as superstitious. The press seemed surprised when black citizens obeyed the law, such as when the mother of one defendant, "to the surprise of all," told others that her son had committed murder.[44] The white press also raised no questions about hangings of juveniles. The press's failure to raise questions about executing juvenile black women continued in the early twentieth century.

Most of the executions of black women in the twentieth century received only cursory notice in the press. Although some of the coverage can be explained because it occurred during the World War II years, that does not fully explain the differences. Some executions were after the war, although executions in general drew much less attention during wartime.[45] However, some white women received substantial news coverage, such as Beatrice Annie "Toni Jo" Henry, who died in Louisiana's electric chair in 1942. The *New Orleans Times-Picayune* ran her execution story on page 1, and ran other front-page stories about her. She also received relatively prominent and substantial coverage in the *Memphis Commercial Appeal*. One article featured the "26-year-old slim brunet" with a photo of her sitting and smiling. The lighthearted article said the photographer "wrestled with the focus-pocus rituals," and Henry said to him: "I've smiled twice, mister. You haven't shot yet. Have you any idea how much talent is being wasted here today?"[46]

During the twentieth century, even the wire services in the South en-

44. "Two Necks Broken," *Atlanta Constitution*, 23 November 1895.
45. World War II had a more direct effect on executions in some states. For example, the War Production Board refused Warden G. Norton Jameson's request for materials to build an electric chair in South Dakota. Two men were said to appear safe from execution for the duration of the war. The state legislature had failed to make provisions for building an electric chair when it enacted the death penalty in 1939. "War Priorities Stay Execution of Killers," *Raleigh News and Observer*, 26 December 1942.
46. See, for example, "Mrs. Henry Dies Calmly in Prison at Lake Charles," *New*

gaged in racial stereotyping. The Associated Press and the United Press International had stories in which they referred to black women by their first names on second reference, used black dialect in stories, and referred to a twenty-nine-year-old black male defendant as a "boy."

The coverage of the only black woman executed in more than fifty years in the United States indicates that the newspaper press is more even-handed than in earlier years. Wanda Jean Allen, executed in Oklahoma in 2001, received relatively similar coverage to that given her white counterparts in the late 1990s. The race distinction in coverage of the execution chamber seems to be disappearing, if one case can be an accurate guide.

Because executions of women are rare, they might be seen as likely stories to sensationalize. For example, David A. Copeland points out that coverage of women and children in colonial America sometimes concentrated on violence and emotion. Because of these factors, he says, "executions became especially powerful forms of sensationalism," and news of executions "often used women as its focal point." Even the earliest of colonial newspapers used such news. Copeland says the *Boston News-Letter* filled half of one early issue with reports about the hangings of six pirates. Yet, sensationalism was not limited to the colonial era. Some newspaper coverage about condemned female (and male) defendants in the twentieth century can rightly be termed *sensational*, and one study showed that "popular [media] outlets focus more on violence as a staple for the dramatic structuring of their news items."[47]

During most of the twentieth century, the public had to rely on the press for information about the death penalty because executions have for years been removed from public view. Executions had been public spectacles, drawing thousands of people and sometimes resulting in drinking and property damage. By the 1830s, many northeastern states were carrying out executions in private. The development of mass-circulation newspapers played an important role in keeping executions private by providing the working-class public with information. Nevertheless, public executions continued in some places, and it was not until 1936 that the last public hanging in the United States took place in Owensboro, Kentucky, although a 1937 hanging in Galena, Missouri, was public for all practical purposes. In most states, executions were moved years earlier from local

---

Orleans Times-Picayune, 29 November 1942; "Annie B. Henry Admits Slaying Texas Salesman," ibid., 21 November 1942; "Slim Slayer Still Wisecracks while Awaiting Electrocution," *Memphis Commercial Appeal,* 4 August 1942; "Fast Life Come [*sic*] to Quick End for Toni Jo in Electric Chair," ibid., 29 November 1942.

47. Copeland, *Colonial American Newspapers,* 82. For reference to the hanging of the pirates, see John D. Stevens, *Sensationalism and the New York Press,* 9. For reference to violence in popular media outlets, see Richard V. Ericson, Patricia M. Baranek, and Janet B. L. Chan, *Representing Order: Crime, Law, and Justice in the News Media,* 244.

communities to state prisons. Missouri, Mississippi, and Louisiana—in the 1930s, 1940s, and part of the 1950s—were the last states to perform executions in the counties in which the crimes had occurred, with Mississippi and Louisiana having portable electric chairs that were taken from place to place. Few people throughout most of the twentieth century ever witnessed an execution—or ever will. About the only experience most of the public has with executions is through news reports, or through columns and editorials in print or on newscasts. Accordingly, the press most often serves as a surrogate for the public, a stand-in witness to a government function. This also means that what the public knows about executions, or, for the most part, about the criminal defendant, it receives from the press. This is important because it raises the question of how or whether "the press embodied, [or] transmitted norms of behavior," and whether the press, by its reporting, might influence social norms concerning women and their roles in society and in capital punishment. *New York Times* writer Peter Applebome believes the press will become even more important, because as federal courts limit death row inmates' appeals, more cases will be played out in the press.[48]

---

48. Louis P. Masur, *Rites of Execution: Capital Punishment and the Transformation of American Culture, 1776–1865*, 114–17. Mississippi moved its executions to a central location in 1955 with the opening of Parchman Farm; see Oshinsky, *"Worse Than Slavery."* For the press as surrogate, see Leon S. Sheleff, *Ultimate Penalties: Capital Punishment, Life Imprisonment, Physical Torture*, 153–56. For press transmission or embodiment of norms, see Hazel Dicken-Garcia, *Journalistic Standards in Nineteenth-Century America*, 21. Applebome, "Virginia Execution Highlighted Politics of Death," *New York Times*, 29 May 1992.

PART I

Murdered Family

Members and Other Schemes

Chapter 1

Viragos and Unnatural Mothers

Nineteenth-Century Mothers

THE NUMBER OF HEADLINES ON the first story indicated its importance. Twelve subordinate headlines streamed down beneath the lead headline, and some of them said: "Confession of the Murder," "A Mother and Son the Murderers," and "Threaten to Lynch the Perpetrators of the Horrible Tragedy." Vermonters rarely lynched others, but this crime outraged the people. The *Burlington Daily Free Press* said a mob's fury grew by the hour. The two defendants were kept under guard. "No event of recent years has so wrought up our people and nothing else is thought of or talked of, the current of the popular feeling running strongly against the accused parties."[1] Emeline Meaker and her son, Almon, were accused of murdering an eight-year-old girl whom they had agreed to care for.

Many people probably consider a child's murder to be the worst type of crime, and when a mother or caretaker is the perpetrator, it is especially heinous. Some people consider mothers who kill their children subhuman.[2] In early 2001, at least two women were on death rows for killing their children or aiding in their murders: Darlie Routier in Texas and Deborah Jean Milke in Arizona. Other women executed for murdering their children include Christina Riggs in Arkansas, executed on 2 May 2000, and Sarah Whiteling of Pennsylvania, executed in 1889.

Emeline Meaker: The Virago of Vermont

Emeline Meaker, and her son, Almon, did not murder eight-year-old Alice Meaker for insurance money. The press put forth two motives: First, and most benign, Alice was a nuisance. Twenty-year-old Almon helped

---

1. "Another Vermont Tragedy," *Burlington Daily Free Press*, 28 April 1880.
2. "Former Nurse Scheduled to Die Tonight," *Jonesboro (Ark.) Sun*, 2 May 2000.

his mother murder her niece; he later confessed and said of Alice: "She wasn't a very good girl; no one liked her, and she was hard to get along with. I thought she would be better off if she were dead, and so I killed her." Second, the *Free Press* speculated, Alice knew Emeline and Almon Meaker were "guilty of the revolting crime of living in incestuous intercourse." That rumor circulated for more than a year, and Alice, "having observed that they [*sic*] two occupied the bedroom while Horace [the husband] slept up stairs, declared that she would tell, and that this made the little girl the victim of terrible abuse, ever after, till she was finally killed."[3] (Horace was also known as E. C. Meaker.)

The murder attracted enormous press interest in Vermont and New York. The *New York Times* wrote: "Probably no murder ever committed in Vermont created more interest than the Meaker murder, which was partly owing to the atrocity of the crime and partly to the fact that the principal criminal was a woman."[4]

The *Free Press* called the crime "one of the most cold-blooded murders known in history or fiction." The first day the story broke, the *Free Press* made clear it would be big news. Its story said Emeline and Almon Meaker were guilty and he had confessed to the killing; eventually, the newspaper published allegations of incest and violent beatings, including two times when Emeline stripped off Alice's clothing and beat her until she bled.[5] The *Free Press* published morning and evening editions, and stories ran in each of the editions for the first several days.

Alice's father had died two years earlier and left Alice, her mother, and her younger brother paupers. E. C. Meaker was the children's uncle, and the town of Duxbury gave him and his wife, Emeline, $400 to care for the children. Shortly before the murder, Alice was "let to the service of a farmer" and was to begin work the next week, a form of indentured service that was not unusual, even for an eight-year-old child. Emeline and Almon Meaker gave Alice strychnine in a dipper of "sweetened water," and then stashed her body in the muck of a swamp. Police discovered the murder because Alice's disappearance concerned some neighbors. Emeline Meaker told her husband that Alice had "stepped out." Actually, Emeline went to the girl's bedroom at about nine one night and spirited her away; then she and Almon gave Alice the poison while riding in a horse-drawn wagon. Emeline Meaker told the neighbors that Alice had

3. "The Duxbury Horror: Some Additional Details," *Burlington Daily Free Press,* 29 April 1880; "The Waterbury Horror," ibid., 11 May 1880. The newspaper did not repeat the incest allegations in subsequent stories, even in a retrospective account of the murder just before Emeline Meaker was hanged.

4. "Emeline Meaker Hanged," *New York Times,* 31 March 1883.

5. "Another Vermont Tragedy"; "Mrs. Lucy E. Meaker," *Burlington Daily Free Press,* 30 March 1883.

run away, and when they asked if a search for her should be organized, Almon told them, "Let the _____ critter go; I will not search for her."[6]

Emeline and Almon Meaker were arraigned on the day of their arrest, and both pleaded not guilty. Almon changed an earlier confession, and claimed he alone had murdered Alice. The newspaper described him as "a harmless appearing young man not over bright." When he changed his story, Deputy Sheriff Frank Atherton became suspicious. Almon first said he had hired a team of horses to drive to Moscow, Vermont, but after questioning he told authorities he and Emeline Meaker had driven Alice to Richmond, Vermont, and given her $6.50 for fare to Montreal. Police questioned Almon again the next day, and he confessed. Atherton later testified that when Almon told his mother about his confession, she "cried and screamed and said 'Almon is innocent, I am the guilty one.'"[7]

Both E. C. and Emeline Meaker were deaf. The *Free Press* described E. C. Meaker as poor but of good character. Emeline Meaker received few accolades. She was described as a "strong energetic" woman "with prominent features and anything but an amiable expression." Worse, the newspaper said, "She is known to be a virago, and her will was the law of the household, Horace being a feeble man and a mere cipher." The *Free Press* extrapolated criminal character when it wrote that her "personal appearance indicates capacity for the cruelty practiced upon the child." It reported that neighbors said Alice and her brother were "shamefully abused by their guardians." The newspaper said Emeline Meaker severely whipped Alice on several occasions; neighbors testified she had once threatened to beat Alice to death, and struck her with sticks and a barrel stave. When police found her body, the newspaper said, there was a "black spot," apparently meaning a bruise, about the size of a man's hand on Alice's hip, and the bruise seemed "conclusive evidence" that Alice had been terribly beaten. In a story three years later, just before Emeline's execution, the *Free Press* termed her "a coarse, brutal, domineering woman" who had taken delight in "abusing, and maltreating," Alice.[8]

According to the *Burlington Daily Free Press,* Alice, a "timid, shrinking child," seemed to invite more abuse from Emeline Meaker, who had forced her "to do far more household drudgery than the child's slender strength was equal to." The *New York Times* said Emeline seemed to despise Alice from the beginning, "beating her without cause." A *Free Press*

6. "The Duxbury Tragedy," ibid., 28 April 1880.
7. "Later. Additional Particulars," ibid., 28 April 1880; "The Duxbury Horror"; "The Waterbury Horror."
8. "The Waterbury Horror." A virago is a woman regarded as noisy, scolding, or domineering. A cipher is one who has no influence or value, a nonentity. "The Duxbury Horror"; "The Meaker Murder," *Burlington Daily Free Press,* 14 May 1880; "Mrs. Lucy E. Meaker."

story published when Emeline was executed said Almon had treated Alice better than had his mother, but he had not dared show Alice too much sympathy because he "was completely under the control of his vicious mother."[9]

The *Free Press* reported that neighbors knew Emeline Meaker abused Alice, but said nothing for fear the abuse would increase. For this, the *Montpelier (Vt.) Watchman* criticized the community, saying every community member had unwritten duties and defined obligations owed to society. It said the "recognized officers of the law" were not the only ones responsible for preventing harm to others, and added, "If individuals, if our churches and social institutions generally, will adopt more aggressive methods" to bring religion and morality to the community, then it might result in fewer crimes. The editorial ended: "The Duxbury people who allowed the Meaker woman to torture, unchecked, the little waif placed under her care, were guilty of culpable neglect, and must take a share of the blame as well as of the disgrace which this horrible crime has brought upon their community."[10]

The Crime

The *Free Press* outlined the crime as follows. Almon rented a team and bought the strychnine used to poison Alice on the same day; she was murdered that night. Emeline and Almon Meaker went to Alice's bedroom, where she slept, tied a sack over her head so she could not be heard, and took her downstairs to the carriage. The three drove for a short distance until they came to the top of Henry Hill, where they gave Alice the poison. The newspaper wrote: "The cup in which the infamous draught was pressed to her lips was the child's own china mug, the gift of her mother, and bearing on it in gilt letters a motto of maternal affection." The inscription read, "Remember Me."[11]

The *Free Press* said Almon told police he and his mother had waited at the spot until Alice died: "He made the remark as coolly as one might speak of the death of a rat." A story published after Emeline Meaker's execution said that as the poison began to work, Alice screamed in pain while suffering convulsions. Almon stopped the carriage under a covered bridge, where he and his mother held their hands over Alice's mouth to muffle her screams until the convulsions stopped and she quit breathing. They buried her body in the muck under two feet of water, and later re-

9. "Mrs. Lucy E. Meaker"; "Emeline Meaker Hanged"; "Mrs. Lucy E. Meaker."
10. "Individual Duty in the Prevention of Crime," *Montpelier (Vt.) Watchman,* as reprinted in the *Burlington Daily Free Press,* 14 May 1880.
11. "The Meaker Murder," *Burlington Daily Free Press,* 3 May 1880; "The Meaker Tragedy," ibid., 7 May 1880; "The Waterbury Horror."

ports said Almon stomped on the body to push it down so it would not be seen and then covered it with brush. After Almon confessed, he took Deputy Atherton to the body, and the *Free Press* said Atherton made him help carry Alice out of the swamp. During the ride back, Atherton told Almon to hold the body, but he refused.[12]

Almon eventually blamed his mother. He first pleaded guilty and was sentenced to hang, but while imprisoned he wrote another confession that gained him a commutation. He claimed he had no motive to kill Alice and had not realized what he was doing, or the consequences of his action, and added that if he had known how horrible her death would be, he would have never participated. The *Free Press* said of his second confession: "Undoubtedly, this retraction on Almon's part was due to the threat or entreaties of his unnatural mother, who now saw no means to escape except by fastening the crime upon her weak accomplice."[13]

If Emeline Meaker admitted guilt when Almon first confessed, as Deputy Atherton testified, she soon recanted and denied guilt to her death. A headline in the 31 March *Free Press,* the day after the hanging, said, "She Meets Death with Little Emotion, Protesting Innocence to the Last." She blamed Almon for the crime. Almon wrote his mother, urging her to confess and saying she would feel better and would be better prepared to meet God. The *Free Press* said that when Almon visited his mother the day before she hanged, they shook hands, but she showed "a slight excitement over the letter," which she claimed contained lies and which she said brought her near to her death. Emeline Meaker said Almon would regret to his death his participation in the crime. Judging from the news reports, she never believed herself responsible for the crime.

Not a Model Prisoner

The *Free Press* reported that prior to her trial, when jailed at Montpelier, Emeline Meaker once attempted to set fire to the jail, and at another time attacked the sheriff "with all the ferocity of a wild beast." After her imprisonment at Windsor Prison, the *Free Press* said she feigned insanity, screamed, and attacked attendants, and because she was a "strong and muscular woman," she was hard to ward off. As the execution day approached, "Mrs. Meaker has gradually grown less and less violent, and has spent much of the time quietly knitting in her cell."[14]

Her execution was big news. The *Free Press* said: "One of the most remarkable executions of modern times was the hanging of Emeline Lucy

12. "The Meaker Tragedy"; "The Duxbury Horror."
13. "Mrs. Lucy E. Meaker."
14. Ibid.

Meaker in the State jail to-day. Such wonderful nerve and composure on the scaffold is seldom seen." The *New York Times* called the hanging "the most remarkable case in the criminal records of this State."[15]

The *Free Press* described in detail Emeline Meaker's behavior and her sleeping and eating habits. It said she "completed her toilet" by doing her hair in a different style, combing it "over her temples and parting it in the middle," a slight but well-accepted change. When officials told her "she looked not over sixteen," she laughed heartily and replied that she also believed she looked good. Despite its detailed report, the *Free Press* did not report on Meaker's attire, which usually is standard fare in any woman's execution story. However, the *Times* filled the void, reporting that she wore a dress "made for the occasion of black cambric, with white necktie and ruffles." The *Free Press* said she had a healthy appetite, and ate a breakfast of "a large beefsteak, three potatoes, a slice of bread and butter, a piece of meat pie," and a cup of coffee. For lunch she had two boiled eggs, two slices of toast, a potato, a doughnut, and a cup of coffee.

When the prison chaplain visited, Meaker showed "stolid indifference." She wanted to see the gallows before her execution. She reportedly showed no fear, and when asked what she thought, she said, "Why, it is not half as bad as I thought it was." Later in the morning, Deputy Sheriff Atherton visited her, and she told him, "Frank, tell them I am to be murdered to-day, an innocent woman." The *Free Press* used the quotation as a subordinate headline in its execution coverage. This meeting marked one of the few times, if not the only time, the *Free Press* described Meaker as showing any emotion other than rage. The newspaper said that as Atherton rose to leave, Meaker began to cry. As her execution day approached, press descriptions of her softened. Where the newspaper earlier described her as a virago and as brutal, she now seemed almost warm and emotional. Many of the harsher descriptions were before her trial. Perhaps she did change.

The *New York Times* said about 125 people, including reporters, witnessed the hanging. There were many requests because, "[b]eing the first woman ever executed in Vermont, much interest had been manifested to see her, and Sheriff Amsden was besieged for passes to witness the execution." Two deputies escorted her to the gallows; she "walked firmly" but looked pale and sad. "Her face was pallid, lips compressed and she showed no emotion except by her hurried breathing. Her hands were clenched and were red as if blood had settled there." Meaker's last words were: "May God forgive you all for hanging me, an innocent woman. I am as innocent as that man standing here," referring to a deputy sheriff stand-

---

15. "A Life for a Life," ibid., 31 March 1883; "Emeline Meaker Hanged." All of the following account of the hanging is taken from these two sources.

ing nearby. Her ankles were tied, the noose was adjusted around her neck, the black cap was placed over her head, and the trap was sprung. The *Free Press* said it was "at precisely 1:36 P.M., Boston time, or 1:30 Windsor time."

Seven doctors witnessed the execution, and the *Free Press,* somewhat ghoulishly, reported pulse rates for Meaker at intervals that sometimes were less than a minute. It wrote: "First minute, 90; 2d, 90; $2\frac{1}{2}$, 67; 5th, 130; 6th, 125; $6\frac{1}{2}$, 55; 7th, 60; $7\frac{1}{4}$, 55 (they could not now get it distinctly); $8\frac{1}{2}$, 25; 9th, 70; 16th, 1. At 1:43 one strong throb was noticed and at 1:44 the sheriff pronounced the woman dead."

Within the news story detailing Meaker's pulse rate at various intervals, the *Free Press* ironically ran a boldface text line that read, "Morbid Curiosity." The text related, "No execution in the past has excited the community as this one" and said that large numbers of people "thronged the jail corridors to look at the gallows." The newspaper said a Waterbury man sought a pass for his wife, "which request of course was refused," and another man wrote to request that one inch of the hangman's rope be cut off and sent to him, "properly certified to, for his collection."

Meaker's husband and daughter refused to visit her, and they also denied her last request to have her remains taken home for burial; instead, she was buried in the prison cemetery. "The wretched woman died friendless and alone, not a relative being present to offer consolation in her last hours," according to the *Free Press.*

The Philadelphia Press Labels an "Unnatural Mother"

Sarah Jane Whiteling, forty, of Philadelphia, had a vermin problem in her home in the late winter of 1888.[16] The family lived in the rear of the residence, located on a small thoroughfare. Whiteling, a "short, stout rather coarse-featured woman," said she purchased some rat poison to kill the vermin, but on the trip home from the store she became possessed. "[T]he devil got into my head and told me to give it to my husband," she later told police.

Her husband, John Whiteling, thirty-eight, was "sick," Sarah Jane Whiteling said, although the *New York Times* described him as "an invalid." The Whitelings had two children: nine-year-old Bertha, who was fathered by another man, and two-year-old Willie. Sarah Jane believed John's death would help alleviate the family's poverty. So she poisoned him.

John Whiteling died on 20 March 1888. Dr. George W. Smith attributed the death to "inflammation of the bowels." Whiteling's $145 in insurance

16. The first portion of this story describing the crimes is reconstructed from stories in the *Philadelphia Inquirer* and the *New York Times.*

and an $85 death benefit from Herd No. 2 of the Benevolent Order of Buf-
faloes, an organization to which he belonged, did help his family financially. Sarah Jane Whiteling used the money to pay for her husband's funeral, and to pay some bills the family owed. She also bought a sewing
machine and a watch for herself. Nonetheless, she soon ran short of money again.

Bertha was a difficult child, Sarah Jane Whiteling said. Bertha had at
various times stolen pennies from others, and once she even stole some
pennies from her teacher. Whiteling worried that her daughter, already a
sinner at age nine, might grow up to be a great sinner. So she poisoned
Bertha.

Bertha died on 24 April, almost one month to the day after her stepfather's death. Dr. Smith attributed Bertha's death to "gastric fever," and
Whiteling collected $122 in insurance.

With her husband and Bertha both dead, only Whiteling was left to care
for Willie. Whiteling wanted to get out of the house and go to work, but
having to take care of Willie made that difficult, if not impossible. She later said the child had become a burden for her, and he was always in her
way. So she poisoned Willie.

Willie's illness baffled Dr. Smith, who suggested that Dr. George Dietrich tend to Willie. Smith believed he had not had good luck treating John
and Bertha. Dietrich fared no better and attributed Willie's death to "congestion of the bowels." Whiteling collected $47 in insurance. Willie died
on 26 May, one month and two days after Bertha's death.

The news coverage about Whiteling's crimes burst upon *Philadelphia Inquirer* readers on 13 June 1888 with a front-page headline that read: "Appalling Revelation." Subordinate headlines were: "Mrs. Whiteling Tells
How She Killed Her Children," "Admits It Was a Terrible Crime," and
"The Wretched Woman Relates the Story in Circumstantial Detail, but Denies That She Poisoned Her Husband."

Maybe because the Whitelings were poor, none of the deaths was noted
in the *Inquirer*. None of the deaths was considered suspicious, although
all three died of what the *Inquirer* termed "singularly similar" symptoms.
No investigation was deemed necessary because all the deaths were attributed to natural causes, even though three people in the same family
died within two months under remarkably similar circumstances.

Whether she was guilty or innocent, the first story possibly damaged
any chance Whiteling might have had for a fair trial. The lead paragraph
of the *Inquirer* story said there had been "a full and absolute confession
from the murderess," and published her lengthy confession within the
news story. The *Inquirer* said Whiteling had lied to the coroner during
the investigation when she told him she was a longtime member of the
Methodist Episcopal Church, and that she was active in its Sunday school.
The coroner, the newspaper said, became interested in the case after learn-

ing of the three deaths. Police questioned neighbors, which, the newspaper said, resulted in an order of exhumation. Officials ordered Whiteling to be present at the exhumations, and when she arrived, she was greeted with the macabre sight of "Professor [Henry] Leffman in the act of removing the viscera from the remains." Leffman's examination, the newspaper said, revealed "large quantities" of arsenic in each victim. Police searched Whiteling's home and found nothing, but she was charged with "the appalling crime" and jailed. The *Inquirer* reported that Whiteling later confessed. The confession ran almost a full column in agate (a small type size). It seems remarkable today that the newspaper would be given the full confession of a defendant to publish before trial. However, published confessions were common at that time, and it was not unusual for reporters to observe police interrogations. The *Inquirer* led into the confession with: "[T]he unnatural mother detailed the particulars of her fiendish work as follows." The motive "apparently" was to collect the insurance money on each of the victims. The *Inquirer* added that an examination into Whiteling's past in Chicago "shows that she had not led a correct life." The newspaper did not say who had conducted the investigation or what it showed Whiteling had done.

The next day's edition carried a headline of "The Modern Borgia." The lead paragraph called Whiteling a murderess and an unnatural mother. The remainder of the lead left little doubt about her guilt, although a coroner's inquest had not yet been held.

> With the full knowledge of her heartless cruelty she now professes repentance and prays for forgiveness for fiendish crimes. Her bearing does not at all partake of insanity, but leaves the impression of a deliberate, calculating woman, who killed her offspring for the sake of a few hundred dollars. While she realizes her present situation, her appetite is said to be not impaired, and even the reflections on the revolting manner in which she administered poison to the two innocents do not appear to keep her from sleeping.

Although the newspaper had all but pronounced her sane, it did speculate about her sanity, saying that she seemed to have been gripped by "a mild form of religious frenzy." If she was sane, then she certainly seemed evil and without conscience. The *Inquirer* speculated about evidence when it wrote that "the neighbors" had told stories about Whiteling giving poisoned candy to children in the neighborhood. There were no sources for the information, other than the aforementioned vague reference. In a lengthy quotation, the *Inquirer* explained that Whiteling had killed her family for the insurance money. The newspaper introduced this section of the story with a boldface line that read, "Unable to Stand Prosperity." The damning story ended by publishing memorials Whiteling had written to her husband, Willie, and Bertha. She had framed and hung the memorials in her home. The *Inquirer* introduced this section of the story with the boldface line, "A Consummate Hypocrite."

A headline in the next day's *Inquirer* was "The Child Poisoner," and the story again called Whiteling an "unnatural mother" and the "poisoner of her two children." Much of the story was an explanation of a pest poison known as Rough on Rats, which the story said had killed "many" people in Philadelphia, and it said one box would kill twenty persons.

Before the inquest or formal charges were filed, the *Inquirer* reported that Whiteling had confessed, had lied during the investigation, was heartless and showed no emotion, ate and slept well despite her crimes, was sane, and had poisoned neighborhood children. The newspaper termed her a "fiend," an "unnatural mother," a "child poisoner," a "Modern Borgia," a "murderess," and a "consummate hypocrite." The state would now consider whether Whiteling should be indicted.

The story about the coroner's inquest contained quotations from Whiteling's confession. She claimed the "devil must have put it in my head" to poison her husband. The story had heavy moral overtones, focusing on the coroner telling Whiteling that if she wished to be forgiven, then she must confess her sins. Whiteling dressed "in deep black—as mourning for the husband and children." The inquest obviously was public because the newspaper said the small hearing room was filled to capacity "with a sweltering curious crowd." The hearing took on a bizarre tone when one of Whiteling's neighbors, who claimed to be a clairvoyant, testified that Whiteling had come to see her about the allegations that the children had been poisoned. The neighbor, identified as "Mrs. Walls," but in a later trial story named Emily Walz, "indignantly denied that she had charged 50 cents for the sitting. She said 50 cents wasn't her price." Twice during the inquest, Whiteling was asked to raise her veil so that witnesses could identify her. About the first instance, the *Inquirer* said Whiteling's face "was without the least trace of grief in it anywhere." Of the second instance, it reported that when Whiteling raised her veil, "she had a half silly smile on her face." Not surprisingly, the coroner's jury, "after a brief deliberation," returned a verdict that Whiteling had killed her husband and children.[17]

The *Inquirer* laid out the state's case in detail within seventy-two hours after the first story about the crimes. The *Inquirer* in its news stories also made its opinions known about the case. Whiteling would now face a jury of her peers in Philadelphia.

The *New York Times* also covered the crime. It published a front-page article about Whiteling's arrest and confession, with a headline that read: "A Mother's Awful Crimes." The *Times*'s story about the inquest con-

---

17. "The Triple Tragedy," *Philadelphia Inquirer*, 16 June 1888.

tained information that did not run in the *Inquirer*. The *Times* said that after the inquest, some of the crowd had lingered and threatened to lynch Whiteling. Police had taken her out an entrance other than the one that had been used to bring her in. The *Times*'s reporter said some women in the crowd were so enraged, they had made a motion as if to hit her, but police prevented them. Only quick and brave action by the police had saved Whiteling from being attacked by the crowd, according to the *Times*.[18]

Lynchings in Pennsylvania were unusual, but not unknown. Between 1882 and 1944, eight people, two of them white, were lynched in Pennsylvania. Women, and especially white women, were seldom lynched, but again it was not unknown. The heinousness of Whiteling's crimes accounted for the public outrage. The *Times* said in its first news story about the case that Whiteling's crimes would "rank in conception and execution with the most diabolical murders on record."[19]

Readers learned much about Whiteling's background in an *Inquirer* story that reported her hanging on 25 June 1889, a little more than one year after the first reports about the crimes. Whiteling's first husband died in a Pennsylvania prison after being convicted of highway robbery. She then married Whiteling in 1880. Bertha, born after the marriage, was the child of a saloon keeper in Philadelphia. Whiteling also had a fifteen-year-old son in Philadelphia who did not know that she was his mother, and the *Inquirer* said this "added to stories of bad reputation in the West," but did not relate any of the stories.[20]

Whiteling went on trial on 26 November 1888 for murdering Bertha. The trial's first day drew a number of local celebrities, including attorney Carrie B. Kilgore, "who is counsel for Mrs. Burroughs, now awaiting trial for disemboweling her husband"; "Mrs. Dr." Mary Pratt; and Dr. Alice Bennett of the Norristown Insane Asylum. The impressive medical and legal celebrity lineup dominated the *Inquirer*'s lead.[21] The newspaper's first paragraph was about 175 words long, astounding by today's journalistic standards, when fledgling reporters are admonished to write a "terse opening paragraph" of not more than 35 words for most "hard news" stories.

18. "A Mother's Awful Crimes," *New York Times*, 13 June 1888; "Killed Her Husband Too," ibid., 16 June 1888.

19. The lynching figures were compiled by Tuskegee University and cited in Mark Curriden and Leroy Phillips Jr., *Contempt of Court: The Turn-of-the-Century Lynching That Launched a Hundred Years of Federalism*, 353. An example of the lynching of a white woman can be found in "Judge Lynch," *Cheyenne Democratic Leader*, 20 January 1884. "A Mother's Awful Crimes."

20. "Mrs. Whiteling's Fate," *Philadelphia Inquirer*, 26 June 1889.

21. "Her Life in Jeopardy," ibid., 27 November 1888.

The *Inquirer*'s second-day coverage again paid close attention to the celebrities at the trial, saying that the courtroom was "thronged with insanity experts and well-known doctors." Dr. Pratt again occupied the same seat, and the clairvoyant, Emily Walz, "was dressed in the height of fashion." The *Inquirer*'s monumental lead paragraph of 252 words and 9 sentences summed up the opening of the day's testimony, Whiteling's reactions, the celebrity attendees, and the clairvoyant Walz's testimony. Whiteling showed more anxiety on the second day of the trial, the *Inquirer* said, because she "gnawed her finger nails and wiped her inflamed eyes." The *New York Times* reported that throughout the trial, Whiteling dressed in deep-mourning black, which made a good impression on spectators. The *Inquirer* added that the crowds in the courtroom were larger than the first day's crowds because of the "great publicity given to the case."[22]

Because Whiteling had pleaded insanity, her mental status was the key issue in the trial. She was apparently going through menopause—which in those days was equated with insanity in some women. The *Inquirer*'s story explained the testimony of at least six witnesses. One said Whiteling was "in a physical condition" and "at an age when insanity sometimes manifests itself." A "well-known expert on insanity" testified that "insanity often comes on at a particular period of female life." The newspaper repeatedly referred to Whiteling's "physical condition" but discreetly never explained its nature. Adult readers were probably expected to read between the lines.

The theories about Whiteling's possible insanity illustrate the state of scientific knowledge in 1888, and also raise the question of whether the experts' testimonies confused jurors more than enlightened them. The idea of a link between menopause and insanity seems laughable but for the reality that Whiteling was on trial for her life. Another expert testified that sanity could be determined by looking into the patient's eyes and that Whiteling's eyes had "lost their sensitiveness and power" and had "congestion" in the retinas. Dr. Alice Bennett said Whiteling had "low mental organization" and heart disease. The latter, she said, was often closely associated with insanity. Bennett said Whiteling was insane, and also was functionally deranged because Whiteling had told her so. After the experts' testimonies, Whiteling's chance of being declared insane seemed slim, although some did describe her behavior as bizarre. The undertaker said Whiteling had tried to bathe her dead son, Willie, and had alternately laughed and cried over the child.[23]

22. "Her Defense Insanity," ibid., 28 November 1888; "Convicted of Murder," *New York Times,* 29 November 1888.
23. "Her Defense Insanity."

The jury deliberated two hours before finding Whiteling guilty. The next day's headline in the *Inquirer* told the story: "The Penalty Is Death." The lead paragraph said Whiteling was only the second woman in Philadelphia's history to be convicted of first-degree murder. Later in the story, the *Inquirer* confusingly reported on two other Philadelphia women who had been convicted of first-degree murder, meaning Whiteling would have been the third. Hester Vaughn, the newspaper said, was convicted about twenty years earlier but never executed for murdering her child, and Annie Cutler, described by the *Inquirer* as "a colored woman," had more recently been sentenced to death, but later received a commutation to life in prison. The *Inquirer* said in the last paragraph that Whiteling would be the first woman in Philadelphia's history to be executed, which was erroneous: the *Philadelphia Pennsylvania Gazette* of 30 June–7 July 1737 reported the hanging of Catherine Conner.[24]

The press described Whiteling as being on an emotional roller coaster. She alternated between being calm one minute and "bellowing" and crying the next while waiting for the verdict. News reports in the *Inquirer* and the *New York Times* differed about how Whiteling had reacted to the verdict. The *Inquirer* said she had not seemed to realize what had happened. She "merely placed her handkerchief to her eyes and bowed her head as she had been wont to do during the course of the trial." The *Times* described the scene differently: "A dead silence fell on the throng, and every neck was craned to see the 12 men who held Mrs. Whiteling's fate in their hands. Every eye was directed to the prisoner as she was led to the prisoner's dock and told to face the jury." When the jury pronounced her guilty, Whiteling covered her face with a white handkerchief and burst into tears, the *Times* reported.[25]

Whiteling did not show the same emotion at her execution, and the *Inquirer* criticized her for it. The first words of the story said she was "[c]allous-hearted to the last," and then described her as "perfectly calm" and showing no emotion "beyond a sort of religious ecstasy." The *Inquirer* said her courage and resignation "disappointed all who looked for Mrs. Whiteling to faint." During her walk to the gallows, "calmly raising her skirts," the *Inquirer* said, she walked up the steps and stood on the trap. She paid no attention to those who offered her comfort, but "[h]er eyes were turned heavenward and with the faintest indication of a smile she prayed inaudibly." The nearly thirty witnesses were "overcome by emotion, and, with blanched faces and half-averted heads," watched Whiteling die. She made no statement, and had a short, silent prayer; the trap

24. "Philadelphia, July 7," *Philadelphia Pennsylvania Gazette*, 30 June–7 July 1737.
25. "The Penalty Is Death," *Philadelphia Inquirer*, 29 November 1888; "Convicted of Murder."

fell at 10:07 A.M., less than one minute after she stepped onto the gallows. The *Inquirer* said that "the woman who ruthlessly destroyed three lives fell into the abyss of eternity."[26]

The *Inquirer* took a mere 2 paragraphs and 183 words to describe the uneventful hanging, but the newspaper devoted 2 full columns to the story. Boldface lines used within the story provide an outline of its content and flow. They read, in order, "How She Spent the Morning," "The Eye-Witnesses Assembling," "In the Line to the Scaffold," "The Murderess Joins the Line Boldly," "The Woman's Life and Crime," "Are Such Poisonings Frequent?" and "The Fate of Other Murderesses." A related story, with the grotesque headline "The Brains of Mrs. Whiteling," detailed the autopsy done on her brain.

The religious angle of the hanging story provided readers with the message that Whiteling had left this world for a better one. Such descriptions were common in execution stories of the time and seemed designed to help assure readers that although the defendant had committed a terrible crime, she had nonetheless repented and likely was forgiven. The people, in the form of the state, were actually doing her a kind of favor by dispatching her from this world of sorrow into the heavenly world, where she would know only happiness. The *Inquirer* reported each hymn sung, including "Jesus, Lover of My Soul," "The Fountain Filled with Blood," and "I Am Coming." The newspaper said the "religious exercises" took more than three hours.[27]

The *Inquirer* melodramatically described the death cortege's trek to Whiteling's cell and then from the cell to the gallows: "Out into the long whitewashed corridor wound the line, with uncovered heads and hearts freighted with fearful expectancy and suspense." The reporter ventured into the unknown when describing prisoners who were locked behind oak doors to prevent them from seeing what was happening. The *Inquirer* said it was the first time that wooden doors had covered the iron bars of the cells, so the prison officials must have believed the sight of a woman walking to her death would be too much for the prisoners. Nonetheless, the *Inquirer* reporter wrote: "Yet each prisoner knew the meaning of the solemn tread, and what agonies they experienced must remain untold." Perhaps it had to remain untold because the reporter could not see the

---

26. "Mrs. Whiteling's Fate."

27. Gallows speeches and execution sermons were intended for those witnessing the execution, as well as the condemned. Execution sermons originated in Puritan Massachusetts in the middle to late seventeenth century. They survived as a literary form even after Puritanism. These sermons often were published, including thirty-three between 1751 and 1798. They were precursors to the news reports of gallows speeches that came later. See Ronald A. Bosco, "Lectures at the Pillory: The Early American Execution Sermon."

prisoners, nor could they see him, and the story did not indicate he had interviewed them.

The *Inquirer* contradicted itself when it said Whiteling's death was "quick and almost painless" and that she had died of strangulation. The reporter had no way of knowing whether she was in pain. The *Inquirer* also contradicted itself when it described in vivid detail every part of the hanging, and then wrote: "The horrors of the first execution of a woman are indescribable," and speculatively added that the execution "will remain everlastingly vivid upon the memories of the witnesses." The newspaper praised officials for their efficiency.[28]

An *Inquirer* reporter apparently attended Whiteling's autopsy because the paper described it in detail. It said the indentation on the neck caused by the rope was "deep." Several of the doctors at the autopsy had never seen a hanging victim's body. Doctors examined Whiteling's skull and brain, and the *Inquirer* said the skull appeared to be "ordinary" although small, which was understood at the time to be often associated with less intelligence, although the newspaper did not specifically say so. Whiteling's brain "showed marked evidences of enous congestion," the newspaper said, although it did not explain what that meant. The *Inquirer*'s report could have been written for a medical journal instead of for a daily newspaper. One of the coverings of the brain "known as the dura mater was rather tightly adhered to the interior of the skull. The brains were natural in appearance. Their convolutions were regular, except in a few of them where slight irregularities were noticed."[29]

Presumably, all of the detailed description of Whiteling's brain was to prove or disprove that she had been insane, which seemed decidedly beside the point now that she was dead. However, the *Inquirer* never explained what all of the description meant, so readers were left to decipher for themselves and to draw their own conclusions.

Eventually, Whiteling was buried beside her husband and two children.

28. The depiction of officials as responsible and efficient is common in execution stories. One book discussing crime news said that much news consists of moral-character portraits, one of which is that of responsible authorities (Ericson, Baranek, and Chan, *Representing Order*, 8).

29. For a description of how craniology was used, see Stephen J. Gould, *The Mismeasure of Man*, chap. 3. The dura mater is a tough membrane that covers the brain and spinal cord and lines the inner surface of the skull.

Chapter 2

The Demons Decline

Twentieth-Century Mothers

WOMEN WHO POISON CHILDREN HAVE also been executed in the twentieth century, including two of the three women executed in Alabama. One, Rhonda Martin, died for poisoning her fourth husband, but she admitted she had also poisoned three of her children and her mother. Mrs. Earle Dennison died for murdering her nieces; she poisoned them to collect insurance money. The nature of the crimes usually results in extensive news coverage. Although murdering a child during a fit of rage might be understood, poisoning a child seems so premeditated that the crime is considered especially heinous, and killing a child for no apparent reason appears even more evil. This type of murder violates every social norm about women being primary caretakers and nurturers of children.

However, the twentieth-century press did not label women who murdered children as fiends, demons, or unnatural mothers.

Earle Dennison: "The First White Woman" Ever Executed in Alabama

Two-year-old Shirley Diann Weldon seemed happy that her aunt Earle Dennison visited on the first day of May 1952. Dennison took Shirley to get an orange soft drink for her and her brother, Orvil. Dennison carried the child into a general store near where the Weldons lived, patted her on the head, and said, "Bless your little heart." Back at the Weldons' home, Dennison poured some of the drink in a cup and gave it to Shirley, and gave the bottle to Orvil. One-half hour later, Shirley convulsed and died that night. Dennison watched as an autopsy showed that Shirley had died of arsenic poisoning.[1]

---

1. "Poisonings in Weldon Family Topic of Day in Wetumpka," *Montgomery Advertiser*, 17 May 1952; "Poison Death Is Admitted by Wetumpkian, Sheriff Says," ibid., 18 May 1952.

The low-key story began with a "Deaths" headline on page 6 in the B section of the 3 May 1952 edition of the *Montgomery Advertiser*, where it said Shirley Diann Weldon, age two and one-half, had died Thursday afternoon. Seven days later, the *Advertiser*'s front-page headline said: "Wetumpka Nurse Held in Death of Niece Takes Sedative Dose." Police arrested Dennison, a widow and a nurse, for poisoning Shirley.

Although the *Advertiser* covered the crime well, the story did not draw the attention one might have expected. Between 10 May and 28 May, the story ran on the *Advertiser*'s front page four times, never as the lead story and only once on the top half of the page. This was unusual not only because of Dennison's heinous crime, but also because nurses are supposed to save lives, not take them, especially those of young children.[2]

Dennison was not just any nurse; she was the head nurse at the Wetumpka General Hospital in Wetumpka, Alabama, a small town near Montgomery. Police took her to the hospital where she worked because she had swallowed an overdose of sedatives just before deputies came to arrest her. The first news story included details that made the crime perhaps even more horrible. Shirley's three-year-old sister, Polly Ann, had died two and one-half years earlier under similar circumstances. Dennison had visited that day and given Polly Ann an ice cream cone; the child fell ill and died about a week later. The similar circumstances aroused the Weldons' suspicions.[3]

As Dennison's condition slowly improved, the *Advertiser* published additional information, including that she had purchased an insurance policy on Shirley worth five thousand dollars about one month before the child died and had taken out a thousand-dollar policy on Shirley with another company just a day or so before she died. Shirley's parents had consented to the policies and to Dennison being the beneficiary.[4] Curiously, the story about the insurance policies ran inside the *Advertiser* under a one-column headline.

Officials exhumed Polly Ann's body, and the *Advertiser* reported it contained traces of arsenic. Dennison's husband had died about a year before, and his remains were also exhumed, but no arsenic was found.[5]

Dennison apparently gave no indication she might be a murderer. The

2. When nurses kill children, especially their own children, it is seen as especially horrifying. See, for example, "Arkansas, Texas Cases Have Similarities," *Jonesboro (Ark.) Sun,* 26 June 2001, which relates the similarities between nurse-mothers Christina Riggs of Arkansas and Andrea Yates of Texas, both of whom murdered their children. Riggs was executed in 2000.

3. "Wetumpka Nurse Held in Death."

4. "Wetumpka Nurse Shows Response," *Montgomery Advertiser,* 11 May 1952; "Nurse Insured Alleged Victim of Poisoning," ibid., 12 May 1952.

5. "Poison Report Issued As 2nd Body Exhumed," ibid., 16 May 1952; "Poison Death Is Admitted."

head of the hospital where she worked called her an excellent nurse and a nice person; each day she cut flowers from the hospital's gardens and gave some to the patients and put others on the reception desk. Coworkers said she was cheerful, and even the Weldons, who had lost two children, said that nothing in Dennison's past indicated she would harm the children. One part of the otherwise somber story seemed inappropriate, saying that Sheriff Lester Holley, who investigated the poisoning deaths, "turned up on the sick list himself today—food poisoning." The newspaper lightheartedly reported there was no suggestion of foul play.[6]

Later news reports indicated that contrary to her coworkers' comments, all was not well in Dennison's life. After the death of her husband, Lemuel, in 1951, some people said Dennison acted strangely. She became nervous and depressed. She reportedly visited her husband's grave site every day, sometimes weeping and refusing to leave for hours. Some of her relatives said they believed her husband's drinking and an unhappy home life had taken a toll; nonetheless, she refused to leave her hospital job.

About two weeks after Shirley's death notice, the *Advertiser* published a front-page story stating that Dennison had confessed to poisoning the child. In a curious twist, she also admitted she had brought arsenic to the Weldons' home shortly before Polly Ann died, but denied she had intentionally poisoned Polly Ann. Dennison said she had inadvertently left on the table a salt shaker containing arsenic that she used to make ant poison. She admitted she had come to the house the next day and given Polly Ann some ice cream, but denied it contained poison. Sheriff Holley revealed that Dennison had purchased insurance policies on Polly Ann and on Orvil worth five thousand dollars each, and that she had collected on Polly Ann's policy, although she told the sheriff that she did not know why she had taken out the policies.[7]

The *Advertiser* said she "stood mute and down-faced" at her arraignment, looked shaky, "and shrank back as the photographer's bulbs flashed." The otherwise straight news story carried an ending more suited to a feature story: "This peaceful unhurried town has talked of little else since the disclosures in the case electrified its citizens. Brought to its own doorstep were facts which heretofore Wetumpkians had merely read about in far-off places."[8]

In August 1952, an all-male jury convicted Dennison of Shirley's murder; she was never tried for Polly Ann's murder. She was distraught when

6. "Poisonings Topic of Day."
7. "Poison Death Is Admitted."
8. "Mrs. Dennison Bound Over on Charges of Poisoning Nieces," ibid., 28 May 1952.

sentenced to die in Alabama's electric chair, and on two separate occasions she took an overdose of sleeping pills; she also slashed her wrists in efforts to kill herself.

The *Advertiser* described Dennison as frail, haggard, and gaunt at a clemency hearing, and also mentioned that her hair had grayed. She sat impassively. When she spoke, she asked the governor, "Have mercy on me. Save my life." The governor denied clemency, and matrons were assigned to an around-the-clock watch because it was feared Dennison would attempt suicide.[9]

A reporter for the *Birmingham News* wrote a highly personalized account of the execution. The lead paragraph said: "The night is clear and starry as you begin the steps that will carry you 'through the valley of the shadow of death'—the death that waits for Mrs. Earle Dennison, the first white woman ever executed by the state of Alabama." A bright-yellow electric chair, sitting in a small black-and-white twelve-foot-by-twelve-foot room, would be used for Dennison's execution. Officials gave her a mild sedative to ease her nerves. The Reverend J. E. Franks, the prison chaplain, told reporters that Dennison was calm, had her Bible with her, and held no ill will toward anyone. At midnight, Dennison entered the death chamber, her head completely shaved. Of the twenty-four witnesses, eleven were newspaper and radio reporters. One reporter said that as he filed into the room, he was inches from Dennison's face. Two guards led her to the electric chair and lifted her into it; her feet dangled about six inches above the floor. Her head jerked as the guards tightened the straps to restrain her. Among her last words were, "I feel I am with God. . . . Please forgive me for everything I have done. . . . He has forgiven me. . . . I forgive everyone," the *News* reported. As guards adjusted the helmet, Dennison winced and said, "Oh, you're hurting," in a barely audible voice. A guard tightened a large nut on the death helmet with a pair of pliers, and at 12:07 A.M. the switch was thrown. *News* reports said it took only one jolt to kill her; she died in twenty-seven seconds, and an acrid odor of burning body hair and flesh filled the room.[10]

Five guards dressed in gray removed the straps, while two inmates dressed in white waited with a stretcher. Witnesses and journalists left the room as Dennison's relatives waited outside for her body to be put into a black hearse.

9. "Clemency Is Denied, Nurse Must Die in Chair," *Birmingham News*, 3 September 1953.

10. "Mrs. Dennison Goes Quietly to Electric Chair—in Span of 27 Seconds She Pays for Poisoning Niece," ibid., 4 September 1953.

Rhonda Belle Martin: A Multiple Murderer

Only three people attended Rhonda Belle Martin's burial in Montgomery, Alabama, on a mid-October day in 1957. That was less than the number of Martin's family members buried near her; she had murdered many of them.

Martin confessed to poisoning and killing three of her seven children, her mother, and her second and fourth husbands. Two other children—Adelaide, age four; and Judith, age one—died with symptoms similar to arsenic poisoning, and she poisoned, but did not kill, her fifth husband, who became paralyzed and "a hopeless cripple." Authorities considered charging Martin with incest because they believed her fifth husband was her stepson; however, it was determined that when Martin married her fourth husband, she was not legally divorced from her third husband. That made her fourth marriage bigamous, and therefore she was not legally married in Alabama, which meant her fourth husband's son, her fifth husband, was not legally her stepson and her marriage to him did not violate Alabama law. Such circumstances might attract the interest of the press.

Unlike Earle Dennison's story, which gently eased its way into the *Montgomery Advertiser*'s news columns, Martin's story screamed at readers and dominated the front page for days. Beginning on 10 March 1956, Martin's story ran on the front page for six consecutive days, three times as the lead story and in every instance on the top half of the page.

The headline on the *Advertiser*'s first report said, "Mobile Waitress, 49, Booked at City Jail in Mate's Poisoning." Police arrested Martin for poisoning her fourth husband, Claude Martin, in 1951, and she was eventually executed on 11 October 1957 for his death. The first story also said officials would exhume and test the bodies of six other family members. The crimes spanned a long period: five of her children, her mother, and her second husband died between 1934 and 1944. Police became suspicious when her fifth husband, Roland Martin, was hospitalized and tests showed arsenic in his body, which led police to exhume Claude Martin's body. He had died in 1951. When arrested, Rhonda Martin reportedly said, "I don't know why you're doing this. There's nothing to it."

Police told the *Advertiser* that she was sullen and smoked continuously. The newspaper said she weighed 175 pounds and had reddish brown hair. The *Advertiser* described her as "plain looking," apparently drawing its information from observation when police brought her to Montgomery's city jail. The story said police would not allow her to be photographed because of "unusual circumstances," but the rule did not last long because her picture ran on the *Advertiser*'s front page the next day, with a caption that said she was en route to the jail.

The *Advertiser* had extraordinary access to Martin; about three hours after she was jailed, *Advertiser* city editor Joe Azbell spent more than two hours interviewing her in her jail cell, and he wrote a remarkably detailed story, "Jailed Waitress Vows Innocence in Mate's Death," published on 11 March 1956. Azbell's lead sentence said Martin wore gold wedding bands on both hands (one for her fourth husband and another for the fifth), and she told him "she never dated a man she didn't marry." Martin said her fifth husband, whom she called "Bud," "will be heartbroken when he finds out what happened to me." She said she had recently visited Bud in Biloxi, Mississippi, where he was hospitalized and that "he was glad to see me and hated to see me go. He kissed me tenderly. . . . I love him so much. He's a good looking man. He's young. . . . We've been so happy together." Three days later, Martin confessed she had poisoned Bud.

In the story, Martin said her family members had died of a heart attack, pneumonia, a throat disorder, or "infirmities." She said, "Everybody always said I spoiled my husbands and everybody always said I spoiled my children. That's the way I am. I always spoil anybody I love." The story described Martin in detail:

> Mrs. Martin was dressed in a white uniform which cost $3 at a bargain sale and a $4 pair of teen-age white shoes. She wore a yellow coat.
>
> She is a plain woman with a rather kindly appearance. Four large moles stand out on her face, three on the cheek and one above the eye, and there is a circle of pock marks from pimples at her mouth line. She wears false uppers, modern brown-rimmed glasses. Her 170 pounds is shaped well for a woman of her age. Her fingernails are painted a fire engine red and her eyebrows are streaked with black shade lines. The rouge on her face was light against a faint, pasty powder. Dime store earrings, three clusters of flower buds, hung from her pierced ears. She had a hard stare in her dark eyes but her voice was tired and sugar coated.

Martin described herself as "a poor woman" who had seen more than her share of tragedy. "Somebody I loved dying almost every year. I always thought if Bud (her fifth) didn't come through his sickeness [*sic*], I would never marry again. I always wanted a home but it looks like everytime I get married, there's some tragedy."

Martin claimed to be ill, although she reportedly chain-smoked throughout the interview, and had had a heart attack and pneumonia in 1950. "I still have a weak heart, very weak, and I can't stand excitement," she said. She told Azbell she had never worn a dress that cost more than ten dollars or a pair of shoes that cost more than five dollars. She had been jailed on two previous occasions, once for drunkenness and once for reckless driving, although she claimed she had never drank or smoked until she married her fifth husband. She said she had always tried to be a "good Christian" but had not been to church in a long time. "I think I will start going again regular when all of this is over."

Martin's "stepdaughters" did not approve of her marriage to Bud, who was their brother. They had lived with her but moved out soon after the marriage. Martin said one of the stepdaughters had received more than two thousand dollars from an insurance policy after the fourth husband's death, but the women claimed they had never gotten "the first penny" of the money.

Martin's involvement with men began early, according to Azbell's story. She married the first time at fifteen, divorced that husband at nineteen, and married again at twenty-one. Martin later admitted poisoning her second husband, George Garrett. She married a third time, but divorced after five months; she apparently married her fourth husband, Claude Martin, before the divorce was final. After having six of her seven children die, losing her mother and two of her husbands, suffering through two divorces, and seeing her last husband paralyzed, what did Martin regret? "It's that Ronald and I couldn't have children. We both wanted children but we couldn't have any. I regret that so much."

The story was the lengthiest that the *Advertiser* published about Martin. It ran two full columns down the left side of the front page and jumped to three additional columns on an inside page. The story showed Martin as a curious, almost delusional person who seemed self-centered to the extreme, worrying about herself while discussing so many deaths in her family. If she had done what police claimed, she seemed in the story to be either a clever liar or someone with no feelings about or understanding of her crimes.

Even if Martin did murder the family members, the story surely damaged her trial chances. It seems remarkable today that police would give a reporter such access to a criminal defendant in a sensational case before that person's case had gone before a grand jury, and apparently before she even had an attorney. However, such circumstances were the norm during the 1950s, and therefore the *Advertiser* cannot be too harshly judged. It seems ironic that a story about United States Supreme Court Chief Justice Earl Warren ran just below Martin's story. The Warren Court in the 1960s for the first time overturned convictions of defendants because of pretrial prejudicial publicity, and thus established stricter constitutional protections for defendants' due-process and fair-trial rights. But those decisions were not made until years after the published interview with Martin.

The story apparently attracted much public interest. A front-page story the next day said the exhumations of Martin's family members were delayed because officials feared a crowd might gather at the cemetery. Azbell recognized the irony of the situation when he reported that of the eighteen hundred people buried in the cemetery, "Mrs. Martin has the largest number of family members buried there of any person." Any reader who kept up with the story knew that police believed Martin had put most of her family members there. Azbell wrote that the graves were "near the entrance of the beautifully landscaped, tree-lined burial grounds." In what seems an attempt at imagery, he added: "On a hillside above these graves is a beautiful engraved monument by pine trees in a quiet setting. It is the scene of the Last Supper." Officials forbade photographers to take pictures of the exhumations, and, curiously, local officials clammed up. The *Advertiser* reported that police kept Martin "incommunicado from the press," and it also said state investigators were "mum" on a report about checks at drugstores to see if Martin had purchased poison. That action seemed too little too late after the *Advertiser*'s jailhouse interview, but if police and prosecutors were trying to shut off information, then their efforts had little or no effect on the *Advertiser*. Its story explained that an *Advertiser* reporter had checked several drugstores in the Montgomery area, and none had any records showing Martin purchased poison.[11]

Perhaps the most damaging story to Martin prior to her trial was on 14 March, when the headline of the *Advertiser*'s lead story said: "Waitress Admits Guilt in Seven Poison Cases; Six Victims Met Death." Another "high official in the investigation" told the *Advertiser* he understood that Martin had confessed to eight murders. The *Advertiser* used unnamed sources with some regularity during the first several days. The 14 March story also contained a quote from one of the stepdaughters, who said when told of Martin's confession, "She's just crazy, that's all."

Another lead story the following day left readers with little doubt about Martin's guilt, although a grand jury had yet to indict her. The first sentence said: "The cold-blooded calculating methods which Mrs. Rhonda Bell [*sic*] Martin admitted employing to kill her children, two ex-husbands and mother were revealed yesterday by investigators." Police and prosecutors laid out in detail for the press and the public how Martin had killed her family members. The story said one child, Ellyn, was crippled after being given poison for more than a year, and that Martin had expressed sorrow to neighbors that the child lost the use of her limbs. It said she murdered a three-year-old daughter, Emogene, on a whim after the child asked for a drink of water. Martin instead poured powdered poison into milk and gave it to her. Martin also put poison in her second husband's whiskey for several days, and when "the father of her five children" came home from his job sick, "she allowed him to stagger about in

11. "Graves of Martin Family Due to Be Opened Today," *Montgomery Advertiser,* 12 March 1956; "2 Bodies Exhumed Here to Test Cause of Death," ibid., 13 March 1956.

the backyard. Soothing him, she took the man inside the house and fed him another shot of whisky mixed with ant poison. The next day he was dead." Investigators changed their ideas about why Martin killed so many members of her family, saying they believed she was emotionally insecure and that no one wanted her, perhaps because her father had deserted the family when she was twelve. Police also said they considered her "fascinated by the effects of poison." However, none of the officers believed Martin to be insane. They said she had "superior intelligence" and planned each murder of the adults. Collecting insurance money was not discounted as a motive, but police said she had collected only a small amount on most victims. Police said Martin, who told them she avoided detection by not using the same doctor for any of her victims, remained mostly calm during the interrogations.[12]

The *Advertiser* located Martin's third husband, whom she divorced after five months, and the headline on the front page said: "Rhonda Bell [sic] Martin's Third Husband Thinks Early Separation Saved Him from Poison." In the story, Talmadge J. Gipson told the *Advertiser*'s Joe Azbell that he believed the only reason he had not been poisoned was "that I got shed of her too quick (they were married five months) or I didn't have no insurance." Gipson said that in his former job as an attendant at a veterans' hospital in Montgomery, he had seen "all kinds of crazy people, alcoholics and dopeheads," but, he added, "I ain't never seen a shrewder, more smart person in the whole country than Rhonda Bell. . . . She ain't no good-looking woman but she's got personality and she's smart. I know a crazy person when I see one and she ain't crazy." Gipson said he considered Martin a sadist who poisoned others because she liked to watch them suffer. He said she had often talked to him about getting married, but he had resisted until one night when they were drinking heavily and he consented; however, soon after the marriage, she began going out at night. Gipson said she drank heavily when they were married. "When she got drunk, and she liked to drink a lot, she would sing. She sings real pretty." Gipson said he would like to ask his former wife "how she missed me. I sure have been wondering about that. Maybe it just wasn't my time."[13]

In nine days, police and prosecutors had fed the *Advertiser* every imaginable detail about Martin and her crimes, including a confession to multiple murders for which she would not face trial. A grand jury had not yet indicted her for the murder of her fourth husband, the crime with which she was eventually charged.

Not surprisingly, Martin was indicted, tried, and convicted for murdering her fourth husband. She was executed nineteen months and one

12. "Grand Jury to Review Waitress' Case in May," ibid., 15 March 1956.
13. "Martin's Third Husband," ibid., 18 March 1956.

day after the first story broke in the *Advertiser* about her arrest. At a clemency hearing, her attorney argued that her sanity had not been clearly established and she needed additional mental examinations. One psychiatrist said he believed she suffered from schizophrenia, but other psychiatrists and doctors who examined her said they found no evidence of insanity. When she died, Martin left a note in her cell. The note, written one year earlier, asked that her body be given to science when she died, whether by execution or natural causes: "At my death, whether it be a natural death or otherwise, I want my body to be given to some scientific institution to be used as they see fit, but especially to see if someone can find out why I committed the crimes I have committed. I can't understand it, for I had no reason whatsoever. There is definitely something wrong. Can't someone find it and save someone else the agony I have been through?"[14]

The note raises an interesting question: if Martin was trying to save herself at the clemency hearing with an insanity argument, then why did she wait until after her death to reveal the note she had written a year earlier? The second point is that the note indicates a certain degree of self-centeredness. Instead of saying that science might find out things that would save others from being murdered by someone such as herself, Martin said it might save someone from the "agony" she had been through. The only way Martin's wish could be granted was for relatives to not claim her body, the *Advertiser* reported. Her remains then would go to the University of Alabama Medical Center at Birmingham. However, her relatives chose to have her buried.

Even at the time of her execution, and after, the *Advertiser* could not keep from writing about Martin's weight and hair color. In its execution story, it referred to her as the "heavy-set, red-haired former waitress," and a story about her burial termed her the "husky ex-waitress." The story also had a subtle racial overtone, which certainly was not unusual for 1950s Alabama. It called Martin the "second white woman" to be executed in Alabama. It also said in a subhead that the "first white woman" had been executed in 1953, and gave details of Earle Dennison's death. However, the story never mentioned the names or the circumstances of black women executed in Alabama. They remained invisible.[15]

14. "Governor Holds Murderess' Fate," ibid., 10 October 1957; "Waitress' Final Wish Rejected by Relatives," ibid., 12 October 1957.

15. "Mrs. Martin's Life Ends in Kilby's Electric Chair," ibid., 11 October 1957. Such invisibility of African Americans was the theme of Ralph Ellison's famous novel *Invisible Man*. Studies have found continued "invisibility" of African Americans in mainstream media.

Chapter 3

Husbands and Other Family Members

POISONINGS OR OTHER WAYS OF MURDERING family members might have also gotten much press attention in the nineteenth and twentieth centuries because of the rise of feminism. One author contends that fear of wives poisoning their husbands was associated with feminism, and that the reported cases of such poisonings increased during the 1800s. "As agitation for women's rights increased, men (and antifeminist women) shrilled that the traditional marriage relationship, established by God, would be destroyed," Ann Jones wrote. Women would turn against their husbands, if the men were seen as oppressors. "The poisoning wife became the specter of the century—the witch who lurked in women's sphere and haunted the minds of men."[1]

At the end of the nineteenth century, Cesare Lombroso and Guglielmo Ferrero described in a book titled *The Female Offender* how a "born criminal" could be identified among women. The book, which focuses on anatomical characteristics, states that many factors make women less likely to become criminals, but when women do act criminally, they could be more ferocious than their male counterparts. This role of killer was an unexpected one for women, who were supposed to be virtuous, gentle, and kind, especially to their families. Society protected women in many ways, legal and otherwise.[2] With such social norms in place, women who broke the norms and killed family members were candidates for much public and press interest—and for the death penalty.

1. Jones, *Women Who Kill*, 76.
2. The Lombroso and Ferrero material is cited in Friedman, *Crime and Punishment*, 421. For protection of women, see esp. 211–23. For example, in the 1830s some post offices in large cities had a separate window to be used only by women to pick up their mail, which protected them from mixing with male patrons (Patricia Cline Cohen, *The Murder of Helen Jewett: The Life and Death of a Prostitute in Nineteenth-Century New York*, 125).

Dovie Dean: The Woman Who Could Not Cry

Dovie Blanche Dean, accused of murdering her husband of four months, awaited on 13 December 1952 the jury verdict of seven men and five women. The newspaper press said her composure during the trial had been "uncanny." She half rose from her chair as the jury foreman announced the guilty verdict with no recommendation for mercy. The *Cincinnati Enquirer* said Dean "uttered a low moan, then fell back with head bowed and hands covering her eyes." Her daughter screamed and ran and fell on her knees in front of her mother, who patted her daughter's shoulder. Dean quickly regained her composure, or at least outwardly so. She did not cry; the *Enquirer* reported she was heard to say, "I cannot cry."

The prosecution made much of Dean's seemingly cold demeanor during the trial, although press reports never made it clear why she could not cry. An *Enquirer* story said a psychologist who testified on her behalf said she had a psychological disorder; however, a later story in the *Cleveland Plain Dealer* said she had no tear ducts, and had never cried.[3]

Judging from news reports, the inability to cry worked against Dean. The *Enquirer* said the prosecuting attorney told jurors during closing arguments that Dean was cold and cunning and had treated the trial "as though this whole thing were a joke." He said to the jury: "I wonder if her happiest moments were not on 22 August when she stood and watched the last breath of Hawkins Dean." Dovie Dean later said she believed her inability to cry had hurt her at trial. However, news reports about this inability came after the trial, and she said that when she testified, the prosecution "made light of me because I couldn't cry."[4]

The *Plain Dealer*, in a story about Dean's execution, flatly said the jury was influenced: "She was taken by her jury to be a woman with no feeling of sympathy or sorrow." The newspaper said few people at Batavia knew why Dean could not cry, although it gave no indication how it had acquired that information. The newspaper, in another unattributed statement, said it was "quite uncommon" for someone to have no tear ducts. Dean told the *Plain Dealer* that her inability to cry caused others to perceive her as hard-hearted. "Like at my son John's funeral two years ago come February. He was 21. I heard someone say: 'Just look, his mother isn't taking it very hard—she's not even crying.' But so many times I want to cry and can't."[5]

3. "Dovie Dean Is Doomed by Jury," *Cincinnati Enquirer*, 4 December 1952; "Mrs. Dean Pays Death Penalty," *Cleveland Plain Dealer*, 16 January 1954.
4. "Doomed by Jury"; "Dovie Dean Will Die Tonight; Lausche Refuses to Intervene," *Columbus Dispatch*, 15 January 1954.
5. "Dean Pays Death Penalty."

Dean was reared in a broken home and married twice, the first time when she was young. That marriage ended for practical purposes in 1938 when her husband was sentenced to serve seven years in a West Virginia prison for raping a daughter. Dovie Dean's life continued along a miserable vein: Ohio newspapers reported that the daughter who was raped later died giving birth, one of Dean's sons died in a boiler explosion, and Dean herself worked mostly as a domestic in others' homes and never had much money.

On 12 April 1952, Hawkins Dean, sixty-eight, a farmer in Owensville, Ohio, made out a will leaving his $27,106 estate, including a 115-acre farm, to his future wife, Dovie Dean. The next day, Dovie married Hawkins; she was his third wife. On 22 August 1952, Hawkins died. Some neighbors said that shortly after his death, someone threw a wild party at the Dean farm and shots were fired. Dovie Dean said there was no party, but several of her children had come over and they went to a drive-in movie and drank several beers afterward. She said shots were fired, but not during a party: she said she had fired two pistol shots at strangers outside her home, and her son-in-law had also shot at the intruders.

A pragmatic Dovie Dean described her marriage to Hawkins: "He needed a housekeeper and I needed a home." The *Cleveland Plain Dealer* described the marriage as "almost a business arrangement." The *Cincinnati Enquirer* reported that Dean had said her husband could not perform "his husbandly duties." She also said at her trial that Hawkins had threatened her life. Despite the problems, Dean said just before she died that she had kept house well for Hawkins: "I papered rooms that hadn't been papered in 33 years, painted woodwork that had never been painted."[6] Dean's son Carl Meyer Jr. also worked on Hawkins's farm.

After Hawkins's death, his only child demanded an autopsy, which showed arsenic in his body—more than twice the amount necessary to kill him. In September, police arrested Dovie Dean and Carl Meyer Jr. Police said she confessed orally and in writing after what the *Cleveland Plain Dealer* described as "intensive questioning." Carl was released. The trial in December 1952 lasted six days, and prosecutor Ray Bradford termed Dean's crime "the most gruesome crime in Clermont County history." In her confession, Dean reportedly said of her husband: "I got him before he got me." Prosecutors said Dean confessed she had given Hawkins rat poison in his milk. In a *Plain Dealer* story, Dean told the newspaper that before police arrested her, they questioned her for nine days in London, Ohio, and again in Batavia. Dean told the newspaper that she spoke out at such a late date—it was only a day before her scheduled execution—

6. "Lausche Weighs Mrs. Dean's Death in Ohio Chair Tonight," *Cleveland Plain Dealer,* 15 January 1954; "Doomed by Jury."

because her lawyers were not able to present what she termed her "theory" at her trial.[7] The theory apparently was that she believed Hawkins would have killed her. Left unsaid is why Dean did not tell the press her story earlier.

A story in the *Columbus Dispatch* about Dean's execution said that only she could name the brand of poison that matched what was found in Hawkins's body, and that she told police where they could find a bottle she had hidden in a woodshed. That admission "sealed her doom" because poison crystals in the bottle were identical to poison found in Hawkins, and in a glass of milk at his bedside.[8]

The *Cincinnati Enquirer* announced the verdict with an alliterative banner headline across the front page: "Dovie Dean Is Doomed by Jury." The *Enquirer* said that following the verdict, Dean walked back to her cell, but was stiff and walked erect with a "firm step" and a "fixed, shocked expression." The "firm step" description has been used for so many years in execution stories that by 1952 it had become a cliché.

Two days before Dean's execution, Gov. Frank J. Lausche told the press he had worried about Dean's death sentence and had studied her case for hours during the two previous nights. He said he would announce his decision on 15 January, the day Dean was to die; if he decided against commutation, Dean would die that night. The *Columbus Dispatch* reported "no hint as to what his decision will be."[9]

The events leading up to the execution received prominent news coverage in the *Cleveland Plain Dealer*, although not front-page coverage until the execution story ran. The *Plain Dealer* ran a 15 January story about Lausche's consideration of commutation at the top of page 2, with Dean's picture. The paper's other big story ran about a week earlier on page 2 and reported that Betty Butler and Dovie Dean were scheduled to die on the same day. Governor Lausche delayed Butler's execution.[10] It seems incredible in hindsight that the story about two women possibly being executed on the same day in the same state did not receive more press coverage. The *Plain Dealer* did run a headline that said "2 Mothers to Go to Chair Jan. 15."

The *Columbus Dispatch* on 15 January said in a six-column two-line headline: "Dovie Dean Will Die Tonight; Lausche Refuses to Intervene." News reports said the governor agonized about the decision. In a statement, Lausche said, "I wanted to help her." The governor's secretaries

7. "2 Mothers to Go to Chair Jan. 15," *Cleveland Plain Dealer*, 7 January 1954.

8. "Dovie Dean Dies Silently in Chair," *Columbus Dispatch*, 16 January 1954.

9. "Dovie Dean to Learn Fate from Gov. Lausche Friday," *Columbus Dispatch*, 13 January 1954.

10. "2 Mothers Go to Chair."

said he worried about any death sentence case, but "this one caused him more emotional disturbance than all the rest of the cases." Lausche said he had conferred with the trial judge, but could find no way to justify intervention. Like other governors before him in other states, Lausche seemingly wanted to prevent a woman's execution—or at least he claimed he did—but he did not believe he could justifiably do so. Such statements must be taken at face value, but they do limit political damage. There was, however, some political reaction. A Democratic Party city councilman from Cincinnati resigned as chairman of the Fifteenth Ward, saying he would not campaign for Governor Lausche's reelection, and a representative-elect called the execution "positively uncivilized," and said he would introduce a bill at the next legislative session to abolish capital punishment in Ohio.[11]

Shortly before her execution, the *Columbus Dispatch* described Dean as calm and "almost unconcerned," and eating and sleeping well. From one description, Dean seemed almost ridiculously unaware of what might happen to her. The *Dispatch* quoted Marguerite Reilly, the superintendent at Marysville, as saying that Dean "doesn't really seem to have any idea that anything's going to happen." Press descriptions two days before her execution made Dean seem a gentle grandmother instead of someone who had methodically poisoned her husband. The *Dispatch* said she had made arrangements to give away books, clothing, and hand-crocheted items that "she [kept] in her pleasant room" at Marysville. Dean instructed that the items go to "her aged father, her four living children or her eight grandchildren." In addition, in an emotional and heartwarming sentence, the *Dispatch* reported that Dean had willed "her pet parakeet, Charlie, to Velma West, notorious Cleveland murderess." Prison officials took Dean's radio from her and decided not to tell her about the governor's commutation decision. The *Dispatch* reported the obvious: "While she will not be told here of the Governor's decision, Dovie probably will be able to figure it out . . . when she leaves Marysville" to go to Columbus. The paper quoted Reilly, the superintendent, as saying, "She will leave here with us telling her we hope for the best."[12] The press did not question the decision not to tell Dean of her fate.

The *Columbus Dispatch* said Dean had earlier seemed almost uninterested in what the governor might do, placing her fate entirely in the hands of God. Readers might have correctly or incorrectly gotten the message that Dean was resigned to her death; the *Cincinnati Enquirer* reported just that.[13] Conversely, readers might have gleaned from Reilly's statements

11. "Dean Will Die Tonight"; "Dean Dies Silently."

12. "Dovie Dean to Be Fitted for Her Execution Dress," *Columbus Dispatch*, 14 January 1954.

13. "Dovie Dean Dies in Electric Chair," *Cincinnati Enquirer*, 16 January 1954.

in at least two stories that Dean had little clue about what was happening. That she did understand seems evident: she disposed of her worldly possessions, was baptized and received communion, thanked the prison officials at Marysville for being "more than good" to her, and apparently did not care what the state did to her. She would not even request a last meal; she told Reilly that "anything would do." Most of the major Ohio newspapers gave an item-by-item account of her meal.

The *Columbus Dispatch* made the reformatory for women, even for those women who were condemned, sound more like a motel than a prison. It referred to the "pleasant" second-floor room that "the gray-haired grandmother" occupied. Not to be outdone, Warden Ralph W. Alvis of the Columbus prison where Dean was to die said she would be served coffee, if she wanted it, just before her execution.[14]

The *Cincinnati Enquirer* and the *Cleveland Plain Dealer* announced Dean's execution with banner headlines in the 16 January editions. "Dovie Dean Dies in Electric Chair," the *Enquirer* said; "Mrs. Dean Pays Death Penalty," the *Plain Dealer* reported. The *Columbus Dispatch* played the story on the front page, but not as the lead; however, three pictures covered five of the eight columns at the top left side of the front page, and the story ran two columns beneath the photos. The photos showed Dean reading "her worn" Bible, eating her last meal, and leaving Marysville for the short trip to Columbus.[15] Interestingly, the *Enquirer* ran a shorter and less detailed Associated Press account of the execution than the *Plain Dealer*'s or the *Dispatch*'s staff-written stories. One might have expected the *Enquirer* to staff the execution for several reasons: The murder was committed near Cincinnati, and Betty Butler, convicted in Hamilton County, would soon be the third woman from the Cincinnati area executed. Furthermore, no Ohio women from anywhere other than the Cincinnati area had been executed during the twentieth century.

Twelve reporters witnessed the execution. The Associated Press story in the *Cincinnati Enquirer* depicted Dean as either a cold-blooded murderer, a quietly confident woman who believed she would attain life after death, or a woman who apparently did not believe she had anything to be sorry for. Dean steadfastly denied murdering her husband. The story obviously juxtaposed the stony, unfeeling murderer and the composed, kindly grandmother. Each newspaper's coverage used her composure as a major element in its story. The *Columbus Dispatch* described her as "grim-faced but outwardly calm." It said she never showed "the slightest trace of excitement or hysteria." The newspaper termed her a "grandmother-

14. "Dean Will Die Tonight." The women's death row could have been just as described. Modern death row facilities for women have been so described by one researcher. See Robert Johnson, *Death Work*, 86–87.
15. "Dean Dies Silently."

slayer," as composed "as an elderly woman sitting down to her knitting."
The chief prison steward at the state penitentiary described Dean sitting
in the death cell adjacent to the execution chamber: "Sitting there with her
hands folded in her lap, she looked just like Whistler's Mother."

Her newly found religion accounted for her composure because she believed God had forgiven her, the Reverend G. W. Wilcher said. If Dean indeed said she believed God had forgiven her, then there is implied doubt
about what she meant. The *Columbus Dispatch,* in a later paragraph, said
no one who had spoken to Dean "could think of anything" she had said
that resembled a confession. The *Dispatch* reported Wilcher's and Dean's
statements but failed to tie together the obvious question: if she denied
committing the murder, then what did God forgive her for?

The *Columbus Dispatch* referred to Dean's inability to cry, but offered no
explanation of why or whether it had contributed to her seeming calm.
Although Dean was described as calm, others were not. The *Dispatch* reported "a nervous tension" at Marysville, saying a prisoner serving a life
sentence there "screamed hysterically." Two matrons who accompanied
Dean to the death chamber and witnessed the execution were described
as "visibly broken" afterward. Dean, on the other hand, seemed more concerned about her hair and about the welfare of others. The afternoon of
the execution day, Dean had her hair done at the Marysville reformatory
beauty salon, and she later told reporters she was sleepy but did not want
to lie down because it might muss her hairdo. The *Cleveland Plain Dealer*
said that just before her execution, Dean's hair "still had curls in it."

Even though the execution seemed relatively cut-and-dried, the *Columbus Dispatch* managed to get seventeen detailed paragraphs from her walk
to the death chamber until the removal of her body. The paper said Dean
wore a "simple green dress buttoned down the front, white anklets and
brown shoes." The *Cincinnati Enquirer*'s description agreed, but it said her
dress was blue. The *Cleveland Plain Dealer* agreed—the dress was blue.

The *Enquirer*'s short wire story described her as small and plump. The
Plain Dealer also commented on her physical size, saying that when Dean
entered Marysville in March 1953, she had weighed 120 pounds, but
weighed 161 pounds at death. Only five paragraphs of the *Enquirer*'s story were devoted to the description of the execution; the rest was background.

The most dramatic and detailed story ran in the *Plain Dealer.* Staff correspondent Sidney E. Elsner used a form of narrative lead: "Head down,
she walked alone. She mounted the wooden platform, sat down in the
electric chair, was strapped in . . . and died."[16] He then shifted to a sum-

16. "Dean Pays Death Penalty."

mary of the execution, and provided background about the case. The two matrons who attended Dean and witnessed her execution were "dressed in white" and stood beside her, giving the metaphor of a clean, efficient, almost surgical procedure. The *Plain Dealer*'s story was more emotional in tone primarily because Elsner emphasized what seemed the most interesting aspect of the story: Dean's inability to cry.

The description of Dean as lonely, perhaps misunderstood, and stoical permeated the story. It also created the image of a woman seemingly without emotion. Up to the point of the execution, Elsner wrote, Dean never uttered a word. Even the description of her dress reflected Dean's quiet lack of flair. "Mrs. Dean was wearing a new blue print dress, nothing fancy." Elsner also noted the silence and somber tone in the death chamber, saying it was "still as death" in there. He even used the weather to hammer home the tone. He described it as "a rainy, nasty night," and said that despite the weather, many onlookers gathered outside the office entrance to the prison, although not nearly as many as for Anna Hahn's execution.

Elsner re-created the scene of Wilcher praying as Dean waited to die, playing upon the rising dramatic tension and using a staccato sentence structure as a technique to maintain pace and increase tension. He wrote: "'He leadeth me . . . ' The preparations continued. 'Yea, though I walk in the valley of the shadow of death . . . ' 'Oh, what a needless pain we bear,' said the preacher. There was a buzz, the flash of a red electric light. It was the beginning of the end and it was 8:03½ P.M."

The next words spoken, Elsner wrote, were by prison physician R. H. Brooks, who officially announced, "Warden Alvis, the electricity has passed through the body of D. B. Dean, 94–211, sufficient to cause death at 8:07." The use of Dean's initials masked her femininity, and the use of the prison number lent the effect of a cold, efficient process. Brooks's words stood in sharp contrast to most of the rest of the story. Elsner vividly described the prison officials at Marysville who had comforted Dean throughout the day and had kept her at the reformatory until 6 P.M. that day "to spare her a more agonizing wait in the prison here." Elsner's description of the control room where the electricity was turned on to kill Dean also conveyed the execution's technological efficiency. The warden spoke no words. He gave hand signals both to start the current and to cut it off, and there were three men at three sets of controls in the room adjacent to the death chamber; only one actually electrocuted Dean. Elsner's description illustrated the state's attempt to shield the executioners from knowing who actually killed her. He achieved this by inserting into a sentence, "and who can say which controls actually were connected to the chair?" The execution was the electrical equivalent of a firing squad, in which one rifle has no live round, and therefore none of the marksmen knows if he fired a blank.

Anna Antonio: "Nobody Can Know How Terrible It Is to Be in Here"

On the day Marie Antonio turned seven years old—9 August 1934—her mother died in New York's electric chair. The next day's *New York Times* reported that Marie wrote her mother to say she intended to have a birthday party if she got good news from the prison. The newspaper added that Anna Antonio had sent Marie a birthday box of candy and a dress she made in the prison.[17]

Marie and her nine-year-old sister, Phyllis, saw their mother once during her fifteen-and-one-half-month confinement in Sing Sing Prison. The girls were put in a home for orphans in Albany, and their three-year-old brother, Frank, lived with Anna Antonio's brother, Pasquale Capello, in Schenectady.

Antonio, twenty-eight, died for having her husband, Salvatore, murdered on Easter Sunday 1932, in connection with a scheme to collect five thousand dollars in life insurance.

She faced near death on several occasions, and hers is accordingly a particularly emotional case. "Nobody can know how terrible it is to be in here except someone who had been through it," she said. Her brother, Pasquale; his wife; and Frank, who the *Times* said "was ignorant" of the fate awaiting his mother, visited her just before her first execution date on 28 June 1934. Frank played with a kitten during the visit, and prison officials allowed him to go inside and kiss his mother, presumably for the last time. Antonio had hoped her daughters would also visit before she died, but they went on an excursion with the orphanage instead.[18]

The strain of death row wore on Antonio; she had not eaten or slept in days and weighed only ninety pounds, having lost more than ten pounds from her already tiny body. The *New York Times* said the strain exhausted her. She made out a will, leaving her few belongings to her children and asking that her brother, Pasquale, have custody of them. Sing Sing Prison warden Lewis Lawes told the *Times* that Antonio, although worried and quiet, was holding up. That seems an extreme understatement. The *Times* reported she had told a prison matron she was "discouraged, ill, broken-hearted," but still hopeful she would not be executed. For her execution, she wore a pink cotton dress trimmed with a white collar, a dress she made while in prison.[19]

New Yorkers suffered for days, and some died from a "hellish" heat wave as New York City's temperature reached ninety-seven degrees. As

17. "Mrs. Antonio to Die in Chair Tonight," *New York Times*, 9 August 1934.
18. "Woman Gets Stay after 2-Hour Wait at Execution Time," ibid., 29 June 1934.
19. "Condemned Woman Feels More Hopeful," ibid., 1 July 1934; "2-Hour Wait."

if the heat was not enough, at 10:45 P.M., just fifteen minutes before Antonio and the two men she had hired to kill her husband were to be executed, one of the men, Vincent Saetta, began what the *Times* described as a "long statement" that exonerated Antonio. Saetta claimed he had shot Salvatore Antonio and that Antonio had had nothing to do with it. Officials delayed the executions as Saetta's statement was typed, but the heat, the strain of the long wait, and the nearness of death caused Antonio to faint.

New York governor H. H. Lehman received word of Saetta's statement, and he granted all three defendants a twenty-four-hour reprieve at 1:15 A.M. on 29 June, about two hours after the scheduled executions. Warden Lawes said that when Antonio was revived, she looked around in surprise and began talking weakly to a matron. "I am sure she thought she was dead, and needed the reassurance of a human voice to convince her that she was still on earth," Lawes said.[20]

The next day, just ten minutes before the reprieve was to expire, Governor Lehman again granted a stay, this time for ten days; Antonio sobbed when told. The *New York Times* said anxiety and a lack of food and sleep had weakened her, but she "clung tenaciously to the hope that her life would be spared." She won a slight victory when prison officials allowed her to grow back hair in the spots they had shaved so the electrodes would have better contact. She burned candles next to a crucifix in her cell, and the *Times* said she "seemed more buoyant and optimistic" than she had the day before.[21]

Her mood improved after a doctor treated her for exhaustion and fatigue. The Men's League of Mercy sent her two bouquets of carnations, and the Mutual Welfare League sent roses—gestures of support that left her more hopeful. Several private groups tried to stop her execution; the Men's League was the most active. That group claimed that a five-week investigation showed Antonio's innocence, and it asked President Franklin Roosevelt, Cardinal Hayes of New York, and Clarence Darrow to help try to save her. In a public statement, Darrow asked Lehman to grant clemency, but Antonio did not have much luck with Hayes. The Men's League said it had given a copy of the investigation to the cardinal and hoped he would deliver it to the Vatican. In a story that used unnamed sources, the *New York Times* reported it had learned Hayes had received the report but did not deliver it to the Vatican because it was the church's "policy" to let the governors and courts act. This was not unusual at the time. It was not until 1963 that Pope John XXIII issued his encyclical *Pacem in Terris,* which provided the basis for the church to eventually stop supporting the death penalty. Darrow's involvement brought Antonio hope for clemency, and flowers, letters, telegrams, and religious articles

20. "Woman Again Gets Stay of Execution," ibid., 30 June 1934.
21. "Antonio Plea Granted," ibid., 12 July 1934; "Woman Again Gets Stay."

flowed in to her from supporters, which led her to believe the public supported clemency.[22]

Others shared the emotional anguish, especially Governor Lehman, who gave three stays of execution and on two occasions issued lengthy public statements about the case. Lehman said carrying out the death penalty for a woman distressed him, and he had looked for a reason to interfere, but found none. Antonio could not be granted clemency simply because of her gender; the law made no such distinction, and neither would "my own conscience or the duty imposed upon me by my oath of office permit me to do so." Lehman said, "I am certain that in the history of the State there are very few instances where the case of any person tried for murder in the first degree has been given greater study and examination."[23]

The *New York Times* empathized with the governor and showed little sympathy for Antonio in an editorial two days after the execution, saying the governor had faced a "painful duty" that must have been "excruciating to a man of his tender heart." Lehman had no choice but to let the executions take place, and "if anyone ought ever to be executed for murder, these three should have been."[24]

Antonio, convicted of arranging her husband's murder, reportedly promised Saetta and Samuel Feraci, a father of ten children, $800 of the $5,000 she would collect as beneficiary of her husband's life insurance policy. Saetta later claimed he killed Salvatore Antonio because he had loaned Antonio $75 and Salvatore would not repay it. Saetta said Anna Antonio knew nothing about the murder.

Antonio's last day was an emotional roller coaster: she often asked the matrons if Governor Lehman had said anything about her case, and she was frustrated at his lack of action. She was despondent—"Only God can help me"—and she most seemed to fear what her execution would mean for her children's future. She was described as dazed during the afternoon and evening; she had not eaten or slept in days, and she refused a last meal, drinking a cup of coffee instead.

Antonio fooled many at her execution because she calmly walked unassisted to the chair, and paid no heed to either the wardens or the witnesses. She wore a blue gingham dress and sat in the electric chair, her lips moving "in prayer," but she reportedly said nothing audible, which rais-

22. "Condemned Woman"; "Mrs. Antonio Fails in New Trial Plea," ibid., 6 July 1934; "Pleads for Mrs. Antonio," ibid., 9 July 1934. For comment about *Pacem in Terris*, see James J. Megivern, *The Death Penalty: An Historical and Theological Survey*, 289–90. "Antonio Fails."

23. "Mrs. Antonio Gets Third Death Stay," *New York Times*, 11 July 1934; "Lehman Is Distressed," ibid., 10 August 1934; "Mrs. Antonio Dies in Electric Chair; Hoped to Last," ibid., 10 August 1934.

24. "A Painful Duty," ibid., 11 August 1934.

es a question about how the reporter knew she was praying. The *New York Times* reported, "Contrary to expectations, she did not break down." Antonio was noteworthy partly because Sing Sing officials said the state had spent $4,650 in fifteen and one-half months, the most money the prison had ever spent to maintain and supervise an inmate.[25]

Just before she died, Antonio told Warden Lawes that she wanted her brother to have custody of her three children, and Lawes said he believed that would happen. Despite Antonio's wishes, her sister-in-law, Mary de Sisto, received custody of the children. The youngest child, Frank, had lived with Antonio's brother, Pasquale Capello, since the child was ten months old. When police went to the Capello home to get Frank, Capello almost became hysterical when he learned about the court order. He calmed down and asked the police if he could bathe Frank before sending him away; they consented and waited outside. After twenty minutes, Capello and Frank had not come out; police searched the home, but the two were gone. A warrant for kidnapping was issued against Capello, but the next day a judge issued a restraining order ceasing all criminal and civil actions against Capello, and ordering de Sisto to show why the custody order in her favor should not be revoked. Capello's friends told the *New York Times* he would return with the boy as soon as he knew about the court order, and he did return with Frank the next day. He said neighbors had brought him his car when he fled with the child, and he and Frank spent two days driving around New York.[26]

Marie Porter of Illinois: "If I Go to the Electric Chair It Will Be with Sealed Lips"

Marie Porter did go to the electric chair for having her brother murdered, and she did not live up to her promise not to talk, although she was not the most forthcoming death row defendant. She had her chances to make her case in the press because *St. Louis Post-Dispatch* reporters had access to her every step of the way.

Readers who did not closely follow the stories about Porter would have been confused. The *Post-Dispatch* first reported that she had shot her brother in the head, a report based on young accomplice Angelo Ralph Giancola's confession. Several days later, Giancola said he had killed William Kappen and Porter had not been at the death site. Giancola lied

25. "Antonio Burial Will Be Monday," ibid., 11 August 1934.

26. "Antonio Dies in Chair"; "Uncle Disappears with Antonio Boy," ibid., 18 August 1934; "Court Stops Hunt for Antonio Boy," ibid., 19 August 1934; "'Kidnapper' Returns Mrs. Antonio's Child," ibid., 20 August 1934. The *Times* did not report on the outcome of the custody hearing in the edition I read.

to try to protect his brother, John, also an accomplice. Newspaper reporters sat in with police at each of the first two confessions and seemingly interviewed the defendants at will throughout the process. About four months later, at the trial, Ralph Giancola testified he had shot Kappen on Porter's orders and that she had been in the automobile at the time of the killing.[27] Two months later, and about six months after the crime, the point about Porter's participation became moot when she and Ralph died in the Illinois electric chair.

Although the murder was committed in Illinois, the crime occurred in the St. Louis metropolitan area and involved St. Louis residents, so the *St. Louis Post-Dispatch* covered the crime and trial more thoroughly than did the *Chicago Tribune*. The *Tribune* paid little attention to the murder and not much more to the trial, devoting much more attention to Anna Hahn's Cincinnati trial, which was being held at the same time. The *Tribune* did give Porter's execution prominent coverage.

The story did not begin with a bang in the *Post-Dispatch,* which, despite a couple of interesting twists, ran an early report of the murder on page 9. Unusual was that Kappen's murder occurred on the day he was to be wed. Passersby found his body in a field on a Saturday afternoon in St. Clair County, Illinois. Police said they knew he had visited his fiancée's home until about midnight on Friday; the two were to be married Saturday morning. Police found in his apartment a freshly pressed suit, laid out on the bed for the wedding, and water drawn for a bath. The second unusual part of the story had nothing to do with the murder, but did have to do with those involved. The victim, William Kappen, was the son of George Kappen, who two years earlier had shot and killed his son-in-law, William H. Porter, and wounded his daughter, Marie Porter. The Porters were caring for George Kappen, and he believed they were going to desert him. He was declared insane and had been a patient at the St. Louis City Sanitarium since the murder.[28]

The story of William Kappen's murder hit the front page of the *St. Louis Post-Dispatch* in a big way just three days later when a headline at the top of the page said police had arrested Kappen's sister, Marie Porter, in connection with his murder. A large two-column picture of an expressionless Porter accompanied the story. Her arrest was based on Ralph Giancola's confession. He had been undone in part by poison ivy; the field where Kappen's body was found had a lot of poison ivy in it, and Ralph had a bad case of it on his arms. He told police Porter had encouraged him to kill her brother for about three months. Kappen's insurance policy was

27. "Sister Held in Killing of Man Near Belleville," *St. Louis Post-Dispatch,* 9 July 1937; "Woman Admits She Hired Boy to Murder Brother," ibid., 12 July 1937; "Testifies Sister of Victim Aided in Insurance Killing," ibid., 4 November 1937.
28. "Trying to Learn Man's Errand on Night of Murder," ibid., 6 July 1937.

worth thirty-three hundred dollars and named Porter as beneficiary, and she offered Ralph eight hundred dollars to help with the murder. Ralph Giancola, twenty-one, worked for Porter—thirty-seven and the mother of four daughters—at a confectionery. Shortly after Kappen's body was found, a *Post-Dispatch* reporter talked to Porter at her home, and she said she believed her brother had been murdered because of a fight. "He was a quiet, unobtrusive man when he was sober, but he used to go on some terrible benders on the East Side. He often got into fights." She also reportedly told the reporter she had not been invited to her brother's wedding, and when she heard police had found a suit in his apartment ready to wear to the wedding, she reportedly said: "You say that he had a suit ready? Was it a new one? Then he might be buried in it."[29]

After her arrest, *St. Louis Post-Dispatch* described her as "sullen" and "silent" and opposed to extradition to Illinois. The reporter sat in and described her as unmoved when police told her about Ralph Giancola's confession. Porter's weight did not escape the notice of the *Post-Dispatch* or the *Tribune* throughout the story process. The *Post-Dispatch* said that while she listened to Ralph's confession, "[t]he tight-lipped woman moved the knuckles of her left hand from her pudgy, unrouged cheek." She "might have been listening to some twice-told tale of neighborhood gossip by a loiterer in the confectionery she formerly operated." Ralph told police that after he had shot her brother, Porter had said, "Well, that's over with," and they dragged his body to the field. Perhaps even more damning was that Porter's fifteen-year-old daughter got married "while [Porter's] brother's body lay" at the undertaker's. When a *Post-Dispatch* reporter stopped at Porter's house to interview her, he found "revelry," "singing and accordion music," and wedding guests drinking beer and eating sandwiches. The Giancolas' mother told the newspaper that her son Ralph had been "taken in by a witch."[30] Neighbors and others agreed that Giancola was a good young man who had never been in trouble.

When Ralph Giancola and John Giancola changed their confessions, they said they had gone alone to Kappen's home and forced him at gunpoint to accompany them, and Ralph had shot him. They said they had planned to buy an automobile with the money. The boys' confession led Porter to confess—also in the presence of reporters—that she had hired the young men. She did not seem too upset, a *Post-Dispatch* reporter wrote: "Occasionally she dabbed at her red eyes with her handkerchief but her tears were few." She told police she had needed money, and Kappen would not help her, although she had helped him earlier. "I had supported Willie during the depression when he was out of work. When things

29. "Sister Held."
30. "'It's a Lie' Says Woman Held As Brother's Killer," ibid., 10 July 1937; "New Evidence in Killing Laid to Victim's Sister," ibid., 11 July 1937.

picked up for him, he moved out on me without offering to pay his back rent or assist me in any way."[31]

Reporters seemed to favor Ralph Giancola because he would talk, whereas the press described Porter as sullen and quiet. When jailed in St. Louis, she sat in her cell wearing a black dress with "a bunch of bedraggled violets at the neck," and refused to answer reporters' questions, according to the *St. Louis Post-Dispatch*. Ralph, on the other hand, "maintained a light air," and talked with reporters while he played solitaire in his cell. "Do you think I'll fry?" he reportedly asked them.[32]

The story faded in July from the *Post-Dispatch* columns, but weakly blossomed in November when the trial started—although the newspaper gave the trial little prominence. Reporters who had sat in on the confessions had to testify to that fact, one story said. The convictions dominated the *Post-Dispatch*'s front page. Porter heard the verdict with little emotion, whereas the Giancolas' mother reportedly shrieked when she heard that Ralph would be executed and John sentenced to ninety-nine years in prison. The *Post-Dispatch* described Porter, who declined to make a statement to reporters after the trial, as "a heavy-set phlegmatic woman." The *Chicago Tribune* hardly noticed the death sentences, running the story on page 17 under a one-column headline.[33]

Illinois governor Henry Horner refused to intervene, but a controversy arose when the lieutenant governor, John Stelle, granted a one-week reprieve while Horner was out of state. Stelle said he had based his decision solely on a request from the Giancolas' mother, who said she had new evidence about her son Ralph. Horner had earlier said he opposed capital punishment, especially for women, but believed he had "no right to amend the statutes to read that the penalty for murder shall not apply to women." Stelle's action drew an editorial rebuke from the *St. Louis Post-Dispatch*, which called it "a sentimental act without sound basis" and an "impertinent interference." The "new evidence" was that Ralph Giancola's association with Porter had lowered his "will power and resistance."[34]

The *Post-Dispatch* gave the executions prominent display, running the otherwise routine story at the top of page 1. The newspaper made a point about Porter's size, saying the guards had "struggled to support her 250

31. "Woman Admits She Hired Boy."

32. "Governor Horner Signs Requisition for Brother-Killer," ibid., 13 July 1937.

33. "Testimony Begun in Murder Trial of Mrs. Marie Porter," ibid., 2 November 1937; "Woman and Man Get Death for Kappen Murder," ibid., 5 November 1937; "Two Get Chair, Third 99 Years in Murder Case," *Chicago Tribune*, 6 November 1937.

34. "Gov. Horner Refuses to Spare Mrs. Porter," *St. Louis Post-Dispatch*, 19 January 1938; "Mrs. Porter and Youth Receive Week's Reprieve," ibid., 20 January 1938; "Mr. Stelle's Interference," ibid., 21 January 1938; "Appeal for Murderer Reprieved from Chair," ibid., 25 January 1938.

pounds as she shuffled" to the chair. She had few last words, saying only, "I hold no malice toward anyone and may God have mercy on my soul," and she died quickly. The *Chicago Tribune* ran a screamer headline on page 1 that read: "Execute Woman for Murder"; the story began with the words, "Pudgy faced Marie Porter." The *Tribune* said Ralph Giancola had been described as Porter's lover, something the *Post-Dispatch* never reported.[35]

The *St. Louis Post-Dispatch* praised Governor Horner and the Illinois justice system. It said Horner had done "the right thing" by allowing Marie Porter and Ralph Giancola to die, and added that those who opposed executing women should try to get the legislature to change the law. "Meanwhile, countless persons will agree that if ever a woman should have been required to pay with her life for a crime, it was Mrs. Porter." The newspaper added, "The sordid records of criminality contain few entries so repulsive" as the murder of William Kappen. The *Post-Dispatch* also praised the swift justice, pointing out that Missouri law would have required separate trials for the three defendants, whereas Illinois had tried them together, sentencing one to life and executing the other two, all within six months of the crime.[36] Since 1976, the *Post-Dispatch* has been among the most vocal of anti–capital punishment newspapers.

May H. Carey: Loose Lips Sink Ships

May Carey and her sons almost got away with the perfect crime. After she and two of her sons murdered her brother in 1927, almost seven years passed with no hint of what was to come. Unfortunately for May, police arrested a third son, Lawrence, in December 1934 for assault and battery, and during questioning he gave police information that convinced them to reopen the murder case. Lawrence, who was fourteen when the murder occurred, told police he had overheard his mother and brothers, Howard and James, plotting the crime. Police soon arrested the three.[37]

The case was a big story for the *Wilmington Morning News* because May Carey would be only the second woman executed in Delaware, and the first since 1860, according to the newspaper. The *New York Times* said she would be the first "white woman" executed in the state. In 1860, Sara Jane

35. "Mrs. Porter and Youth Executed in Electric Chair," ibid., 28 January 1938; "Mrs. Porter and Youth Executed in Electric Chair," ibid., 28 January 1938; "Execute Woman for Murder," *Chicago Tribune*, 28 January 1938.

36. "The Lesson of a Criminal Case," *St. Louis Post-Dispatch*, 28 January 1938.

37. "Woman and Her Son Sentenced to Hang," *New York Times*, 27 April 1935; "Careys Sing Hymns, Pray All Night As They Await Noose," *Wilmington (Del.) Morning News*, 7 June 1935.

Bradley, a "negro girl," was hanged for murdering a child, and the *Morning News* said Delaware had executed only one other woman: Catherine Bevans, who was burned at the stake under old English law in 1731 for murdering her husband.[38] The few executions of women, the heinous nature of the crime, and the years of mystery about the murder made the story a natural for prominent news coverage.

May Carey's brother Robert Hitchens was murdered in 1927 in his home in what was described as the "hamlet" of Omar, near Frankford, Delaware. Carey and her sons waited for him to return to his home and struck him with a cudgel; then May gave Howard a pistol and ordered him to shoot Hitchens. Howard shot him twice in the head. Then the Careys poured liquor in the house and on Hitchens's clothing "to give the appearance that the slaying had climaxed a drunken brawl." Reportedly, Hitchens was murdered for two reasons: he had been "mean" to May, and, more important, she believed she stood to collect $1,954.36 in life insurance. *Believed* is the key word because the *Morning News* reported that after other heirs got their inheritance and the outstanding bills were paid, May Carey received only $457.59.[39] If she had contracted the murder out, she perhaps would have gone into the red.

In the week before the execution, the story received only modest play in the *Wilmington Morning News;* however, on the day before the execution, and the following two days, the newspaper ran front-page stories. The most prominent coverage was on the day of the hangings. The story had a three-line, three-column headline accompanied by two drab pictures: One was a three-column photo of an empty prison yard, with a wire fence in the foreground and some buildings in the background. It showed the corner of the prison yard where the two would die. A one-column mug shot of May Carey ran beneath the main photo. The rather useless photos probably resulted from the trial court judge's order barring the press and others from access to the prison or the Careys.

Just three days before the execution, the *Morning News* ran a story on page 6 that read in part like a "society section" account. It said May Carey would go to the gallows "attired in a black dress with a white ruching at the neck," whereas Howard would die in a dark-blue suit and a white shirt with a soft collar attached.[40] James had been convicted of second-degree murder and had been sentenced to life imprisonment.

A story two days later gave hanging aficionados the technical details about the gallows. It was a single gallows, which meant the Careys would die separately. It was made of heavy oaken beams, and a trap door was held shut by a bolt to which a forty-foot rope was attached. The rope went

38. "Sentenced to Hang"; "Careys Sing Hymns."
39. "Careys Sing Hymns."
40. "Single Gallows for Two Careys," *Wilmington (Del.) Morning News,* 4 June 1935.

to a windowless structure where the hangman, Warden Hugh D. Brown, would "officiate." The *Wilmington Morning News* stressed the security for the hangings, saying a fifteen-foot-high board fence would be around the scaffold, and a heavy canvas across the top of the scaffold would prevent the execution from being photographed from the air. Prison officials later increased the security by raising the fence to twenty feet and erecting two wire fences around the entire jail. Reporters would be allowed into the jail yard but had to "give their word of honor" that they would not attempt to see the executions. Even the Careys' burials were to be "under the protection of a special detail of state and local police." The *Morning News* raised no questions about the restrictions, instead confidently reporting that once the last of the defendants was executed, Warden Brown would "give the detailed information to the reporters."[41]

Some of the reporting was melodramatic, saying May Carey and Howard Carey prepared for their deaths "with Bibles in hands," and ordered their funeral garb and caskets, and that May's other two sons visited and there were "farewells said, tears shed and protestations of forgiveness."[42]

Georgetown and Omar residents did not seem too worked up about the hangings, the *Morning News* said. A corps of reporters lodged in Georgetown's only hotel, but otherwise nothing seemed unusual in the town. Residents did seem opposed to hanging a woman, and did not believe the hanging would take place, according to the newspaper.

The *Wilmington Morning News* published its lengthiest story on the day of the hangings. It had heavy religious overtones, was laden with emotion, and was packed with detail. The first paragraph contained almost biblical phraseology: "Singing hymns and praying with rising fervor, Mrs. May H. Carey, 55 years old, and her first born son, Howard, early today awaited the coming of another dawn—their last." The tone reflected a somber aura of death, created by description and metaphors. "Outside the cells, the measured tread of the death watch beat a requiem for the mother and son while outside flood lights bathed the prison and the awaiting gallows in an eery glare." Howard's last meeting with his wife and three children gave the story emotion. They wept, and he gave his wife a last gift, a necklace he had made in jail by punching holes in small coins and stringing them together. The coins had "a total face value of $1." The *Morning News* had repeatedly reported that the Careys were resigned to their fates and that they were calm, but the story on the day of the executions, which related the previous day's happenings, presented another picture. May and Howard showed effects of "nervous hysteria" that came

41. "Gallows Set for Mother, and Her Son," *Wilmington (Del.) Morning News*, 6 June 1935; "Careys Sing Hymns."
42. "Single Gallows."

over them early the previous morning "during a violent thunder storm." The *Morning News* consistently tried for a more "literary" approach than did the *New York Times*. For example, the *Times* described the day of the hangings as "hazy," but the *Morning News* created a more foreboding scene, describing the "dim light of a mist-laden dawn" and the "fog-shrouded gallows."[43]

Details about the hangings were published the next day. The *Wilmington Morning News* used words that carried strong emotional connotations, such as choosing to describe May Carey first as a "grandmother"; the lead paragraph never referred to her or to Howard by name but instead said the state had "exacted from a grandmother and her eldest son the price of murder." The newspaper called the hangings a "grim drama." The *Morning News* especially played on irony in the hanging story. It reported that "side by side in little St. Georges cemetery near here there are two fresh mounds" for the defendants; nearby was "the grave of Robert Hitchens, the woman's brother, the man who a jury decided she bludgeoned and shot to death." Meanwhile, Lawrence waited in a cell for his trial, while "his mother and brother walked to the doom he had brought them." The newspaper also noted that the Careys were buried near a small house where "a mother gathered her three children [Lawrence's children] about her and prepared to face life without their father." The children had been christened the day before in their father's cell, the *Morning News* reported, and, in a final stroke of irony, the newspaper said residents of the "peaceful county seat . . . slept peacefully while the sentences of the court were executed."[44]

News reporters did not receive the detailed information from Warden Brown that the *Wilmington Morning News* had so confidently predicted. The following excerpt from the newspaper story gives the flavor of the warden's "detailed" briefing:

> "Mrs. May Carey, she went first," he said in a flat, emotionless tone. "Left cell 5:02. Trap, 5:07. Pronounced dead 5:24. She said: 'My way is clear. I have nothing else to say.'"
> A reporter asked the warden: "Did she walk?"
> He answered curtly: "Walked," and tossed a slip of notepaper into his wastebasket, and started reading from another.
> "Howard J.—he left the cell 5:31 . . . "

Apparently, reporters learned additional details from other witnesses, although the story said the witnesses were "whisked out a back gate" af-

43. "Careys Sing Hymns."
44. "Mrs. Carey, Son Die on Gallows; Are Calm at End," *Wilmington (Del.) Morning News,* 8 June 1935.

ter the hangings. It seems evident that state officials wanted to get the executions over in a hurry because the story said the two were buried less than an hour after the hangings, "the bodies not yet cold." The cortege drove rapidly to the cemetery, took the bodies to the grave sites, offered brief prayers, and buried them.

The *Wilmington Morning News* described Howard's widow, Myra, in sharply different ways. At the burial, she was "the weeping wife," but twenty minutes later, she and her two sisters "chatted amiably, and smiled frequently, Myra's jaws incessantly busy with that wad of gum" at the hanging site. Myra showed neither tears nor emotion. In a statement that used no named sources, the newspaper reported "it was said" by state troopers that Myra, shortly before her husband's execution, attended a firemen's carnival in a small nearby town. The newspaper then noted: "With her husband's death, she will receive the proceeds from a life insurance policy for $1000."[45]

45. Ibid.

Chapter 4

Other Schemes

Marie Beck: The Press Homes In on a Defendant's Weight

Marie Beck was overweight. *New York Times* readers who overlooked that the first time the newspaper published her weight had plenty more opportunities. In staff-written and wire stories, she was called a "200-pound mistress," a "200-pound sweetheart," a "200-pound thrice-divorced aide," a "plump defendant," a "plump suspect," "stocky," "bulky" and "the corpulent Mrs. Beck." When the *Times* first published a story about Beck's arrest in connection with three murders, it called her a "200-pound divorcee." One might wonder if her greatest fault was being fat or being a killer. She was executed for her part in what the press termed "lonely hearts" murders.

Near the end of her trial, the *New York Times* called her "the 180-pound divorcee." Previous and subsequent references always had her weight at 200 pounds, and the *Times* never explained the rapid weight loss, or how quickly she regained it. But, then, the *Times* never really indicated why her weight made any difference at all.

The *New York Times* did practice equal-opportunity stereotyping, tagging Beck's cohort, Raymond Fernandez, as a "smooth operator," the "smooth-talking Fernandez," "dark," and "swarthy." The *Times* termed Fernandez either Hawaiian or Spanish, not seeming to notice the obvious cultural difference. Fernandez's "Latin suavity was the chief stock in trade of the couple."

Martha Jule Beck made the *New York Times*'s news agenda in 1949; she went off the agenda in 1951 when the State of New York electrocuted her. Between 2 March 1949 and 9 March 1951, the *Times* ran eighty-one stories about Beck and her lover, Fernandez; the story about their arrests was on page 1 under a two-column headline, but the story about their executions ran on page 52 under a one-column headline.

According to news stories, either Beck abandoned her two children or they were taken from her because of her love for Fernandez. Of the eighty-one stories about Beck and Fernandez, only the arrest story ran on the *New York Times*'s front page, despite their controversial extradition fight to avoid being taken from Michigan to New York. Michigan, a state that had no death penalty, also charged them with murder. New York governor Thomas Dewey forged a pact with Michigan governor G. Mennan Williams to return Beck and Fernandez to New York, where they could be tried for capital murder.

Their trial lasted two months. The *New York Times* reported the first juror's selection on 10 June 1949; the story about the verdict ran on 19 August. During that time, the state called 600 potential jurors before seating 12 and 2 alternates, the jurors heard 43 days of testimony, and police on one occasion had to quell a near riot when 150 people fought for the 70 available seats in the courtroom. The trial court judge was enough of a celebrity to be voted in a straw poll as the top mayoral prospect in New York City.

That the story remained totally off the front page after the first story about the arrests might seem odd in hindsight because Beck's mug popped up in the *New York Times* as late as the year 2000. However, while Beck and Fernandez were being tried, there was a hung jury in the Alger Hiss case, and by the time the two were executed, the Korean War dominated the *Times*'s news coverage.[1] The *Times* sometimes seemed almost bored with the whole affair, fed up with the defendants, and ready for the case to end.

How the Story Broke

Michigan authorities arrested Beck and Fernandez in connection with the murders of Delphine Downing, twenty-eight, and her twenty-month-old daughter, Rainelle. Police said Beck and Fernandez had confessed to three murders, the third being that of Janet Fay of Albany, New York. Police dug up the bodies of Downing and her daughter "from cement-filled graves" in the cottage of their Grand Rapids, Michigan, home. Police found Fay's body buried in the basement of an apartment building in South Ozone Park, Queens, New York, where it had been for almost two months.

After contacting women through "Lonely Hearts" clubs, Fernandez either married them or gained their trust so they would give him money or sign over their assets to him. Then he bilked them. For Downing, her child, and Fay, the end result was murder. The *New York Times* appropriately

---

1. Hiss was accused of espionage and convicted of perjury during a highly publicized, controversial trial.

termed the case "bizarre." Beck and Fernandez traveled as brother and sister, although in reality they were lovers. She had been a registered nurse in Pensacola, and her Florida relatives said she had been married three times and had two children, but a Florida judge had found her an unfit mother and taken the children from her.[2]

Although there were three known murder victims, the *New York Times* said police suspected there might have been others. Using unnamed "neighbors" as sources, the newspaper reported that Fernandez corresponded with between fifty and seventy-five women. Police said he carried "a list of sixteen more potential victims" when arrested.[3]

The Fair-Trial Controversy

Information published prior to the trial resulted in a change of venue. Judging from the stories in the *New York Times*, that newspaper was not part of the reason for the motion, although press reports in Nassau County, New York, were. Fay had been murdered in Nassau County, and her body was brought to Queens. The judge granted a change of venue to Bronx County, ruling that newspaper coverage in Nassau County had made a fair trial there impossible. However, the judge did not criticize the newspapers, and said his ruling should not be taken to mean the press had done anything wrong. The judge said the newspapers had used legitimate sources to get information from police and the district attorney. He said sensational cases made publicity inevitable. The stories about the jury selection make it evident that the case was sensational in Bronx County. The court summoned 450 potential jurors, and 1 juror and 2 alternates remained to be selected after 434 potential jurors were questioned. An additional 150 were called, and it took ten days of questioning to select the jury. According to "courtroom attendants," the number in the jury pool was a record.[4]

The publication of confessions prior to trial—which some scholars today believe is the most damaging to fair-trial rights—could have caused the change of venue. The *New York Times* on many occasions wrote that Beck and Fernandez had confessed, and a third party told the *Times* that Fernandez had reportedly said, "I ought to be killed. I deserve it," though the newspaper did not report who had provided Fernandez's words.[5]

2. "3 'Lonely Hearts' Murders Trap Pair; Body Dug Up Here," *New York Times*, 2 March 1949.

3. "Two Slayers Face Trial in Nassau," ibid., 3 March 1949.

4. "Will Aid in 'Hearts' Trial," ibid., 12 May 1949; "Jury Nears Completion," ibid., 21 June 1949; "'Hearts' Jury Completed," ibid., 25 June 1949; "Row on Alternates Delays 'Hearts' Trial," ibid., 22 June 1949.

5. "Two Slayers Face Trial."

The Extradition Fight

Beck and Fernandez stayed in the news after their arrests because of the extradition fight. They were arrested in Michigan and could have been charged there, but the Michigan legislature had days earlier voted down a bill that would have provided for capital punishment. The *New York Times* said that the Michigan governor held an extradition hearing, which was related to the legislature's vote against capital punishment. Beck and Fernandez obviously did not want to return to New York: she said she was afraid of the electric chair, and Fernandez later confessed to the Michigan murders but denied the New York one. The two states finally agreed to return them to New York, but if they were not convicted then they would be returned to Michigan and tried there.[6]

In what seems a far-fetched justification, Michigan attorney general Stephen Roth said Michigan might become a "sanctuary state" if it failed to extradite Beck and Fernandez. He said people who committed murders in other states that had the death penalty might come to Michigan and commit a murder there in order to be arrested and tried, and to have legal sanctuary against the death penalty.[7]

The *New York Times*'s stories before the trial rarely received prominent placement and often amounted to only a few short paragraphs. The *Times* also published speculative stories about trial testimony, but cannot be too harshly faulted because its sources were the defense counsel and the assistant district attorney.

For the most part, the *New York Times* seemed bored or frustrated with the tedious legal process. The newspaper seized upon moments of drama, such as when Beck, "usually a placid spectator," blurted out that a witness was "being paid to sit there and tell those lies about me." For the most part, though, the trial seemed dull. Adding insult to injury, Fernandez's 73-page confession was read into the record, and later, attempting to establish Beck's insanity, her attorney read 225 pages of material into the record. The *Times* headlined that story: "Mrs. Beck's Story Read." The headline writer showed restraint by not inserting "Life" after her name. The public obviously followed proceedings closely. During the middle of the trial, a "mayoralty straw poll" showed Judge Pecora as almost dou-

6. "Michigan Delays Action in Slaying," ibid., 5 March 1949; "Defense Loses Point in 'Hearts' Trial," ibid., 13 July 1949; "Two Slayers Face Trial"; "Michigan Agrees to Shift Slayers," ibid., 9 March 1949.

7. "Dewey Pact to Get Two Killers Here," ibid., 10 March 1949. The attorney general's idea played out in fiction some years later in a television presentation that had a somewhat similar scenario. Philip Hamburger, in a 1953 article in the *New Yorker*, reviewed a television show in which a killer murdered his cell mate because the murderer was incarcerated in a state that had no death penalty. The inmate was to be released from prison and feared being indicted for murdering his wife in a state that had a death penalty. See Hamburger, *Friends Talking in the Night*, 325–27.

bling the total for second-place Joseph T. Sharkey, the majority leader of the city council. Franklin D. Roosevelt Jr. finished third.[8]

Once the defense began its case, the *New York Times*'s stories were longer, although the story play remained about the same. Fernandez's testimony about his relationship with Fay and "sex relations with women he met" through the lonely-hearts connections packed the courtroom. Many spectators, "predominantly women," did without lunch so as not to lose their seats.[9]

Nonetheless, Beck drew the most rowdy crowds when she testified about trying to commit suicide six times in one and one-half years; she said she had attempted suicide because she feared Fernandez would leave her. On 25 July, a "near riot" broke out when "a pushing, shouting crowd" of about 150 people vied for the seventy courtroom seats. When they "attempted to elbow past court attendants," a special detail of about a dozen policemen restored order.[10]

The trial's final hours were controversial because of the length of jury deliberation. The case went to the jury, the *New York Times* reported, at 7:56 P.M. on 17 August, and a verdict was reached at 8:30 the next morning.[11] Although spectators packed the courtroom throughout the trial, only about a dozen people waited through the night for the verdict. The trial record reportedly was four thousand pages. When the judge announced the verdict, and later at sentencing, the *Times* described both Beck and Fernandez as calm and impassive; they were also called "weird schemers."

The two defendants for the most part dropped out of the *New York Times*'s columns until January 1951, when various courts refused to intervene. Beck and Fernandez scarcely drew any press attention during the final days before their executions. The 9 March 1951 story about the execution ran on page 52 under a one-column headline.[12] The length and placement of the story probably illustrate how routine state executions had become in the 1930s and 1940s. New York that day executed four people in twenty-two minutes. Only on rare occasions had New York executed more people in a single day, and never before had multiple executions included a woman. It is unlikely that multiple executions in New York ever resulted in so little news coverage.

---

8. "'Hearts' Prosecution Enters Confessions," *New York Times*, 30 June 1949; "'Hearts' Pair Hear Statements Read," ibid., 14 July 1949; "Mrs. Beck's Story Read," ibid., 6 August 1949; "Pecora Wins Poll for Mayoralty, Sharkey and Roosevelt Jr. Next," ibid., 9 July 1949.

9. "Fernandez Denies Slaying Mrs. Fay," ibid., 22 July 1949.

10. "'Hearts' Defendant Tried Suicide 6 Times," ibid., 27 July 1949.

11. "'Hearts' Case Goes to Jury in Bronx," ibid., 18 August 1949.

12. "'Lonely Hearts' Lose," ibid., 3 January 1951; "Two Sentenced to Die," ibid., 18 January 1951; "2 'Lonely Hearts' Pay Death Penalty," ibid., 9 March 1951.

In its last story about Beck, the *New York Times* reported: "Mrs. Beck, who weighed 200 pounds, was the eighth woman executed in New York."[13]

Eva Coo of New York: Did She or Didn't She?

Regardless of whether Eva Coo was a cold-blooded, scheming killer or a not-too-innocent participant in a murder, she died almost friendless. On 27 June 1935, she became the fifth woman to die in New York's electric chair; she died for killing a handyman who worked for her. The three matrons at her execution—her "darlings"—and the prison warden's wife helped bury her in a small private cemetery owned by a prison welfare league. Her family wanted nothing to do with her. Coo's sister, Mrs. William A. Baker, said the family had considered her dead for seventeen years before her execution.[14]

A jury convicted Coo of being primarily responsible for murdering a handyman; her motive was to collect insurance money, although press reports varied about how much. Martha Clift, who earlier confessed that she had killed the handyman, was the prosecution's main witness.

Police arrested Coo on 21 June 1934; she died in the electric chair on 27 June 1935, one year and two weeks after the murder. She became one of 1935's infamous statistics, when the United States executed 199 people, more than in any year in modern times.

Coo's story was confusing as reported, and raises questions about the truth of the information used to send her to the electric chair. A handyman's death brought about her arrest and that of Clift. Harry Wright, forty-nine, died after being run over by an automobile several times, and the two women were arrested the next week.

The *New York Times* relied mostly on Associated Press coverage, and readers must have had difficulty discerning the relationships among individuals and among the facts in the stories because there were many discrepancies. The *Times* initially reported Coo's age as forty-five, but later said she was forty-two; stories described her as a widow and as a "blond divorcee." Her roadhouse was called "Little Eva's Place" and the "Woodbine Inn."

Coo became an early suspect because she held insurance on Wright, variously described as a "crippled handyman," a "crippled odd-jobs worker," and a "shuffling, crippled handyman" at her roadhouse. Al-

13. "'Lonely Hearts' Pay."
14. "Mrs. Coo Is Buried," ibid., 29 June 1935; "Long 'Dead' to Relatives," ibid., 28 June 1935.

though press reports said Coo was not the beneficiary in any of the insurance policies, Wright had left everything to her in his will. The *New York Times* did not adequately explain why Wright would leave everything to Coo, never indicating they had been lovers. The women were jailed at Cooperstown, New York. The murder was near the small village of Maryland, not far from Oneonta, New York.

The relationship between Clift and Coo was never exactly clear. Clift reportedly worked as a hostess and frequently stayed at Coo's roadhouse. Clift's story about the murder changed several times. The first news story after the murder said she had told police that she, Wright, and Coo went for a ride and stopped on Crumhorn Mountain. Clift and Wright got out of the car, and Coo drove over Wright three or four times. The women put Wright's body in the auto and dumped it on the roadside about nine hundred feet from Coo's roadhouse. In a news story three days later, Clift claimed she had driven the car over Wright's body, and she said Coo had struck him in the head with a mallet. Clift said Coo had promised her two hundred dollars for helping with the murder. Authorities said Wright was murdered for three thousand dollars in insurance. Clift claimed she and Coo had planned the murder for two or three months, an allegation Coo denied.[15] As the stories progressed, even regular *Times* readers must have had difficulty making sense of the amount of insurance involved. The sum was "a large amount" on 21 June; $3,000 on 24 June; $1,800 on 12 August; $12,900 on 14 August; and $10,000 on 18 August.

One day before the trial began, the *New York Times* said police had exhumed Wright's body to determine if he had been hit with a mallet, but reburied his body after the inconclusive examination. Five days later, Coo's attorney filed a motion opposing the introduction of her confession because police had "tortured" her for two days and a night by not allowing her to sleep and by forcing her to reenact the crime. The attorney's allegation had a ghoulish twist. He said police had exhumed Wright's body six days after the murder and forced Coo to lift it. The reenactment had taken place at a "haunted house," which the *Times* said was a "tumbledown and bat-infested farmhouse." The allegations were grotesque because it seemed police had dug up Wright's body once within a week of the murder and then again two weeks later. If police forced Coo to hold the body, then the allegations are especially disturbing.[16]

15. "Two Women Held in Auto Slaying," ibid., 21 June 1934; "Woman Ran Over Man in Death Plot," ibid., 24 June 1934.

16. "Body Exhumed on Eve of Trial of Woman," *New York Times,* 12 August 1934. Police reenactments were common into the early 1960s, and often police invited the press along; they would take pictures and write stories about how the defendants reenacted the crime and confessed. At times, the pictures were obviously posed. Marlin Shipman, "Forgotten Men and Media Celebrities."

The press might have figured into the case in a couple of ways. First, Coo sought a change of venue, although it is not clear if prejudicial publicity played a role in the motion, which was denied. When denying the motion, the trial court judge predicted that potential jurors would not be prejudiced against her, but instead would "lean the other way" to be fair. Second, the court sequestered the all-male jury. The judge told them at the beginning of the trial: "Do not feel we are locking you up. Enjoy yourselves. Laugh and chat; get plenty of exercise. You are good sports and good citizens, and I appreciate what you're doing."[17] Although the news story gave no reason for the sequestration, it must have been to shield jurors from outside information, either from others in the community or from the press.

Cooperstown's first murder trial in thirteen years resulted in tourists and townspeople jamming the courtroom on the trial's first day, when, according to the Associated Press, about one hundred people could not find a seat and stood against the back wall. The first day shocked Coo because, according to the *New York Times,* she discovered for the first time that Clift would testify for the prosecution and would be allowed to plead guilty to second-degree murder.[18]

The press did not raise questions about Clift being a witness, although she obviously had much to gain from her plea bargain. Clift had given conflicting confessions. Another witness, Gladys Shumway, also called a "surprise" witness against Coo, testified that she had ridden in the automobile before the murder, but was not in it at the time of the murder. She also said Coo had told her it would be easy to get behind Wright and knock him in the head with a mallet.[19]

Public interest waned as the trial progressed, and not more than two hundred people attended the last day's testimony. The *New York Times's* story about Coo's death sentence was the first time she made the front page. The jury deliberated for two hours, took eight ballots, and deadlocked ten-to-two for conviction before it finally reached a verdict. Moments after the jury announced Coo's sentence, Clift pleaded guilty to second-degree murder and received a twenty-year sentence, the *Times* reported. The only time during the trial that the *Times* described Coo as upset was at the sentencing when she "shuddered violently" and "walked unsteadily."[20]

Coo received press attention when she arrived at Sing Sing because she was assigned to the "centre cage," a description with a Wimbletonian ring,

17. "Jury Panel Filled for Trial of Mrs. Coo," ibid., 16 August 1934.

18. "Guest of Mrs. Coo to Be State Witness," ibid., 17 August 1934.

19. "Guest at Coo Inn Tells of Death Car," ibid., 21 August 1934; "Witness Identifies Mallet in Coo Trial," ibid., 23 August 1934.

20. "Eva Coo Convicted; Sentenced to Die," ibid., 7 September 1934.

as spelled. The *New York Times* said that Ruth Snyder, among the most famous of women executed in the United States, had occupied the "centre cage" seven years earlier.[21]

More direct press involvement came about a month later when the *New York Daily Mirror,* a tabloid with past questionable reporting techniques, published articles purported to be Coo's life story, written by her from her cell. If this were so, then it would have seriously violated prison regulations, and the State Department of Correction appointed a three-person committee to investigate. Coo claimed she had not written the articles, and she was almost hysterical because she worried the publication might damage her chance to avoid the death penalty. Her attorney and John Kobler, a reporter for the *Daily Mirror,* had visited her, and Sing Sing warden Lewis Lawes and a prison matron said Kobler had been introduced to Coo as a court stenographer. She claimed she asked several times during the four-hour interview if it was for a newspaper and was told it was not. A prison chaplain told the committee that Coo had told him she heard her attorney would receive three thousand dollars for the articles. Lawes told the committee he believed the attorney had taken "unfair advantage" of Coo because the stories were obtained by misrepresentation.[22]

Coo's case took a bizarre turn when her attorney filed an affidavit saying that before her trial, a man posing as the governor had visited Clift at the Cooperstown jail and promised her she would receive a governor's pardon after Coo was executed.[23] The story was not enough to convince Gov. H. H. Lehman, who denied the commutation request.

Coo made the front page of the *New York Times* one more time, this being the report about her execution. The paper described her as calm, steady, and prayerful; she walked unassisted to the electric chair. Matrons stood in front of her, screening her from witnesses. The matrons put their hands over their eyes, and Coo told them, "Goodbye, darlings." She was dead minutes later.

Judging from the news stories, only two people knew what happened when Wright was murdered, and Coo was convicted largely on the testimony of the other person involved in the murder. To her death, Coo proclaimed her innocence.

Sue Logue: How the Press Covered a Family Feud

A sheriff, a deputy sheriff, a storekeeper, a farmer, and a sharecropper: all were shot to death during a fourteen-month period. Three more people died in South Carolina's electric chair as a result of the shootings. One of

21. "Mrs. Coo Gets Cell of Ruth Snyder," ibid., 8 September 1934.
22. "Deny That Mrs. Coo Wrote Story of Life," ibid., 10 November 1934.
23. "Affidavit Charges 'Hoax' in Coo Trial," ibid., 25 June 1935.

those executed, Sue Logue, was called the "mastermind" of the southern feud. "Oh, what a line of murder and assassination have come from the spleen of that master mind," a prosecutor said of her.[24] It all began with an argument about a yearling calf.

Logue was a rarity: a white woman condemned to death in the twentieth century who received little press attention when executed. The former schoolteacher's misfortune in this respect can be attributed to being executed during the middle of World War II when interest in capital punishment waned because thousands of U.S. soldiers were dying. Logue's story did garner a good deal of local press coverage during the events that spawned the case, and during the trial.

Readers unfamiliar with the Logues, Timmermans, and Allens in Edgefield County, South Carolina, might have needed a scorecard to determine who was who. The trial judge granted a change of venue because the three families involved were the largest in the county, and "no section of the county could be found that did not include a relative of theirs."[25]

Those involved were: Wallace Logue, shot to death by Davis Timmerman; Sue Logue, Wallace's widow; George Logue, Wallace's brother; Joe Frank Logue, George's nephew and a Spartanburg police officer (Sue Logue was termed Joe Frank's "aunt-in-law" by the local press); Sheriff W. D. Allen, the Logues' cousin; and Clarence Bagwell, a Spartanburg, South Carolina, plasterer.

The "fearful Timmerman-Logue family feud" heated up with a disagreement between Davis W. Timmerman and Wallace Logue, a farmer, about who was responsible for the death of Logue's yearling calf. Timmerman later shot Wallace Logue to death, but was acquitted after arguing he had acted in self-defense. Sue Logue threatened to kill Timmerman or have him killed, and six months after her husband's death, Clarence Bagwell, the Spartanburg plasterer, shot Timmerman to death in his store. Joe Frank Logue had hired Bagwell to kill Timmerman for five hundred dollars. Bagwell, down and out and in need of money, told Joe Frank he "would kill every damn body in Spartanburg county for $500."[26] Joe Frank later testified that Sue Logue and George Logue had constantly pestered him to hire Bagwell.

After Timmerman's death, Sheriff Allen and Deputy W. L. Clark went to George Logue's home to serve him and Sue Logue with warrants for being accessories to Timmerman's murder. Allen was fatally shot in the head, and a sharecropper on Logue's "five-horse farm," Fred Dorn, was

24. "Logues Granted 7-Day Reprieve by Governor," *Aiken (S.C.) Standard and Review,* 6 January 1943.

25. "Edgefield Trial Site Changed," *Augusta Chronicle,* 6 January 1942.

26. "Two Killed in Edgefield Gunfire," ibid., 17 November 1941; "Timmerman Slain for $500, Joe Frank Logue Testifies," ibid., 23 January 1942.

also killed. Clark was wounded and died days later. George Logue was wounded but recovered. Sue Logue, George Logue, and Clarence Bagwell were executed on 15 January 1943.

The Gun Battle

The biggest story in the case was the shoot-out at George Logue's home. The *Augusta (Ga.) Chronicle,* the largest daily newspaper near Edgefield County, ran an all-capitals banner headline that read: "Two Killed in Edgefield Gunfire." The story said the shootings were "a bloody new chapter" in the family feud. Three pictures accompanied the front-page story. Sheriff Allen went to the Logue home unarmed, according to the newspaper, and when he said he would have to take George Logue and Sue Logue into custody, George and Dorn left the room. They returned with guns, and George reportedly shot Allen, his cousin, in the head, then shot Clark, who returned fire. Dorn shot Clark again with a shotgun, and Clark shot Dorn to death. Clark stumbled from the house, and one of the Logues's cousins found him and took him to a hospital where he died two days later; he was shot on his fiftieth birthday.[27] The coroner, reportedly one of the first people to reach the shooting scene, was the sheriff's brother-in-law. Dorn, before he died, claimed Clark had shot him without cause. He said he had been outside carrying a bucket of water when he came around a corner of the home and saw Clark, and the deputy had shot him.

Curious onlookers flocked to the Logue home. The *Chronicle* said police from throughout South Carolina were stationed at intersections to keep traffic moving, and heavily armed police patrolled near the home.

The stories were mostly big news in the *Chronicle* until December 1941 when the Japanese attacked Pearl Harbor. Then the paper almost exclusively ran wire stories about the murder, and although many were on the front page, they did not receive the prominent news play they had, and they usually consisted of only a few paragraphs. Other than the murder stories, the *Chronicle* gave the most attention to the trial, and most stories prominently featured Sue Logue. Prior to the trial, reports about confessions and about her role in the crimes were often published, and the story about her conviction, which automatically carried a death sentence, ran on page 1 under a one-column headline.[28]

The local weekly, the *Aiken (S.C.) Standard and Review,* did not give much coverage to the case in the weeks before the execution. The paper

27. "Two Killed"; "Deputy Clark Dies of Gunshot Wounds," ibid., 19 November 1941.
28. "Bagwell, Logues Are Found Guilty," *Augusta Chronicle,* 27 January 1942.

did not publish a story about the 15 January 1943 executions in its issue after the executions. Perhaps the editors believed the dailies had amply covered the case. One of South Carolina's leading newspapers, the *Columbia State*, located in the state capital, ran a short story on page 2 under a one-column headline.[29]

The murders put Sue Logue's case onto many front pages, but the press paid little attention to her death. Despite her involvement in the murders of two police officers, the deaths of thousands of U.S. soldiers overshadowed her execution.

29. "Logues and Bagwell Die in the Chair," *Columbia State*, 16 January 1943.

PART II

Jazz Journalism and the

Execution Story As Drama

Chapter 5

Excesses in 1920s Louisiana

WHEN ADA LEBOEUF AND DR. THOMAS DREHER were hanged in 1929 in Franklin, Louisiana, for murdering LeBoeuf's husband, it was a story of national proportions. Spokane, Washington, is almost as far from Franklin, Louisiana, as one can get in the United States. Yet, the *Spokane Daily Chronicle* blared forth with a front-page, two-line, all-capitals screamer headline: "Woman Begs for Mercy As Gallows Trap Drops." Stories about the executions, or about events during the two days before the executions, ran on the front pages of newspapers in Chicago; Charleston, South Carolina; San Francisco; Miami; Tulsa; and Washington, D.C.[1] The story about the murder of James J. LeBoeuf of Morgan City, Louisiana, was never routine, and the major newspaper in the state, the *New Orleans Times-Picayune,* almost never covered it in a routine way.[2]

The story came at the end of the jazz-journalism era, during which some historians say tabloid editors "built sordid murder cases into national sensations." Two murder cases that are often used as examples are the Judd Gray and Ruth Snyder case in New York and the Hall-Mills murder case in New Jersey. New York executed Snyder in 1928, and the *New*

1. "Woman Begs for Mercy," *Spokane Daily Chronicle,* 1 February 1929; "Louisiana Pair, Thrice Saved, to Hang Today," *Chicago Tribune,* 1 February 1929; "LeBouef Killers Die, Protesting Their Innocence," *Charleston (S.C.) News and Courier,* 2 February 1929; "Love Killers Hang Praying for Enemies," *San Francisco Examiner,* 2 February 1929; "Doctor and Woman on Death's Brink," *Miami Herald,* 1 February 1929; "Woman, Doctor Go to Death for Slaying Husband," *Tulsa World,* 2 February 1929; "Widow and Doctor Hanged for Killing," *Washington Post,* 2 February 1929. The *New York Times,* 2 February 1929, discreetly ran the story about the execution on page 19.

2. In 1930, the *New Orleans Times-Picayune* had a substantial circulation advantage, with the Audit Bureau of Circulation showing 100,000 sold daily and 130,000 Sunday. The *New Orleans Item* sold 67,000 daily and 85,000 Sunday, the *New Orleans States* 50,000 daily and 91,000 Sunday, and the *New Orleans Morning Tribune* 47,000 daily (Thomas Ewing Dabney, *One Hundred Great Years: The Story of the "Times-Picayune" from Its Founding to 1940,* 444).

York Daily News published about 1 million extra copies because the newspaper had a front-page picture of Snyder surreptitiously taken at the moment she was electrocuted.[3]

Reports of crime, courts, and executions have been standard fare since the first successful U.S. newspaper, the *Boston News-Letter,* featured news about violence and hangings. According to Dan Schiller, "Local news, human interest news, and, above all, crime news" became staples for the first mass-circulation newspapers in the 1830s. But the so-called Penny Press did not invent the sensational murder story. Frank Luther Mott contends that even some of the six-cent commercial newspapers published before 1830 gave considerable space to such stories. One definition of sensationalism, Mott says, was detailed descriptions of crimes. Sensationalism especially marked the jazz-journalism period. Vivid descriptions of crimes, the use of literary techniques, bold headlines, and large photographs were some of the techniques.[4] The techniques were restricted neither to New York nor to the tabloid press; some elements are found in news reports of famous crimes during the period in such newspapers as the *New York Times.*

The murder case involving Ada LeBoeuf illustrates the brash, flashy style of jazz journalism in the *New Orleans Times-Picayune.* The reporting of LeBoeuf's case is different from any other case in this book, except perhaps that of Anna Hahn. How the stories were displayed and the sensational and subjective coverage are different from cases either before or after. Nonetheless, LeBoeuf's case has not had the "staying power" that the Snyder-Gray or Hall-Mills cases have had, and it is for that reason that I chose her case. Before, during, and after the trial, it was national news. LeBoeuf's execution resulted in headlines across the United States. Today, her story and how the *Times-Picayune* covered it are largely forgotten.

The "Angle-Iron" Murder

A Morgan City youth said today he is writing a seven-verse song to be titled "Boat Riding Mamma, Don't You Try to Angle-Iron Me."

—New Orleans Times-Picayune, *17 July 1927*

3. Emery and Emery, *The Press and America,* 267.
4. Stevens, *Sensationalism,* 9; Schiller, *Objectivity and the News,* 7; Mott, *American Journalism,* 297, 442. About the narrative style, Roy Edward Lotz noted, "Probably the most attractive characteristic of newspapers long ago was their use of narrative instead of the inverted pyramid" (*Crime and the American Press,* 31). News was more in the nature of stories.

Sweet piroguing mamma, don't you
angle iron me.
That you, Jim?
Uhhuh boom zim!
Oh, please sweet mamma, don't you
Angle iron me.

—New Orleans Times-Picayune, *26 July 1927*

The *Times-Picayune* wrote of the murder trial of Ada LeBoeuf, Dr. Thomas Dreher, and James Beadle: "Selection of a jury probably will be difficult, on account of the wide publicity the case has attracted."[5]

By any standard, the story was sensational: sex, money, prominence, murder, and intrigue had to attract readers' attention. The *Times-Picayune* recognized that and wrote about it in a front-page news story that read more like a personal-opinion column. "For such, dear children, is the spectacle of criminal justice in an American city, large or small, the morbid desire to see things and hear things, seen in an exaggerated and caricatured miniature in night court at New Orleans, and seen full size when Peaches Brownings sue 'Daddies,' or when a good sex murder trial is staged."[6]

The coverage of the arrests, trial, and executions of two principals in the case drew almost daily front-page attention in the *Times-Picayune*, and also attracted much of the regional press. From 8 July to 8 August 1927, the story ran every day on the front page of the *Times-Picayune* except on 20, 21, and 22 July, and that was because in the last days before the trial there was nothing new to report.[7] On twelve occasions during the period, the story ran as the lead, often under headlines that streamed across the width of the page, screaming at readers. Despite the attention the case received in the late 1920s, it and the newspaper coverage are not mentioned in many, if any, journalism histories, nor is the case mentioned in some histories of Louisiana. Nonetheless, the *Times-Picayune* called the case the South's equivalent of the Hall-Mills case or the Gray-Snyder case.[8] The

5. "Court Orders Better Spelling in Indictment," *New Orleans Times-Picayune*, 19 July 1927.

6. "Trio in LeBoeuf Case Face Trial for Life Today," ibid., 25 July 1927.

7. Commerce Secretary Herbert Hoover's levee plan, in response to the 1927 Mississippi river flood, ran as the lead story on 21 July, and the Jack Dempsey–Jack Sharkey heavyweight prizefight led the 22 July edition.

8. The Hall-Mills case began in 1922 with the murders of the Reverend Edward W. Hall and Mrs. James Mills. The case was sensational and especially so in the New York tabloid press. Prosecutors were unable to produce an indictment in 1922, but the case was reopened in 1926, with the *New York Times* first reporting it on 17 July 1926. The reopening resulted in a sensational trial. According to Frank Luther Mott, more than

comparisons reached far out of Louisiana. Some four hundred miles to the north, the *Memphis Commercial Appeal* on the first day the story was reported in the newspaper said in a headline: "Parallel of Snyder Case, Sheriff Thinks."[9]

The story interested the local and regional press for several reasons. First, it involved sex, murder, and mystery—subjects with natural appeal, especially when a female killer is involved.[10] Second, it involved well-to-do people, and the media have always concentrated much coverage on society's rich and famous because they have reader appeal. Third, the action took place during an extremely short time period. Only one month elapsed from the 8 July arrests until the 6 August convictions. That led to a rapid-fire release of information on an almost daily basis—a natural serial approach. Readers did not have time to get bored with the story. Furthermore, despite the *New Orleans Times-Picayune*'s lamentations about the slowness of the trial process, the trial moved quickly. Finally, the story presented itself in terms of a neat three-act drama. The two primary reporters covering the case for the *Times-Picayune* often noted the theatrical nature of the story, and on some occasions used Middle English words to emphasize the case's Shakespearean nature. In describing the closing argument of the district attorney, *Times-Picayune* reporter Kenneth T. Knoblock said the attorney argued that the defendants "should be hanged by the neck until they are dead, dead, dead. They should be punished, forsooth, . . . because it is the law."[11]

---

200 reporters covered the trial, and about 5 million words were reported. Mrs. Hall and James Mills, the husband of the slain woman, were not convicted.

The Snyder-Gray case was in 1927 and involved the murder of Albert Snyder. His wife and her lover, Judd Gray, were convicted and executed. The *New York Daily News* published a picture of Snyder's execution, taken with a hidden camera. The Snyder case was the closest in time to the LeBoeuf case. The murder was first reported in the *New York Times* on 21 March 1927, and the story about the two being convicted ran 10 May 1927. By 28 July, when the LeBoeuf trial was beginning, the *New York Times* had run more than 100 stories about the Snyder-Gray case. By the time Snyder was executed in early January 1928, the *Times* had published more than 150 stories. The *New York Times Index* during the period between 21 March 1927 and 13 January 1928 shows 148 entries, some of which include multiple stories. For information about the cases, see Mott, *American Journalism,* 670–71.

9. "Parallel of Snyder Case," *Memphis Commercial Appeal,* 8 July 1927.

10. There is some evidence that sensational news coverage has value for readers and that for some people it is more informative than nonsensational coverage because it contains more details. See Richard Hofstetter and David Dozier, "Useful News, Sensational News." Others, such as Ray Surette, say most extensively covered criminal trials more appeal to voyeuristic instincts than provide education ("Media Trials," 299). Still others, such as Doris Graber, say that although the media are a prime information source, readers pay little attention to stories, ignore many stories, and forget the information from most (*Crime News and the Public,* 50).

11. See, for example, Wendy Lesser, *Pictures at an Execution: An Inquiry into the Subject of Murder;* and Ericson, Baranek, and Chan, *Representing Order,* for a discussion

The LeBoeuf murder case occurred during a time when newspapers were much more likely to interject opinion into a news story, or to use literary techniques to the extreme. The *Times-Picayune* reporters and editors reflected these techniques in the coverage.

As described by the *New Orleans Times-Picayune* in its stories, the principals in the story line included: James LeBoeuf, a somewhat prominent, hardworking family man; Ada LeBoeuf, his flighty, cold, unfaithful, scheming wife; Thomas Dreher, a wealthy, aging, well-regarded local physician who was Ada LeBoeuf's lover; Jim Beadle, a poor, basically honest, uneducated, and easily manipulated hunter and trapper; Mrs. Willie Husband, James LeBoeuf's elderly, long-suffering, saintly mother; and Sheriff Charles Pecot, a strong, honest lawman. Others included lawyers, the judge, Beadle's "pioneer woman" wife, and children who were mature beyond their ages.

It seems unlikely the story would have received the coverage it did had it not involved Ada LeBoeuf, around whom the coverage revolved. In its reporting, the *Times-Picayune* freely speculated, used questionable sources and techniques of attribution, reached for story angles, wrote misleading headlines, and certainly made a substantial contribution to the circus proceedings of the case by sensationalizing the story. Such was the stuff of the jazz-journalism era, and the *Times-Picayune* was not alone in using such techniques. The case and how it was reported must be viewed in the context of the time.

The Crime

The area where the crime occurred and some of that area's history were important parts of the *New Orleans Times-Picayune*'s coverage because the newspaper attempted to capture the romance, history, and aura of south Louisiana and made those elements metaphors.

Morgan City is almost as far south as one can go in Louisiana. Just below Morgan City are Atchafalaya Bay and the Gulf of Mexico. Morgan City is directly south of Baton Rouge, and it is in the heart of what is known as Cajun Country, where descendants of the Grand Pré Acadians settled after the British evicted them from what is now Nova Scotia. Longfellow's epic poem *Evangeline* popularized the area's lore. There are today the Evangeline oak, Evangeline's grave site, and a monument to the Acadians in St. Martinville, a few miles northwest of Morgan City. The Bayou Teche flows nearby the oak, grave site, and monument. The land is

---

of crime reporting as theater. "Mercy Asked for Beadle As State Demands Three Lives," *New Orleans Times-Picayune,* 6 August 1927.

flat, and the growing sugar cane waves when the wind blows across the fields. Spanish moss hangs from the trees. The area exudes mystery, romance, and history.

These places and south Louisiana's mystique were not lost on *Times-Picayune* reporter Kenneth T. Knoblock, who covered much of the LeBoeuf murder case. His front-page news story about the opening day of the murder trial contained the following description of Franklin, near Morgan City where the trial was held, and the environs:

> The moon, when there is one, silvers the waters that spread everywhere to the horizon, rank with saber-tooth varieties of giant grass, cane and stunted oaks, cypress and willows all strangely sepulchral, by day as well as by night—tombstones of a people, perhaps, commemorating that other loved one of the Teche, Evangeline.
>
> And on these trees, or rather on the live oaks among them, for cleaner trees refuse to support so parasitical a growth, on all these trees hangs—ah fatal word, perchance prophetic—a sickly fringe of Spanish moss, ghastly in the moon and leprous in the sun.[12]

James J. LeBoeuf, forty-two, disappeared on 1 July 1927 from Morgan City, but his absence caused little alarm because it was believed he was away on business in nearby Lafayette. LeBoeuf was the superintendent of the Morgan City power plant. The *Times-Picayune* said he was the father of five children and a good citizen. When he did not show up in Lafayette, a search began, although no one suspected foul play. Still, it seemed curious to some, at least in hindsight, that LeBoeuf's wife, Ada Bonner LeBoeuf, made no early inquiry about her husband's whereabouts. The *Times-Picayune* later reported that she did not seem too interested. On the night of 6 July, some men cruising in a motorboat in about three or four feet of water on Lake Palourde struck a submerged object. It was James LeBoeuf's body.[13]

The Arrests

The *New Orleans Times-Picayune* broke the story about the murder on 8 July under a one-column headline at the top of the right side of the front page, an inauspicious start for a story that would dominate the front page for weeks to come. The headline featured Ada LeBoeuf by naming her first among those arrested. The story said LeBoeuf, a trapper named James

12. "Trio Face Trial Today."
13. "Wife of Murder Victim, Trapper, Physician Jailed," *New Orleans Times-Picayune,* 8 July 1927. Later trial coverage made it clear that John Beadle was among the group. He testified at trial, and he also was a third cousin to defendant James Beadle. "Widow's Collapse in Crowded Court Ends Night Session," ibid., 30 July 1927.

Beadle, and a prominent Morgan City physician, Thomas E. Dreher, forty-eight, had been arrested and jailed. LeBoeuf was termed her dead husband's "handsome wife." Beadle, forty-five, was said to be "noted for his cunning as a hunter and a trapper." The story devoted more attention to Dreher. He was called "a leading practicing physician" and "one of the sterling citizens of Morgan City." Dreher had a wife, two daughters, and a son who attended Tulane University in New Orleans. Police released a lot of information to the press in the first reports. They said James LeBoeuf had been shot with two buckshot loads, and a long incision made in his abdomen. The newspaper speculated that the incision was apparently made to ensure that the body sank. A source identified as a member of the coroner's staff said an expert in such work evidently made the incision. Left unsaid, but still obvious, was that a medical doctor might fit that description, or a skilled trapper and hunter. To help ensure the body would not float, railroad angle irons—each weighing about 150 pounds, the *Times-Picayune* estimated—had been tied to LeBoeuf's head and feet, and his body dumped into Lake Palourde. Coroner C. M. Horton said he could not explain why LeBoeuf's body had come to the surface. An Associated Press story said that the body had been dropped into deep water, but the weights were "insufficient to hold the body," which apparently floated into shallow water, where it was found near the edge of the lake.[14]

Although it might be a minor point, it seems unbelievable that a body with 300 pounds of iron tied to it could "float" anywhere. The story did not say the weights had come loose; it said they were insufficient. Later trial testimony showed the body had not floated at all. Enormous floods on the Mississippi River in 1927 caused the water level in the lake to rise. The body, thrown into what was at the time deep water, was in shallow water when the river receded. *Times-Picayune* reporter Knoblock used a biblical analogy in a later trial story, noting: "And the floods passed away from this Ararat, that carried such a mountainous crime, and some crab fishermen came along."[15]

Shortly after the arrests, the *New Orleans Times-Picayune* said police termed the murder "one of the most brutal crimes in Louisiana history." Not to be outdone, a story in the *Memphis Commercial Appeal* said the slaying was "one of the most strikingly brutal murders in the crime history of the south."[16]

14. "Victim, Trapper, Physician"; "Dead Body of LeBoeuf Cut and Sunk in Lake," *Memphis Commercial Appeal*, 9 July 1927.

15. For a good account of the flood, see John M. Barry, *Rising Tide: The Great Mississippi River Flood of 1927 and How It Changed America*. "Three Defendants' Counsel Ask Public to Keep Open Mind," *New Orleans Times-Picayune*, 1 August 1927.

16. "Victim, Trapper, Physician"; "Law Moves to Punish Slayers of LeBoeuf," *Memphis Commercial Appeal*, 11 July 1927.

Police put forward in the press a sketchy theory for the murder, saying they believed Dreher had hired Beadle to kill LeBoeuf. The *Times-Picayune* developed two major story angles: First was a love affair between LeBoeuf and Dreher. Second was the depiction of the characters, with LeBoeuf a cold, calculating woman; Dreher a weak or simpering man; and Beadle a strong, silent outdoorsman, probably fooled by the more worldly LeBoeuf and Dreher.[17] Ada LeBoeuf was the star of the show.

The Love Affair

The *New Orleans Times-Picayune* approached the love affair angle with some caution on the day the story broke, but soon flung caution to the wind. The first story said Dreher and James LeBoeuf had been good friends, but Dreher's interest in Ada LeBoeuf, and her interest in him, resulted in hatred between James LeBoeuf and Dreher. Attributing the information to no source, the newspaper said "gossip" in Morgan City had linked Ada LeBoeuf and Dreher for some weeks. A later *Times-Picayune* story said that more than two years earlier, James LeBoeuf had reprimanded Dreher for the attention paid to his wife. The newspaper, again naming no sources, said Dreher's interest had started about six years earlier, far earlier than the aforementioned "some weeks," and that "it is believed" that the slain man and the doctor had more trouble weeks before the murder. James LeBoeuf was quoted as having said he would kill his wife if he could prove the relationship, but there was no source attached to a direct quotation from a man who was now dead. In a statement attributed only to "close friends," the newspaper said the LeBoeufs' marriage came close to the breaking point, although the couple was seen only two days before the murder and seemed happy.[18]

Developing the Characters

One hallmark of sensational crime reporting is a concentration on personalities and personal relationships, often raising the main characters in stories to celebrity status.[19] Although there were many characters developed in the story, Ada LeBoeuf was the central figure.

17. "Swift Justice Seen As Men and Matron Confess in Murder," *New Orleans Times-Picayune,* 9 July 1927. The character development in the LeBoeuf case fits within Surette's description of "media trials" ("Media Trials," 294).

18. "Swift Justice Seen"; "New Arrests Near As LeBoeuf Death Boat Is Discovered," *New Orleans Times-Picayune,* 12 July 1927.

19. Surette, "Media Trials," 294.

Ada LeBoeuf

The *New Orleans Times-Picayune* gave Ada LeBoeuf a myriad of monikers. The newspaper termed her "the bucolic Lorelei"; "The Lady of the Lake"; the "plain Jane Lorelei of the swamplands"; "Louisiana's love pirate"; a "small-town Cleopatra"; "Ada, she of the raven tresses and the small, odd and ancient eyes, compressed lips and angle-iron ways"; "the siren of the swamps"; "the automobile riding vampire"; and Dreher's "automobile-ride paramour." From the time of her arrest until the beginning of the trial, LeBoeuf was most often depicted as cold and emotionless or as silly and girlish and preoccupied with her appearance.

The cold and emotionless LeBoeuf developed early in the story process. The *Times-Picayune* said she had claimed she did not know who had killed her husband, although she said she had been present when the murder occurred. The newspaper termed her response "coy," and said she was "an unmoved spectator" to the murder. Moreover, she told her story about the murder "without emotion," and was "cool and self-possessed." The newspaper, in one of many opinion comments made in news stories, asserted, "If the killing of her husband by the physician has caused her remorse she has concealed it well."[20] No one had yet been charged with the murder.

During the trial, the *Times-Picayune* continued its portrayal of LeBoeuf as cold. Toward the end of the trial, Knoblock wrote that LeBoeuf had "just sense enough to fight to save her skin." He said her testimony in her defense had been flat and emotionless. "What little anger Ada did show was a thwarted, plebeian anger under inhibitions of good breeding, vicarcously [sic] acquired," he added. Even when convicted, LeBoeuf was described as emotionless. "She might have been listening to a not particularly interesting sermon by her pastor or a lecture by her husband," Knoblock wrote.[21]

It was evident from the start that of the three defendants, LeBoeuf was the star of the show in the press. The *New Orleans Times-Picayune* at times stretched its descriptions of her behavior. For example, the headline on the lead story about the arraignments read: "Mrs. LeBoeuf Defiant As Defense Loses Fight to Delay Murder Trial."[22] However, the text cited no instances of LeBoeuf's defiant behavior. One part of the story said she had worn "a mourning dress of black satin and stylishly cut, [and] *appeared* almost defiant" (emphasis added). The newspaper took a purely subjective statement by the writer and turned it into a headline seemingly based

20. "Swift Justice Seen"; "Quick Indictment of Trio in LeBoeuf Murder Demanded," *New Orleans Times-Picayune,* 10 July 1927.
21. "LeBoeuf Murder Case Will Reach Jury Tomorrow," *New Orleans Times-Picayune,* 4 August 1927; "Ada, Doctor to Hang; Life for Beadle," ibid., 7 August 1927.
22. "LeBoeuf Defiant," ibid., 24 July 1927.

upon fact. Adding to the possibility that the *Times-Picayune* occasionally wrote speculative or misleading headlines was an Associated Press story that ran the same day in the *Times-Picayune*. That story, also about the court appearance, said LeBoeuf had a "sad demeanor" in court, which is almost the antithesis of defiance. The headline that the *Times-Picayune* put on the story also seemed to reach to show LeBoeuf in a certain way: "Children Shun Woman Who Confessed Luring Husband to His Death." It was not until near the end of the story, which jumped from the front page to page 2, that it said children who had been playing near the jail ran away when LeBoeuf called to them from her cell window. Because none of the children was interviewed—at least no interviews were apparent in the story—it would have been impossible for the headline writer to know if they had "shunned" the infamous accused killer or if they would have run away from anyone who hailed them from a jail window.

A 17 July news story described the three defendants meeting with their attorneys, and said LeBoeuf, Dreher's "paramour," had been nonchalant. Why newspaper reporters were apparently allowed to witness an attorney-client meeting was not explained, nor was it evident that anyone had so described LeBoeuf for the newspaper. The next day, at a court hearing, the newspaper said LeBoeuf had a handkerchief in her hand "but never once placed it to her eyes," implying an unproved fact that she carried the handkerchief for show. At the hearing, the newspaper said, LeBoeuf's facial expression was "masklike, inscrutable." When the three defendants left the court, after their attorney had asked the judge to order newsmen to stop harassing the defendants, LeBoeuf reportedly "giggled and covered her face with a handkerchief" when photographers outside the courtroom tried to photograph them. "They did not appear to be 'harassed,'" the newspaper said in the story. The next day's edition of the *Times-Picayune* contained a one-column picture of LeBoeuf trying to cover her face with the handkerchief, but the caption declared "the photographer was too fast for her." The caption also said that it had been claimed that newsmen were harassing the defendants, but, "[r]unning the gauntlet of lenses, however, Mrs. LeBoeuf giggled. Dr. Dreher grinned," implying the two defendants were actually enjoying the press attention, despite their protestations to the contrary.[23]

The *Times-Picayune* also used a suspect technique of attributing direct quotations to anonymous groups. One article attributed direct quotes to "four kinds of prophets and four sets of partisans."[24]

LeBoeuf seemed a socialite instead of an inmate, more concerned with her looks than with her situation. The *Times-Picayune* described her as "en-

23. "Trio in Murder Case Permitted to See Lawyers," ibid., 18 July 1927; "Court Orders Better Spelling"; "Chemist Unable to Analyze Knife Stains by July 25," ibid., 20 July 1927.
24. "Pecot Discovers Two Witnesses in LeBoeuf Trial," ibid., 24 July 1927.

tertaining" friends in her jail cell while wearing a stylish white organdie dress. She seemed vain because when some of her guests suggested she have her "long black hair" bobbed, she reportedly replied, "No, indeed. Bobbed hair is becoming for some women, but I don't think I would like it. I never had my hair cut, and I don't suppose I ever will."[25]

Dr. Thomas Dreher

The *New Orleans Times-Picayune* depicted Dr. Thomas Dreher as weak and perhaps easily manipulated, the antithesis of the strong and collected Ada LeBoeuf. He confessed "with tears streaming down his face"—not a manly attribute in 1927 America. A special guard was assigned to watch Dreher because it was feared he would attempt suicide, an allegation his attorney denounced as untrue. At a 13 July court hearing for arraignment, the newspaper portrayed Dreher as a weakling and LeBoeuf as a calm, unconcerned defendant.[26]

During the trial, the descriptions of Dreher changed, and he was termed cool and collected when he testified. Knoblock also believed Dreher to be devious, and editorialized or attempted to read Dreher's mind on more than one occasion. Knoblock said testifying concerned Dreher as much as "he used to mind those days in the little coupe with the sporty wire wheels, or in the green pirogue's ancestors with Fidus Achates Jim Beadle at his side, the little man who, the doctor once said, shot a fellow for him just out of the friendly feeling in his heart." Knoblock virtually declared that Dreher was lying.

> The physician continued as cold-blooded, phlegmatic and lethargic as an eel, but didn't squirm or wiggle under the conscience microscope adjusted by the district attorney. He stepped down as serenely confident as he was when he climbed up. It is seldom that such an anomaly is seen in a prisoner's dock, a man heartless and chicken-hearted, kind and heartlessly cruel, gentle and brutal—absolutely contradictory in every detail of his nature.

Knoblock said drama critics could have discerned that the "acting was better than the script, that verisimilitude was there, but not plausibility."[27]

Despite the unflattering descriptions of Dreher, he was also called "one of the sterling citizens of Morgan City." A news source identified only as "a parish official" noted—to illustrate how prominent and involved

25. "State Checking Doctor's Story by Fingerprints," ibid., 16 July 1927.
26. "Swift Justice Seen"; "Quick Indictment Demanded"; "Fourteen Called for Grand Jury's Probe of Murder," ibid., 11 July 1927; "LeBoeuf Defiant."
27. "Beadle to Take Stand As Ada and Doctor Close Case," ibid., 5 August 1927.

Dreher had been—that the doctor had once held high office in the Ku Klux Klan and was always active in civic work. In some parts of the country, active Klan membership was considered a sign of good citizenship.[28]

James Beadle: The Silent, "Plain Man"

In contrast to the other two defendants, James Beadle's press persona developed as the strong, silent trapper, and as the unwitting foil of the devious Dreher and LeBoeuf. He was also consistently described as uneducated. It was a classic story line of the well-to-do using the poor, less educated common man: one story said Beadle was Dreher's "Good Man Friday." The newspaper emphasized Beadle's plain, folksy ways, calling him "Plain Jim Beadle."[29]

Press accounts made Beadle seem a better person than Dreher or LeBoeuf. At arraignment, he wore "a clean, neatly pressed blue coat and spotless black trousers" and was "attentive." He accommodated photographers more than did Dreher or LeBoeuf, and he once stopped before going into his cell so photographers could take his picture. He said he would help because he was innocent. The newspaper said this won him a huge following, although it was not clear whether it was because of his willingness to oblige the press or his generally unassuming demeanor. "I can't see how that poor man can be guilty," a woman spectator reportedly said. "He was entirely different from that brazen woman, and he wasn't worried like Dr. Dreher." One day before the trial began, the *Times-Picayune* called Beadle the "silent handy-man," and during the trial referred to him as "big-hearted" and possessing a "primitive soul."[30] Beadle's lack of education as a theme of the coverage prior to trial might have created public sympathy for him because he seemed the dupe in the case.

Beadle's Family

Beadle's family received some of the most sympathetic coverage. One early story reported that Alice Beadle and her seven children had attended a preliminary proceeding, "their hearts aching for their husband and father." The newspaper account stressed the family's poor circumstances:

28. "Victim, Trapper, Physician"; "Trio to Face Trial July 25 As Slayers of James LeBoeuf," ibid., 13 July 1927. United States Supreme Court Justice Hugo Black made a similar point about his own Klan membership in Alabama in the 1920s. See Howard Ball, *Hugo L. Black: Cold Steel Warrior*, 60–63.

29. "State Checking Doctor's Story."

30. "Court Orders Better Spelling"; "Eve of LeBoeuf Trial Finds Franklin Keenly Expectant," *New Orleans Times-Picayune*, 24 July 1927; "Widow's Collapse"; "Beadle to Take Stand."

"The Beadle family returned this evening to their humble little home in Morgan City, where they will talk with friends until they can come again to the jail." Alice was depicted as a small but brave woman who had a heart problem. During the trial, she came to the court against the advice of her doctor, the newspaper reported. She was also called "thin, scrawny, worn but indomitable—a pioneer mother, working and fighting to bring up her children decently." The children were "slim and pretty," or youngsters bored with the proceedings who would "much rather be shooting marbles on the courthouse walk."[31]

Mrs. Willie Husband: The Grieving Mother

An important character in the unfolding story process was James LeBoeuf's mother, Mrs. Willie Husband. She was described in one story as "a tragic, pitiable figure." Her persona contrasted sharply with the all-important Ada LeBoeuf, perhaps making LeBoeuf seem even more evil. Early in the story process, the *New Orleans Times-Picayune* quoted Husband, James LeBoeuf's "aged mother, who is matron of the Jesuit school near Franklin," as saying that she believed someone had tried to poison her son two years earlier. She said James suspected that he had been poisoned. "He would have left his wife then, but I begged him to try to get along for my sake." The implication was that the son had died because he was trying to please his elderly mother. The information also contributed to Ada LeBoeuf's persona as a scheming wife who tried to get rid of her husband over a period of years, all the while frolicking in bed with a well-to-do, prominent doctor.[32]

Husband later described her daughter-in-law as a rotten housekeeper and a terrible cook, unpardonable faults for a proper wife: "My poor boy hardly ate at home at all for the past year. . . . And when I went to see them I used to carry my lunch in a paper bag, because I never could tell when she was going to have a hot meal and when she wasn't. She used to give those children nothing but grits and butter for supper, and Jim never did eat butter, not even when he was a little fellow."[33]

The *Times-Picayune* reported that Husband had offered her "scanty savings" to Sheriff Pecot to aid the prosecution, but he did not accept. The newspaper said James LeBoeuf's "aged mother" had tears "rolling down her cheeks." She came from work, "[d]rying away her tears with the cor-

31. "LeBoeuf Defiant"; "Grim Questions to Jurors Rend Mother's Heart," ibid., 29 July 1927; "Mercy Asked for Beadle."
32. "Ada Uses Rouge, Wearing White Dress to Court," ibid., 28 July 1927; "Trio Face Trial July 25." Some contend that the media like different types of conflict, such as the brute offender and saintly victim (Lotz, *Crime and the Press,* 55).
33. "Grim Questions."

ner of an apron as she talked of her only son." After offering her meager savings, Husband returned to her school and work. It was not easy: "It is mighty hard keeping on with my cooking and sewing and cleaning when I have to stop ever so often to think about my dear boy."[34]

Juxtaposed in the story with the grieving Husband were LeBoeuf and her codefendants, who, the *Times-Picayune* said, "entertained friends and relatives while the jury commission was in session." The newspaper, naming no source, said all who visited the jail reported the three were in good spirits. The word *entertained* made it seem as if the trio were having a party in the jailhouse while LeBoeuf's mother was working herself to the bone, offering her small savings to the prosecution and suffering all the while. The newspaper reported that Dreher never asked about his own wife or family. His first words were "How is Ada?"[35] All of the descriptions might have been accurate, but even so, the prosecution could not have hired a public relations team to concoct stories that would more enrage the public—and potential jurors.

Other Characters

Sheriff Charles F. Pecot personified order and authority. The *New Orleans Times-Picayune* described him as a powerful yet "courtly" man, a man of action, "big and broad," and accustomed to being obeyed. "He is direct and straightforward, yet his manner is flavored with the courtliness characteristic of the state's 'French' parishes." Pecot used the press to make a case against the defendants prior to trial. The sheriff informed the *Times-Picayune* about evidence—possible evidence—and predicted that he would hang the defendants.[36]

Defense attorneys unsuccessfully tried to control the pretrial publicity. Sen. James R. Parkerson, the chief defense attorney, objected three days after the arrests about newsmen talking to his clients, and Judge James Simon ordered newsmen not to talk to them. About a week later, the defense asked the court to prevent newsmen from "harassing" the accused, and Simon ordered the escorts to protect the defendants from being bothered by photographers. The orders might have slowed the reporters and pho-

34. "Loophole to Save Trio Seen in Attack on Drawing of Jury," *New Orleans Times-Picayune*, 15 July 1927.
35. "Grim Questions"; "Loophole to Save Trio."
36. "Court Orders Better Spelling." Ericson, Baranek, and Chan say murder stories often portray police as people of action (*Representing Order*, 106). Police providing such information to the press was common at the time. For the past several decades, the American Bar Association has listed confessions, potential evidence, and the personal feelings of officials about the defendant as among those things that often should not be reported prior to trial. See, for example, Don R. Pember, *Mass Media Law*, 400–401.

tographers, but it was not noticeably evident in the coverage. One day before the trial, Parkerson said he would get an acquittal for his clients, "and when we get through with the district attorney and the sheriff's office those fellows will be sorry they have had so many photographs appear in the newspaper."[37]

Published Confessions before Trial

On 9 July, the day after the press reported the arrests, confessions were also reported. The *New Orleans Times-Picayune* said Dreher had tears streaming down his face as he said Beadle had killed James LeBoeuf. Beadle claimed innocence. The *Times-Picayune* said Ada LeBoeuf had aided in the murder "without emotion." During her confession, she was "cool and self-possessed" and "weighed each word carefully." The story about the confessions ran on page 1, and the headline said that swift justice was expected and that both Dreher and LeBoeuf had confessed. A grand jury had not yet assembled to consider indictments. Two days later, the *Times-Picayune* again quoted from LeBoeuf's confession, indicating that either the news reporter sat in on the confession or police gave a copy of the confession to the press. Despite the reported confessions, all three defendants pleaded not guilty.[38]

The "Science" Aspect

Although the use of science in law enforcement was not well developed when compared to current standards, the use of "science" in the case was evident in the stories. A knife was sent to New Orleans for experts to examine for fingerprints and to chemically analyze a "foreign substance," presumably blood, on the blade. Beadle said the stains were pineapple juice, but Sheriff Pecot said he was confident they were blood. Pecot assembled reporters in a room at the Jung Hotel in New Orleans and showed them the knife before giving it to the chemist for analysis. It was impossible to do the analysis before the trial's start, so the expert chemist did not testify. Sheriff Pecot said it did not matter because the state had an "airtight" case.[39] The stories about the pending chemical examination,

37. "LeBoeuf Defiant"; "Court Orders Better Spelling"; "Pecot Discovers Two Witnesses."

38. "Swift Justice Seen"; "Fourteen Called"; "LeBoeuf Defiant."

39. "Orleans Experts May Help Solve LeBoeuf Murder," *New Orleans Time-Picayune,* 14 July 1927; "Trio Permitted to See Lawyers"; "Court Orders Better Spelling"; "Chemist Unable to Analyze Stains."

and about the sheriff's confidence that the stains would prove to be blood, ran on page 1, whereas the story about the inability to analyze the knife stains before trial ran on page 2.

Furthermore, experts were reportedly checking the "dim outline" of three fingerprints taken from the port side of the pirogue, near the bow. The *Times-Picayune* said that if the prints were Dreher's, he would be charged with the actual shooting of "his paramour's husband." Fingerprints on the pirogue—and on a gun that police believed was used to kill LeBoeuf—were too dim for use.[40] In sum, the reporting on possible bloodstain analysis and fingerprint analysis was speculative.

The Indictments

A 12 July story about the indictments produced by a special grand jury ran as the lead on page 1 of the *New Orleans Times-Picayune*. Judge Simon called a special jury because he believed public interest demanded it.[41] Whether the public interest preceded or followed the news play is arguable, but the *Times-Picayune* had run the story every day on the front page, and on four of the five days it had been the lead.

The newspaper described the defense challenges as seeking "loopholes." Defense attorney Parkerson challenged a state law that restricted summoning women for jury service to only those who had filed a declaration saying they wanted to serve. No women in St. Mary's Parish had filed. Parkerson argued that the provision was discriminatory and violated Fourteenth and Nineteenth Amendment constitutional guarantees. The *Times-Picayune* headline writer said this action was seeking a "loophole," a term that when used in this context had a derogatory connotation. A later story clarified the status of the 1924 law, which had been upheld by the Louisiana Supreme Court, but had never gone to the United States Supreme Court.[42]

The lead paragraph of the story about the indictments focused only on LeBoeuf. A picture of her, with Deputy Sheriff Arthur Martel at her side as she left the courtroom, accompanied the story. For the first time in any of the stories, Beadle was described as concerned. The *Times-Picayune* said

40. "State Checking Doctor's Story"; "Murder Charge against Three to Be Amended," ibid., 17 July 1927.
41. "Trio Face Trial July 25."
42. "Loophole to Save Trio." "Protection" of women from jury duty was common at the time. For a brief description of women serving on juries, see Friedman, *Crime and Punishment*, 419–21. In regard to women not serving on juries, as late as 1961, the United States Supreme Court found no constitutional defect in such laws (Lucas A. Powe Jr., *The Warren Court and American Politics*, 180). "Trio Permitted to See Lawyers."

he was a "veteran Acadian trapper" and a working man, whose "clothes were immaculately clean." Dreher was depicted as a nervous mess. He was visibly weary and worried; his gray summer suit was unpressed, which "gave him the mark of a careless man, far different from the debonaire Dr. Dreher, whom Morgan City had known as one of its most prominent physicians." The *Times-Picayune* said one newsman had sat beside Dreher in the courtroom. Dreher reportedly said, "The newspapers are painting me up as a pretty hardened criminal." Not so, said the reporter, who might have been correct. As painted in the press, Dreher seemed a rich, arrogant playboy type who cavorted with another man's wife, and now, when he might have to answer for it, was a weak, whining nobody. The story never explained how a newspaper reporter came to be seated beside a criminal defendant during a court proceeding.

An exchange of words between Dreher and LeBoeuf illustrated the *Times-Picayune*'s remarkable access to the defendants. The newspaper said the two were allowed a few seconds together before being returned to their cells, but the seconds apparently were anything but private. Dreher was quoted as telling her, "Don't break down, Ada, keep your nerves together." She replied, "All right, doc, you can depend on me." Attorney Parkerson declined to talk to the press about his clients, but he did say he would object to a proposal to install telegraph wires for reporters in the courthouse. He said he wanted to keep the trial from becoming a circus.[43]

A Circus in Franklin

With LeBoeuf as the leading character, press scrutiny of the upcoming trial was intense, and it naturally affected those involved. Mrs. Dreher reportedly would not come to the jail because she feared it would result in her picture being in the newspaper. The day before the grand jury hearing, Dr. Dreher reportedly told a barber who was shaving him not to scratch him before he went before the grand jury because reporters would believe he had attempted suicide.[44]

Public interest grew as the days passed. The judge had to ask on several occasions for court officers to clear the aisles of spectators. The *New Orleans Times-Picayune* reported there would be seats for the press at the trial, but no photographers would be allowed in the courtroom. Telegraph wires would be installed in offices in the courthouse to help reporters more quickly file their stories. The telegraph would allow stories to be

43. "LeBoeuf Defiant."
44. "New Arrests Near."

"flashed to newspaper offices all over the United States." No such instruments would be allowed in the courtroom. Reporters would have to write with pencil and paper. A long table was put in the front of the courtroom for the reporters.[45]

Two days before the trial began, the *Times-Picayune* reported that a "record crowd" was expected in Franklin.[46] The few hotel rooms were sold out. Restaurants and lunch stands "heavily stocked provisions." However, not all businesses were expected to profit. The *Times-Picayune* said the case afforded "opportunity for recreation other than the usual visits to bathing beaches or the main street movie house."[47]

The newspaper reported that Franklin residents were "like children with new toys" because of the attention the town received. The newspaper noted that although the murder was in Morgan City, Franklin was getting all the publicity. The effect of the case also extended to Morgan City, for "it is in Morgan City that the Drehers and the LeBoeufs lived, and loved, it is charged, both licitly and illicitly." The newspaper said the case was "Louisiana's own Gray-Snyder love murder bared in court," and noted the day before the trial that Franklin was "getting all set to out-Somerville Somerville N.J., seat of the notorious Hall-Mills trial." The first day of the trial, the newspaper reported that the crime was "elected, almost unanimously, to succeed the Snyder-Gray case in the public interest." It seemed evident that public officials and the newspaper press had elected the case, because "a score" of newspapermen were to attend. The *Times-Picayune* noted it was the first time Franklin had drawn such national attention. The courtroom could seat three hundred, but conservative estimates were that more than five thousand would seek admittance.[48]

The day before the trial started, a headline on the lead story read: "Eve of LeBoeuf Trial Finds Franklin Keenly Expectant." The story was accompanied by a five-column picture of the town of Franklin, taken from the air. Mug shots of Dreher, LeBoeuf, Beadle, and Pecot were superimposed into each corner. The *New Orleans Times-Picayune* announced that "news butchers" hawked newspapers from train windows at all the stops between Franklin and New Orleans. They shouted, "Read about the murder," but they did not use the names, Knoblock wrote, "for that would be redundant, as well as tautological, irrelevant, incompetent and immaterial."[49]

---

45. "Court Orders Better Spelling"; "Pecot Discovers Two Witnesses"; "LeBoeuf Defense May Try to Get Trial Continued," *New Orleans Times-Picayune,* 23 July 1927.
46. "Mother of Slain Man to Adopt Two Children," ibid., 22 July 1927.
47. "Franklin Expectant." The financial boon for small towns apparently was not unusual. For a Pennsylvania description, see Hugh Manchester, "Executions Were Good for Business," *Centre (Pa.) Daily Times,* 19 March 1996.
48. "Trio Face Trial Today"; "Franklin Expectant."
49. "Franklin Expectant"; "Trio Face Trial Today."

The *Times-Picayune,* almost giddy about the beginning of the trial, opened its story about the first day of trial this way: "Sweltering on the edge of a prostrating heat wave, Franklin today faces what, with luck, may be the most sensational criminal trial in the history of Louisiana." Given the enormous advance publicity, one part of a story the day before might have been interpreted as symbolic or ironic, even if the newspaper had not planned it that way. The *Times-Picayune* reported that the scales of Miss Justice, who stood atop the courthouse dome, had blown away in a storm the previous year and had not been replaced.[50]

The *Times-Picayune* recounted that early in the trial, the defense counsel had to ask for a chair in which to sit because all the chairs were taken. At the afternoon session that same day, even the space behind the judge's bench was filled with standing spectators. A line of girls reportedly squeezed between the front rail and the front row of seats, and spectators in the front row complained that the girls blocked their view. The girls did not leave, but instead "dropped to their knees as if they were going to say their prayers, and chins on the railing, there they remained." The crowd was not the "ordinary courtroom riff-raff," but instead included "leaders of business, society and politics" fighting for spots with "the farm hands from along the bayous."[51]

Speculation and Gossip Prior to Trial

Speculation about potential evidence and witnesses often occurred in news stories before the trial. The *New Orleans Times-Picayune* also used other questionable reporting techniques, including statements that would have been hard to substantiate. For example, "Franklin, eagerly looking forward to the trial, is quiet, but the murder case still is the subject of conversation at almost every dinner table and on every street corner."[52] How the reporter determined the subject of conversation at dinner tables was left unsaid and was unattributed, but the report was followed by a statement that, if true, made it unlikely that the *Times-Picayune* had found out much from interviewing local adults. "On account of the prominence of principals in the case, older Morgan City residents do not discuss the matter with strangers." However, the newspaper said young people in town did discuss the case, but named no youths as sources.

One day before the trial, the *Times-Picayune* used a "man-on-the-street" statement, saying that the consensus was that none of the defendants

50. "Trio Face Trial Today"; "Franklin Expectant."

51. "Widow's Collapse"; "Record-Breaking Throng Crowds into Courtroom," *New Orleans Times-Picayune,* 30 July 1927.

52. "Defense May Get Trial Continued."

would hang. "Louisiana has never hanged a white woman," the newspaper noted, and added that Dreher was either too rich or too popular to be executed. No sources were used to support the views of the "consensus" of Morgan City residents.[53]

The trial began on 24 July 1927 in Franklin. The opening day resulted in little of news interest, so the *Times-Picayune* focused on speculation and rumors. The story theorized about what motions would be filed, whether the state would ever be able to convince jurors to vote for the death penalty, and what the defense would be. The best bet, it said, seemed to be an insanity defense. The *Times-Picayune* used no named sources, but instead attributed the speculation to "professional legal guessers," which could have been the reporters themselves.[54]

Two *Times-Picayune* reporters covered the trial. Kenneth Knoblock handled most of the "straight" reporting from the courtroom, and Gwin Bristow wrote features. Each had front-page stories every day from 25 July until 7 August, when a story about the previous day's verdict was announced. Knoblock's stories indicated he was excited about the trial. He commented in a story that LeBoeuf did not "look the part of a temptress. . . . Still, neither did Ruth Snyder, nor, for that matter, was Judd Gray the perfect sheik."[55]

The Trial

The trial that the *New Orleans Times-Picayune* had predicted would be one of the most sensational in Louisiana history opened not with a bang but with a thud for the newspaper. Legal motions and jury selection bored and disgusted Knoblock. His opinions came through in the news story. About motions heard prior to jury selection, he wrote: "The case is obviously to be used as an excuse for a demonstration by defense attorneys of their virtuosity as lawyers, exactly as violinists use the compositions of Sarasate or Paganini." He reported that the first morning had been devoted to "quibbling argument" about qualifications of the jury pool. He ridiculed defense efforts: "And so, to prevent such a contretemps, a morning of a murder trial was spent in straining at gnats. Whether any camels will be swallowed later remains to be seen."[56]

As the jury selection dragged on for several days, Knoblock described the proceedings as dull, and as a "drab and endless procession of venire-

53. "Murder Charge Amended."
54. "Franklin Expectant."
55. "Trio Face Trial Today."
56. Ibid.

men from the halls or the spectators' seats to the jury box and back again."
He later described jury selection as a "horrible day in court." He groused
that such a colorful case had been brought to a grinding legal halt. "[It is
a] case that has attracted parish, state and national attention, the LeBoeuf
angle iron murder and mutilation, that srange [sic] Thomas Hardy sort of
tragedy of the swamp lands that now, brought to court, is becoming such
a horrible, drab, dull and commonplace affair."[57]

Nevertheless, the *Times-Picayune* had columns to fill on its front pages,
and Knoblock could always break up the boredom of accounts of the proceedings with his observations about the people who attended. These remarks came within the text of the news stories, and at times he simply
broke away from describing the jury selection or motions. For example,
he dropped into a story this description:

> Genial Arthur Martel, the jailor and a happy bachelor, perhaps hap-
> pier since all this happened because he has seen first-hand to what
> depths marriage may bring one, is among the guards by courtesy and
> later beams as bailiff from the bench at Judge Simon's right. His sun-
> tanned phiz is a Pickwickian picture of contentment. He seems to ooze
> the optimism that "God's in His Heaven, all's right with the world,"
> if that's what Browning wrote, the library of the local Browning Club
> being out of range at the moment of this writing.

Later in the story, he broke from a blow-by-blow description of the questioning of jurors to say: "The prettiest girls of the trial, and the largest
crowd, attended. One, in particular, wore a green dress with white buttons and a boyish bob. Her companion was trimmed in black embroi-
dery."[58]

Knoblock longed for more drama. He wrote on the first day of the trial that "thus far no single 'pig woman' has appeared to tell of trysts in
lovers' lanes, or out on sleepy, eerie bayous in the moonlight." Knoblock
was referring to testimony in the famous Hall-Mills case in 1926. As the
jury selection ground on, Knoblock's longing for mystery and drama
grew. "One longs for a 'pig woman,' a cache of love letters; liaison, if told,
probably won't make much of a 'true confession.'"[59]

57. "One Juror Chosen at Night Session of LeBoeuf Trial," ibid., 26 July 1927;
"Missing LeBoeuf Witness Reported in New Orleans," ibid., 27 July 1927.
58. "New Venire Called to Complete Jury in LeBoeuf Case," ibid., 28 July 1927.
59. "Missing Witness." The "pig woman" was the dramatic climax to the Hall-Mills
trial. She was Jane Gibson, and her testimony was published as the lead story in the
New York Times on 19 November 1926. Her testimony was widely published, especially
by the tabloid press. However, even the comparatively conservative *Times* was drawn
into the sensational coverage.

The lack of defendants who would talk, to Knoblock's mind, caused a problem. They needed to reveal their motivation for the killing, he said. "As Pepys might have said to Trail, with a hope at least, that there'll be a little more motivation revealed in the trial than there has been thus far in the murder and its investigation."[60]

Reaching for Stories

On the days when there was little to write about, Knoblock and Bristow would range far afield for stories. Two such stories were about the jail in which the three defendants were housed, and readers got starkly different perceptions from the two writers. Knoblock, flexing his literary imagination, wrote this lead on a news story: "Hard by the Teche high in its banks but dreamy with its cargo of green islands floating lazily down to the sea there is a pretty little jail, green too, as all this Teche land is green, and gold, as far as the eye can see, in trees green and undergrowth green of cane and then blackish, brackish, ominous green of swamp country, way back, a mile, two miles." Knoblock said the jail had no "grim, forbidding look," and "within it is as immaculate, as cheerful and as restful as without." The jail was more a manse than a jail, he believed. For additional color, and so that "we might know from experience the other side of this ordeal," Bristow asked to be housed in a jail cell. She described the light as pale and the jail as "[w]hite walls surrounding an inner cell of iron grating, like a white cage in a white box, walls staring blankly down at an iron cot and an unpainted pine table." It hardly was the pristine, almost idyllic place Knoblock had described two days earlier. Bristow said she wanted out and noted it was little wonder that the prisoners' faces had become so lined. "You wonder only at the power that makes them endure and endure, and flinch so little."[61] Bristow, of course, could have no idea about what being in jail was like for the defendants because she could leave whenever she wished. She used an old, and phony, journalistic technique of "experiencing" what a criminal defendant experiences by playing at being locked up.

Once the trial began, Knoblock had less time for "color." His reports were more restricted to almost-verbatim accounts of the trial testimony, but he still moralized about the crowd attending the trial. On one occasion, he wrote, "The courtroom ghouls got their morning thrill when Ada

60. "Missing Witness."
61. "Ada, Doctor and Trapper, Awaiting Destiny in Tiny Jail, Talk of Little Things," *New Orleans Times-Picayune*, 1 August 1927; "Prisoners Pass Hours in Silence in White Case of St. Mary Jail," ibid., 3 August 1927.

kissed her darkly handsome son, Ernest, a long, touching, sad-eyed kiss full on the mouth."[62]

Knoblock warmed up his imagination when LeBoeuf took the stand in her defense. The first paragraph of the lead front-page news story read: "Ada, she of the raven tresses and the small, odd and ancient eyes, compressed lips and angle-iron ways, that Ada took the stand in her own behalf as the first defense witness tonight, told her story of innocent participation in a justifiable homicide, and bore up nobly like one of Fox's most Tony martyrs, under the strain of cross-examination." Knoblock termed LeBoeuf "the siren of the swamps" and called her "sphinx-like" on the stand.[63]

Bristow, as the primary feature writer, found plenty of material. Most of her articles focused on descriptions of the defendants, especially LeBoeuf. Some focused on the community, such as her description of how the trial was economically affecting Franklin's movie theater. "Girls come to court with their boy friends, decked out in their flowery summer organdies, and have their dates in the courtroom, while the boy friends are gleeful over having the town provide an evening entertainment that costs them nothing." Boys no longer asked girls if they "[w]anna take a ride," but instead said, "Let's go piroguing."[64]

Scornful of Spectators and the Jury

Both Knoblock and Bristow at times openly scorned the spectators' behavior. Bristow said of them, "You might reasonably think that it was a marathon endurance contest, or that they were being paid by the hour." She claimed the spectators were rude, shoving, pushing, and gouging for seats. She said none of them minded Beadle's constant chewing of gum, "for the courtroom habitues are as much addicted to it as he." Knoblock became harder on the spectators as the trial progressed. Near the end of the trial, he wrote about "Big-hearted Jim" Beadle and his chance to testify, but then said Beadle would have a chance to sit in "the one chair in the courtroom that isn't surrounded by perspiring and morbid fat ladies who, with the hot air contributed by all the lawyers, manage to make the place give a daily imitation of the fiery furnace of Holy Writ." Knoblock also skewered others. Of Dreher's testimony, Knoblock maintained: "Oh, the doctor made a ghastly witness for the sob sisters and others taking a high

62. "Mercy Asked for Beadle."
63. "James Beadle Shot Husband to Death Says Ada on Stand," ibid., 3 August 1927; "Murder Case Will Reach Jury."
64. "Murder Trial Driving Movie Shows to Wall," ibid., 27 July 1927.

Binet test. But, as for the jury, you can never tell about juries, no matter how closely you watch them. They may be thinking about a lost quid of eating tobacco when you think they're thinking about a gallows."[65]

Ada's Attire

During each day of court, LeBoeuf was the center of the *New Orleans Times-Picayune*'s fashion attention. "Ada wore a new dress into court Tuesday morning, a soft black and white voile with a white organdie roll collar ending on her right shoulder in a bow whose long ends fell almost to her waist in front, and organdie cuffs tied in chic little bows on her wrists." Even headlines stressed how LeBoeuf looked or what she wore. One read: "Ada Uses Rouge, Wearing White Dress to Court." A subordinate headline read: "Mrs. LeBoeuf Tints Lips and Cheeks in Timid Fashion." The story, of course, focused on those aspects: "Wednesday morning in came Ada fresh and cool in a new dress of white handkerchief linen. Her lips were faintly pink, and so were her cheeks. The rouge had been very timidly applied, but there it was." Bristow also criticized LeBoeuf's makeup in an earlier story: "She uses too much powder, does Ada. Any girl 20 years younger than she could tell her that anybody who is as much addicted to white powder ought to use more rouge to complete the effect." Later in the story, Bristow noted that during the trial, "Mrs. LeBoeuf's floury make-up began to get speckly" before day's end.[66]

LeBoeuf's attorneys might have determined her wardrobe, to a point. Bristow reported that defense attorney L. O. Pecot said, "'We've warned Ada not to show off too much of her wardrobe,' whereat a howl went up from the girl reporters. The consensus of their opinion was that if they were on trial for their lives they'd be in style." Moreover, LeBoeuf's dresses provided deeper meaning, when Bristow reported that LeBoeuf changed from her dress of "pirogue green" to one of "virgin white" for her testimony. Even during preliminary proceedings, readers might have believed they were reading a fashion story: "Mrs. LeBoeuf, the attractive and matronly woman, . . . wore a dress more becoming to her than that of black satin which she wore Wednesday. Her simple dress of today was of white organdie, with a belt and a brown collar."[67]

65. Ibid.; "Record-Breaking Throng"; "Beadle to Take Stand."
66. "Driving Movie Shows"; "Ada Uses Rouge"; "Three on Trial for Lives Face Ordeal Calmly," ibid., 26 July 1927.
67. "Driving Movie Shows"; "Jury to Decide Which of Trio Has Told Truth," ibid., 6 August 1927; "Court Orders Better Spelling."

The Anguished and the Brave

Sometimes Bristow concentrated her efforts on others' bravery or their anguish. Ada LeBoeuf's mother, Virginia Bonner, personified the anguish. "Mrs. Bonner, with her tired face, her ill-fitting, home-made dress, her work-hardened hands, they are questions of fearful tragedy."[68]

A later story detailed that Bonner wept as she said her daughter had suffered too much. "She was so pitifully unhappy with Jim LeBoeuf. He wasn't good to her. Ada's a good girl, a good girl. They say such horrible things about her, but I can't believe them. Ada is not bad." Through the stories about Bonner and others, a more sympathetic portrait of LeBoeuf emerged, but not too sympathetic. Bristow understood the tragic theater that the case represented. She said there was "a sardonic tragedy in being born a thousand miles away from one's background," pointing out that fate had placed a Cleopatra-like Ada LeBoeuf in a small town. Bristow contended that if LeBoeuf had been born rich, had been rich during the days of Louis XV, or had been in Hollywood, she "would not have been the village gossip. Ada would have been the toast of the town. There's a difference." Bristow admired some of LeBoeuf's qualities: "You may call Ada a scarlet woman, a brazen enchantress, a small-town Cleopatra, or any of the other names popular gossip has thrown at her, but you've got to hand her one thing. Ada is game."[69]

Bristow became personally involved in the case when LeBoeuf, near the end of the trial, gave a jailhouse "confession" of sorts to two newspaper reporters. The defense heard of it and quickly summoned the two reporters as defense witnesses, precluding their use by the prosecution. However, Bristow was overlooked and was summoned by the state. Not a great deal was made of it in the press, although the defense did later move for a new trial based upon spectators holding up newspapers in the courtroom so that jurors could read the headlines about LeBoeuf's confession.[70] Although this stunt might seem remarkable today, and would almost certainly be cause for a mistrial, in 1927, defendants' due-process and fair-trial rights were not so clearly defined.

As the trial neared its end, Bristow's focus shifted from the "color" to the trial itself. Her coverage was interpretive and highly descriptive. She reported that when Dreher was testifying, LeBoeuf held her head high, but as the testimony progressed, she "crumpled weakly in her chair, her head turned completely away from the witness stand, her face suddenly

---

68. "Grim Questions."

69. "Ada Suffering Too Much, Says Loyal Mother," ibid., 1 August 1927; "Mrs. LeBoeuf's Iron Nerve Still Refuses to Yield," ibid., 31 July 1927.

70. "LeBoeuf Slayers Ask Judge Borah to Halt Hanging," ibid., 31 January 1929.

flushing crimson, her handkerchief tensely over her lips as though to hide their quivering." She then began to weep silently.[71]

Bristow's commentary occasionally focused on things other than the testimony, such as the cost of the trial. She stated it cost St. Mary's Parish six hundred dollars per day, and noted that large crowds had damaged more than fifty chairs. Although ten thousand dollars was appropriated to pay for the trial, Bristow believed it would have been easier "to sell tickets to the courthouse and turn the proceeds into the parish treasury, but nobody seems eager to suggest it." Bristow added: "Ten thousand dollars—and all for a sordid love affair that has been back-alley gossip in Morgan City for years."[72]

Bristow's story about the guilty verdict was straightforward until the second half, when she focused on LeBoeuf's eight-year-old daughter, Liberty. Bristow used LeBoeuf's reaction to "Libby" as a metaphor for her own indifference to others, or for LeBoeuf's preoccupation with her own fate. The child sat in her mother's lap, Bristow wrote, but LeBoeuf looked only at the jury. Even when thunder caused the child to jump, LeBoeuf did not look at her. (Ominous thunderclaps at premonitory times were reported on at least three separate occasions in Bristow's stories during the course of the trial.) Only when LeBoeuf's attorney pleaded in his closing statement to allow her to go back to her family did she seek to comfort the child. Bristow said LeBoeuf's efforts seemed timid, "as if it were somebody else's little girl." She said LeBoeuf straightened the child's clothing "with faltering fingers, as if she had forgotten how." When the child became too tired, her grandmother took her and her brother from the courtroom. LeBoeuf did not watch them leave. Bristow wrote: "Their mother had turned her head away." Knoblock's version differed somewhat from Bristow's account of the slowly crumbling LeBoeuf. Knoblock remarked that "the marble Ada Bonner LeBoeuf" showed no emotion from the beginning of the trial to the end, and she heard the verdict without emotion. Knoblock, however, read something into LeBoeuf's movements. He wrote that her tongue flickered across her lips as the jury came in to announce the verdict. "It was the barest of indications, but there it was. The iron in the woman's soul had conquered, the stupid courage that caused her to entice her husband to his death, and mayhap, to watch while his body was butchered, slit open, weighted with iron and turned like a sack of meal into the waters of Lake Palourde."[73]

Knoblock's enthusiasm for the case waned when the trial ended, but he seemed haunted by the reaction of James Beadle's wife when he was sen-

71. "Beadle to Take Stand."
72. "Mercy Asked for Beadle."
73. Articles by Knoblock and Bristow both appeared under the headline "Ada, Doctor to Hang."

tenced to life in prison. Alice Beadle screamed "the screams of a woman hurt to her death." Knoblock had written favorably of Alice on several occasions. It was apparent he admired her, or at least saw her as a tragic figure in a play—especially tragic when juxtaposed with LeBoeuf. One day earlier, Knoblock said Alice "proved to be the most human figure of the trial." Whether Knoblock actually knew Alice or had met her was never indicated in the stories, but that did not matter. When she broke down, Knoblock's pity for her, or his capacity for imagination, showed. He termed James Beadle "shiftless" and far from the ideal husband. Alice's life had been difficult. Knoblock stereotyped and dealt in conjecture: "Her husband, simple, unaffected, probably within the sacrosanct precincts of his home, like all who live much in the silences of an overwhelmingly silent land, the bayou land, probably was far from demonstrative. When had he kissed her last, when had he bought her anything as attractive as the costumes the Drehers wore? What could his absence mean to her, he whose presence probably meant as little?" In the next day's edition, Knoblock wrote that two thousand people in Franklin must have heard Alice Beadle's screams, and "he who heard them could not help but remember them."[74]

Knoblock wrapped up his reporting with a harsh assessment of LeBoeuf, who "is said to have seen the body of James J. LeBoeuf butchered as a calf is butchered in an abattoir." He saved his harshest words, though, for those who attended the trial. He declared the case had brought out "the worst side of human nature, the slimy, crawling atavistic desire, to see a trio tortured." People had "robbed Franklin of its peace, and their own souls of quiet." He noted, too, that there had been "obscene gloating" by the people at the trial.[75]

Knoblock never acknowledged in his stories any responsibility on his part or on the part of his newspaper for the circus surroundings at the trial, or for the morbid fascination of the crowds. He wrote as if he stood above the fray, an omniscient narrator observing mere mortals engaging in legal debauchery. He summarized in the story about the death sentences: "And so, except for more law and one last climax, so endeth the great LeBoeuf murder trial, about which more words have been written than go to make a thousand novels."

Bristow wrapped up her coverage of the case with the following statement:

> The LeBoeuf trial has been big, but not great. It is the biggest affair that has happened in St. Mary parish in this generation; it has focused the

74. Knoblock, ibid.; "Franklin Quiet As People Avoid Talk of Trial," ibid., 8 August 1927.
75. "Franklin Quiet."

flashlight of public notice on St. Mary as no new public buildings or good roads campaign or overall king's palace on the bayou could have done; it has made the principals famous as they never would have been if they had maintained reputations of peace and sobriety and good behavior. But it has not been noble. It has not been magnificent. It has been sordid.[76]

Knoblock's and Bristow's bylines quickly vanished from the LeBoeuf coverage. The case, however, remained in the news for days, with stories about appeals and a bizarre account of a "witness" to the crime who purportedly would exonerate LeBoeuf and Dreher. The witness turned out to be a man who claimed to have witnessed many murders.

On 1 February 1929, Ada LeBoeuf and Dr. Thomas Dreher were hanged. Some in the newspaper press were horrified. Arthur Brisbane, in his "Today" column on 2 February in the *San Francisco Examiner*, asked: "Does a great State deserve to have on its records the first hanging of a white woman, or black woman, either?"

The *New Orleans Times-Picayune* wrote early on that the case was "elected, almost unanimously, to succeed the Snyder-Gray case in the public interest." However, it failed in that respect, at least when judged as a national story, because the Hall-Mills case, and especially the Snyder-Gray one, trumped the LeBoeuf case in the national consciousness and in the important New York newspaper market. New Orleans was a large newspaper market, but it was not New York City.

The LeBoeuf murder plot occurred in the wrong media market and at the wrong time to achieve lasting national prominence. Nonetheless, the story is an example of the excesses of the jazz-journalism period, and illustrates how the deadly serious business of three people on trial for their lives can be trivialized.

76. Articles by Knoblock and Bristow, "Ada, Doctor to Hang."

Chapter 6

Female Mass Murderers

KILLING WITH POISON SEEMS MORE SINISTER and premeditated than other methods of murder. It is less direct and spontaneous than a more violent shooting, ax murder, stabbing, or beating, which could be done during a moment of rage. Poisoning usually takes planning. Furthermore, the death seems slower and more agonizing and lingering for the victim than does a more violent demise. Poison seems more evil, more underhanded, because the killer often seems to be offering the victim what might be considered a gift—nourishment or something to quench the thirst. (The word *gift* in German means poison.) Hence, there probably is more public fascination and revulsion with poisoning cases, and likely there also is a good deal of press attention. For example, the *New York Times* wrote in 1866 of Martha Grinder, convicted of killing a boarder with poison: "[T]he accused was unremitting in her attentions to the sufferer, and exhibited so much apparent kindness and sympathy as to completely disarm suspicion. After the death of the person whom she with her own hands destroyed, none were more careful in the preparation for the funeral than the murderess herself."[1]

Anna Hahn was not as indiscriminate a killer as Grinder, but she was perhaps as prolific, although that is arguable. A prosecutor described Hahn as the most prolific mass murderer in the United States in 1937. There were only three women executed in Ohio in the twentieth century, and all were convicted in counties in the Cincinnati area.[2] Hahn was one of them.

---

1. "The American Borgia," *New York Times*, 20 January 1866.
2. Certain areas produce more death sentences or executions than others. Cincinnati is an example. As of January 1999, Hamilton County, Ohio, had about five times more death row inmates than did Franklin County, where Columbus is located, even though the latter had 14 percent more population. Sometimes a prosecutor might more actively seek the death penalty. For example, a prosecutor in Robeson County, North Carolina, reportedly obtained in twenty-three months "death sentences for

Anna Hahn: "There Isn't Another Human Being Like Her"

Police and prosecutors in 1937 called Anna Hahn, the first woman to die in Ohio's electric chair, the perpetrator of "the biggest mass murder in this country" and a "female Bluebeard." Police suspected she had murdered thirteen people with poison, and they told the press that Hahn had "bought enough poison to kill half" of Cincinnati.[3]

Hahn saw herself differently. "If I'm in trouble it's because of my goodness to old people. I am so-o-o big hearted," she said. She said she had not killed anyone and that her one ambition in life was to have enough money to care for "the poor unfortunates, the old people and the children."[4]

According to the *Cincinnati Enquirer,* Hahn claimed during her trial that she was born in 1906 in Fussen, Germany.[5] She immigrated to the United States in 1929, and settled in Cincinnati, although she never became a U.S. citizen and spoke English with a marked German accent. Her twelve-year-old son, Oscar, was reportedly born out of wedlock. She married Philip Hahn in April 1930, but he never legally adopted Oscar.

Anna Hahn liked to gamble on horse races, frequenting the track three or four times per week, and she said that the first time she went she won $300. She was not always as successful and soon piled up debt, although she claimed she never lost more than $50 in a day. In fact, she said she won $540 on one horse on 5 July 1937; on 6 July, George Gsellman of Cincinnati died after eating a dinner with a massive amount of poison in it. Prosecutors said Hahn had prepared it for him.[6]

Authorities claimed Hahn had gained the confidence of elderly German men in Cincinnati and then murdered them. Ernest Kohler died in

---

more people than resided on the death rows of two-thirds of the states that embraced capital punishment" (Jerry Bledsoe, *Death Sentence,* 1). Political, legal, and economic conditions can shift the "geography" of the death penalty. For example, in Arkansas between 1913—when the state began executing prisoners in a single location—and 1964, about 73 percent of the 172 men executed were from the 42 Delta counties. Most defendants were black. Since 1990 when the state resumed executions, 23 people have been executed, and only 5 of them were from Delta counties. Most of those executed since 1990 are from the northwest part of the state, which is heavily populated by whites. Almost all of the defendants have been white, whereas a huge majority of those executed between 1913 and 1964 were black. The geography has shifted dramatically. The difference, I would argue, is because of increased political, legal, educational, and economic opportunities for black Arkansans.

3. "13th Friend of Widow Dies in Midst of Probe," *Chicago Tribune,* 20 August 1937.

4. "Charge Murder to Ex-Teacher; Poison in Body," ibid., 14 August 1937; "11 Deaths Studied for Link to Woman," *New York Times,* 16 August 1937.

5. "'Lies, All Lies!' Anna Hahn Exclaims under State Grilling in Murder Case," *Cincinnati Enquirer,* 2 November 1937.

6. "Mrs. Hahn in Collapse, Dies in Chair," *Cleveland Plain Dealer,* 8 December 1938; "Mrs. Hahn on Stand, Closing Her Defense," *New York Times,* 4 November 1937; "Mrs. Hahn Denies 4 Murder Charges," ibid., 2 November 1937; "13th Friend of Widow."

1933, and Hahn inherited his $12,000 house in Cincinnati. When police arrested Hahn, she, her husband, and her son were living in Kohler's house. Unproved reports from South Bend, Indiana, said Kohler had left a hidden fortune of $60,000.[7]

During her trial, the *Enquirer* detailed how Hahn had killed four of the men and left another paralyzed. They included the second suspected victim, Albert Palmer, seventy-two, who died on 26 March 1937; Jacob Wagner; George Gsellman; George Obendoerfer; and George Heis, who was paralyzed but lived. Hahn said that Palmer was among "the finest men I ever knew. He was more like a father to me and my boy. He was so kind and good. He tried to do everything for us." She even used "My Dear Sweet Daddy" as a salutation on correspondence to Palmer because she said she had regarded him as she would a father. Hahn met Palmer at a bookmaking establishment, and later received about $1,500 in checks and $500 in cash from him. She claimed she spent only about $500 of the money and repaid the rest.[8]

She said she had met Wagner when he came to her house and told her he believed they were related. At trial, several witnesses testified that Hahn had gone to the building where Wagner lived and asked if there were "any old German men" living there. Wagner visited her often, although he later accused her of stealing his bankbook. After the bankbook was found, Hahn asked Wagner to come the next day for dinner, but she said he did not, and when she went to his house the next day he was sick. Wagner had given her his bankbook and asked her to write a check, she said, and she had forged his signature because she knew he wanted her to have some money to pay his bills. Wagner died on 3 June 1937, and a will left all of his property to Hahn. Two handwriting experts later testified that Hahn wrote the will.[9]

George Gsellman, sixty-seven, died 6 July 1937. Witnesses placed Hahn in Gsellman's room, and prosecutors said she had cooked him a meal and he died soon after. Leftover food found in the room contained enough poison to kill three or four people, authorities contended.[10]

Newspapers described Obendoerfer, sixty-seven, as a "well-to-do" Cincinnati cobbler and as "moderately well-to-do." Whatever his financial status, he died on 1 August 1937, in Colorado Springs, Colorado, with Hahn at his side. She said she had met him in Cincinnati four days before he left for Colorado Springs. She told him she planned to go to Colorado Springs, and he said that, ironically, he also planned to go. He later asked her and Oscar to accompany him. Before leaving, Hahn signed Wagner's

7. "Woman Faces Court Today for Poison Deaths," *Chicago Tribune,* 18 August 1937.
8. "'Lies, All Lies!'"; "4 Murder Charges."
9. "'Lies, All Lies!'"
10. Ibid.; "4 Murder Charges."

name to a $1,000 check, saying later she had needed money and knew Wagner "wanted me to have the money." When Hahn, Oscar, and Obendoerfer boarded the train, she registered for them and indicated Obendoerfer was from Chicago; she later said she had done so because she did not want to be responsible for his bills. Obendoerfer became ill on the train trip, and his condition worsened in Colorado Springs. Hahn said he had asked her to write to his Cincinnati building-and-loan association for money and that she had done so, but signed her name A. Felser because she did not want to have anything to do with his affairs. Hahn did help Obendoerfer by registering him as a charity patient at a Colorado Springs hospital, but she denied knowing him. As the hospital staff tried to find out who he was, she leaned over him and said, "Old man, why don't you tell these people who you are?" witnesses testified.[11]

The press identified other possible poison victims. Julia Kresckay, forty-eight, of Cincinnati, became ill while Hahn ministered to her for another illness. Hahn received $800 from Kresckay but did not repay it, and Kresckay threatened to prosecute. Soon thereafter, Kresckay became ill and was paralyzed. Ollie Luella Koehler, seventy-nine, of Cincinnati, died on 19 August 1937 after eating ice cream that Hahn had given her. Newspapers said police found a bag in Hahn's home that contained Koehler's valuables and a document signed by her that gave Mrs. A. Felser—Hahn's maiden name—the power of attorney.[12]

Thus, newspapers reported that in a period from 26 March to 19 August, police suspected Hahn had killed at least five people and paralyzed another. They also suspected she had poisoned George Heis, her coal dealer for several years, who claimed he was paralyzed shortly after drinking beer with Hahn. Heis later told her, as he was seated in his wheelchair, "You did this to me." He also claimed she stole $140 in cash and a $75 ring, which police said they had found on Hahn when she was arrested.[13]

Hahn also faced fugitive-from-justice warrants stemming from her trip to Colorado Springs. A motel owner in Colorado Springs testified that she believed Hahn had stolen $305 worth of diamond rings. Hahn's arrest on this complaint led to the discovery that she had accompanied Obendoerfer to Colorado Springs, which led to the additional investigation.[14]

The stories of the poisonings broke daily during the first week after Hahn's arrest, which caused her lawyer to accuse the prosecution of "trying the case in the newspapers," and her attorneys also asked for a change

11. "Laboratory Work Led to the Chair," *Cleveland Plain Dealer*, 8 December 1938.
12. "Mrs. Hahn Indicted in 2 Ohio Slayings," *New York Times*, 17 August 1937; "13th Friend of Widow."
13. "'Lies, All Lies!'"; "Federal Aid Asked in 'Mass Murders,'" *New York Times*, 15 August 1937.
14. "Federal Aid"; "Mrs. Hahn Guilty; Faces Execution," *New York Times*, 7 November 1937.

of venue, which the court denied. Police and prosecutors did use the newspaper press to good advantage. They released to the press much of the evidence against Hahn before her indictment, and, judging from trial stories, newspapers published almost all of it before her trial. Hahn also used the press. She proclaimed her innocence to reporters in an interview published just days after the story first broke. "Why don't they go out and find the real criminals?" She said she had learned "it is wrong to be good to people—that it doesn't pay to be good to them." The press interviewed her while she ate breakfast at the Hamilton County jail, dressed in a navy-blue frock that had a pink piqué collar. Her nails were carefully manicured, and she insisted on dressing up for "the oddest breakfast table chat I ever had."[15]

When prosecutors charged Hahn with murdering Gsellman, she confidently predicted: "This is one case I'm going to win. I am not guilty. I can face anything there is to come." Lt. George W. Schattle of the Cincinnati Police Department told the press he had found a small bottle of a "violent dysenteric poison," but a story in the *Chicago Tribune* said Hahn's husband had given the bottle to police, indicating Schattle had not "found" it. Prosecutor Dudley M. Outcalt told the press that Hahn had used two poisons in Gsellman's death. Cincinnati authorities also told the press they had received a report from the Colorado Springs coroner that Obendoerfer might have died of oil poisoning, and police said they were checking the deaths of Palmer and Kohler.[16]

Police and prosecutors talked in the newspapers as if Hahn had been convicted, although she would not stand trial for two months and had not yet been arraigned. Police continued building a case in the press, showing reporters a box with a "poison" label on it, but refusing to say where they had found it. To shore up their case, one day before Hahn's arraignment, police told the press they had found in Hahn's home jewelry, money, and a bond reportedly stolen. An assistant prosecutor said he had "fairly definite proof" that Hahn had fed Kresckay poisoned ice cream. Moreover, the *Tribune* reported that a "supposed suicide note" found under Wagner's bed shortly after he died was written in English, although Wagner could write only in German.[17]

Fifteen minutes after hearing evidence, the grand jury indicted Hahn for murdering Gsellman and Wagner. Press reports said she did not laugh or smile, and was not the composed, nonchalant person she had been. She

15. "Mrs. Hahn Asks Venue Change in Poisoning Trial," *Chicago Tribune*, 19 August 1937; "Trail 11 Strange Deaths; Find All Point to Widow," ibid., 16 August 1937; "11 Deaths Studied."

16. "Woman Is Accused; Five Deaths Sifted," *New York Times*, 14 August 1937; "Fifth Death and Poison Vial Spur Quiz in Mystery," *Chicago Tribune*, 13 August 1937; "Charge Murder to Ex-Teacher."

17. "11 Deaths Studied"; "Woman Faces Court Today."

pleaded not guilty, and her attorneys asked for a change of venue, which was denied.[18]

Hahn's case continued to be played out in the press before her trial. A police official told reporters that thirteen prescriptions for poison and narcotics were traced to Hahn, and she had forged a doctor's name to get them. Police said Hahn had taken prescription blanks from the doctor's office in Ernest Kohler's home, which she had inherited. In addition, the *Tribune* soon published a front-page story about Ollie Koehler's death, the first time Hahn appeared on that newspaper's front page, which indicated her travails were gaining notice outside Cincinnati and Ohio.[19] Although Hahn never made the front page in New York, she was major news in Chicago; the *Tribune* gave her banner front-page headlines five times.

Shortly before her trial, prosecutors told the *Tribune* they had evidence "definitly [sic] linking her with George Gsellman."[20] Although Hahn was to be tried only for Wagner's murder, newspaper readers in Cincinnati, elsewhere in Ohio, and probably most of the Midwest and East were aware of the other murders. Although Hahn's arrest and indictment attracted much press attention, her trial, which began on 11 October 1937 in Hamilton County Circuit Court, attracted more.

Eleven women and one man were on the jury, apparently a rarity. The *Chicago Tribune* dwelled on trivialities about the single male, John Granda, whose presence on the jury almost overshadowed Hahn's murder trial, according to reporter Virginia Gardner. Gardner said Granda was "young, well set up, and sprucely garbed." She often described him as having his chin thrust out, and as being admired by the women. When jurors left the courtroom while attorneys argued what could be used in opening statements, Granda "glanced furtively toward the counsel table where the defendant sits, and showed his dimples in a smile as he went out, flanked on all sides by virtuous womanhood." The eleven women selected him as jury foreman "as the one concession to masculinity, and then only after an hour's debate." Gardner wrote that because the jury was primarily women and was sequestered, Mrs. Granda and the wife of alternate juror Frederick Juergens "are keeping an eye on their husbands by attending the sessions."[21]

After the trial's first week, Gardner ceased commenting about how the male and female jurors were getting along, but she did not stop com-

18. "Hahn Indicted"; "Mrs. Hahn Denies Guilt," *New York Times*, 19 August 1937.
19. "Hahn Denies Guilt"; "13th Friend of Widow."
20. "Link Mrs. Hahn with Gsellman; She Faces Trial As His Slayer," *Chicago Tribune*, 25 August 1937.
21. "1 Man, 11 Women on Hahn Jury," ibid., 15 October 1937; "Jury Hears of Potions Dealt by Anna Hahn," ibid., 16 October 1937; "Tales of Agony Fail to Upset 11 Women Jurors," ibid., 17 October 1937.

menting on the women jurors. She emphasized two things in the stories: the women's strength and what they wore. In regard to the first, Gardner said the opening statements were not softened "to spare the sensitive feelings of the women." When a witness spoke too softly, Alice Peters, "the social leader of the jury," stood and "haughtily" said the jurors could not hear. "She resumed her seat with perfect calm and dignity, her flat bosom unagitated beneath its correct navy blue sheer crepe ensemble." The lead paragraph on the story stressed the "women's strength" angle: "Women jurors proved here today that they can take it." Gardner added, "Not an eyelash flickered" among the jurors when prosecutors displayed samples of Wagner's organs in a row of bottles for the jury. The jurors reportedly sat calmly when attorneys said another exhibit was "the brain of Albert J. Palmer."[22]

At other times, stories described the women in ways that today seem frivolous and condescending, although the reports were probably not taken in such a way in the 1930s. Gardner related, "Meanwhile a big issue to the eleven ladies of the jury . . . is the failure of the county to date to produce a hairdresser for them." On another occasion, she said the women jurors especially looked forward to evidence about love letters between Hahn and Albert Palmer.[23]

The dress and appearance of the jurors, Hahn, and some female witnesses and spectators did not escape notice. Gardner described Hahn as plump, blonde, garrulous, stolid, and cheerful. At the beginning of the trial, Gardner included this opinionated lead in a report: "Mrs. Hahn, whose reputation is about as unblemished as that of Lucrezia Borgia during her early career . . . " A huge all-capitals, bold-faced headline at the top of one edition of the *Chicago Tribune* called Hahn "Arsenic Anna." Gardner described Hahn's dress and makeup several times during the trial, as in this lengthy description:

> Her bright hair, brighter on top than the strands showing through, was elaborately and freshly curled. Lipstick moderately applied, but noticeable in contrast to the makeupless faces of the jurors, softened the thin lines of her mouth. Her cold pale blue eyes were arched over with brows scarcely darkened by an eyebrow pencil. She wore a conservative tailored suit of navy blue, a high necked demure white blouse, sheer stockings, and high heeled pumps. Her skirts were long for the prevailing mode, but her slim ankles nevertheless were not

22. "Jury Hears of Potions"; "Tales of Agony"; "Poisoned Liver of Victim Shown to Hahn Jurors," ibid., 20 October 1937; "Women Jurors View Evidences of 3d Poisoning," ibid., 26 October 1937.

23. "Anna Pales at Failure to Dent Poison Stories," ibid., 21 October 1937; "Women Jurors Look Forward to Love Letters," ibid., 25 October 1937.

overlooked by at least the alternate juror, a male, who sat outside the jury box on the floor level with her.[24]

Scarcely a day passed that readers did not get a description of Hahn's "brown crepe dress with tiny birds of gold poised in flight," or her "altered color, which became a pasty shade marked only by rouge and the bluish tint her lips assumed."

In fact, the *Tribune*'s coverage often resembled a story about a fashion show. For example: "The young and charming little laundress, Miss Georgia McDonald, 22 years old, had on a change of costume, a tightly fitting burnt orange suit with a round collar. Mrs. Florence E. Bartlett, one of the town's more prominent matrons, appeared in a colorful blouse." In another instance: "On his other side stood the most socially prominent member of the jury, Mrs. Alice Peters, tall, aristocratic looking, her gray hair in careful waves, her attire navy blue, sedate and faultless." Yet another statement began this way: "In a special night session to which the 11 women jurors came attired in becoming costumes . . . " And finally: "It is a sharp jury of women. Only one, Mrs. Preston Thompson, wife of a salesman and mother of two girls, a front row juror, could be described as actually comfortable looking with ample curves. Two are substantial, and the others downright thin."[25]

The *Chicago Tribune* described handwriting-expert Katherine Keeler of Chicago as "a blonde and attractive witness," "[d]ressed in a modish black dress which was super-fashionably short." The story contrasted Hahn with the fashionable Keeler, calling Hahn the "blonde defendant, whose ankles are slender and shapely but whose skirts are long."[26]

Some dramatic moments during the trial attracted special press interest, such as when George Heis testified from his wheelchair during the second week of the trial and accusingly said to Hahn, "You did this to me." Another was when Outcalt said of Hahn, "This woman killed so many people there isn't another human being like her on the face of the earth." When Hahn's son, Oscar, testified, Gardner depicted him sympathetically; she said he had made "a greater effort than his years and size warrant [*sic*] to save his mother from the death penalty." Oscar's testimony added a "pathetic touch" when he referred to Philip Hahn as "my daddy," although Hahn's first husband, not Philip, was Oscar's father. Gardner termed the moment "pathetic" because earlier in the trial, the defense counsel had "branded [Oscar] as illegitimate." Gardner said Oscar's tes-

24. "Accused 'Mass Killer' Pale As She Faces Jury," ibid., 15 October 1937; "Jury Hears of Potions."

25. "Jury Hears of Potions"; "Jury Hears of Money Willed to Mrs. Hahn," ibid., 19 October 1937.

26. "Hahn Defense Hunts Expert to Beat Chair," ibid., 29 October 1937.

timony perhaps ironically damaged rather than helped Hahn because it allowed the prosecution to introduce into evidence a bottle of croton oil, which Oscar had found and his stepfather, Philip, had turned over to police. The evidence had not been admissible until Oscar's testimony. *Cincinnati Enquirer* reporter Joseph Garretson Jr. also depicted Oscar as a sympathetic figure, and added that even Hahn's early testimony "was not so absorbing as the testimony of her handsome, eleven-year-old [*sic*] son, Oscar."[27]

Anna Hahn's testimony resulted in the biggest headlines in both the *Enquirer* and the *Tribune*. The latter ran an all-capitals screamer across the top of the front page that read: "Jury Hears Anna's Denial," illustrating her celebrity status by using only her first name. The *Enquirer*'s two-line headline stretched across the front page; the *New York Times* discreetly played the story on page 9. Hahn testified for two days, and Cincinnati news coverage can be described only as immense. The headline "'Lies, All Lies!' Anna Hahn Exclaims Under State Grilling in Murder Case" screamed at *Enquirer* readers. The story ran a full column on the front page and jumped inside where it covered page 8 and jumped again to page 9. *Enquirer* reporter Garretson said Hahn "pictured herself as the victim of a cruel coincidence."

The jury got the case late on 5 November. After deliberating fifty-two minutes, the jury retired to a hotel for the night; the next day after two hours and thirteen minutes and two ballots, the jury found Hahn guilty and made no recommendation for mercy. The *Enquirer* said Hahn's hands trembled and her face flushed, but she showed little other emotion. Three jurors cried when the verdict was announced, and one "sobbed audibly." After the verdict, eleven jurors spoke to the press; some said they sympathized with Oscar. The *Chicago Tribune* ran mug shots of five of the jurors, with small phrases inserted into the photos such as "She Smiled," "She Wept," or "Seemed Nervous," depending on the individual juror. The story said the jurors had formed a "Murder Jury" club and planned to meet every 11 October. The trial produced a record of sixteen hundred pages, and cost Hamilton County an estimated twenty-five thousand dollars, according to the *Enquirer*. Jurors agreed that Hahn's purse, which contained arsenic, most damaged her. Gardner foresaw the importance; her story's lead sentence on the day after the purse was introduced began: "The state today for the first time placed arsenic in the hands of Anna Marie Hahn."[28]

27. "Anna Hahn Is to Die for Murder," *Cincinnati Enquirer,* 7 November 1937; "Jury Hears Anna's Denial," *Chicago Tribune,* 2 November 1937; "'Lies, All Lies!'"
28. "Hahn to Die for Murder"; "Jurors Serene after Vote of Death for Anna," *Chicago Tribune,* 7 November 1937; "Women Hear Purse Yields 35 Pct. Arsenic," ibid., 28 October 1937.

When police took Hahn back to her jail cell, reporters and photographers crowded into the elevator with her, but one of her attorneys shielded her. She said nothing to the press, but once in her cell she broke down, and the *Enquirer* said her sobs could be heard down the corridors of the jail.[29]

Hahn's fate eventually rested with Ohio governor Martin L. Davey. The governor's decision produced banner headlines in Columbus, Cleveland, and Cincinnati. The *Columbus Dispatch* published an extra edition on 6 December with this screamer headline: "Anna Hahn Must Die in Chair." Governor Davey refused to intervene. A bulletin on the front page of the 7 December *Cleveland Plain Dealer* described Hahn's reaction: "Anna Marie Hahn late last night was reported to have collapsed in her cell in death row at Ohio Penitentiary, according to an Associated Press dispatch. Hysterical sobbing preceded the collapse, her matron said." Governor Davey's decision was not easy; if executed, Hahn would be the first woman to die in Ohio's electric chair, and the governor's personal beliefs compounded the difficulty. "Something inside of me has sort of rebelled against the idea of allowing a woman to go to the chair." Davey said he was raised "to respect womanhood," and he added that he believed "there is a little difference when a woman is involved in a tragedy of this kind." He acknowledged that some might argue, with a "measure of logic . . . in these days of equal rights," that women should be treated the same as men. "I do not hold to this view, because it seems to me that woman is cast in a finer mold than man." Davey went far into the past, asking what had become of chivalry. "Is that merely a fantasy of some forgotten age? I cannot believe that chivalry has become lifeless and meaningless in this modern world." Hahn's heartless crimes, that she committed them for money and carefully planned them, her lack of remorse, and his need to be fair to other defendants influenced his decision to allow her execution.[30]

Hahn had been so confident of receiving a commutation that she packed all her clothing and belongings for a trip back to Marysville. She first heard of the decision from her attorney, Joseph Hoodin, who told her, "I've bad news for you." She screamed, "Oh! my God, I didn't think he would do that to me," and collapsed into a chair. Her son Oscar rushed into the cell and embraced her. The *Cincinnati Enquirer* said Hoodin gave interviews to reporters and, after "posing for numerous photographs," went back and got Oscar to come out for interviews. *Enquirer* reporter Garretson wrote that Oscar faced "a battery of flashbulbs" and "was

29. "Hahn to Die for Murder."
30. "Mrs. Hahn Dies Tonight in Pen Chair," *Cleveland Plain Dealer*, 7 December 1938; "Text of Davey's Statement Dooming Anna Marie Hahn," *Cincinnati Enquirer*, 7 December 1938.

chewing gum and there was a faint grin on his face. There were no tears in his eyes." Despite others' press appearances, Hahn gave no final interviews, said state welfare director Margaret Allman, who noted that she "both personally and officially opposed" them. The *Enquirer* said the *Columbus Citizen* had angered Allman in an earlier article.[31] Reporters who covered Hahn's case speculated she would go to her death with the same composure she had shown at trial. They could not have been more wrong.

Almost all the newspapers noted Hahn's disheveled appearance on execution day, contrasting it with her previously immaculate grooming. To the end, her physical attractiveness, or lack thereof, interested the press. A reporter described the scene in her jail cell just before her execution: "Her usually beautifully-groomed golden brown hair was disheveled. Her tear-swollen face was the color of ashes. She appeared to be more dead than alive." When guards came to her cell door to get her, she reportedly cried, "Oh, heavenly Father! Oh, God! Oh, God! I can't go. I won't go. I won't go."[32]

Two matrons lifted Hahn to her feet. She reportedly looked "almost childlike" in blue cotton pajamas, a brown-and-tan-flowered silk robe, black oxfords, and tan silk hose rolled to the ankles. Matrons had slit the right leg of her pajamas the day before so an electrode could be attached to her skin; Hahn was so upset she had not noticed. Matrons clipped a small patch of hair on the back of Hahn's head an hour before her execution; she did not protest: "She was still expecting to be spared."[33]

Hahn leaned on two matrons who accompanied her to the death chamber. The cortege included prison chaplain John A. Sullivan, another matron, the assistant deputy warden of the prison, an attorney, and six prison guards. At least two female reporters from Columbus walked with the cortege to the death chamber. Sarah Dush of the *Columbus Ohio State Journal* and Dorothy Todd Foster of the *Columbus Dispatch* recorded every sight and sound. Dush said Hahn seemed shorter than her diminutive five feet; Foster contended Hahn's moans "sounded like a chant." As Hahn walked past the condemned men on death row, the reporters said she cried, "Heavenly Father . . . Oh, God . . . Oh, God, help me."[34]

When Hahn crossed the death chamber's threshold, she collapsed. Guards carried her and placed her in the electric chair. They began to strap her into the chair, and she cried, "Don't do that to me." She pleaded with

31. "Hahn to Die for Murder."
32. "Anna Hahn Falls and Is Carried to Chair; Dies after She Cries Appeal to Spectators," *Cincinnati Enquirer,* 8 December 1938.
33. "Pictures Breaking of Blond's Iron Nerve," *Cleveland Plain Dealer,* 8 December 1938; "Hahn in Collapse"; "Hahn Falls."
34. Foster, "Anna Hahn Loses Iron Nerve on Her Last Walk to Chair," *Columbus Dispatch,* 8 December 1938; "Hahn in Collapse."

prison warden James C. Woodard. "I'm sorry, but we can't help it," Woodard told her. She asked prison officials to "[t]hink of my boy. . . . Is nobody going to help me?" She quit struggling when guards placed a black mask over her face, but she continued to sob, and said, "Nobody's going to help me."[35]

As she sat in the electric chair, she asked Father Sullivan to "come close to me." However, when he gripped her hand, she whispered: "Be careful, Father. You'll be killed." He recited the Lord's Prayer, and she repeated each verse, her voice reportedly strained but steady. When Sullivan reached the portion of the prayer that said, "Lead us not into temptation," Warden Woodard pushed a button to signal three guards in another part of the building to turn on the power.[36] Only one switch was connected to the chair so that none of the guards would know who had pushed the button that electrocuted her.

A blue light and then a red light came on above the chair. Hahn's praying stopped; her hands clenched, and her body strained against the straps. The red light went off, and the blue light came on. Two doctors listened with stethoscopes for a sign of life; one said, "current sufficient to cause death has passed through her body at 8:13 and a half." As witnesses left the room, they passed an undertaker's basket, into which Hahn's body would be deposited.[37]

The *Columbus Dispatch* used the swiftness of the execution and the interruption of the Lord's Prayer as its lead. The story began, "Deliver u— . . . " Reporter George Kienzie also made several references, perhaps for dramatic effect, to the fact that Hahn died alone. The *Cleveland Plain Dealer* likewise made the Lord's Prayer angle prominent in its lead. Reporter Ralph J. Donaldson's use of dialogue as a literary technique increased the inherent drama and tension. He wrote out the Lord's Prayer, with Father Sullivan reciting lines, and Hahn repeating them, up to the point of the electricity entering her body.[38]

The hometown *Enquirer* had little sympathy for Hahn, terming her "a pitiful, whimpering creature" in the first sentence, and adding in the third paragraph: "The murderer's death was more merciful than the agonizing deaths she dealt to at least four men through the administration of arsenic."[39] Others were not so harsh in their assessments.

The *Plain Dealer*, in an editorial, blasted the execution process, saying there should be legal or moral restraints "to prevent such an exhibition of

35. Dush, "Death Cells," *Cincinnati Enquirer,* 8 December 1938; Foster, "Hahn Loses Iron Nerve."
36. "Anna Hahn Dies in Chair with Prayer on Her Lips," *Columbus Dispatch,* 8 December 1938; "Hahn Falls."
37. "Hahn Falls"; "Hahn in Collapse."
38. "Prayer on Her Lips"; "Hahn in Collapse."
39. "Hahn Falls."

maudlinism [*sic*] and positive cruelty as marked the last hours of Anna Hahn's misspent life." The editorial also condemned Hahn's defense attorneys, saying they had used Oscar by posing him for photographs, by his personal appeals for clemency, and by his repeated visits to the death house. The newspaper said these acts were "taking liberties with childhood, which ordinary decency condemns." The *Plain Dealer*'s wrath also fell on Hahn. The editorial said she had used Oscar to "pull chestnuts out of the fire."[40]

Father Sullivan presided at a simple burial ceremony for Hahn. Three defense attorneys, the three prison matrons who were the first women in Ohio history to witness an execution, Warden Woodard's wife, and six newspapermen attended. The reporters almost outnumbered the others present. Hahn lingered in the press for a time as newspapers speculated about whether letters she had left with Hoodin contained a confession. Hahn died steadfastly claiming innocence.

For some fifteen months, the story captured the attention of the Ohio press, and a good deal of the midwestern press. The celebrity status it took on was illustrated by a paragraph buried in a 10 December story in the *Cincinnati Enquirer*. It reported Hoodin doubted Oscar Hahn would accept an invitation from actor George Raft to spend the Christmas holidays with him in Hollywood.[41]

The Pittsburgh Press Finds a Fiend Incarnate

Newspapers in Pittsburgh and New York termed Martha Grinder an American Lucrezia Borgia, "a woman who was fully the peer, not the inferior in crime, of the world-renowned" Borgia. Grinder's execution on 19 January 1866 in Pittsburgh was a major news story there, in Philadelphia, and in the *New York Times*. She died for poisoning a boarder, although she was suspected of poisoning as many as twenty people. During her trial, the *Pittsburgh Post* said the facts "all stamp this as an [*sic*] unique and marvelous case." The newspaper went on: "Never . . . has any murder case produced so intense and lasting an interest as this." As the writer continued, his exuberance, and the case's importance, grew: "[T]he case of Martha Grinder is, without exception, the most extraordinary that ever was written down in the annals of murder, not only in our vicinity, but in the entire country, and perhaps in any country."[42] Pittsburgh, according to the *Post* and other newspapers, had itself a world-class murderer.

40. "Sorry Exhibition," *Cleveland Plain Dealer*, 8 December 1938.
41. "Confession," *Cincinnati Enquirer*, 10 December 1938.
42. "The American Borgia." Lucrezia Borgia was renowned as a master of political intrigue. "Execution of Mrs. Grinder," *New York Times*, 21 January 1866; "The Sixth Day," *Pittsburgh Post*, 30 October 1865. For a full account of the case, from start to finish, see "Another Hanging," ibid., 20 January 1866.

Martha Grinder might have been that rare species, the female serial killer. She seemed, according to news reports in the Pittsburgh newspapers, to be an ingratiating sociopath; the *Pittsburgh Post* termed it "monomania," and the *New York Times* said she was a "homicidal monomaniac"—killing without feeling or intent, seemingly indiscriminately, poisoning people for no apparent reason. She killed while pretending to care for her victims, much like Anna Hahn, but Grinder received no apparent gain from her murders.

The pretrial publicity bothered Grinder's attorney, who, on the first day of her trial, criticized the press, saying that the coverage had made it impossible for his client to receive a fair trial.[43] The *Post* ran verbatim accounts of Grinder's trial for six days. The stories all ran on page 1 and totaled about fourteen columns with no illustrations. It was high drama, and the *Post* covered it as such. The story about Grinder's conviction ended by saying: "And now the curtain has fallen on the second act of this startling drama. We have seen the wretched victim die; we have seen the wretched torturer convicted, and we leave her waiting for Justice to write for her the rest of the part she is to play."[44]

Grinder was convicted of murdering Mary Caroline Caruthers, a newlywed who had accepted Grinder's offers of food and drink. When Caruthers fell ill, Grinder was always there with tea or soup and insisted that she alone care for her. Just before she was hanged, Grinder confessed to murdering Caruthers and Jane Buchanan, who had worked as a domestic in Grinder's home. Although she denied killing anyone else, the *Post* suggested there might have been many others. "The number of deaths which had taken place at her house, and the extraordinary symptoms of sickness manifested by those associating with her intimately, made people imagine all was not exactly right."[45]

The *Pittsburgh Post* said Grinder was suspected of having poisoned two of her husband's brothers, a child left with her by a poor woman, and one of her own children. Besides Caruthers, the *Post* said, Grinder might have murdered as many as "twenty others, equally black and dreadful." The

---

43. "Trial of Martha Grinder," *Pittsburgh Post*, 28 October 1865. It should be pointed out that it was the state's legal responsibility, not the newspaper's, to provide Grinder a fair trial. For a discussion of this viewpoint, see Rodney Smolla, *Free Speech in an Open Society*. Also, it is unfair to judge nineteenth-century newspapers by today's standards. In 1866, the idea of what constituted a fair trial or due process of law was vastly different from today, although the basic legal standards of what constituted juror prejudice were established much earlier in U.S. history (see *United States v. Burr*). For a discussion, see Roger G. Kennedy, *Burr, Hamilton, and Jefferson: A Study in Character*, 347–48.
44. "Conclusion of the Trial of Martha Grinder," *Pittsburgh Post*, 29 October 1865.
45. "Another Hanging."

Pittsburgh Gazette-Times was more conservative, saying Grinder was suspected of at least seven murders.[46]

News accounts described Grinder as a person without emotion, or even as a demon. The *Post* said her soul seemed "for all time, a demon embodied." The paper declared her crimes were "committed under the guise of tenderest friendship" and said that she indiscriminately killed old and young, chance victims and those she knew well. She had, the paper asserted, "fiendish, inexorable persistence." The *Post* also reported that she showed no emotion when the jury announced its verdict. She almost seemed uninterested. "The only person in the room who seemed utterly unimpressed by the situation of the prisoner at the bar was Martha Grinder."[47]

Those descriptions sharply contrasted with descriptions of Grinder when she left the courtroom and wept bitterly in her jail cell. The *Gazette-Times* said she wept and wailed loudly when the death warrant was read. The *Post* reported that "she exhibited the greatest emotion, and listened to the reading with tears and sobs and protestations of innocence. After the reading, as the party were [*sic*] leaving the cell, she fell into violent hysterics and finally fainted on her bed."[48]

Hanging a woman apparently repulsed some because the *Gazette-Times* said someone gave Grinder poison while she was in prison, but the newspaper claimed she would not take it. The *Post* disputed the contention that she refused to commit suicide, saying that she attempted it on two or three occasions while jailed. About two or three weeks before her execution, Grinder did take poison, and it "was only after repeated efforts that she could be persuaded to take an emetic to throw off the poison." Once, when Grinder became hysterical, the warden believed that she had taken poison but found "the drug" wrapped in paper with a note attached: "We have done all for you that we can. This is a last resort. A Friend."[49]

After Grinder's arrest, the *Pittsburgh Post* also reported, people began recollecting "how strange at times had been her conduct," how people who had accepted her hospitality had fallen ill, and "how quiet and terrible [were] the deaths which happened to those she nursed."

The *Pittsburgh Gazette-Times* suggested that Grinder became a suspect not because of any person she had poisoned but because of the chance poisoning of a dog. The newspaper said suspicions were aroused when some

46. "Conclusion of Trial of Grinder"; "Execution of Mrs. Grinder," *Pittsburgh Gazette-Times*, 20 January 1866.

47. "Conclusion of Trial of Grinder."

48. "Execution of Mrs. Grinder," *Pittsburgh Gazette-Times*; "Conclusion of Trial of Grinder."

49. "Another Hanging."

veal soup that Grinder had made was thrown out and a dog ate it and died.[50] The *Post* did not report this information.

Grinder's trial drew big crowds each day, and the *Post* reported that many spectators were women. The trial was a major local event, according to the newspaper. "The utmost excitement prevailed during the trial. The terrible character of the crimes with which the prisoner had been charged, together with the publicity which had been given to them, awakened an intense curiosity on the part of the public to get a glimpse of the prisoner." The *Post* did not like the "morbid curiosity" of the female spectators at the trial. The paper reported that the women's presence and unseemly behavior drew a sharp rebuke from the court, but that did not lessen the number of women wanting to see the trial.[51]

The *Post* discussed in detail Grinder's sanity, saying she was "surely . . . the victim of monomania," which the newspaper seemed to define as being an irresistible inclination to kill or to commit some other particular offense.[52] The *Post* discounted Grinder's mental state as irrelevant, and the *Gazette-Times* said that she had to be found so insane as to blind her to moral duty and to distinguishing right from wrong.[53]

Both newspapers described Grinder's execution in great detail, although the *Post*'s story was more descriptive. The *Gazette-Times* devoted four columns to the story, and the *Post* had three. Both newspapers also had detailed accounts of the crimes, the arrest, the trial, and background information. The execution probably received more than usual coverage because of the rarity of hanging a woman, and because two men had been hanged within the same week in Pittsburgh.

Press descriptions made Grinder seem more concerned about her appearance than about her impending death. The *Post* claimed she had given specific instructions the night before the execution about how she wanted to be dressed. At eleven in the morning, female jail attendants helped her dress, and she seemed "quite anxious" about how she would look on the scaffold. The newspaper reported that early in the day, even

50. "Execution of Mrs. Grinder," *Pittsburgh Gazette-Times.*
51. "Conclusion of Trial of Grinder."
52. A definition in the modern-day *American Heritage Dictionary of the English Language* defines *monomania* as, "Pathological obsession with one idea or subject, as in paranoia." The way the Pittsburgh newspapers described Grinder might lead a modern-day reader to "diagnose" her as being a sociopath.
53. The modern legal test for determining insanity is that a defendant must understand the nature of the charges against him, and be able to assist in his own defense. To legally qualify for execution, the prisoner has to know the nature and effect of the death penalty, and why it is to be imposed upon him. See Kent S. Miller and Michael L. Radelet, *Executing the Mentally Ill,* 19. In addition, the United States Supreme Court ruled in 1989 that execution of a mentally retarded person is not categorically prohibited by the Eighth Amendment (174).

while talking about the Gospels with her spiritual advisers, Grinder was having her hair oiled and platted and "seemed more anxious about her personal appearance than the dread event so soon to take place." Like many executions of the period, the language and descriptions newspapers used to convey the formality and precision of the event made it seem almost a ceremony. A "procession" went from the cell to the scaffold. During the walk, Grinder carefully surveyed the prison, "and it seemed to us she was mentally bidding it goodbye." The story also conveyed a strong religious tone. Grinder was described as prayerful, repentant, and calm in the self-assurance of salvation. On the scaffold, she had a face that "wore a benign smile full of sweetness and resignation, which won for her the sympathy of many who had set her down as a fiend incarnate"— which included the Pittsburgh newspapers.[54]

The *Philadelphia Inquirer* correspondent made Grinder seem positively angelic, both before and after her death. His story, reprinted in the *New York Times,* said Grinder's face wore a "pleasant smile" from the time she left her cell until the black cap was put over her head: "There was nothing like a forced determination to appear calm and composed; it was evidently natural, and entirely unaffected." Just before the cap was put over her head, "she glanced pleasantly around at the spectators, and then cast her expressive blue eyes upward." After Grinder was dead and the cap was removed, "to the astonishment of every person who saw it, the face wore exactly the same placid, cheerful, smiling expression which characterized it on the scaffold." Even her eyes still looked "bright and animated."[55]

The later reports in the Pittsburgh press and in New York made Grinder seem redeemed. As with many other condemned defendants in the nineteenth and early twentieth centuries, the press described her in ways that are almost the embodiment of the promise of Christianity: a horrible sinner who in the end apparently repented, confessed, and would win eternal salvation. In this sense, coverage about her did not greatly differ from any other defendant, male or female. Readers surely noticed the story's pedagogical nature. A sentence from the *Pittsburgh Post*'s story on the first day of her trial perhaps best illustrates the shift in the way Pittsburgh newspapers described Grinder before her trial and after it. Before trial, she was often described as almost inhuman, as a fiend and a demon. However, on the day the trial began, the *Post* said that regardless of her guilt, she "has still the right to claim a place in the great sisterhood of womankind." In his execution story, the *Inquirer* reporter expressed admiration for

54. "Another Hanging."
55. "Execution of Mrs. Grinder," *New York Times.*

Grinder: "There is something inexplicable in the entire conduct of the woman. Something more than courage, physical strength, or even faith has conduced to enable her to bear herself with such astonishing, not only fortitude but meekness, gentleness, and childlike cheerfulness. She has been a marvel and a wonder to all who have had association with her since her conviction."[56]

56. "The Trial of Martha Grinder," *Pittsburgh Post*, 24 October 1865, quoted in "Execution of Mrs. Grinder," *New York Times*.

Chapter 7

Execution Stories As Serial Dramas

WHEN FRANCES CREIGHTON WAS EXECUTED in New York in 1936, the case attracted enormous interest in the New York City press, and how the *New York Times* reported it resembled a four-act Broadway drama. It actually involved two separate dramas: one in 1923 in New Jersey and the second in 1935–1936 in New York. The first is an integral part of the second, and was recounted in the 1930s stories.

Newspapers were the main source for information, and somewhat for entertainment, before television became a widespread communications medium. The present-day equivalent of television soap operas ran in many newspapers, with fictional stories presented in serial fashion. When one story line ended, another began, much like some comic strips even today.

Some news stories fitted the serial presentation, especially a crime that was sensational enough to merit almost day-by-day coverage. Ray Surette calls them "media trials," in which drama supercedes legal facts in the news reports, and the stories concentrate more on personalities, relationships, appearances, and idiosyncrasies.

Creighton's story fitted within this format because it contained popular-fiction elements, including sexual intrigue, strong emotional qualities, and mystery. The way these types of stories progressed to a final dramatic moment—the execution—had built-in tension. Sometimes the stories were bizarre. When such facts presented themselves, newspapers quickly publicized them. In a study about death row inmates, one scholar claims that the "popular media . . . typically transforms [*sic*] complex human tragedies into simple morality plays."[1]

---

1. The media are still fond of presenting some execution stories almost as a "playbill," complete with a cast of characters. In 2000, just before Tennessee had its first execution since the 1960s, some newspapers presented their Internet news about the execution in such a format, using "thumbnail sketches" of the major people

In earlier years, a defendant might be arrested, tried, convicted, and executed in less than one year, unlike today when most defendants are on death row for a decade or more.[2] Although the justice system's speed might not have produced the best way to find truth, it was advantageous to newspapers because it was easier to present information to readers in a serial format.

Creighton's story unfolded for *New York Times* readers in four distinct segments, almost resembling acts in a play. There were time periods between each, somewhat like intermissions, although the time between the first segment, in 1923, and the second, in October 1935, was too far removed for most readers to make the connection. Still, the *Times* recounted enough of the 1923 case to make it a part of the 1935–1936 episode. The parts of the whole were: the allegations of poisoning deaths and two criminal trials in 1923, with distinct "miniacts" within; the arrests and additional poisoning charge in October–November 1935; the trial for murder in January 1936; and the execution and events leading up to it in June–July 1936. The main portion of the story took place in less than one year. Creighton's execution in mid-July 1936 came less than one year after her October 1935 arrest.[3]

Some scholars criticize the "drama" structure, saying the only time condemned prisoners get public attention is at the time of the crime, at trial, and near the date of execution. Death row inmates are otherwise anonymous.[4] The fact is that executions of women were and are more likely to

---

involved. For the comment about media transformation of tragedies, see Robert Johnson, *Condemned to Die: Life under Sentence of Death*, 22.

2. In one case in Arkansas in the 1930s, defendant Tom Hutto was executed forty-three days after killing a police officer in El Dorado, Arkansas. Likewise, in Chicago in the 1930s, during an outbreak of murders of police officers, there were a number of criminal defendants who were executed less than a year after the commissions of their crimes.

3. Creighton's case is not the only one that fits the serial presentation. Other examples in this book include Martha Grinder of Pennsylvania, 1860s; Catharine Miller of Pennsylvania, 1880s; Mary Rogers of Vermont, early 1900s; Ada LeBoeuf of Louisiana, 1920s; Irene Schroeder of Pennsylvania and Anna Hahn of Ohio, 1930s; Barbara Graham of California, 1950s; Elizabeth Duncan of California, 1960s; Velma Barfield of North Carolina, 1980s; and Karla Faye Tucker of Texas, 1990s.

4. Johnson, *Condemned to Die*, 22. This is a valid criticism if the public needs to know more about the penal system, because the press does not provide as much information as perhaps it should. However, the lack of a constitutional right of access to prisons or prisoners, and few laws that require such access, make the press's job difficult. See *Richmond Newspapers, Inc. v. Virginia* for access to criminal courts, and *Houchins v. KQED* for access to prisons or jails. Usually, prison policies define the amount of press access, and those policies vary from state to state. Thus, either for reasons of convenience or because of government roadblocks, the press does in fact usually report major crimes in what almost amounts to a three-act-play format.

receive press scrutiny because of their rarity. Many male defendants, then and now, receive little press attention at any stage of the process.

There also is criticism that the ad hoc way these cases are reported means that neither the press nor the public pays much attention to possible flaws in the system. Questions about cultural values, the state, and the news and legal institutions themselves get short shrift because the crimes are reported as popular narrative. The criticism usually comes, if at all, in the form of editorials or columns.[5]

Act 1: The 1920s Case

Scene 1: Annie Creighton's Death

On 1 December 1920, Annie Creighton, forty-seven, died. She had become ill on 30 November, and Dr. Thomas Boyle diagnosed the cause of death as a cerebral hemorrhage, induced by ptomaine poisoning.[6] The Creightons had hired Florence Morris, a nurse, to care for Annie. On 30 November, Morris gave Creighton her medicine, and her condition seemed satisfactory. She had recently shown improvement after a long illness. The next morning while Morris fixed Creighton's breakfast, Annie's daughter-in-law Frances Creighton said she would look after her. About twenty minutes later, Morris went upstairs and found Annie terrified. She could not speak; she could make only gurgling noises. She became extremely nauseated, and a short time later suffered paralysis in her legs and in her left arm. She died at half past eleven.[7]

Several months later, Annie Creighton's husband, John C. Creighton, had his wallet containing $150 stolen while he slept. A few days later, his wallet was returned through the mail with a note: "Here is your wallet. It will not do you any good to hunt for your $150." Shortly after the theft, on 24 September 1921, John Creighton became ill and died the next day. Dr. Boyle said the symptoms "were of the acute gastric type."[8]

5. Ericson, Baranek, Chan, *Representing Order,* 9, 106; Tim Chavez, "News Media Drop the Ball While Man's Life Hangs in Balance" (http://www.tennessean.com/sn/99/10/09/chavez09.shtml). There was much press interest in 2000 as Tennessee prepared for its first two executions in almost fifty years. Columnist Tim Chavez of the *Nashville Tennessean* wrote a column sharply criticizing some reporting. His lead illustrates the tone: "For proof that the death penalty brings out the worst in us, look no further than WSMV–Channel 4's 10 P.M. Thursday newscast."

6. "Boy of 18 Murdered with Slow Poison; Sister Is Accused," *New York Times,* 13 May 1923.

7. "Tells Death Scene at Creighton Trial," ibid., 11 July 1923.

8. "To Exhume Bodies of the Creightons," ibid., 14 May 1923; "Boy of 18 Murdered."

Scene 2: A 1923 Murder

A year and a half later, on 20 April 1923, eighteen-year-old Charles Raymond Avery died suddenly. He was Frances Creighton's brother, and he lived with her and her husband, John, both twenty-four. Avery paid the Creightons five dollars per week for board; out of that money came about sixteen dollars per year for a life insurance policy on Raymond's life worth one thousand dollars, with Frances Creighton the beneficiary.[9] With Frances within weeks of giving birth to her second child, the Creightons needed the rent money; they already had a daughter, Ruth.

Dr. Boyle treated Raymond Avery for the first time on 2 April for a minor digestive ailment. Eight days later, his illness was worse. By 20 April, though, Avery seemed to have recovered; however, late that night he fell seriously ill. At the Creightons' house, Dr. Boyle found Avery near death and Frances Creighton standing near her brother's bed. "I think he had a love affair. He may have taken something," she told Dr. Boyle. Avery died that night. The suddenness of his death, especially after he had seemed much better earlier that day, puzzled Dr. Boyle. He sought the help of county physician George H. Warren, and they diagnosed the cause of death as "gastro-emeritis," according to the *New York Times*.

Sometime before Avery's death, his sister Helen received a letter from Frances, who said that Dr. Boyle had told her Raymond had kidney trouble and needed an operation. One of the Creightons' neighbors later told Helen that Raymond had not complained about kidney problems but had complained that Frances forced him to eat a lot of chocolate pudding, which he did not like. When Helen asked Dr. Boyle about Raymond's kidney ailment, the doctor said he had not found any symptoms of kidney trouble.[10]

Four days after Avery died, Essex County prosecutor John O. Bigelow received an anonymous letter signed, "A Friend of Justice." The letter, written before Avery died, asked Bigelow to investigate Avery's illness, and said Frances Creighton was a liar, a thief, and "bad at heart." It also said her mother-in-law and father-in-law had died under suspicious circumstances nearly two years earlier. Two days later, a second anonymous letter to Bigelow asked him to investigate Avery's death. The notes aroused Bigelow's suspicion, and an investigation resulted in grand jury indictments against John and Frances Creighton for Avery's murder.[11]

On 12 May, police arrested Frances Creighton at her home for murdering Raymond. She reportedly showed no surprise. She removed her

9. "Boy of 18 Murdered"; "To Exhume Bodies."
10. Author's note: The time sequence of this episode is unclear as to whether Raymond Avery was still alive or was dead.
11. "Boy of 18 Murdered."

apron, put on a hat and coat, and asked no questions, police told the *New York Times*.[12] Police arrested John Creighton at his office. A dozen Newark and Essex County detectives searched the Creighton home and took about thirty vials, medicine bottles, and pillboxes; sealed them; and turned them over to a laboratory for chemical analysis.

At the arraignment, an emotional Frances Creighton wore mourning clothes for her brother; she carried her child, Ruth, in her arms and another child in her womb. Her condition stirred the courtroom spectators' sympathy, the *Times* reported. The Creightons pleaded not guilty.

The judge ordered the Creightons held without bail. Ruth was taken to a family friend. Frances Creighton wept and said that she did not know what she was supposed to have done. She said Raymond had been sick about ten days. "All I know is that he was taken sick. . . . The night he died the doctor had said he was all right." She said her brother could not keep a job. "I promised him if he would work steady I would take out a policy for him. I know people . . . said I didn't treat him good. But I couldn't buy him $45 suits when he wasn't working."[13]

Police told reporters that Frances Creighton persuaded Avery to take out the insurance policy and that she also stood to profit from his death because she would inherit his portion of their parents' estates. Police theorized that Avery had died from arsenic put into his chocolate pudding. Bigelow said three doctors told the grand jury that chocolate pudding would have been an ideal medium for administering poison.

Scene 3: Grand Jury–Testimony Leaks

The *New York Times* reported that the grand jury proceedings were unusually secretive, but published plenty of testimony on the day after the arrests. Testimony leaked to the *Times* included that Avery's body had been exhumed and an autopsy showed arsenic in many of the vital organs. In addition, the manager of an office of the Metropolitan Life Insurance Company told the grand jury that a life insurance policy for one thousand dollars had been made out for Avery, with Frances Creighton as the beneficiary.[14]

The *Times* might have known more about the grand jury testimony than did the Creightons' attorney, James W. McCarthy of Jersey City, who criticized the lack of secrecy and access to the grand jury minutes. McCarthy proclaimed the Creightons' innocence. "Nobody would kill a person for a $1,000 insurance policy," he said. Authorities obtained an order for the exhumation of Annie and John C. Creighton, but when they brought it to

12. "To Exhume Bodies."
13. "Boy of 18 Murdered."
14. Ibid.

the jail, John refused to sign it. "Are they going to drag my parents into this?" he asked. Judge-ordered exhumations and an autopsy were performed under a tent at the cemetery, and the bodies were reburied. A minor confrontation occurred when police tried to keep the press away. A photographer for a Newark newspaper refused to leave, and police arrested him for disorderly conduct, according to the *Times*. Bigelow, sensing trouble, immediately ordered that all newspapermen be allowed to attend. The exhumations moved the story in the *Times* from page 40 to page 1 in a single day.[15]

Several other aspects of the case made news. First, Frances Creighton was taken to the Newark City Hospital on the night before the autopsies, and she gave birth to a nine-pound boy, whom the couple named John, after his father. Creighton asked to be allowed either to stay at the hospital until her June trial or to keep the baby in her cell. Eventually, she was allowed to keep the child with her.[16] Second, police revealed that three years earlier, Frances Creighton had charged several items at a Newark department store to another customer's account. Police also disclosed that when her father-in-law died, Creighton had attempted to get the same store to put his charge account into her name. The store refused, police said, because of the earlier incident.[17]

As the case developed in the courts, both the prosecution and the defense also developed their cases in the newspapers. The *Times* published information questioning McCarthy's argument about Creighton having had little financial gain from the insurance policy on Avery. Days later, Bigelow told the *Times* that a report on the estates of John and Annie Creighton showed his worth $6,368 and hers $3,500.[18] Frances Creighton was indicted early in June for murdering Annie.

Scene 4: The First Murder Trial

The Creightons' trial for murdering Avery began 18 June in Newark. Stories ran every day in the *New York Times* from 18 June to 23 June, and so many wanted to attend the trial that it was moved to a larger court-

15. "To Exhume Bodies"; "Creighton Autopsy Aids Poison Theory," ibid., 17 May 1923.
16. "Autopsy Aids Theory"; "Hints Young Avery Was Poison-Suicide," ibid., 20 May 1923. There are examples of children staying with their mothers not only in jails, but also in prisons. A one-year-old child, Furlough Latin, was reported to have made "more or less permanent residence" at Camp Four in Arkansas's Cummins Prison Farm in 1946. The child's mother, Pinkie Mae Latin of Warren, was imprisoned for the murder of her husband. Furlough was cared for by the twenty women murderers of Camp Four. "Baby Girl Is Pet of 20 Women Murderers," *Little Rock Arkansas Gazette*, 28 November 1946.
17. "Autopsy Aids Theory."
18. "Testifies to Poison in Body of Youth," *New York Times*, 19 June 1923; "Explain Why Search for Poison Is Slow," ibid., 23 May 1923.

room.[19] The *Times* provided detailed reports for those readers who could not attend.

The trial moved quickly. When the state rested its case, the defense called no witnesses. After deliberating fifty-three minutes, the jury returned, according to the *Times*. Frances Creighton appeared nervous for the first time during the four-day trial. The Creightons stood, and the jury foreman read the verdict. Frances looked straight at the foreman. "We, the jury, find the defendants not guilty." Frances smiled, then collapsed, fainting into her husband's arms. He caught her as she fell. John Creighton was free. He went to Kearney, New Jersey, and got Ruth, now four, while the baby, John, remained with Frances in jail.[20]

Scene 5: The Second Trial

The next part of the 1923 drama opened on 9 July with Frances Creighton's second murder trial about two weeks after the first trial. John Creighton told the *New York Times*: "I know that Fanny is guiltless of killing my mother. If my mother died of unnatural causes I know in my innermost heart that my wife is innocent of responsibility for her death." The assistant prosecuting attorney, Victor D'Aloia, who had also helped prosecute the first trial, told the jury the state would show that Annie Creighton became ill after drinking a cup of cocoa given to her by Frances Creighton, and that Frances had worn silk underwear bought for Annie Creighton's body. D'Aloia's allegation visibly upset Frances; she flushed and breathed sharply at such a scandalous allegation, the *Times* reported.[21]

The defense relied solely on the testimony of experts, including Dr. Alexander O. Gettler, a toxicologist for the New York County District Attorney's Office and a professor of sciences at New York University, and two other doctors.

The jury deliberated three hours and fifty-five minutes. Frances Creighton appeared pale, worn, and tired, according to the *New York Times*. The longer the jury deliberated, the more strained she appeared. Curious spectators packed the courtroom. Judge Caffrey asked the jury for its verdict. The *Times* described in detail what happened. "What is your verdict?" Judge Caffrey asked. As the foreman began to speak, Frances Creighton swayed, moaned, and collapsed into her lawyer's arms. The jury announced its verdict, and John Creighton, concentrating on his wife's collapse, heard the word *guilty*. He cried out, started for-

19. "Creighton Trial on Today," ibid., 18 June 1923; "Testifies to Poison."
20. "Creightons Freed of Murder Charge," ibid., 23 June 1923.
21. "Tells Death Scene at Creighton Trial," ibid., 11 July 1923; "Mrs. Creighton Calm As New Trial Begins," ibid., 10 July 1923.

ward, then fell back into a chair and sat, seemingly in a trance. Then he was told the foreman had said "not guilty." Frances had not heard the verdict, and her husband had misunderstood it. She remarked, "I shall never forget Friday the 13th," the day she was acquitted. The next day's *Times* ran the story on page 1.[22]

Act 2: 1935

Scene 1: Sharing a House Twelve Years Later

Twelve years later, in September 1935, John and Frances Creighton, and their daughter, Ruth, sixteen, an attractive high school student, and their son, John Jr., twelve, lived in a cramped five-room green-stucco house on Long Island. John Creighton worked as a surveyor in the county engineer's office in Nassau County, where the Creightons had lived for twelve years. Frances was medium-size, dark-haired, and energetic. Ruth was blonde and later described as "rather shy" and as still wearing "her hair with ribbons."[23]

The four lived with Everett C. and Ada Applegate, and their daughter, Agnes, twelve. Everett Applegate had met the Creightons about nine years earlier while investigating their application for relief, and he invited them to move into his house. Applegate was an investigator for the Veterans' Bureau and was active in American Legion affairs. The *New York Times* described Ada Applegate as a large woman, weighing about 220 pounds; she took diet pills to control her weight. She shared her husband's enthusiasm for the American Legion, and was the founder and past president of the Ladies Auxiliary of the Baldwin Post.[24]

Despite the cramped living conditions, the Creightons and the Applegates seemed to get along well. Everett took an especially active interest in Ruth and Agnes. He took the two girls on auto trips with him when he investigated veterans' applications for home relief, and he showed concern for Ruth's welfare, and objected to her attending high school dances because she would be exposed to bad influences. Oddly, the previous February, the Creightons had received six anonymous letters urging them to "get rid of the Applegates."[25]

22. "Jury Again Acquits Mrs. Creighton of Murder," ibid., 14 July 1923.

23. "Arsenic Victim Held Murdered," ibid., 8 October 1935; "Death of Woman a Poison Mystery," ibid., 7 October 1935; "Woman Confesses Arsenic Slaying, Clears Applegate," ibid., 9 October 1935.

24. "Arsenic Victim Held Murdered"; "Woman Confesses Arsenic Slaying"; "Poison Mystery."

25. "Arsenic Victim Held Murdered"; "Creighton Says Wife Is Innocent of Crime," ibid., 21 January 1936.

In early September 1936, Frances Creighton bought a twenty-three-cent box of poison that was called Rough on Rats. On 19 September, Ada Applegate became ill and was hospitalized until 25 September. Frances visited her daily. Shortly after Ada returned home, she asked her husband to mix her an eggnog. Frances volunteered to mix the drink, and Everett took it to his wife. On 26 September, Ada Applegate became violently ill, and died the next day.[26]

Scene 2: Rumors and Investigation

Soon after, rumors reached William Vaughn, a Nassau County detective, that Ada Applegate's death was suspicious. Vaughn sent newspaper clippings about Frances Creighton's 1923 trials to the Nassau County district attorney, and an investigation began. Ada's organs were sent to Dr. Alexander O. Gettler, who the *New York Times* said was the same toxicologist who had testified in Creighton's defense twelve years earlier. Dr. Gettler said that there was about three times more arsenic in Applegate's vital organs than an average fatal dose. Police searched the Creighton-Applegate home but said they found no Rough on Rats poison. They later stated that Frances Creighton told them that she had thrown it into the garbage, which had since been taken away.[27]

Scene 3: "An Improper Relationship"

On 6 October, police booked Everett Applegate, and he was arraigned for criminal assault on sixteen-year-old Ruth Creighton. Police said Ruth had admitted to "an improper relationship" since April with Applegate, and his attorney confirmed to reporters Applegate's confession. Police inspector Harold R. King was convinced Ada Applegate had been murdered, the *New York Times* reported. King said police had ruled out suicide because three loaded revolvers were in the house and had ruled out accidental poisoning because none of the other people in the house was affected. Everett Applegate reportedly told his attorney that he did not believe his wife had committed suicide because she was not depressed and had no reason to kill herself. Frances Creighton told reporters that many of Everett's actions with Ruth that had not previously seemed significant now seemed so.[28] A murder-by-poison mystery emerged with a bizarre sexual angle involving Ruth Creighton and Everett Applegate.

26. "Poisoning Is Denied by Mrs. Creighton," ibid., 23 January 1936; "Poison Mystery"; "Woman Confesses Arsenic Slaying."
27. "Poison Mystery"; "Woman Confesses Arsenic Slaying"; "Arsenic Murder Now Held Solved," ibid., 10 October 1935.
28. "Poison Mystery"; "Arsenic Victim Held Murdered."

Scene 4: A Confession

On 9 October, a headline at the top left side of the front page of the *New York Times* read: "Woman Confesses Arsenic Slaying, Clears Applegate." District Attorney Martin W. Littleton told reporters that Frances Creighton had confessed that she had blamed Ada Applegate for rumors about Ruth and Everett's relationship and put rat poison in her coffee, milk, and tea. Littleton said Creighton had mixed an extraheavy dose of poison into the eggnog, which Applegate gave to his wife, not knowing about the poison. Creighton said she had known about Ruth and Everett's relationship for several months, but never told her husband because of what he might do. Police also said that during the questioning, Creighton admitted poisoning her brother Raymond, saying she had done so because he was a "cripple" and she had wanted to relieve his suffering. Littleton said Creighton showed no "nervousness, confusion, unhappiness or emotional upset of any kind."

Creighton was jailed on 9 October and held without bail on a charge of first-degree murder. Before her confession, she implicated Applegate, but later said she had done so because she wanted to avenge what he had done to Ruth. Creighton said she, too, had had a sexual relationship with Applegate.

Creighton's "confession" relieved Applegate. "I'm very glad to know she had told the truth. I had no ill-feeling toward my wife. I was always kind to her. When she was sick I helped her in and out of bed."[29] Although the grand jury had not heard the evidence, and no indictment had been issued, the *New York Times*'s headline on 10 October read, "Arsenic Murder Now Held Solved."

Scene 5: "I Wish to Marry This Girl"

On 11 October, Applegate and Creighton were indicted for first-degree murder, she for the actual poisoning and Applegate for being an accessory after the fact. Applegate was also indicted for criminal assault on Ruth. The *New York Times* said the two alleged criminals sat about thirty feet apart, but neither looked directly at the other. When asked to enter a plea to the assault charge involving Ruth at the arraignment, Applegate said, "I plead guilty to this charge." Then he added, "I wish to marry this girl." Judge George Johnson refused to accept the plea and ordered a plea of not guilty entered, the *Times* reported.[30]

29. "Arsenic Murder Solved."
30. "Husband Indicted in Arsenic Murder," ibid., 12 October 1935.

Act 3: The Trial

Scene 1: The State's Case

The trial began on 13 January 1936 amid great public interest. The jury pool consisted of 170 people, from which 25 prospective jurors were chosen. Despite the pretrial publicity, a jury was seated in two days.[31]

Some thirteen years after he testified in Frances Creighton's defense during her New Jersey trial, Dr. Gettler testified for the prosecution. He estimated arsenic quantities in Ada Applegate's vital organs were almost four times more than necessary to kill her, more than his earlier assessment. A New York City handwriting expert testified that Creighton had written the six anonymous letters that came to the Creighton-Applegate home in February, urging that the Applegates be gotten "rid of." The *Times*'s blow-by-blow description of the trial also noted that John Creighton testified that he did not believe his wife had anything to do with Applegate's murder. He said he considered Ruth a child, and he had never suspected she was having an affair with Applegate.[32]

Scene 2: Frances Creighton Takes the Stand

Creighton's testimony repudiated her three earlier statements that she and Applegate had killed his wife. She now blamed only him. Creighton said she had bought the rat poison at his request, and she denied knowing anything about Ruth's relationship with Applegate.[33]

The next day, Creighton's cross-examination provided the most dramatic moment in the trial, and marked the first time that a trial story made the *Times*'s front page. The paper's reporter and editors recognized the tension that had built to the single most dramatic moment. They did not summarize or paraphrase that portion of the story, but reported it as dialogue.

> LITTLETON: "When you took the milk to Mrs. Applegate and waited for her to drink it, you knew then there was arsenic in it, did you not?"
> CREIGHTON: "Yes, I did. Applegate told me."
> LITTLETON: "Knowing this, you took it to her to drink?"
> CREIGHTON: "Yes."

31. "Applegate on Trial Today," ibid., 13 January 1936; "Three Jurors Selected in Applegate Case," ibid., 14 January 1936; "Applegate Jury Ready," ibid., 16 January 1936.
32. "Dr. Gettler on Stand at Applegate Trial," 18 January 1936; "Wife Is Innocent."
33. "Poisoning Denied."

LITTLETON: "You stood by and watched this woman, who was your
best friend, die?"
CREIGHTON: "Yes."[34]

Creighton broke under cross-examination, admitted she knew Applegate's drink was poisoned, testified she had given it to her anyway, and
said she had told no one.

Scene 3: Applegate's Testimony, the Verdict, and the Sentences

Applegate denied ever causing poison to be given to his wife. He said
he had never suspected that Frances Creighton had poisoned her. He denied any relationship with Frances, and denied that his relationship with
Ruth had anything to do with his wife's murder. Testimony about the sexual escapades and the murder drew big crowds. One woman fainted, and
several others were knocked down and bruised during the rush for seats,
according to the *New York Times*. About two hundred people, half of them
women; twenty uniformed police; and fifteen police detectives reportedly were in the courtroom. During closing arguments, Creighton's attorney
described her as "putty" in Everett Applegate's hands and termed him a
dominating "man of steel." Littleton denounced both the defendants and
said they had committed "so hideous a crime that no classic statute has
been written to cover it."[35]

The jury began deliberations at nine o'clock and returned a verdict at
12:47 the next morning. The court clerk warned spectators about dem-
onstrations, which indicates that people perhaps sat in the courtroom
during the night to await the verdict. Creighton and Applegate were convicted of first-degree murder, which meant, the *Times* reported, mandatory death sentences; however, the judge would still formally pronounce the
sentences at a later date. Frances Creighton sobbed softly when the verdict was announced, but quickly regained her composure.

Judge Cortland Johnson sentenced Frances Creighton and Everett Applegate on 30 January. He asked them if they had anything to say, and
Creighton shook her head no. Applegate, however, said he had neither
bought poison nor given it to his wife, and he claimed he never had an affair with Frances. Johnson sentenced Creighton and Applegate to die in
early March in New York's electric chair at Sing Sing Prison. Before leaving for prison, Creighton left a note for Ruth with her attorney. The *New
York Times* obtained and published it: "Dear Ruth: Mother is going away.
No matter what has happened to you in your life, be a good girl and look

---

34. "Admits Poisoning in Applegate Case," ibid., 24 January 1936.
35. Ibid.; "Applegate, Woman Guilty of Murder," ibid., 25 January 1936.

after the best man you will ever have, your father. Whatever the judge tells you to do, be sure to do it, because it is for your good. You and Jackie [John Jr.] are all that daddy has. Make every effort to help in this trying situation. I love you all. Please pray for me. Lovingly, Mother."[36]

Act 4: The Executions

Scene 1: Frances Creighton Becomes Ill

In early June 1936, *New York Times* readers got their first indication that Frances Creighton might not be holding up well. The newspaper reported she had a "serious mental and physical condition," citing as sources "persons who have access to her." She had partly lost the power of speech, and prison officials feared she perhaps had a stroke, although there had been no medical diagnosis. Sing Sing warden Lewis E. Lawes refused to discuss Creighton's condition. The *Times* reported two days before Creighton's execution that she had been in a state of collapse for eight weeks, had been unable to leave her bed for a week, appeared to be paralyzed, and could hardly retain food. On 21 June, she refused to allow her son to visit her, and she persisted in this decision to her death.[37]

Scene 2: Ruth's Letter Is Revealed

One week before the execution, Creighton's attorney, Elvin M. Edwards, said Ruth had sent him a letter in April in which she said Applegate had told her he "would do away with Aunt Ada and have me for himself and that he could talk Dad into letting us be married." The *New York Times* called the letter's revelation a surprise because Ruth had testified at her mother's trial and said nothing about it. Edwards said Applegate had told Ruth that if she revealed their relationship, she would go to jail. That proved true in the sense that, at the time Edwards revealed the letter, Ruth was termed an "inmate" at the Brooklyn Training School for Girls. Ruth also said she had not told because the investigators had frightened her, the *Times* said.[38]

The next day, the *Times* also reported that Judge Johnson refused to confirm or deny that he had written a letter asking Gov. H. H. Lehman to com-

36. "Two Sentenced to Die in Poison Murder," ibid., 31 January 1936.
37. "Mrs. Creighton Is Ill," ibid., 1 June 1936; "Mrs. Creighton Gets Special Examination," ibid., 15 July 1936; "Slayer Bans Son's Visits," ibid., 22 June 1936.
38. "Applegate Bared Plot, Girl Charges," ibid., 7 July 1936. Near the time of the execution, Applegate said his last name was spelled "Applegate." The *Times* used that spelling in this headline.

mute Applegate's death sentence. In the letter, he reportedly told the governor that Creighton was guilty beyond a reasonable doubt.[39] Governor Lehman, who was deciding whether to seek another term, had not reported his decision for clemency, and the scheduled executions were one week away.

One day before the scheduled executions, a five-man commission appointed by Governor Lehman said Creighton's physical and mental condition were caused by "hysteria." Creighton insisted she was paralyzed below her waist.[40] The executions were scheduled for the next day.

Scene 3: The Final Curtain

On 16 July, Frances Creighton and Everett Applegate died in Sing Sing's electric chair. The *Times*'s front-page story said Creighton was, according to Sing Sing warden Lewis E. Lawes, the first condemned person in the history of the prison to be taken by wheelchair from her cell to the death chair. Attendants lifted her from the wheelchair and placed her in the electric chair. Physicians and prison attendants formed a human screen between Creighton and the newspapermen and other witnesses to ensure that no secret photographs would be taken. The *New York Times* said Creighton had "adopted the Catholic religion" shortly before her execution. She claimed she had done so to make it easier for her to die. "Just before the current was turned on she dropped the rosary beads that had been given to her when she adopted the Catholic religion this afternoon." Moments later, she was dead. To the end, she refused to see Ruth or John Jr., although she did visit with her husband.[41]

39. "Mrs. Creighton Signs Plea for New Trial," ibid., 8 July 1936.
40. "Mrs. Creighton Found Suffering Hysteria," ibid., 16 July 1936.
41. "Mrs. Creighton Dies for Poison Murder," ibid., 17 July 1936. Creighton's condition might be an illustration of a statement by French philosopher Albert Camus, who said people condemned to death die two deaths. One is during the process of waiting, and the second is the actual execution. Camus said the first death is the worst. Camus, *Resistance, Rebellion, and Death,* 191. Lawes later was an active reformer against the death penalty (Mackey, *Voices against Death,* xxxvii).

PART III

Race, Ethnicity, and Sexual Preference

Chapter 8

Pre–Civil War Press and Slave Executions

AFTER JANE WILLIAMS WAS SENTENCED to death in 1852 in Richmond, Virginia, for murdering the wife and son of her master, the *Richmond Daily Dispatch* reported that her value had been fixed at five hundred dollars. The state would compensate the man who owned her for taking his private property. The newspaper reported the fact as routinely as if the state had taken land or animals. The *Dispatch* later said no felon ever deserved the gallows more than did Williams. The newspaper termed her "a fiend" and "a wretched murderess," and it said she had no motive for the crime and would die "without the smallest particle of sympathy from any human being possessed of the ordinary feelings of justice."[1]

Race played a large part in determining newspaper coverage given to Williams and to other condemned women. Black women usually received neither the amount nor the prominence of coverage as whites. This was especially true in the twentieth century. During the nineteenth century, a few hangings of black female slaves got some news coverage, but most were barely mentioned.

Hangings of slaves helped maintain the southern system of social control of African Americans and were virtually rituals to inform slaves that they could not practice violence against whites, who often made sure blacks attended.[2] The same probably was true in northern states before they abolished slavery. Two black women and a black man, all slaves, were hanged in 1793 in New York after a fire destroyed several homes in Albany. As late as the 1850s, even in northern cities such as Boston, and among some intellectuals, the idea of black equality was not widespread.[3]

1. "Hustings Court," *Richmond Daily Dispatch*, 10 August 1852; "The Execution," ibid., 8 September 1852.
2. Friedman, *Crime and Punishment*, 88.
3. Bernard A. Weisberger, *America Afire: Jefferson, Adams, and the Revolutionary Election of 1800,* 99. For comment on Boston, see Louis Menand, chap. 1 in *The Metaphysical Club.*

Some southern newspapers probably did not report hangings of slaves in much depth because the majority white-owned and -operated newspapers in the South certainly did not consider blacks part of their readership; some southern states made it a crime to teach slaves to read. Furthermore, white readers might not have considered slave hangings big news.

After the Civil War, and especially in the late nineteenth century, newspapers generally reported hangings of black women more fully than the earlier executions of female slaves, and later executions of black women in the twentieth century. Peter Kolchin, in his book about U.S. slavery, contends that emancipation increased racism, whereas slavery lessened it because white slave owners took a paternalistic attitude toward what they considered their property.[4] Kolchin's contention is strengthened if one looks at lynchings as well as legal executions. More African Americans were lynched after slavery than before.

Two other authors contend that few slaves were lynched because they constituted valuable property: "[I]f a black slave committed a capital offense and was [legally] executed, the state had to reimburse the owner for the fair market value of the slave." This is not to say that slaves, or free blacks, were not subjected to horrible punishments during slavery. Nor were women immune from lynching. In 1898, in the small town of Clarendon, Arkansas, a woman was one of four African Americans lynched in connection with the murder of a prominent young white businessman. The man's wife, who had conspired to have her husband murdered, later killed herself by taking poison.[5]

Almost all women executed in some states, such as Virginia and Mississippi, were black. In other states, such as Florida, few women have ever been executed. Until 1998, the only woman executed in Florida was a slave, Celia, hanged in 1848. A retrospective article in the *Miami Herald* said Celia had been hanged for killing her white owner, who also was her father, and he probably fathered four of her children. The jury recommended clemency, but the judge overrode the recommendation and sentenced her to die. The *Herald* reported that the *Jacksonville News* called for her execution, saying clemency might encourage other slaves and might produce "dangerous consequences." Thus the newspaper supported the plantation system, despite the white victim's revolting behavior. Lawrence Friedman contends that maintaining the caste system mattered

4. Kolchin, *American Slavery, 1619–1877*, 58, 234–35. See especially his description of the punishment of a free black girl in Louisiana who was convicted of torturing and killing a white girl.
5. Oshinsky, *"Worse Than Slavery,"* 209–13; George C. Wright, *Racial Violence in Kentucky, 1865–1940: Lynchings, Mob Rule, and "Legal Lynchings"*; Curriden and Phillips, *Contempt of Court*, 215; "Lynched," *Little Rock Arkansas Gazette*, 10 August 1898.

more than guilt or innocence. If a black such as Celia murdered a white, no matter what the circumstances, she had to be punished harshly or the system would crumble.[6]

The societal norms of the nineteenth century that placed white women on a pedestal and carried expectations that they were to be more virtuous and pure than others did not apply to black women.

Executions of Slaves

Slavery's pernicious nature is illustrated by the news coverage about Jane Williams's execution on 10 September 1852 in Richmond. Jane Williams and her husband, John, died for murdering the wife and infant of their master, Joseph P. Winston. Jane Williams had reportedly attacked the Winstons with a hatchet while they slept. Joseph Winston survived.

The 20 July 1852 attack was big news. The 24 July issue of the *Richmond Daily Dispatch* said: "Extra copies of the *Dispatch*, containing a full report of the examination of the negroes charged with the Winston family murder can be bought at the office for 2 cents each."[7]

About thirty years later, the *Petersburg (Va.) Index-Appeal* called Williams's hanging "[t]he most noted execution of a female that ever occurred in this State."[8] The same could be said today because no subsequent executions of Virginia women received as much prominent coverage.

The *Dispatch* reported the gory details, saying Joseph Winston and his wife were found in their beds with "deep brain-cuts upon their heads." Although alive when found, the mother soon died, and "the infant was soon after laid a bleeding corpse by the side of its mangled mother." Important happenings were reported daily under the headline "Local Matters." An all-capitals leader in text face said "Murder," and led readers into the story, which ran more than three full columns of text. The testimony of three doctors at an inquest provided readers with graphic descriptions of the crime. The newspaper concluded, "The testimony thus far proves that Jane Williams has perjured herself, and that there are strong circumstantials of the guilt of both John and Jane Williams." The *Dispatch* added: "It seems to be agreed by all who were acquainted with

6. Lori Rozsa, "Woman on Death Row: Echoes of a Slave's Hanging in 1848," *Miami Herald*, 29 March 1998; Friedman, *Crime and Punishment*, 376. Such caste systems were not exclusive to African Americans. Executions in Arizona's early history show a preponderance of Hispanic defendants. See http://www.adc.state.az.us:81/Death Row/Death PenaltyHistory.htm.

7. *Richmond Daily Dispatch*, 24 July 1852, p. 2.

8. "The Death Penalty," *Petersburg (Va.) Index-Appeal*, 23 April 1881.

the family, that the negroes who are on trial for this horrible crime, are the most indulged in the whole city of Richmond."[9]

Six days later, the *Richmond Daily Dispatch* published an opinionated and emotional story, reporting that Jane Williams had confessed that only she committed the murders. The *Dispatch* disagreed. It called the murders "hardly paralleled in history" and said the killers were "more than demons" and that the crime "must wind up with the execution of the murderer or murderers." The *Dispatch* said John Williams deserved the death penalty even if he only knew about his wife's plan. "We see but little difference between the failure to stay the uplifted arm, and the striking of the blow." The newspaper made grotesque reference to the crime when it said Jane Williams "stands forth as the confessed murderess of the mistress who had never been any otherwise than kind, trusting and forgiving to her, and the crusher of the skull of her innocent babe, so that the physician said that when he pressed its head to discover its injuries, he heard the broken pieces of bone grating against each other!"[10]

The *Dispatch* for the first time reported a motive, saying Williams believed the Winstons treated her badly, and she wanted revenge. A later story said Winston had once threatened to sell Williams without selling her child. This was the first reference to a child.

The *Dispatch* reported a rumor that Jane Williams had confessed that she murdered another of the Winstons' children, who had died some months earlier. The newspaper sent a reporter to ask her, and she denied making the confession and said she was sick at heart. The *Dispatch* added in a news story: "Well she may be. The fires of her eternal future doom are just being enkindled in her fiendish heart."[11]

A crowd estimated at six thousand, composed of "persons of all sexes, colors, and ages," watched Williams hang. The pastor of the local African church told the crowd that she should be given the consolation of religion during her last moments, but the *Dispatch* demurred: "Never before in this city, perhaps, did religious ceremonies of so serious and impressive a character, fall upon more unwilling ears. The thick-crowding thoughts of the diabolical murder of two innocent, guileless beings, committed by Jane with the coolness and deliberation of a fiend, rendered unimpressive, cold, and tedious, those ceremonies."[12]

The statement is not surprising because some whites might not have applied Christian sentiments to blacks, especially black slaves. In the early 1900s, a Baptist church congregation in Chattanooga, Tennessee, "vot-

---

9. "Local Matters," *Richmond Daily Dispatch*, 20 July 1852.
10. Ibid., 26 July 1852.
11. Ibid., 2 August 1852.
12. "The Execution of Jane Williams," *Richmond Daily Dispatch*, 11 September 1852.

ed seventy-four to seventy-one that black people do have souls and can go to heaven." If white Christians in the early twentieth century had to vote about blacks having souls, similar or even more outrageous beliefs about blacks could easily have existed in the mid-nineteenth century. The *Dispatch* ended its story by saying: "It is to be hoped that her merited and summary execution will operate as a warning to the fractious portion of our negro population."[13]

Mississippi Hangings of Slaves

The extensive coverage given Williams was unusual. The newspaper coverage in Mississippi seems more the norm. Mississippi has executed at least eighteen women, none of whom is known to be white. Most were executed between 1833 and 1861; all of them were slaves. News coverage is sparse or nonexistent; stories often were a paragraph or two. For example, the *Woodville (Miss.) Republican* reported the hanging of a slave named Nancy, who had poisoned two members of her master's family, in 1833 in one long sentence of fifty-nine words. The *Jackson (Miss.) Daily News*'s entire story about the hanging of a slave named Eliza in 1860 said: "The negro woman Eliza, who has been for some time under sentence of death for the burning of the gin house of Mrs. McCann, was hung in Yazoo City, the 2d inst."[14]

An 1838 hanging of another slave named Eliza merited more coverage. She had assaulted "her mistress" with intent to kill her, the *Natchez Mississippi Free Trader* reported. Because of her youth, the jury recommended the governor grant her mercy. The news stories did not give her age, but she apparently was a juvenile. The judge overruled the jury's recommendation and sentenced her to death. The *Free Trader* made clear the intent of the hanging: "The blacks on the ground [witnessing the hanging] appeared suitably affected." The report made it seem the perfect hanging— almost. Near the end of the story, it said Eliza had slowly strangled. "The struggles of the culprit were protracted and severe, as if she died of strangulation rather than dislocation of the neck and the head of the spine." Nonetheless, the newspaper reported, "It was one of the most sober and well-behaved public, outdoor assemblages we ever saw. Not a jest, nor an

13. Curriden and Phillips, *Contempt of Court*, 23; "Execution of Jane Williams."

14. "Execution," *Woodville (Miss.) Republican*, 7 December 1833; *Jackson (Miss.) Daily News*, 14 March 1860 (no title). Execution records in Mississippi are especially sketchy and hard to obtain. I am using a list compiled by Jan Hillegas of Jackson, Mississippi, and supplied to me. The state of Mississippi has no good records, to my knowledge, of executions prior to 1955, when the executions were moved to Parchman Farm and defendants were no longer executed in the counties. Prior to that, from 1940 to 1954, a portable electric chair was taken from county to county.

oath, not an obscene, nor an irrelevant remark did we hear during the melancholy transaction."[15]

Post-Slavery Coverage

After emancipation, newspapers usually gave more coverage to black women's executions. When Lucinda Fowlkes hanged in Lunenburg County, Virginia, on 22 April 1881, about four months after murdering her husband with an ax, the nearby *Petersburg Index-Appeal* and *Lynchburg Virginian* both reported the execution. The Petersburg paper played the story on page 1 and gave it reasonably substantial coverage. Lynchburg's newspaper had a brief account on page 2. The substantial coverage might have been because white-owned newspapers saw more of a need after emancipation to let black citizens know that they were subject to harsh punishment.

The hanging attracted little attention in the white community. A crowd of about one hundred who gathered outside the county jail for the private hanging "consisted principally of negroes. The white people in the county seem to manifest but little interest in the matter." Fowlkes died about four months after killing her husband with an ax. The Petersburg newspaper called her crime "cold-blooded and brutal," and added that the "fiendishness of [the crime] has few parallels in that section" of Virginia. Lucinda Fowlkes reportedly killed her husband to be with her lover, Isaac Dean, with whom she had been intimate "at the house of the deceased." The Petersburg newspaper said Dean had spent the night at the Fowlkeses' home, and a few days later Mr. Fowlkes "for some reason flogged his wife." The Lynchburg newspaper was more sympathetic to Lucinda Fowlkes. It said her husband's jealousy was "without cause," and that she had murdered him "because he was mean to her, and constantly beating and abusing her."[16]

When Margaret Lashley and her lover, James Lyles, were hanged in Danville, Virginia, on 22 January 1892, the story was front-page news in the *Roanoke Times* and in the *Raleigh News and Observer.* Lyles and Lashley murdered the latter's husband. However, it likely was front-page news only because four people hanged on the same day in Virginia, North Carolina, and Georgia, and two of them were women. A subordinate headline in the Roanoke newspaper read, "Four Souls Jerked into Eternity Yesterday." The *Richmond Times-Dispatch* gave the story prominent display on

15. "Court Calendar," *Natchez Mississippi Free Trader,* 3 July 1838; "The Execution," ibid., 11 August 1838.
16. "The Death Penalty"; "A Woman to Be Hung in Lunenburg Today," *Petersburg (Va.) Index-Appeal,* 22 April 1881; "Execution of Lucinda Fowlkes for the Murder of Her Husband," *Lynchburg (Va.) Virginian,* 23 April 1881.

page 2. Both the Roanoke and Richmond newspapers led the four-person executions with the Danville hangings, but the Raleigh paper led the story with the hanging of Caroline Shipp in North Carolina.[17]

The stories had the usual racial descriptions of "Negro" or "colored" in the lead sentences, even though race had nothing to do with the crimes. The story also referred to the blacks as "darkies." The *Times-Dispatch*'s story questioned whether the Lashleys were married. It said the pair were "supposed to be man and wife." The newspaper also said they "lived happily together, as happily as negroes usually do." The executions were controversial because Lyles said he had committed the murder, and Lashley insisted she was innocent. The *Times-Dispatch* said that "if it was false she died with a lie on her lips." In another story, the newspaper said the hangings "excited" hundreds of black people in Danville because they did not believe a guilty person could act as she did on the gallows. The newspaper also termed blacks "superstitious," and said "a wild rumor" that doctors would give Lashley's and Lyles's bodies for study and dissection concerned some black citizens. The black community's fears apparently had some foundation. The *Times-Dispatch* said a state law allowed the remains of executed criminals not claimed by relatives to be turned over to doctors for dissection; however, the newspaper stated that local authorities rejected such a request in this case. The newspaper also reported that black residents said black prisoners saw the executions in a reflection in a mirror after a preacher, praying on the gallows about the results of sinfulness, suggested that the executions be seen "as in a looking glass."[18]

Lucinda Tisdale's hanging in Kingstree, South Carolina, in 1882 made page 1 of the *Atlanta Constitution*, but again it perhaps was because of the novelty of four people being executed on the same day, all in Kingstree. Tisdale and Anderson Singleton hanged for killing Tisdale's sister—Singleton's wife—Phoebie. Two men hanged for arson and robbery.

The *Constitution* called Singleton "a prosperous and respectable colored farmer," who had become bad when he came under the influence of Lucinda, "an ebon-hued siren" who moved in with the Singletons and quickly trapped him "in the meshes of her fascinations." The newspaper described the sisters as Singleton's concubines despite Phoebie being his wife, although the newspaper said they had wed "after the fashion common among negroes of this part of South Carolina, that is, she was domiciled in his house without any formal marital rites." Singleton denied involvement in the murder, but was convicted after a jury deliberated only twenty minutes. Lucinda later professed that Singleton was guiltless and

17. "Women Hanged for Murder," *Roanoke Times,* 23 January 1892; "A Day of Hangings," *Raleigh News and Observer,* 23 January 1892.

18. "A Double Execution," *Richmond Times-Dispatch,* 23 January 1892; "The Negroes Excited," ibid., 24 January 1892.

she had murdered her sister. "Of course, this statement was not believed," the *Constitution* reported. The newspaper described her as frivolous and "a bad, vicious woman" with "a black, muddy complexion." She "was wholly devoid of the sense of fear or shame."[19]

An Interracial Love Affair

A story about Ann Hunt's hanging in Elberton, Georgia, in 1874 had interracial love as a theme, something that was bound to attract press attention in the South. She was described as a "bright, warm-blooded girl" and a "mulatto," who had "acquired a terrible, all-absorbing passion" for John R. Fortson, "a young man of highly respectable white parentage" with whom Hunt lived. The *Atlanta Constitution* identified the two as lovers. Hunt hanged for her part in poisoning Eliza Brawner. The *Constitution* said the motive was the jealousy of a shunned woman, which "knew no bounds."

Ann Hunt, about twenty-five, reportedly had four or five children by Fortson, who was indicted as an accessory to murder, but "fled the country." Hunt reportedly gave a flask filled with whiskey and strychnine to a friend, America Burden, to give to Eliza Brawner at a party. Burden was arrested the next day and confessed; however, Hunt hid for two or three weeks, "secreted up in the chimney" of Fortson's house before being found. The newspaper said public opinion had Hunt as the primary instigator and Burden as "the silly dupe."

The two attempted to escape from the local jail but were discovered and chained around their necks, with a chain fastened to the floor. The chains were secured with a "strong padlock." The *Constitution* matter-of-factly reported that Hunt and Burden had used "a small rock, a piece of stick and a string" to break the locks from their necks, and reached through the bars and "broke the strong padlock" on their cell door. Authorities recaptured Burden within a week and Hunt within about three weeks. Hunt's hanging constituted a minor part of a lengthy story that recounted all aspects of the crime. The *Constitution* reported that a large crowd watched the hanging and that the "colored man and brother" attended by the thousands.[20]

Large Crowds at Hangings

Other Georgia hangings of black women sometimes attracted enormous crowds. The *Constitution* said an estimated thirty-five hundred to four

---

19. "Four on the Gallows," *Atlanta Constitution*, 24 June 1882.
20. "The Gibbett," ibid., 2 May 1874.

thousand people witnessed the 19 October 1883 hanging of Margaret Harris in Calhoun, Georgia. "Those living at a distance from here came in last night, some even camping on the road. They began to come in long lines of wagons, carriages, buggies, horses and on foot, until by 10 o'clock there was such a crowd as Calhoun has not seen for years." Many of the curious were women who "evinced as much curiosity to see the revolting sight as the men, many of them sitting near the gallows for two and three hours so as to get an unobstructed view." Harris, reportedly only eighteen years old when hanged, was executed for the poison murder of a child, Lela Lewis.

The *Atlanta Constitution* reported that Harris said in her gallows speech: "I am now going to tell the truth. Before God I am innocent of this crime." The *Constitution* said her speech rambled, "and she repeated some sentences over and over." The published part of her speech seemed eloquent, passionate, and grammatical, but other parts of the story made her seem naive, superstitious, and ignorant. The newspaper noticed that she "did not seem to comprehend the enormity of her crime."

The story recounted that she had first tried to murder a woman who raised her "from a babe" because the woman opposed her desire to marry. Harris, the story said, tried to "conjure" the woman's death by placing white beans into a bottle of water and burying the bottle with the neck down. When the beans swelled, the woman was to become sick, and when the beans burst, she was to burst as well. When the bean and water conjure did not work, Harris resorted to poison.

Her execution must have been controversial because the story said that fifty men armed with double-barreled shotguns had escorted her from the jail to the gallows. Later in the story, the newspaper noted that officials suspected an attempt "would be made by the negroes to rescue her." The story never indicated if the victim was white, but one might suspect so, given the report of a possible attempt by blacks to rescue Harris and the heavily armed guards.

The *Atlanta Constitution* described Harris as "coal black" and "heavily built," with a face "not pleasant to look upon." The story added: "[S]he has very large hands and feet, which make her appearance even worse looking." Harris's hanging was the first in Gordon County, Georgia, since 1857, when a crowd of seven thousand reportedly attended the hanging of a man named Hawkins.[21]

Hangings were private in 1895, when Mandy Cody and a man named Florence English hanged in Warrenton, Georgia, but that did not deter some two thousand people from gathering around the jail, the *Constitution* reported, adding that Cody was the first woman ever hanged in War-

21. "Three Necks Twisted," ibid., 20 October 1883.

ren County. The paper asserted that English and Cody were having an affair and had killed her husband, Cicero. They took his body to a swamp and buried it, but about three weeks later, English told his mother, "who, to the surprise of all, told it to the white people living near."[22]

Despite the large crowds and apparent public interest, few executions of blacks in Georgia received the press coverage given to the hanging of a white woman, Susan Eberhart. Even white women's commutations attracted a lot of press coverage in the *Constitution*, as was the case for Ida Hughes in 1925.[23]

Executing a Teenager

The *New Orleans Daily Picayune*, in an 1888 story about the hanging of Pauline McCoy, reported that McCoy was the third woman hanged in Alabama since it became a state in 1818. The newspaper reported that McCoy, a nineteen-year-old black woman, "broke down completely" on the scaffold. She had not eaten for two days and was "kept up" by the use of stimulants. The *Picayune* declared of the murder: "The crime for which the woman was hanged had not its equal in the whole criminal history of Alabama." McCoy had reportedly murdered Annie Jordan—fourteen or sixteen, depending on conflicting news accounts—a white child. Jordan had "strayed away from her home in Montgomery" and was not seen alive again. McCoy was found wearing Jordan's clothing, and reportedly killed her for a pair of red shoes. Years later, the *Birmingham News* termed Jordan "subject to mental aberrations," and the *Picayune* said she was "demented."[24]

22. "Two Necks Broken," ibid., 23 November 1895.

23. "Woman Murderer Escapes Gallows," ibid., 12 April 1925.

24. "Alabama, Montgomery: Execution of Pauline McCoy, the First Woman Hanged in Alabama Since the War—She Murdered a Little Girl for Her Clothes," *New Orleans Daily Picayune*, 13 October 1888; "Woman's Execution to Be Third in Alabama," *Birmingham News*, 5 January 1930.

Chapter 9

Twentieth-Century Black Defendants

THE LOPSIDED EXECUTION RATE OF minorities continued well into the twentieth century in almost all southern states. This imbalance began to change after the United States Supreme Court declared the death penalty as practiced unconstitutional in 1972, but some change had begun even earlier after the passage of the federal Voting Rights Act in the mid-1960s. The act resulted in increased black (read minority) political power, which meant greater political pressure on officeholders but, more important, more minority officeholders.[1] This act, coupled with the Supreme Court's decision about minority exclusion on capital punishment–case juries, surely had an effect on who was executed, and on the geography of executions.

Today, minorities are overrepresented on death rows, and have historically been overrepresented among those executed. Someone is much more likely to be sentenced to death for killing a white person than for killing a black person. Nonetheless, not many black women were executed in the twentieth century. However, among those executed were some teenagers.

Executing a Minor in Virginia

The last execution of a woman in Virginia was controversial outside the state but drew little press interest in Virginia. The victim was white, prominent, and murdered in a horrible way; the defendant was black and seventeen years old when executed. Nonetheless, the *Richmond Times-Dispatch* ran the story about the murder well inside the newspaper, and

---

1. For a description of this effect in the Deep South, see Robert Dallek, *Flawed Giant: Lyndon Johnson and His Times, 1961–1973*, 220–21.

both the *Times-Dispatch* and the *Virginian Pilot and Norfolk Landmark* buried the execution stories.

On 16 August 1912, five months after the crime, Virginia Christian became the only woman ever to die in Virginia's electric chair. Virginia's leading newspapers were defensive about the "northern" press and others meddling in the state's affairs.[2]

The victim, Ida Belote, was the mother of eight children, the daughter of "a former prominent merchant" of Hampton, and "a member of a well-known family" there. The *Times-Dispatch* reported that Belote was "knocked in the head" and a towel was stuffed down her throat, strangling her. She had "had some trouble" with Christian and had "threatened to have the negress arrested on a charge of petty larceny." Although the murder "caused a great sensation in this section," the story ran on page 11, near the back of the newspaper, and the story the next day about Christian's arrest ran on page 3. The first story said police found Belote's pocketbook tied to Christian's body, and bloody clothing "which the negress is said to have worn was also found in her home." According to the newspaper, the police announced that "the woman is guilty of the brutal murder, and that the evidence to-morrow before the coroner's jury will be convincing of that fact." Police alleged "spitefulness and robbery" were the motives for the crime.[3]

Following her conviction, the case attracted much interest in Chicago, where the *Chicago Examiner,* the *Chicago World,* and the *Chicago Defender* all asked the governor of Virginia to commute Christian's sentence. The *Defender,* a black-owned newspaper, editorialized that there had never been such an impassioned plea as that by Val Putnam, managing editor for the *World.* The *Defender* said Putnam argued that the execution would be a blot on the state of Virginia, on the administration of Governor Mann, and on civilization. He said the old law of an eye for an eye was not applicable in the twentieth century. The *Defender* asserted that Christian had committed a horrible crime and should pay for it with life imprisonment. However, the paper also contended she should not be executed because she was so young, was illiterate, and "had no kindly hand to guide her and since birth was immersed in the ignorance and darkness of a little cabin at Hampton, Va." The *Defender* argued that the state and the society were in part responsible for Christian's lot in life.[4]

The *Richmond Times-Dispatch* derided the Chicago press and the efforts of northerners who came to plead with Governor Mann for Christian's

2. This theme has resonated in the southern states, especially Virginia, since early in U.S. history. See Forrest McDonald, *States' Rights and the Union.*

3. "Woman Is Murdered in Home at Hampton," *Richmond Times-Dispatch,* 19 March 1912; "Negro Woman Is Held for Murder," ibid., 20 March 1912.

4. Editorial, *Chicago Defender,* 17 August 1912.

life. The *Times-Dispatch* called the *Chicago Examiner* a newspaper that "specializes in sob stuff and human emotions." The *Examiner* sent Chicago attorney W. J. Anderson to plead with Governor Mann, and the *Times-Dispatch* satirically wrote that Anderson was known as "Habeas Corpus" because he was "an exponent of forlorn hopes."[5]

The *Times-Dispatch* resented a Chicagoan proposing that an alienist from Chicago be allowed to examine Christian. The governor declined, maintaining that if Virginia needed an alienist, it would provide its own.[6]

Although the governor and the *Times-Dispatch* stressed that race had nothing to do with the upcoming execution, coverage in the newspaper indicates otherwise; it also indicates how differently white Virginians and black Chicagoans saw the world. In two stories prior to Anderson's visit to Richmond, the *Times-Dispatch* referred to him in derogatory terms but gave him a prominent position in stories and depicted him as a clever attorney. "This attorney is said to have a reputation for snatching criminals from the deaths which await them. Just what arts he will bring to bear on the Governor remains to be seen." When Anderson arrived, the *Times-Dispatch* summarily dismissed him in a short paragraph: "The representative of Chicago people, heralded by a newspaper of that city, arrived yesterday and saw the Governor. He turned out to be a negro. Governor Mann heard him through."[7] Anderson was not mentioned again.

The newspaper said local "colored lawyers" had tried to save Christian, and the governor had granted her a reprieve based upon requests from her attorney "and other representatives of the colored race." The *Times-Dispatch* blamed the Chicago newspapers for what it called the erroneous opinion that nothing had been done for Christian. "To the contrary, colored people of Hampton and Newport News have put forth many efforts in her behalf." The newspaper noted that "colored" ministers had visited Christian and that "two preachers of her race" attended to her in her last hours. Governor Mann said he did not consider matters of race or gender because "no distinctions are made by law."[8]

Governor Mann and the *Times-Dispatch* deflected criticism by repeatedly stressing the heinous nature of Christian's crime, which they described as one of the most horrible in the state's history. The newspaper dismissed the argument that Christian was too young to be sentenced to death, saying "the murder which she committed might have been the product of the most fiendish mature mind." The *Times-Dispatch* termed

5. "Newspaper Would Save Girl's Life," *Richmond Times-Dispatch,* 14 August 1912.
6. *Alienist* is a term used to describe a doctor who has been accepted by a court of law as an expert to determine the mental condition of a defendant or witness. "Ask Respite for Young Murderess," ibid., 15 August 1912.
7. Ibid; "Christian Girl Must Die To-Day," ibid., 16 August 1912.
8. "Ask Respite"; "Negro Girl Pays Death Penalty," ibid., 17 August 1912.

her "stoical" and indifferent to her fate because, the newspaper speculated, she "possesses little sensibility."[9]

In a curious editorial, the *Times-Dispatch* noted sentiment against the death penalty was increasing, and there was a natural human revulsion at killing another human being. The editorial seemed to agree with the Chicago press, which partly blamed the state of Virginia for Christian's actions. Society "also knows that often by its own failure to provide education and social control, it has been a partner in the crimes of ignorance and unmorality." Nonetheless, the newspaper added that arguments about capital punishment might produce ways to protect society by restraint and punishment; therefore, executions accomplished more than mere revenge.[10]

Early on 16 August 1912, Christian died in the electric chair. Although the *Times-Dispatch* reported the first electric shock had killed her, she was given two additional shocks "as a matter of precaution," which seems unnecessary if a doctor had examined her and pronounced her dead.

The *Richmond Times-Dispatch* ran the story about the execution of a seventeen-year-old girl who was the first female to die in Virginia's electric chair, and who was the subject of controversy as far away as Chicago, under a one-column headline on the last page. The newspaper that served her hometown of Hampton reported her death under a one-column headline on page 5.[11]

Gassing Teenagers in North Carolina

North Carolina executed Bessie Mae Williams, nineteen, and Ralph Thompson, eighteen, on 29 December 1944 for murdering a Charlotte taxi driver. A third person, Annie Mae Allison, fifteen, had her death sentence commuted because she was only fourteen when the crime was committed.[12]

Williams and Thompson were among eight North Carolina defendants scheduled to be executed on the same day, only two of whom were more than twenty years old. That fact caused controversy. News accounts said the Reverend Allyn P. Robinson, in his Christmas Eve sermon, had urged Gov. J. Melville Broughton to commute the sentences of the two youngest

9. "Woman Must Die in Electric Chair," ibid., 6 August 1912; "Negro Girl to Die in Electric Chair," ibid., 19 July 1912; "Ask Respite."

10. "Shall Society Kill?" ibid., 14 August 1912.

11. "Negro Girl Pays Death Penalty"; "Negress Dies for Brutal Crime," *Virginian Pilot and Norfolk Landmark,* 17 August 1912.

12. "Governor Commutes Sentence of One of Taxi Slayers," *Charlotte Observer,* 28 December 1944.

defendants, who were fifteen. Robinson said even North Carolinians who supported executing adults "are disturbed by the thought that our state should take the lives of children, whatever their crime. I think these children on Death Row are something for us to ponder at Christmas time." The governor refused to intervene in Williams's or Thompson's execution, saying they had previous records of serious crimes, they understood their crime, and the crime was especially heinous.[13]

Williams denied killing the taxi driver. She admitted she had taken one dollar off the taxicab seat but said she had not "cut" the driver. In the Associated Press story, the wire service did not refer to her by her last name on subsequent references, as it did others, but instead referred to her as "Bessie Mae." The execution story ran on page 5 of the *Charlotte Observer*, and on page 10, the last page, of the *Raleigh News and Observer*.[14]

Reports of Voodoo and Superstitions

Rosanna Lightner Phillips was the first woman executed by the State of North Carolina, according to several news sources. She and her husband died the same day, 1 January 1943, in North Carolina's gas chamber. The story about their executions ran on the last page of the *Raleigh News and Observer*, where Central Prison is located. They died for the 3 August 1942 ax murder of a Durham farmer, who was the couple's landlord. The *Durham Morning Herald* published an Associated Press account of the execution on page 1.[15]

Some of Daniel and Rosanna Phillips's coverage had racial overtones. A United Press International (UPI) story based on an interview with the defendants one day before their executions relied heavily on black dialect, using "de" for "the," and forms such as "'cause," "'cept'n," and "'bout" for "because," "except," and "about." Although the dialect might have been correctly quoted, no groups other than blacks were usually quoted in dialect, and usually the stories were derisive.

13. "Execution of Minors Protested by Pastor," *Raleigh News and Observer*, 25 December 1944; "Young Negro Girl Saved from Execution by State," ibid., 28 December 1944.

14. "Two Executed for Murder of Minyard, Charlotte Cab Driver," *Charlotte Observer*, 30 December 1944; "Three Executed in Gas Chamber," *Raleigh News and Observer*, 30 December 1944.

15. "Woman and Husband Die in Gas Chamber at Prison," *Raleigh News and Observer*, 2 January 1943; "Negroes Die for Watkins Slaying," *Durham Morning Herald*, 2 January 1943. The stories noted that several women had been executed in North Carolina, when the counties had been responsible for the executions. See, for example, "Caroline Shipp Hanged," *Charlotte Chronicle*, 23 January 1892. Shipp, described as "barely 20 years old," was a black woman convicted of poisoning her eleven-month-old baby. On the gallows she denied the killing, saying her paramour, Mack Farrar, had committed the crime.

The story and headline prominently featured an angle about voodoo. Rosanna Phillips said her husband had put a spell on her, and Daniel Phillips claimed that someone not named in the story had put a spell on him in South Carolina, where they went after the murder. The UPI writer referred to Daniel Phillips as a "boy," although he was twenty-nine years old.[16]

North Carolina governor J. Melville Broughton noted that Daniel and Rosanna Phillips had lived in adultery for almost three years, marrying two days after the murder. Adultery was not a capital offense in North Carolina. The governor rejected the idea that women should not face the death penalty, which he said was the only reason given in Rosanna Phillips's clemency requests.[17]

The *Raleigh News and Observer*'s execution story did not mention a problem with the mechanism that drops the cyanide capsules. However, an article in the *Columbia (S.C.) State* said the mechanism had failed during Rosanna's Phillips's execution, and guards had to enter the chamber and adjust it.[18]

Executing someone on New Year's Day might seem an odd way to bring in the new year. However, the *News and Observer* explained that when the state supreme court denied appeals, the execution date was automatically set for 1 January.

Following the executions, some people said the electric chair in North Carolina should be brought back. Central Prison warden Ralph R. McLean favored the more humane gas chamber and threatened to quit if the state brought back the chair. The headline on a story detailing McLean's remarks must stand as one of the great examples of double entendre: "NC Pen Head to Quit If Electric Chair Came Back."[19]

Differences in Coverage for Blacks and Whites

Like the coverage for Rosanna Phillips, the coverage of the 17 January 1947 execution of Rose Stinnette in South Carolina shows how differently the press treated white and black defendants in news stories, even when the supposedly objective Associated Press wrote the stories.

The *Florence (S.C.) Morning News* never gave especially prominent coverage to Stinnette, despite her being "the first Negro woman to die in the

16. "Negroes to Die Friday, Put Blame on Voodooism," *Raleigh News and Observer*, 31 December 1942.
17. "No Intervention," ibid.
18. "Woman and Husband Die in Gas Chamber at Prison," *Raleigh News and Observer*, 2 January 1943; "NC Executes First Woman," *Columbia (S.C.) State*, 2 January 1943.
19. "Pen Head to Quit," *Columbia (S.C.) State*, 12 January 1943.

electric chair" in South Carolina and the first black woman executed in South Carolina since the late 1800s. Stinnette committed her crime in Florence County, making the story local for the *Morning News.* Nonetheless, the paper relied solely on AP stories. Stories about Stinnette did play on the front page, but always under a one-column headline.

Sue Logue, a white woman, electrocuted in South Carolina in 1943, was the first woman "to expire" in South Carolina's chair. Stinnette's and Logue's executions were covered differently.

Rose Stinnette and Roy Singletary died for bludgeoning to death Stinnette's husband. The AP stories said Rose Stinnette was married, but the wire service did not refer to her as "Mrs. Rose Marie Stinnette" or "Mrs. Stinnette"; references always were to "Rose Marie" or "the Stinnette woman." In contrast, when the AP mentioned Sue Logue in background for several of the stories about Stinnette, she was always referred to as "Mrs. Sue Logue." The AP also referred to Stinnette as the "Florence Negress."[20]

Stinnette's bizarre execution received little news play. When officials threw the switch, a fuse blew, leaving the room in darkness. The AP reported the macabre scene matter-of-factly: "Witnesses then saw sparks from the woman's head and arms dimly illuminate the death scene, before somebody struck a match to provide more light." Likewise, the news article did not make much of the fact that eleven of the twelve trial-court jurors had sought clemency for Stinnette and Singletary. Singletary received a commutation, but Stinnette did not. The governor later said he had commuted Singletary's sentence because Stinnette had exonerated him and because the trial jurors requested clemency. Rose Stinnette died claiming she was innocent.[21]

Relative of Murder Victim Writes News Story

The *Birmingham News*'s report about the electrocution of Selina Gilmore in Alabama in January 1930 ran as a news story but read like an opinion piece. It probably read that way because the victim's uncle wrote it. The headline was: "Uncle of Slain Restaurant Waiter Watches Negro Woman Burn for It." The story's lead was: "I am the uncle of Horace Johnson. . . .

20. "Florence Negroess Goes to Electric Chair Today," *Florence (S.C.) Morning News,* 17 January 1947. Willie Morris notes that when he grew up in Mississippi in the 1940s, it was assumed that no white person, however young, would address any black person as "ma'am" or "sir" (*North toward Home,* 78).

21. "Williams Refers Florence Case to Judge Lide," *Florence (S.C.) Morning News,* 7 January 1947; "Florence Negroess"; "Florence Negress Dies in Chair," ibid., 18 January 1947.

Friday morning I saw Selina Gilmore sit in the death chair at Kilby Prison. I could have reached out my hand and touched her as the 2,300 volts crackled through her rigid body. A great relief has come into my heart."

The emotional and gruesome story made it evident that the uncle relished his chance to watch Gilmore die. He said she had run after killing his nephew, but she could not run once strapped into the electric chair: "She sat there bound by 10 straps while the current burned through her. I watched the blue coil of smoke rise from her shaved head and I smelled the odor of singed flesh. A great peace has come over me."

The writer worried that Gilmore had died too quickly and did not suffer enough, as he claimed his nephew had suffered before dying. The story said Gilmore had walked calmly and unassisted to the chair. The uncle noted that Gilmore had not died after the first electrical shock, and a doctor checked to see if her heart was still beating. Her head moved twice, and her chest rose and fell as if it were "a great puff of wind bursting out from tortured lungs." After another jolt of electricity, a witness clasped his hand over his mouth and ran out. The story ended with these words: "My peace is disturbed only by the fear that maybe they might be able to do something to bring her back to life again. But I don't believe they're smart enough for that."

Despite Gilmore being the first woman to die in the state's electric chair, during the month prior to the execution only three stories ran in the *News*. None was detailed, and none ran prominently in the newspaper.

Gilmore and her victim, Horace Johnson, died because she had reportedly come into a restaurant and ordered sandwiches, brains, and eggs. She got the sandwiches, but the other items had to be cooked. While she was waiting, she became loud and was asked to leave. She returned with a shotgun, cornered Johnson behind the counter, and shot him, opening a "great gaping hole in his side."[22] Johnson and Gilmore died over an argument about brains and eggs.

Mississippi Executes Four

Although not many black women were executed in the twentieth century, Mississippi executed four. At least three things had changed for Mississippi black women since the nineteenth century: executions were private, which meant any "lessons" for the black populace had to come through mass media; stories about the executions received more prominent display and were more detailed; and stories were less opinionated.

It is hard to say why the coverage increased. It is doubtful that white Mississippians held black Mississippians in higher esteem in the 1920s,

22. "Uncle Watches," *Birmingham News*, 24 January 1930.

1930s, and 1940s than in the 1830s or 1860s. All four women were executed with a male defendant, which might have influenced the twentieth-century coverage. Technology also made news coverage quicker and easier, and wire services made accounts of executions available to more people and in a wider area. Whatever the reasons, the executions received more coverage than executions of black women in most other states, including those in the North.

In 1922, Pattie Perdue hanged in Forest, Mississippi, and Ann Knight hanged in Leakesville, in Greene County. Perdue and Knight both claimed innocence on the gallows.

Pattie Perdue and Leon Viverett hanged for murdering a white man in August 1921. The *Forest (Miss.) News Register* reported they had murdered the man, cut up his body, and burned as much of it as they could. They took the remains to a "negro cemetery," where they opened a grave and buried them. The newspaper said lynching threats had been made.[23] Although the hangings occurred near Jackson, there were no news stories in the Jackson newspapers.

Ann Knight and Will Grey hanged for murdering Knight's husband. The *Greene County (Miss.) Herald* made much of how long it took for them to die; Knight died in eleven minutes and Grey in fourteen minutes. "We mention this because some got it mixed and thought that Ann was longer in dying than Will when the reverse was the case." The *Herald* also reported that although Grey's neck was broken during the hanging, it was unclear for Knight because she had "a fat neck." The *Herald* assured readers that even if her neck was not broken, "a vertebra likely slipped" because she died so quickly, although eleven minutes does not indicate a quick death.

The newspaper gave a detailed and graphic description of the hangings, and dramatically reported the scene when the sheriff gave the word to spring the trap to hang Knight. "Both those inside and out of the jail heard the ominous sound of those two metal leaves seperating [sic] as the body darted down to death, the fall being broken as the length of the rope was reached by the jerk on the condemned one's neck."

The story said Grey had claimed his mother was "half Indian" and his father was Italian, but Grey "showed the negro in hair, nose, etc." The story also referred to both Knight and Grey as "colored."[24]

The 1937 hangings of Mary Holmes, thirty-five, and Selmon Brooks, thirty-two, received widespread coverage in newspapers in Jackson, Greenville, and Vicksburg, and in the local *Rolling Fork (Miss.) Deer Creek*

23. "Double Execution Today, Two Negroes Hanged," *Forest (Miss.) News Register,* 13 January 1922.
24. "Double Execution in Leakesville," *Greene County (Miss.) Herald,* 20 October 1922.

Pilot. Holmes and Brooks hanged for murdering prominent Sharkey County planter E. W. Cook in his home, where Holmes was a cook and a trusted employee, the *Pilot* reported. The newspaper said she was the first woman ever to hang in Sharkey County, adding to the news value.

The *Pilot*'s news story provided a moral message, noting that although the two cleverly planned the murder, "there are loopholes, and more than one of these loopholes proved their undoing, which clearly demonstrates once more that 'crime does not pay.'"[25] Holmes and Brooks murdered Cook when he returned home while they were burglarizing it. They set fire to the home, which caused the newspapers to term the crime a "torch murder," although the story indicated Cook had died from the blow to the head, not from the fire.

One of the state's leading newspapers, the *Jackson Clarion-Ledger*, editorialized about the hangings, although it did not mention the defendants' names. It said that although Mississippi had hanged few women, "this one deserved it" because she had betrayed a friendship. The editorial praised Mississippians for not lynching Holmes and Brooks, which the newspaper made seem remarkable.[26] The *Clarion-Ledger* ran the story about the hangings on page 12, but the executions were front-page news in the *Greenville (Miss.) Delta Star*, and in Rolling Fork and Vicksburg. The *Pilot* ran by far the most detailed account.

Mildred James is the only woman electrocuted in Mississippi, which substituted electrocution for hanging in 1940. She is also the last woman executed there.[27]

Mildred James and James S. Hughes were executed on 19 May 1944 for unrelated crimes. She died for murdering a local woman. The executions were in Vicksburg, and the *Vicksburg Evening Post* and the *Jackson Clarion-Ledger* played the story on the front page, which was unusual because

25. "Torch Murders [sic] of Mr. E. W. Cook Executed," *Rolling Fork (Miss.) Deer Creek Pilot*, 30 April 1937.

26. "Justice Is Again Done without Resort to Mobbery," *Jackson Clarion-Ledger*, 30 April 1937.

27. From 1940 to 1955, the state hauled a portable electric chair from county to county; a central execution site at Parchman Farm opened in 1955. The history of Mississippi's electric chair is bizarre because Gov. Paul Johnson fired the first executioner, Jimmy Thompson, an ex-convict and a former vaudevillian, in 1943 because he reportedly drank too much after executions. The *Jackson Daily News*, in an editorial on 11 February 1943, sniffed that Thompson was a far better man than were some of his critics, an obvious dart at Johnson. The *Daily News* defended Thompson, saying he had been "cast adrift in a cold and cruel world where he has small chance to get a job in a similar capacity." The newspaper said that perhaps Johnson lost his temper because he believed it was "highly disgraceful . . . for Jimmy to soothe his jangled nerves with a few alcoholic libations after each successful performance of the electric chair." Still, the newspaper defended Thompson, saying, "He always got drunk after performing his ghastly job, never before, and he was always duly repentant during the sobering-up process."

many executions during World War II received little coverage. Influencing the news play were the facts that James was the first woman electrocuted in the state and that Hughes was white and had murdered a police officer. In the South, a black and a white were almost never executed on the same day. Mississippi reportedly did not hang white and black men together until 1902.[28]

Both the Jackson and Vicksburg newspapers termed James's and Hughes's murders two of the "most sensational" in Warren County in years. James died for murdering Nannie Conklin, whom both newspapers called "an aged spinster." The execution stories in both newspapers were straightforward, containing the usual cliché coverage.[29]

Little Coverage in Atlanta

The Atlanta press did not give much coverage to the first woman to die in Georgia's electric chair. The story about Lena Baker's death ran one paragraph on page 8 of the 6 March 1945 edition of the *Atlanta Constitution*, buried amid advertisements and the radio program listings.[30]

War news dominated the front page: the Allied drive into Cologne, Germany, led on the front page. Stories about condemned defendants commonly received less press coverage during the war, which nonetheless does not entirely explain the skimpy coverage for Baker. Three days earlier, Georgia executed two men, one white and one black. The story ran at the top of page 3 under a two-column headline. Most of the story concerned the execution of the white man, Walter Fowler. Willie Jackson, the black man, received one sentence.[31] Baker received far less press attention than did some of her nineteenth-century black counterparts in Georgia.

Little Coverage in Northern States

Black women executed in southern states were not the only ones who received less press coverage than their white counterparts. Helen Fowler, the next-to-last woman executed in New York, could be termed the "forgotten woman" among those women executed. The lack of press attention to her crime, trial, and execution can in part be attributed to war cover-

---

28. "Mathis and Lester Hung," *Oxford (Miss.) Eagle,* 25 September 1902.
29. "Vicksburg Murderers Pay Death Penalty," *Jackson Clarion-Ledger,* 20 May 1944; "Two Executed This Morning in Local Jail," *Vicksburg (Miss.) Evening Post,* 19 May 1944.
30. "Georgia 'Chair' Takes First Woman Victim," *Atlanta Constitution,* 6 March 1945.
31. "Two Men Electrocuted at Tattnall Prison," ibid., 3 March 1945.

age. At about the time of her execution, Gen. George Patton and the Third Army were less than a mile from the German border. Still, New York had not executed an African American woman since about the mid-1850s or earlier.

Helen Fowler, thirty-six, and her accomplice, George Knight, died for murdering George Fowler (no relation), a white man whom they had killed during a robbery, according to the *New York Times.* The *Times* ran no stories about the crime, or about the arrests or trials for Fowler and Knight. The first story ran on 22 February 1944 on page 25 under a one-column headline, and it said Fowler had been "admitted" to Sing Sing Prison. The story gave almost no background about the murder, not even the date. The *Times* next reported about Fowler on 4 October 1944, saying she was to die in the state's electric chair the next day. The story ran under a one-column headline on page 38, the last page. Fowler was not executed on 5 October. The three-paragraph story about her execution ran on page 13 under a one-column headline. It was a "special" to the *Times,* meaning that the newspaper did not staff the execution.[32]

Pennsylvania executed Corrine Sykes, twenty-two, on 13 October 1946. The story ran on page 1 of the *Philadelphia Inquirer,* but the execution did not receive especially prominent news play. The *Inquirer* erroneously said Sykes was the second woman Pennsylvania ever executed, but should have said she was the second ever electrocuted. The unembellished story said Sykes had made no final statement, and she was almost late for her execution because on the way from Philadelphia, where she was jailed, to Rockview Prison, one of the car's tires blew out.

Sykes died for stabbing to death a Philadelphia woman—for whom she worked for a short time as a "domestic servant"—during a robbery that netted her two thousand dollars in jewelry. Sykes's attorneys appealed her death sentence, saying she was mentally incompetent. Because she was female, the state agreed to shave only a spot on the back of her head for the electrodes to make contact, according to the *Inquirer.*[33]

32. "Woman in Death House," *New York Times,* 22 February 1944; "Woman to Go to Sing Sing Chair," ibid., 4 October 1944; "Woman Goes to Chair," ibid., 17 November 1944.

33. "Corrine Sykes Dies in Chair at Rockview," *Philadelphia Inquirer,* 14 October 1946. Another woman, Shellie McKeithen, is listed as having been executed in Pennsylvania on 7 January 1946, but I could find no information about the execution. The source gives no race for McKeithen, either. See http://www.deathpenaltyinfo. org/WomenExecuted.html.

Chapter 10

The Irish

More Animal Than Human?

A FEW DAYS BEFORE NEW JERSEY executed Bridget Durgan, newspapers in that state and in nearby New York City ran an article describing her as "on the very lowest level" of human intelligence. She concealed her real actions, as did "the fox, the panther, and many inferior animals, whose instincts are more clearly defined than are those of Bridget Durgan." Her head revealed "her strong animal organization," because "she is large in the base of the brain, and swells out over the ears, where destructiveness and secretiveness are located by phrenologists, while the whole region of intellect, ideality and moral sentiment is small." Durgan's eyes winked and wavered constantly, and they "open across, not below, the ball, and the pupil is uncommonly small. . . . It is purely the eye of a reptile in shape and expression."[1]

Killing a human being is more acceptable if the person killed is perceived as less than human. This is true with war or capital punishment. If the public perceives a condemned inmate as more animal than human, then executions are made more palatable. The press plays an important role in this process because most of what the public knows about a condemned defendant, it learns through press reports. How the press "labels" and describes defendants probably are important, especially before trial. Some researchers contend that most people believe that press descriptions of defendants are real and accurate.[2]

The "human garbage" concept has been controversial for hundreds of years. Saint Augustine, one theologian asserts, showed that a condemned person "cannot simply be abandoned to cruel fate like an animal marked for slaughter." Some scholars say news stories have portrayed defendants as psychotic killers, or as normal persons who in reality are maddened,

---

1. "Mrs. Elizabeth Oakes Smith's Account of a Visit to Bridget Durgan—Her Impressions of the Woman," *New York Times*, 25 August 1867; "Bridget Dergan [*sic*]," *New Brunswick Weekly Freedonian*, 29 August 1867.
2. Surrette, "Media Trials," 293.

dangerous killers. One study of Alabama death row inmates revealed that news stories often depict capital offenders as animals or psychopathic killers. News stories described the inmates as "kill crazy," or "sex maddened," although the study showed most of them were not psychotic at the time of their crimes. Another study indicated that some crime news consists of "moral-character portraits" of criminals or "demon criminals," or defendants characterized as "less than human."[3]

Some groups, such as African Americans, have been characterized as more animal than human. Even worse, "studies" were used to support the characterizations, or politicians used the claims to appeal to voters' racial prejudice. David Oshinsky describes some of these early works that labeled blacks "purely animal," or as part of "a wild and tropical race." Minorities, especially African Americans, have more often been executed than whites. However, other groups have also been stereotyped as less than human. Anarchists, mainly immigrants, have been subjects of a public relations campaign in the press and in the pulpit that dehumanized them and termed them criminals, aliens, and madmen.[4]

The Irish, for a time, were stereotyped as savage. Thomas Cahill recalls that British prime minister Benjamin Disraeli described the Irish as a "wild, reckless, indolent, uncertain and superstitious race." Cahill notes that Charles Kingsley, commenting on the famine he saw in Victorian Ireland, called the Irish "human chimpanzees." Kingsley said that seeing "white chimpanzees is dreadful; if they were black, one would not feel it so much." Likewise, the Irish suffered prejudice in the United States. Cahill quotes a distinguished Princeton historian who admitted that prejudices against Roman Catholic culture "persisted in American universities until an uncomfortably recent date." R. F. Foster recalls that Evelyn Waugh once said that "to the Irishman there were only two final realities: Hell and the United States." By the mid-1800s, Irish Catholics emigrated mainly to the United States, and they became easy targets for American nativist and anti-Catholic prejudice: "A 'savage' stereotype was created and in some ways remained."[5]

Among those women executed in the United States in the mid-nineteenth century and early twentieth century were two Irish immigrants: Bridget Durgan, hanged in New Jersey in 1867, and Mary Farmer, electrocuted in New York in 1909.

3. Megivern, *Death Penalty,* 160, 294; Robert Johnson, *Condemned to Die,* 23–24, 35; Ericson, Baranek, and Chan, *Representing Order,* 8, 106.

4. Oshinsky, chap. 4 in *"Worse Than Slavery"*; Paul Avrich, *The Haymarket Tragedy,* 176.

5. Cahill, *How the Irish Saved Civilization,* 6–7; Foster, *Modern Ireland, 1600–1972,* 357–58.

Bridget Durgan: "No More Power to Resist [Her Ferocious Instincts] Than a Tiger Rolling Itself in the Blood of Its Prey"

Bridget Durgan hanged in New Jersey on 30 August 1867 for murdering her employer's wife.[6] New Jersey physician William Wallace Coriell and his wife had hired Durgan as a servant. She stabbed Mary Ellen Coriell to death and set the house afire. Her execution attracted great newspaper interest, especially from the *New Brunswick Weekly Freedonian*, in which city she hanged. The *New York Times* and the *Philadelphia Inquirer* also closely covered the case, and they were more important because they were close to New Brunswick and had large circulations.

The *Times*'s lead paragraph about the hanging said, "Probably the execution of no person, with the single exception of Mrs. Surratt, has attracted such general attention and interest as hers."[7] (Mary Surratt and three other conspirators were hanged in connection with the assassination of President Abraham Lincoln.) Putting aside whether the *Times*'s comparison was hyperbole, there is no doubt that Durgan's hanging attracted much attention. Many people demanded admission tickets to the "private" hanging.

The *New Brunswick Weekly Freedonian* said up to one hundred people per day came to the jail to see Durgan after her death sentence. These visits, the newspaper reported, "annoyed" the sheriff and jailer. The *Freedonian* noted the sheriff received fifty letters per day asking for admission. He issued about five hundred tickets, but many more people came to see the hanging. The *Freedonian* estimated the crowd outside the jail yard at two thousand, whereas the *Inquirer* guessed there were two to three thousand, "constituting a turbulent and excited mob pressing around the prison walls at all points." The *Inquirer* described the places that provided a view of the hanging as "black with anxious would-be spectators," and commented that "even a number of women, armed with tickets of admittance," were seen trying to get into the prison yard and "witness one of their own sex suffer an ignominious death." The *Inquirer*'s front-page story asserted that hanging a woman was a "very revolting spectacle" but resulted "in the vindication of the law." The *Inquirer*'s story ran at the top of the front page and featured a main headline and seven subordinate headlines, which promised readers information about her "last hours," the "Confession of the Murderess," a description of how "the bloody deed" was done, and "Scenes around the Scaffold."[8]

---

6. The subheading quote is from "Bridget Dergan [*sic*]."
7. "Execution of Bridget Durgan," *New York Times*, 31 August 1867.
8. "Execution of Bridget Dergan [*sic*]," *New Brunswick Weekly Freedonian*, 5 September 1867; "The Gallows," *Philadelphia Inquirer*, 31 August 1867.

Newspapers often called Durgan a fiend. The *Times* called her "a fiend incarnate," and the *Inquirer* asked, "Was ever a fouler, more horrible crime than this committed by a fiend in human shape?" Her crime was heinous. She murdered Coriell when her husband was away. The *Inquirer*'s recount of the crime went into gory detail, describing virtually every knife wound in the "mutilated woman," as well as gouged-out flesh, gaping wounds, and teeth marks on Coriell's face. The *Times* was more discreet, merely saying Coriell had suffered from "half a hundred" wounds, which is about double the number reported by the *Inquirer.* Both the *Times* and the *Inquirer* contended Durgan had murdered Coriell to get her out of the way. The *Inquirer* said Coriell had fired Durgan "because of her want of cleanliness," but allowed her to stay for a few days because she was sick. During that time, Durgan murdered Coriell. The *Inquirer* said Durgan "wished to attain a place in the household that she could not reach while Mrs. Coriell lived." The *Times* reported that Dr. Coriell believed Durgan had killed his wife because she wished to "supplant Mrs. Coriell in his affections." She lived in the Coriell home, according to the *Inquirer,* because she suffered from epilepsy, and Dr. Coriell treated her in his home "in order that he might give her complaint all the necessary attention."[9]

The newspapers most differed about the crowd behavior at the hanging. The *New York Times* described men, women, and children swarming the streets, with some of the men and boys walking about with muskets on their shoulders, shouting, and "having a gay-old pic-nic (without provisions)." The *Times* reported that inside the enclosure where the private hanging was to take place, there was "a crowd of a thousand rough and jostling men, and were it not that the gallows stood before us, [we] could have thought that the gathering was for the purpose of witnessing a race or a prize fight." Officials acted no better, behaving rudely and engaging in "many a private row and scrimmage . . . while the wretched woman was mumbling her prayers in the murderer's cell." People crowded into the jail yard, sat on the jail's roof, looked from jail windows, crowded on the roof of a barn adjacent to the yard, and "overloaded a platform until it broke beneath their weight." The newspaper characterized the men as "profane, indecent and ungentlemanly persons who pushed and hauled, and swore and fought." When officials took Durgan into the jail yard, a scene resulted "such as we hope never again to witness." The crowd pushed for position to see, and men cried out oaths and curses "such as one may hear at a circus." While prayers were being offered on the scaffold, officials fought with the crowd in front. Men shouted for others to get down so they could see, and others shouted that Durgan would not "die game."[10]

9. "Execution of Bridget Durgan"; "The Gallows."
10. "Execution of Bridget Durgan."

The *New Brunswick Weekly Freedonian*'s description of crowd behavior differed sharply. That paper remarked that some people had jostled to get a good place to see the hanging, but everyone settled down once Durgan was on the gallows. The *Freedonian* also mentioned that outside the jail yard, "order generally prevailed."[11]

A *Philadelphia Inquirer* editorial condemned the crowd's behavior, calling it "a disgraceful scene." It complained that the sheriff had given out so many tickets that the hanging was, for all purposes, public. More than one thousand people packed inside were "swearing, fighting and quarreling with the officials who were trying to club them into order. The gathering resembled the rabble brought together to witness a horse race or a prize fight." Outside the jail yard, according to the *Inquirer*, "boys and men walked up and down shouting, hurrahing and otherwise making heartless mirth." Hanging day resembled "a sort of gala day," with hotels and boardinghouses filled as "[t]housands of persons flocked to the city from a distance."[12]

Durgan was hanged on a "jerker," which meant she did not drop through a trap, but instead was "jerked" upward. The *Times* said she never moved a muscle on the gallows. Her only remark was, "Don't let them Protestants know what I say." The *New Brunswick Weekly Freedonian* reported the comment as, "Don't let a Protestant touch me." Part of the *Times*'s lead read, "Bridget Durgen [sic], the New-Jersey murderess, was jerked into eternity yesterday morning, in an unseemly manner," and died after dangling for thirty minutes. The *Inquirer* grotesquely wrote: "The neck was not broken, and she died a rather easy death of strangulation." The *Freedonian*'s graphic description said that shortly after being jerked into the air, Durgan struggled violently, made a gurgling sound, and heaved her breast; her hands turned a dark color. She reportedly died after thirteen minutes, much quicker than the *Times* reported. The *Freedonian* expressed surprise that Durgan had strangled. She weighed about 170 pounds, and it was believed that the "sudden jerk she received would have certainly broken her neck." The newspaper gave its readers a ghastly description of Durgan after she was cut down: her eyes were swollen but not bleeding, although there was bleeding around her mouth, and her face was "discolored and turned quite purple."[13]

She was buried in a Catholic cemetery. Earlier in the week, she requested that no postmortem be performed on her because she knew that after a hanging just days before, the body of Joseph Williams, a "colored

---

11. "Execution of Bridget Dergan [sic]."
12. Editorial, *Philadelphia Inquirer*, 2 September 1867; "The Gallows."
13. "Execution of Bridget Durgan"; "Execution of Bridget Dergan [sic]"; "The Gallows."

man," had been dissected in the jail yard immediately after being cut down from the gallows. The *Freedonian* said about thirty news reporters had covered the hanging, and four had been admitted to her jail cell to observe her last moments.[14]

It is hard to say whether Durgan's Irish heritage had anything to do with how the press described her. The *Times* often called her "an Irish girl," and some descriptions might have fitted the stereotype of Irish immigrants as poor, ignorant, and almost less than human. Irish immigrants were not well regarded in the United States. Millions died or immigrated during the great potato famine of 1845–1849, and many who came to the United States were not welcomed. Irish workers were not well liked because of strikes in several U.S. cities just before and during the Civil War. During a strike in Jersey City, New Jersey, in 1859, Irish workers barricaded railroad tracks they had just built; some workers were arrested and sentenced to lengthy prison terms. City officials termed the Irish workers animals. Durgan denied she was a poor laborer, although she did work as a servant girl, according to the *Times*. She claimed to be from a financially well-off family in Ireland.[15]

The *Times*'s descriptions of her were neither flattering nor overly negative. In a story about the beginning of her murder trial, the *Times* called her "an ordinary looking Irish girl, with plain features that are not very expressive." She dressed plainly and showed no sign of nervousness. A *Times* interview shortly after her conviction, but prior to sentencing, depicted her as generally good-humored and laughing. "She is not hideous as some have painted her in appearance. Still she is by no means attractive." The paper further described her as having a large head; a broad, low forehead; and a full, unexpressive face. She was of medium height and "rather fleshy," and had a "bloated look" caused by a lack of exercise and sunshine. The *Inquirer* also reported she weighed about 150 pounds and was "quite stout and full faced."[16]

The oft-repeated description of Durgan as unemotional contrasted with her behavior when she was sentenced. The judge who sentenced her

14. "Bridget Durgan," *Philadelphia Inquirer,* 29 August 1867; "Execution of Bridget Dergan [*sic*]."
15. "Execution of Bridget Durgan." In general, see Foster, *Modern Ireland, 1600–1972;* and Kerby A. Miller, *Emigrants and Exiles: Ireland and the Irish Exodus to North America,* 322. Some authors say that Irish American participation on the side of the Union during the Civil War alleviated much of the class discrimination (Thomas J. Curran, *Xenophobia and Immigration, 1820–1930*), but others disagree, saying that even during the war, Irish troops were used as fodder in lost-cause battles, and that discrimination continued until well after the war (K. A. Miller, *Emigrants and Exiles,* 322–25).
16. "The Coriell Murder," *New York Times,* 21 May 1867; "The Coriell Murder—Her Appearance and Statements—Important Admissions," ibid., 3 June 1867; "The Gallows."

said her crime "attended by circumstances of cruelty and horror is not perhaps exceeded, considering your sex, in the history of crime." The story said some spectators in the packed courtroom had applauded at the end of the speech. When the judge pronounced the death sentence, Durgan sat down and cried, "rocking herself to and fro and uttering screams that could be heard far beyond the Court-house." In the jail, she continued to scream so loudly that people outside the jail could hear her.[17]

By the time of her execution, the *Times* described Durgan as "steady as a ship's mast." Each of the three newspapers described what she wore. She died, according to the *Times*, wearing a plain brown suit with a white collar, and white gloves. The *Inquirer* said she wore a brown "paramatta" frock with long sleeves and a high neck with a lace collar, white gloves, white stockings, and "lasting" slippers.[18]

The three newspapers' stories provide an emotional profile of Durgan: She was not as stoic as described, but instead exhibited a wide range of emotions, depending upon the situation. She was morose, withdrawn, happy, laughing, and angry, among many other emotions. She also was bitter. In an interview, when talking about the large number of Irish immigrants coming to the United States, she said, "They had better stay away from Jersey."[19]

Described as an Animal

A story published in the *Times* five days before Durgan's execution reported in detail her physical appearance. Theories were gaining popularity that physical attributes could indicate innate criminality.[20] The story, reprinted in the *New Brunswick Weekly Freedonian* two days before the execution, showed strong evidence of those theories. The account written by Elizabeth Oakes Smith, savaged Durgan. Smith visited prisons in the United States "not from a morbid and idle curiosity, but that I may better understand my own sex in every respect in which they may be placed."

Smith said Durgan's jaw was large and heavy, and her small mouth had narrow gums, "cat-like in shape," with pointed teeth. "There is not one character of beauty, even in the lowest degree, about the girl; not one ray of sentiment, nothing genuine, hardly human, except a weak, sometimes a bitter, smile." Smith continued, "She was born without moral responsibility, just as much as the tiger or wolf is so born." She charged that the community should have identified Durgan's dangerousness before the

17. "The Coriell Murder: Bridget Durgan to Be Hanged Aug. 30," *New York Times*, 18 June 1867.
18. "Execution of Bridget Durgan"; "The Gallows."
19. "The Execution of Bridget Dergan [*sic*]."
20. For one analysis of such ideas, see Gould, *The Mismeasure of Man*, esp. 123–45.

murder. Smith said Durgan should not be allowed to prey on society again, and added: "But whether it is right to take an irresponsible morally idiotic creature, and she a woman, whose sex had no voice in making the laws under which she will suffer, and hang her by the neck till she is dead, is a question for our advanced civilization to consider." She answered her own question, calling capital punishment "the cruel relic of a barbarism which ought to be expunged from our legal code." The *New Brunswick Weekly Freedonian* said Smith's description "most truthfully described" Durgan.[21] It seems remarkable in hindsight that a newspaper such as the *Times*, which had earlier described Durgan as being rather plain looking but not hideous, would publish such material.

The *Philadelphia Inquirer*'s final sentence in its execution story was, "Thus ended the earthly career of a female fiend."[22] It is small wonder that thousands of people wanted to see Bridget Durgan hang.

Mary Farmer: Seeking Security for Her Son

James and Mary Farmer wanted their infant son, Peter, to have property and wealth someday. Peter's father had neither. Peter's mother, Mary, had emigrated to the United States from Ireland and met James in Buffalo, New York. They wed and moved to Brownville, a small town in northwestern New York.

Sarah and Patrick Brennan also lived in Brownville. Sarah Brennan was, according to news reports, "a woman of some property." In a 28 April 1908 article, the *New York Times* reported that on 23 April, she wanted returned a forged deed that transferred her property to the Farmers. Patrick Brennan said neither he nor his wife had executed the deed, and a 23 March news report said Mary Farmer had impersonated Sarah to sign and acknowledge the deed. The Farmers later rendered the forged deed to Peter to ensure his future.[23]

According to the *New York Times*, Sarah Brennan went to the Farmer home to get the forged deed, but instead she got smashed in the head with an ax. That same day, the Farmers sought possession of the Brennan property; Patrick Brennan objected, but the deed seemed valid, and the Farmers took occupancy. When Sarah Brennan did not return home, a search began. Four days after the murder, during a second search of the former

---

21. "Smith's Account of Visit"; "Bridget Dergan [*sic*]."

22. "The Gallows."

23. "Confesses Brennan Murder," *New York Times*, 29 April 1908; "Woman's Body in Trunk," ibid., 28 April 1908; "Confesses Brennan Murder," ibid., 29 April 1908; "Mrs. Farmer Must Pay Death Penalty," ibid., 23 March 1909.

Brennan home, police opened a large trunk and found Sarah Brennan. That same day, the Farmers were arrested, and one day later a *Times* story reported that Mary Farmer had confessed.[24]

The Farmers were convicted in mid-June 1908 and sentenced to die in the electric chair. During the ride to Auburn Prison, Mary Farmer, according to the newspaper, maintained the stoicism she had shown since her arrest until the prison gates opened. Then she shuddered. Her imprisonment created a headache for state officials. No accommodations for women, and no death row cells for anyone, were available. Auburn's warden, Benham, seeking a solution, tried to get Farmer transferred to the women's prison, but that proved impossible because no state law provided for such a switch, and the court had specifically assigned her to Auburn.[25]

Eight months later, the *Times* ran another story, which briefly reported that after the New York State Court of Appeals denied her appeal, Mary Farmer faced becoming the second woman to die in New York's electric chair.[26]

In late March, just days before Farmer's scheduled execution, Gov. Charles Evans Hughes decided not to intervene, and he used the newspaper press to defend his decision. Hughes explained that because capital punishment was the law in New York, the executive had no right to change the law. Some opponents sought clemency because executing a woman was especially revolting, but the law made no gender distinctions.[27]

The *Times* defended Governor Hughes's decision and his logic. In an editorial, the *Times* acknowledged increasing public opposition to capital punishment, and confirmed that public opinion opposed executing a woman. However, the paper concluded, the proper remedy was with the legislature because the governor had no power to change the law. The editorial said Farmer likely was "what alienists would call a 'moral imbecile.'" Nonetheless, the *Times* saw no reason existing for clemency because the law did not recognize such a thing.[28]

As might be expected, not everyone agreed with the *Times* or Governor Hughes. A letter to the editor from a Francis D. Gallatin said men committed many more murders than women, and therefore the law could be "softened" for women with little effect on society. Furthermore, Gallatin pointed out, the law already made many distinctions between men and women. Another letter, signed simply, "A Man," said sentiment had as

24. "Woman's Body in Trunk"; "Confesses Brennan Murder."
25. "Troubled by Woman Slayer," ibid., 22 June 1908.
26. "Says Mrs. Farmer Must Die," ibid., 10 February 1909.
27. "Farmer Must Pay."
28. "Expresses Sound Doctrine," ibid., 24 March 1909.

much to its credit as did logic in "the long process of the evolution and uplifting of the race," and therefore Hughes might as well have decided the issue on sentiment as on logic. The writer also accused the yellow press and morbid sentimentality of making heroes of murderers, no matter how vile the crime. "A Man" cynically said several flagrant and scandalous miscarriages of justice had characterized recent murder trials of men, and all had escaped the electric chair. Therefore, Governor Hughes could have commuted Farmer's sentence without creating a dangerous precedent.[29]

Times readers might have wondered if Mary Farmer was capable of feeling emotion. She would reportedly visit with her husband the day before her scheduled execution, and prison officials said they did not "look for any display of real feeling on the part of either." The *Times* added that neither James nor Mary had said anything about young son Peter.[30]

The *Times* speculated that Mary Farmer would be the last person executed at 6 A.M. in New York, and that future executions probably would be at 6 P.M. to make it more convenient for witnesses and others to get to the prison and have time to leave that same day. In addition, the *Times* announced that Dr. Edwin Spitzka of Philadelphia would perform a postmortem examination of Mary Farmer. Spitzka had attended more than thirty executions and had done an autopsy on President William McKinley's assassin, Leon Czolgosz.[31]

In the two or three days before her execution, the *New York Times* dwelled on the slightest details about Mary Farmer. The newspaper's detailed coverage included the likelihood that she would have a longer walk to the waiting cell than previous condemned inmates because she would have to go behind the five death cells in the corridor. The chaplain and a prison matron would accompany her. The paper reported that Farmer's skirt would be slit up the side so that an electrode could be attached to her leg. Rumors circulated that Farmer would confess shortly before her execution, and exonerate her husband. The *Times* also said some people believed Farmer would go to the chair "as bravely as any man."[32]

The most prominent coverage the *Times* gave Farmer came on the day before her execution. She exonerated her husband, saying he had known nothing about Brennan's death until the trunk was opened, but she did

29. "Death Penalty for Women," ibid., 30 March 1909; "Sentiment," ibid., 1 April 1909.

30. "Test Death Chair for Mrs. Farmer," ibid., 28 March 1909.

31. Making execution times convenient is still a problem. As recently as August 2000, Oklahoma announced it would switch to early-evening executions to accommodate family members of victims ("Man Who Killed Arkansas Teens Is Scheduled to Be Executed," *Jonesboro (Ark.) Sun,* 7 August 2000). "Mrs. Farmer to Say Good-Bye to Husband," *New York Times,* 27 March 1909.

32. "Test Death Chair."

not confess. The paper also reported that Farmer left a second statement, this to her son Peter, but the statement was not released, and the *Times* relied on unattributed information. However, the newspaper knew a good deal about the content because it described what the letter said, although it cited no source. The *Times* described in detail the meeting between James and Mary Farmer, and its logistics. The Farmers were described as "unemotional" during the meeting, although that might have been in part because prison rules did not allow personal contact between visiting relatives, and thus the Farmers, during their last meeting, were not allowed to touch each other. Officials took Mary Farmer to a cell about twenty feet from the death chamber, and she had a prayer book, a book on the lives of the saints, and other religious readings. The newspaper said there was "a feeling of confidence" that Farmer would make no last statement except to pray or in response to prayers by the chaplain, and that she would die bravely.[33]

The *New York Times* published two related articles: one was a short story that said Farmer would be the second woman to die in the New York electric chair, and the second was a letter from a female attorney, Madeleine Z. Doty, protesting a woman's execution. Doty said women were subject to New York's laws, but could not help formulate them. She also said Farmer had "a red twist" in her brain, a reference to an inherited trait from long-ago ancestors who hunted and "killed for the joy of killing." This trait caused Farmer to murder. Doty shifted to a nature versus nurture argument, saying Farmer "was either born a criminal or made a criminal. . . . She was a monster because of her heredity or her environment." Doty believed Farmer should not be freed but that she and other prisoners should be kept in "clean, wholesome places" where they could have a chance to be rehabilitated and to improve.[34]

The *Times* ran the execution story on page 6, perhaps because after the coverage of the day before, there was little left to say. Farmer did, as the newspaper predicted, die bravely and in prayer, and the execution went "without sensational incident." Five women witnessed the execution; it was rare in 1909 for women to witness. The newspaper played that aspect prominently, using it in the first of three subordinate headlines and in the second paragraph of the story. Female witnesses included the two matrons, a medical doctor, and two nurses.

The *Times* editorialized a second time about the case, using the headline: "Abolition Is the One Remedy." However, the editorial did not follow that line of argument and never dealt with abolition in a meaningful

33. "Mrs. Farmer Dies Praying in Chair," *New York Times,* 30 March 1909; "Mrs. Farmer Calm, Facing Death To-Day," ibid., 29 March 1909.

34. "Second Woman to Die in Chair," ibid., 29 March 1909; "The Case of Mrs. Farmer," ibid.

way. The execution was as successful "as a hideous thing could be," but the paper said such executions were difficult for "modern sensibilities to bear." Although difficult for many people, the newspaper surmised the burden had weighed heaviest on Governor Hughes. In a curious sentence, the *Times* defended the execution, saying, "Society is in greater, rather than less, danger from the woman who kills than from the man." The editorial discourse on "abolition" of the death penalty ended with this statement: "Meanwhile as was long ago suggested to messieurs les assassins, an obvious first step toward the abolition of capital punishment is for mesdames les assassins to begin it by controlling their emotions."[35]

35. "Abolition Is the One Remedy," ibid., 30 March 1909.

Chapter 11

Sexual Preference

Changes during the Past Fifty Years

THE LAST BLACK WOMAN EXECUTED IN the twentieth century was Betty Butler in 1954. She murdered her lesbian lover at a lake in Cincinnati in front of hundreds of people. The first woman executed in the twenty-first century was Wanda Jean Allen. She died 11 January 2001 for shooting to death her lesbian lover in an Oklahoma City Police Department parking lot.

Butler's crime and execution received relatively little news coverage, especially when compared to two white women executed in Ohio in the twentieth century. Allen's crime and trial received little coverage, but her execution received substantial coverage. She was the first woman executed in Oklahoma since 1903, when it was a territory.

The Ohio newspaper press rarely mentioned Butler's sexual preference. The *Oklahoma City Daily Oklahoman* and others mentioned Allen's sexual preference often and prominently. This difference in the coverage is not necessarily indicative of any editorial bias on the part of the *Oklahoman* or the Ohio press; rather, it suggests the cultural difference between 1954 and 2001 and how the press reflected that contrast. The *Oklahoman* could hardly keep from mentioning sexual preference because it was a prominent part of the trial, and because Allen had murdered two former female lovers. She served four years in prison for the first murder, and she was executed for the second.

News about a Black Lesbian Mother of Two

The Ohio newspaper press in the early 1950s did not know exactly what to do when reporting about Betty Butler. How do family newspapers describe a black lesbian mother of two, condemned for murder?

When Butler choked and drowned Evelyn Clark at a public park before two hundred persons on 6 September 1952, the *Cincinnati Enquirer* reported that Butler and Clark had been fighting over a man. On 8 January 1954, in a story about a stay of execution for Butler, the *Cleveland Plain Dealer* reported that court records showed that Butler had "associated with Lesbians" in Cleveland and Cincinnati. The newspaper described Clark, thirty, as Butler's "aggressive girl friend."[1]

According to press reports, Butler left little doubt about whether she had committed the murder. Butler, Clark, and Deezie Ivory were in a boat, fishing on the crowded lake near Cincinnati. The two women argued, and Ivory rowed to shore. The women fought, and the *Enquirer* said Butler twisted a handkerchief around Clark's neck in an attempt to strangle her. Clark lost consciousness, but when Butler saw Clark was still alive, she dragged her into the lake and held her head underwater. Witnesses to the incident claimed they heard Butler say: "If I can't strangle her, I'll drown her." Witnesses also recalled that Butler said, "My work is done," after dumping Clark's body in the lake.[2]

The next day's *Enquirer* reported that Butler had murdered her "love rival," leaving the impression that the women were arguing about a man. According to that newspaper, after Butler choked Clark, she dragged "her unconscious rival" into the lake. The *Plain Dealer* claimed Butler was tried for a "sex revenge" murder. The press never made clear why Butler had murdered Clark. Also unclear is whether Butler blamed the press for her conviction. When sentenced to death, Butler said her trial was "as fair as those things go, I guess." She and her husband, Harry, had separated about a month before the murder. Butler said he had visited her while she was jailed in Cincinnati, but had not come to the women's prison in Columbus. "He has taken to preaching, his sermons emphasizing my sins," the *Plain Dealer* quoted. The newspaper called her bitter. Ohio press descriptions of Butler varied. The superintendent of the reformatory for women described her as "hard," but in the same story, the *Plain Dealer* described her as a remarkably gifted amateur artist, who had taken up charcoal drawing since being imprisoned and "shows a remarkable eye and hand." Butler remarked of her artistic ability: "It's one of those things I didn't know I could do until too late."[3]

The prison superintendent called Butler calm and "very wrapped up in her religion" shortly before her death. She "seems to feel that she will be very happy when it is all over. She feels that there is life in the hereafter and appears anxious to be a part of it." The lead paragraph of the story in

1. "West End Woman Strangled, Drowned in Sharon Woods," *Cincinnati Enquirer*, 7 September 1952; "Mrs. Butler Death Off Till Summer," *Cleveland Plain Dealer*, 8 January 1954.

2. "West End Woman Strangled."

3. "Rival Choked and Drowned, Woman Held for Grand Jury," ibid., 8 September 1952; "2 Mothers to Go to Chair Jan. 15," *Cleveland Plain Dealer*, 7 January 1954.

the *Columbus Dispatch* identified Butler as a "Negro mother of two small children" before describing her in any other way.[4] Butler's artistic sensitivity, religious beliefs, motherly concern for her children, and calm demeanor sharply contrasted with descriptions of her as a hardened killer.

The *Enquirer* played Butler's execution on the front page, giving it prominent display with a "second lead" headline. The brief story said she was the first "Negro woman" to be executed in Ohio. The *Dispatch* played the story on page 11, along with sports news, a weather map, and a community calendar of events.[5]

Prominently Featured Lesbian Relationship

Wanda Jean Allen's crime and arrest merited only brief mention in the *Oklahoma City Daily Oklahoman*. The sentence received front-page coverage, and the execution was big news. The stories about the December 1988 murder were brief and to the point. The first story ran on page 8 and identified the victim as Gloria J. Leathers, who told police Allen had shot her. Leathers reportedly was on her way to the police department to file a complaint against Allen when the shooting occurred. Police had answered a dispute at a shopping center involving the two women that same day, and the shooting occurred fifteen minutes later. The next day's *Oklahoman* reported in a page 14 story that Allen had been charged with intent to kill, and police were searching for her. The story also reported Allen's 1982 sentencing for manslaughter, but little else. Three days later, a short story on page 11 said police had arrested Allen in Duncan, Oklahoma, and that Leathers had died. The newspaper later termed Leathers Allen's roommate.[6]

Allen for the most part dropped out of the news until her April 1989 trial. The *Oklahoman* prominently featured her lesbian relationship with Leathers in its front-page story about the death sentence. The lead said: "Jurors have chosen the death penalty for a woman who fatally shot her lesbian lover outside The Village police station in December." The prosecutor said she had not expected the death penalty because of Allen's gender. However, in a story ten years later when Allen's execution date drew nearer, Oklahoma attorney general Drew Edmondson maintained gender was not relevant to the judicial process, although he said condemned

4. "Lausche Refuses to Save Woman's Life," *Columbus Dispatch,* 11 June 1954.
5. "Mother of Two Dies Calmly in Chair," ibid., 12 June 1954.
6. "Woman Sought in Shooting," *Oklahoma City Daily Oklahoman,* 2 December 1988; "Woman Charged in Village Shooting," ibid., 3 December 1988; "Woman Arrested in Duncan in Connection with Shooting," ibid., 6 December 1988; "Roommate Charged in Death," ibid., 7 December 1988.

women or young inmates tend to draw more media attention. Edmondson said no distinction in punishment should be made for male and female killers, but the story quoted death penalty expert Victor Streib, who noted that executions of women in the United States were rare. In a later story, Edmondson said he did not believe the death penalty served as a deterrent for others, though it did mean those executed would never kill again.[7]

Just three months before her execution, an *Oklahoman* article quoted prosecutors as terming Allen a "hunter" who had tracked down her victims and killed them. The prosecutor at Allen's 1989 trial declared she considered Allen a continued threat to society who likely "would respond in the same way" if future lovers angered her.[8]

Several stories in mid-December, about a month before the execution, revolved around Allen's clemency plea, and local ministers were central figures. One, the Reverend Robin Meyers, spoke at the clemency hearing. Part of his purpose was "to shift the appeal process away from legal arguments, and toward moral and ethical ones." Meyers criticized the process, noting that the pardon or parole board had never granted clemency in Oklahoma, and "in this predominantly evangelical state, it is assumed that the Bible supports capital punishment." The story about the clemency hearing also carried a religious theme. The *Oklahoma City Daily Oklahoman*'s lead on the story read: "Neither Wanda Jean Allen's claim of love for Jesus Christ nor claims that she's brain damaged will keep her from becoming the first woman executed in Oklahoma since statehood." Although the story's lead pertained to Allen's "love for Jesus Christ," there was little in the story to support the lead. Most of the information came from Meyers. The *Oklahoman* did not moralize about the case or about capital punishment, but the sources made the points in the story. The story's other main point related to arguments about Allen's mental capacity. Again, Meyers made the argument to spare her. He pointed out that Allen was "poor, black, female, brain damaged and lesbian," which had contributed to her death sentence. According to Meyers, Allen had suffered brain damage from an automobile accident or a stabbing, and when she was fifteen her IQ had been measured at sixty-nine. The assistant attorney general disputed that claim, saying Allen's IQ had measured eighty during a 1995 test.[9]

---

7. "Woman Sentenced to Death," ibid., 19 April 1989; "Condemned Women Approaching Execution," ibid., 31 January 1999; "State Nears 1st Execution of Woman—'Hunter' Would Kill Again, Prosecutors Say," ibid., 8 October 2000.

8. "State Nears 1st Execution."

9. "Death Penalty Opponents Plan Sermon," ibid., 15 December 2000; "Woman Denied Bid for Clemency," ibid., 16 December 2000.

The *Oklahoman's* story was more detailed than either Reuters or APB-news.com, but the others contained some information not reported in the *Oklahoman,* mainly because both were more oriented toward reaction to the hearing than coverage of the hearing itself. APBnews.com's article led by quoting Allen's attorney, Steve Presson, who called the board a "kangaroo court" and "a joke." He claimed the board had "never voted for clemency." The story also said that board member Currie Ballard, an African American, had criticized Meyers for talking about Allen's poverty, race, sexual preference, and retardation. Ballard reportedly called them "excuses for murder." Presson later said, "If [Ballard] does not think that race, poverty, and mental status have a place at a clemency hearing, he has no business being on the clemency board." APBnews.com's story also said gay-rights groups claimed that the prosecution's statement at trial that Allen was "the man" in her relationship with Leathers had prejudiced the jury.[10]

Allen began reappearing in the *Oklahoman* in October and November 2000, but most of the stories ran inside the newspaper. A front-page roundup story about many condemned inmates ran on 3 October, and a story about the last woman executed in Oklahoma, in 1903, ran on the front page on 19 November. It was mid-December before Allen became a fixture in the newspaper's columns. However, between 15 December 2000 and 12 January 2001, when Allen was executed, the newspaper published fourteen stories in thirteen days, seven of them on the front page.

National media attention also increased. An *Oklahoman* story argued that Allen's story attracted the national press because "[t]he shooting stemmed from a domestic dispute between two gay black women, and the attack took place right outside The Village Police Department." The story noted that groups such as Amnesty International and the Coalition to Abolish the Death Penalty were also pleading Allen's case.[11] Those organizations, and others, no doubt contributed to national interest, but that interest heightened when a national celebrity in the person of the Reverend Jesse Jackson came to Oklahoma City to lead protesters.

In the last days before the execution, the protests drew much of the press attention. Jackson led demonstrators in Oklahoma City to protest not only Allen's upcoming execution, but also the eight executions scheduled within a month in the state. He appealed to Oklahoma governor Frank Keating to examine his own religious beliefs and to stop the executions. Governor Keating did not comment specifically about Allen's case

10. "Oklahoma Woman Loses Clemency Bid," http://www.APBnews.com, 19 December 2000.
11. "Murder Case Stirs Attention Nationally," *Oklahoma City Daily Oklahoman,* 27 December 2000.

in the stories but did say that he believed people facing the death penalty should have good trial representation and scientific evidence that supported guilt.[12]

Jackson and twenty-seven other people were arrested because they crossed a police barricade at the prison where Allen was held. The Associated Press story led with the arrests and then reported that a federal judge had denied Allen's request for a stay. The *Oklahoman* carried a dual lead, first emphasizing the denial and then following with the arrests.[13]

The *Oklahoma City Daily Oklahoman* ran two front-page stories about the execution, accompanied by six photographs. Both stories concentrated on those supporting and opposing the execution. The *Oklahoman* followed standard execution coverage when it published Allen's last words: "Father, forgive them, they know not what they do." She then smiled at her attorneys and spiritual advisers and stuck out her tongue. Two Oklahoma City ministers, including Meyers, called the execution wrong, but Attorney General Edmondson told the press that Allen had victimized the families of the people she had killed. Leathers's relatives criticized Jackson. The *Oklahoman*'s related story focused more on protests to the execution, and carried this headline: "Survivors Speak for the Dead." The story mainly consisted of several interviews with people opposing the execution and those in favor of it. The political angle in the story was obvious. Jackson criticized Keating, saying the governor had chosen politics over his religion. In addition, the president of the Oklahoma City chapter of the NAACP said Governor Keating was "hard-hearted" and sometimes "hard-headed."[14]

The *Oklahoman* story noted that Allen's case attracted national press interest. Coverage of her case resembled reporting of some other late-twentieth-century executions of women in that there was some national media attention but not an overabundance. The execution differed slightly because Governor Keating did not exactly follow the same pattern of governors in the 1990s and 2000 who had few if any soul-searching statements about executing a woman. The governor noted, when he denied a stay of execution forty-five minutes before Allen died, that she had appealed eleven times. Allowing the execution "is not easy because I am dealing with a fellow human being." Governor Keating added, however,

12. "Jackson Fights 8 Executions," http://www.DallasNews.com, 5 January 2001; "Jackson Returning As Protests Begin," ibid., 9 January 2001.

13. "28 Held in Oklahoma Execution Protest," ibid., 11 January 2001; "Inmate Loses Federal Appeal; Jesse Jackson, Others Arrested," *Oklahoma City Daily Oklahoman*, 10 January 2001.

14. "Wanda Jean Allen Executed," *Oklahoma City Daily Oklahoman*, 12 January 2001; "Survivors Speak for the Dead," ibid.

that he also had to consider the victim and her family. "If a person takes another's life premeditated, they take their own."[15]

Oklahoma's Other Execution of a Woman, in 1903

An *Oklahoma City Daily Oklahoman* article about the 1903 hanging of Dora Wright showed that news coverage of that execution was similar to others of the time. Hundreds of people jammed into McAlester, Oklahoma, and those who had no tickets to witness the hanging found viewing points on housetops, in trees, or from other high places. Wright hanged for murdering and mutilating a young girl, apparently her stepdaughter. The *South McAlester Daily Capital* reportedly called the crime "the most horrible and outrageous" ever committed in that area, and termed Wright a "demon" and a "fiend."[16]

The execution was under federal authority, and a controversy arose about whether the hangings (a male defendant was also hanged for an unrelated crime) should be public. A local district attorney argued for public hangings, saying they would serve a deterrent purpose, but a U.S. chief deputy marshal opposed public hangings, and said he was personally opposed to capital punishment. A local Baptist minister opposed a public hanging, noting they "have a tendency to incite rather than prevent crime." Eventually, only the jurors, a few officials, the press, and friends of the defendants were allowed to witness.[17]

15. "Wanda Jean Allen Executed." Oklahoma executed a second woman, Marilyn Plantz, on 1 May 2001. News coverage of that execution is not included in this book.
16. "1903 Execution Has Parallels with Today," as reported in ibid., 19 November 2000.
17. Ibid.

PART IV

Hollywood, Female "Tough Guys," and Love Triangles

Chapter 12

Southern California Defendants

THE *LOS ANGELES TIMES* COMPARED Barbara Graham to a movie queen shortly after a jury found her guilty of murder and recommended she be executed. Graham presided at a press interview arranged by her attorney, and the *Times* said she "met the press and newsreel men yesterday with all the aplomb of a movie queen starring in a colossal production—which it appeared to be." Graham lacked only one thing: "The star of the show was shorn of the glamorous appearance she presented throughout the Mabel Monahan trial."[1] Graham would die in California's gas chamber for her part in murdering Mabel Monahan.

Three of the four women executed in California in the twentieth century were from southern California, all in the Los Angeles area. Of the three, movies were made about two: Barbara Graham, executed in 1955, and Elizabeth Duncan, executed in 1962. Those executed from the film capital of the world were bound to draw more attention than elsewhere, and the cases certainly drew the attention of the *Los Angeles Times.*

Capital punishment has been a theme in Hollywood movies, advertisements, plays, and books. *Paths of Glory, Breaker Morant, In Cold Blood,* and *I Want to Live* were among early films. More recently, *Dead Man Walking* and *The Green Mile* were popular films and books. Literature is replete with examples, including Ambrose Bierce's "Occurrence at Owl Creek Bridge," William Bradford Huie's "South Kills Another Negro," Jerry Bledsoe's *Death Sentence* (a recounting of the execution of Velma Barfield), and Ernest Gaines's *Lesson before Dying.*[2] These are only a few of many examples.

1. "Press Besieges Barbara Graham," *Los Angeles Times,* 25 September 1953.
2. "Death Penalty Is Theme of Three Great Movies," *Jonesboro (Ark.) Sun,* 29 June 1997; Bierce, *Best of Bierce,* 9–17; Huie, "South Kills Another Negro."

Barbara Graham: Mother, Murderess, Mobster, and Moll

Probably the most famous movie made about a death row woman is *I Want to Live,* an account of the life and execution of Barbara Graham. Actress Susan Hayward won an Academy Award for her portrayal of Graham.

News stories said Graham was "trim," sometimes "prim," and a "confessed narcotics user" who frequently "glared malevolently" and sometimes lost her temper. She wept in private, but generally maintained a "stony" exterior; she wore to her execution a "skin-tight" suit and "jangling, dangling" earrings, and had "crimson painted lips." She was a "rattlesnake," a "rat," and a member of an "unholy trio," a "reddish-blond" who liked hot fudge sundaes and hot jazz music. She was a mother, a murderess, a mobster, and a moll.

However, Graham's hair color, more than any other of her features or habits, repeatedly drew the *Los Angeles Times*'s attention. The paper wrote of her death walk to California's gas chamber: "The brashly attractive 32-year-old convicted murderess, her bleached blond hair turned to its natural brown and cut in a short bob, walked to her death as if dressed for a shopping trip."[3] For once, she was not a "reddish-blond."

The story was big news but especially in Los Angeles. Attorneys for the other two defendants argued that the prejudicial newspaper publicity constituted a denial of due process guaranteed by the Fourteenth Amendment.[4]

The *Times* first reported about Graham on 5 May 1953; police had arrested her and two accomplices at a "shabby converted store in Lynwood," where the three had lived for about two weeks. The story said that when Graham was arrested, she was "partly clothed," reportedly had injected herself with a hypodermic needle, and was examined as a possible drug addict. Police arrested her, Albert Santos, and Emmett Raymond Perkins in connection with the beating and strangulation of Mabel Monahan, the mother-in-law of Las Vegas gambler Tutor Scherer. Graham and her accomplices killed Monahan because they believed Scherer had stashed jewels and cash at her home; he had not. Police told reporters they believed the three had also kidnapped and murdered Baxter Shorter, who had told police about Monahan's murder. Shorter was missing.[5]

On several occasions, headlines about Graham were about her health, not the murder. When arrested, she told police she had a heart ailment and

3. Gene Blake, "Barbara Graham Dies Despite Two Last Delays," *Los Angeles Times,* 5 June 1955.
4. "Monahan Murder Trial Nears Finale," ibid., 13 September 1953.
5. "3 Suspects in Burbank Killing Seized," ibid., 5 May 1953; "Shorter Case Suspects Will Be Arraigned," ibid., 8 May 1953.

might die in a few months, but apparently that was not true. She collapsed, fell, and hit her head in her cell during the grand jury hearings; some feared she might have a blood clot on her brain because she "could not or would not" talk. When she fell down a flight of stairs about two months later, during her trial, she had ceased to be taken seriously. The *Times,* using no named sources, reported the fall as a scheme to divert attention and allow one or more of the defendants to flee, or as a staged tactic to delay the trial. The *Times* used an unnamed source to attribute to Graham a quotation she made after she fell in her cell: "When I really get into my act I'm going to make Sarah Bernhardt look like a chump." She also made minor news when she struck a cell mate after the woman made a remark about Graham and the gas chamber. The woman said Graham "had a wallop like Joe Louis," but a deputy who saw the fight said she did not believe Graham had much of a punch because she did not even skin her knuckle.[6]

The *Los Angeles Times* repeatedly said Graham was part of a gang or crime mob, and police took this allegation seriously, using "extraordinary precautions" at her trial. Armed deputies and plainclothes police were in the courtroom because the district attorney's office received word that "the underworld" had offered money to kill a prosecution witness. The most bizarre scheme called for killing John L. True, an important prosecution witness, by turning him "into a human torch" in court. Police arrested two men for plotting to smash a napalm bomb against True. Eleven police surrounded True on his way to the courtroom. Additional stories detailed contracts on witnesses' lives and rumors of bombing plots. One "revealed" threat (the newspaper did not say by whom) resulted in searches of spectators, especially women, because the report said a woman would hurl a "finger bomb" in the courtroom. When a "woman in gray" asked to be seated near the door but left because there was no seat, it was cause for police to search for her.[7]

Police investigative techniques were a major issue in Graham's case. One of the most sensational moments in the *Times*'s trial coverage came when an undercover policeman testified. The officer had posed as a man who would help Graham form an alibi, and the *Times* said Graham's "jaw fell in dismay" when she saw Officer Samuel Sirianni. He came into the case after she had reportedly asked a jail mate, Donna Prow, to help her find someone to frame an alibi; instead, Prow went to the police. Sirian-

6. "3 Suspects Seized"; "Three Meet in Burbank," ibid., 4 June 1953; "Mrs. Graham Hurt; Death Case Delayed," ibid., 20 August 1953; "Barbara Graham and Mrs. Curtis Tangle," ibid., 18 June 1953.
7. "Weird Plan Exposed by Arrest of 2," ibid., 25 August 1953; "Witness Describes Monahan Slaying," ibid., 26 August 1953; "Theft Scheme Told in Monahan Trial," ibid., 27 August 1953; "Alibi Plot Told in Monahan Case," ibid., 28 August 1953.

ni's testimony "exploded like a bombshell," according to the *Times*. Prow, serving a sentence for manslaughter, had her sentence modified to time served, and she was released after police told the judge that other inmates had threatened her life.[8]

Questions about Graham's sexual preferences were raised because the prosecution introduced portions of "amorous notes" she had written to Prow, and the *Times*, reporting about the notes, called Prow the prisoner "friend" of Graham, using the quotation marks for emphasis. When additional notes were later read, Graham for the first time lost her composure; the *Times* said she "gave vent to emotional outbursts."[9]

Graham had served a year in prison for perjury, and she had been in a state reformatory for delinquent girls when she was fourteen. She had been married three times. The *Times* said of her when she testified: "With her hair drawn back into a neat bun and wearing a trim beige-colored suit, Mrs. Graham presented a picture of primness on the witness stand." During her testimony, she admitted using narcotics, "working as a shill" for a gambling game, and writing bad checks. As the trial wore on, the *Times* more frequently described Graham as emotional, and asserted that her "demeanor was in marked contrast to the icy composure" she had shown earlier. The *Times* contended she worried when the jury came back for further instructions on fixing punishment: "The 30-year-old defendant, her reddish-blond tresses curled up in a mass of tiny ringlets, showed signs of worry on her pale, set face. Her eyes were red-rimmed and watery." She had shortly before heard the deputy prosecutor in closing arguments refer to her, Santos, and Perkins as an "unholy trio," "rats," and "rattlesnakes." He said: "Murders of this type are not hatched in the churches or in the homes. They are hatched in the foul caves they infest. Comes nightfall and they crawl out from under their rocks and perform the foul deeds they perform."[10]

Although Graham might have appeared worried, she did not show it when the jury announced the guilty verdict. As reported in the *Times*, "Barbara doesn't kick over the traces. She doesn't leap to her feet to scream vile abuse at the jury. She doesn't swoon. She sits there and takes it with unexpected calm." The newspaper attributed her behavior to previous convictions. "She has heard guilty verdicts before—guilty of prostitution and guilty of perjury."[11]

Press reports indicate Graham was a constant headache for prison of-

8. "Alibi Plot"; "Monahan Case Figure Freed after Threats," ibid., 29 August 1953.
9. "Slaying Denied by Mrs. Graham," ibid., 2 September 1953; "Trial Nears Finale."
10. "Defense to Open at Monahan Trial," ibid., 30 August 1953; "Slaying Denied"; "Monahan Murder Witness Arrested," ibid., 5 September 1953; "Monahan Jury Out; Guilty Verdict Hinted," ibid., 22 September 1953.
11. "Prefers Death to Life Term, Says Barbara," ibid., 23 September 1953.

ficials and others. Officials moved her from Corona Women's Prison to San Quentin because of "a strong possibility" someone might try to free or kill her. While at San Quentin, two inmates were put into solitary confinement for "yelling profane comments" at her. Another inmate whistled at her and had all privileges revoked.[12]

The problems partly stemmed from Graham being the only woman inmate at San Quentin and from continued concerns she would be killed to keep her quiet about other crimes. This meant more security, and cost soon became an issue. A legislative subcommittee refused to approve four special guards for Graham to "keep unknown people" from killing her. This so angered the state director of corrections that he said he would move her back to Corona when the money ran out and added that when she got "her brains blown out," everyone would know whom to blame. He later withdrew the remark. Assemblyman Caspar Weinberger, a Republican from San Francisco, said that thirty thousand dollars would be spent just to guard Graham, an amount he described as "fantastic." After only seven months, officials returned Graham to Corona because there was no more money left to house her at San Quentin. The superintendent at Corona requested special guards for Graham because she had frequent "fainting spells of a hysterical nature" and threatened suicide, but a legislative subcommittee denied the request.[13]

Barbara Graham's execution was as controversial as her life had been. She died on 3 June 1955 after the governor twice delayed her execution at the last minute. She was scheduled to die at 10 A.M., but that was delayed until 10:45, and the second delay was until 11:30. She died at 11:42 A.M., according to the *Times*, seven minutes after the cyanide pellets dropped into the can of sulfuric acid and distilled water.[14]

The *Los Angeles Times*'s Gene Blake, who later won an award for his reporting on Graham's case, said that at each delay she cried, "Why do they torture me? I was ready to go at 10 o'clock." The delays brought harsh responses from the press and from some politicians. *Times* columnist Anne Norman said the execution "was an ordeal not equaled in the civilized world excepting, possibly, behind the Iron Curtain. Brainwashing they call torture there. Here we call it justice." Norman also said Graham never had a chance because at age thirteen she was put into a reform school for girls, where she learned to be a prostitute, a drug user, a forger, and a

12. "Barbara Graham Moved; Prison Fears for Safety," ibid., 26 November 1953; "Prison Pair Punished for Yelling at Mrs. Graham," ibid., 3 December 1953; "Barbara Graham Whistle Costly in San Quentin," ibid., 20 May 1954.
13. "Special Guards Voted Down for Mrs. Graham," ibid., 17 February 1954; "Barbara Graham Changes Prisons," ibid., 24 June 1954; "Special Guards for Mrs. Graham Held Needless," ibid., 19 February 1955.
14. Blake, "Graham Dies Despite Delays."

murderer. Society shared guilt because a thirteen-year-old child "was discarded by society and her feet planted firmly on a road that led, almost inevitably, to the gas chamber in San Quentin."[15]

California state attorney general Edmund "Pat" Brown, an opponent of capital punishment, said the execution delays were part of a "cat and mouse" game played with Graham. He called the delays "cruel and unusual punishment."[16]

Graham's eccentric behavior also drew press notice. Blake reported that she requested for her last meal a hot fudge sundae and a milk shake; she had another sundae the next morning. She spent her last night listening to "hot jazz records," and she went to her death in a "skin-tight" beige skirt that "clung to her 120-pound body" and wore "dangling, jangling" earrings.

In 1958, three years after the execution, the movie *I Want to Live* revived the controversy about Barbara Graham in the *Times*'s columns. The movie won acclaim as critics called it the "most relentless American indictment of capital punishment yet put on film," and an "overwhelmingly powerful" movie. United States Supreme Court Justices William O. Douglas, Potter Stewart, and John Harlan saw a private screening. The film "bowled over" New York critics. Not everyone agreed. *Los Angeles Times* reporter Blake, who had covered the trial and execution, called the movie a "dramatic and eloquent piece of propaganda for abolition of the death penalty," but he said it was not "true," "factual," or a "documentary." Blake termed the film an "insult" to the jurors and to the people of California, and he said he was convinced of Graham's guilt. A prosecutor in Graham's trial called the movie a farce.[17] As late as the early 1960s, the *Times* published stories about Graham.

Louise Peete: "One of Crime's Most Notorious Fatal Women"

Almost everywhere Louise Peete went, someone turned up dead—and she was a much traveled woman.

She went to San Quentin Prison in the early 1920s for murdering a man for whom she had worked as a housekeeper. Twenty-five years later, she

15. Ibid.; Norman, "Must We Share Part of the Guilt?" ibid., 4 June 1955.
16. "Mrs. Graham's Body Prepared for Burial Rite," ibid., 5 June 1955.
17. Philip K. Scheuer, "'I Want to Live!' Taut Film," 16 November 1958; John L. Scott, "'I Want to Live' Grim, Powerful," ibid., 27 November 1958; "High Jurists See Film on Mrs. Graham," ibid., 12 December 1958; "Graham Film Bowls Over N.Y. Critics," ibid., 16 December 1958; Blake, "Barbara Graham—Film and Fact," ibid., 28 November 1958; "Barbara Graham Found Surely Right-Handed," ibid., 1 March 1959.

was convicted of murdering an elderly woman, and it was for that crime that Peete died in 1947. Between the murders, two of her three husbands committed suicide, as did a suitor. People closely associated with her died by her hand or their own hands in Dallas, Tucson, and Los Angeles; in Boston, where she lived with her first husband, twenty thousand dollars worth of jewels disappeared when she left the town and her husband.

The *Los Angeles Times* called Peete "one of crime's most notorious fatal women," and said her execution "ended a saga of murder and suicide rivaling some of the most sanguinary pages of history." Peete was the second woman legally executed in California in the twentieth century; she was the only one of the three southern California women about whom a movie was not made. Her story was big news, and her trial would probably have been bigger news except that Nazi Germany was unraveling in 1945 and war news dominated the front pages of U.S. newspapers. Nonetheless, when Peete was executed two years later, her picture dominated the front page of the *Times*; a caption under the picture called her cold and defiant until her death. The story said that although ninety-one people had seen her executed, she was "alone and haughty."

The *Times* depicted Peete as a mercurial woman who grew up poor in Louisiana but soon learned to use her wiles and men to get what she wanted. Her age perplexed the *Times*. When executed, she was not young; "some say" she was sixty-five, whereas "others believe" she was about fifty-eight. Whatever the case, Peete was not telling her age, gas chamber or no, and the *Times* was left to bemoan that her date of birth was "left blurred in the vital statistics of criminal history."

Peete's first stint in San Quentin came after she was convicted of murdering Joseph C. Denton, described in the *Times* as "a lonely, wealthy Arizona miner" who bought a house in Los Angeles for his wife and daughter, but they died before the house was finished. Peete leased the house and became his housekeeper after she left her husband, Richard, in Denver. A month after Peete moved in, Denton was missing. Peete returned to Denver to her husband and four-year-old daughter, but three months later, Denton's badly decomposed body was found in a crude grave in the basement of the "house of his dreams." He had been shot in the head. The *Times* described Peete's first trial as sensational and said the all-male jury was loath to recommend a death sentence because in 1920, California had never executed a woman. While Peete was in prison, her husband, Richard, shot himself to death in Tucson.

Before Louise married Richard Peete, a Dallas man courted her "with the gallantry men of his State accord women of beauty. For her suitor's ardor he was arrested for complicity in the jewel theft," and he later killed himself. The jewel theft referred to Louise's having left Boston about the time twenty thousand dollars' worth of jewels turned up missing, and she was a suspect. Five years after Louise's release from prison, she married

Lee Borden Judson, but just eight months later, police arrested her for the second murder; Judson was also taken into custody but later released. One month later, he jumped to his death from the twelfth-story stairwell of a Los Angeles office building.

Peete was convicted and executed for murdering Margaret Logan, to whom Peete was "a sort of companion and assistant." Logan was missing in May 1944, and Peete said her employer had gone away for a time. Police found her body buried under her "favorite avocado tree in the backyard" and the grave marked with potted geraniums. The situation was ironic because in 1920 when Peete was on trial for the first murder, Logan had taken care of Peete's young daughter.[18]

The second murder trial lasted almost the entire month of May 1945 and was raucous from the beginning. During the prosecution's opening statement, Peete yelled, "It's a lie" when the prosecutor said she had beaten Logan after shooting her. The *Los Angeles Times* termed her "a plump and graying defendant," and two days later a "steelly-eyed [sic]" Peete angrily shouted and interrupted a prosecution witness.[19]

Peete's behavior seemed bizarre in other ways. A neighbor said when she had asked about Margaret Logan's whereabouts, Peete had told her that Arthur C. Logan had bitten off his wife's nose during an argument and she had gone away for plastic surgery. Another neighbor said Peete had done a hat dance when she learned of Arthur Logan's death in the state hospital. The neighbor said she had erroneously received a telegram about his death, and when she took it to Peete at the Logan house, "She read it and ran into the bedroom. She came out with several hats and started doing a little dance while trying them on. I stood there amazed at her reaction and she quieted down." The neighbor said Peete had asked her not to conclude she was trying on the hats for Logan's funeral.[20]

Near the end of the trial, Peete loudly accused Deputy District Attorney John Barnes of "heckling" her during cross-examination. Barnes was known as "the hatchet man" because of his questioning of witnesses, according to the *Times*. A jury of twelve men had found Peete guilty of murder in 1920 with a recommendation of mercy; in 1945, a jury of eleven women and one man found her guilty of murder and made no recommendation, making the death penalty mandatory, the *Times* reported. After the trial, Peete reportedly thanked reporters for their kindness and told a woman reporter who was about to cry, "Don't weep for me, dear."[21]

18. "Louise Peete Meets Doom, Calm till End," ibid., 12 April 1947.
19. "Denial Voiced by Mrs. Peete at Death Trial," ibid., 2 May 1945; "Mrs. Peete Halts Officer in Midst of Testimony," ibid., 4 May 1945.
20. "Home Life Told in Peete Case," ibid., 5 May 1945; "Witness Reveals Peete Hat Dance," ibid., 8 May 1945.
21. "Mrs. Peete Says She's 'Heckled' by Prosecution," ibid., 22 May 1945; "Louise Peete Found Guilty, Faces Death," ibid., 29 May 1945.

The press seemed taken with Peete, and especially so after her conviction. An interview with her the day after the verdict amounted to a personality profile in which Peete came off as a gentle soul. The reporter said she had sat and talked "just like a kindly serene old lady of threescore years talking with a long-time friend." Although she denied murdering anyone and expressed no remorse for those deaths, she did say she regretted her third husband's death. "Whatever else had been left out of the make-up of this strange woman, she was capable of feeling grief over the tragedy that had come upon a man who had loved her in their later days." When the interview ended, Peete "pertly" walked back to her cell "as if she were a busy housewife turning contentedly to home duties." The reporter, however, did not fully fall prey to Peete's charm, for the story ended: "A strange woman, indeed. Certainly something was left out of her make-up or something blocked off the normal course of human action and reaction."[22]

Just days before her execution, Peete again met reporters; again she mesmerized them with her charm as she "kept a roomful of newsmen guffawing as she sprinkled her final remarks liberally with wit and sarcasm. It was a most amazing interview with a woman about to die." Described as "plump and matronly," she also seemed to have a mercurial temperament. At first, she reportedly would not talk to reporters and blamed them for her troubles, but two hours later, she came to the interview "exuding charm" and with a "gold-wrapped pound of chocolates." She told the press she "wanted to spank all the children to get the bad one" who had written a story alleging she had attempted suicide, and they reportedly all denied having written the story. She told them: "Well, it didn't appear in the Christian Science Monitor." The *Times* reporter described her as calm and said her speech was "meticulous and softened" by "her native Louisiana" drawl. Gene Sherman's story about the interview must have left some *Times* readers believing they were reading about their grandmothers:

> "Now I want you to have some candy—all of you," she said. Looking more like a mother with whom you like to eat fried chicken and biscuits than a woman twice a murderer and doomed to death, Mrs. Peete opened the gold-wrapped box and offered her chocolates.
> "Go on, take one," she smiled, when some hands lingered.
> Then, tucking the box under her chubby arm, she turned to leave. At the door she paused and pointed to one reporter who had lavished compliments on her.
> "And you stop your flattery," she said.[23]

22. "'My Mind above Fear,' Mrs. Peete Tells Herself," ibid., 30 May 1945.
23. "Mrs. Peete Laughs Way through Last Interview," ibid., 10 April 1947.

Gov. Earl Warren refused to commute her sentence, saying he regretted "seeing a woman go to her death in this manner," but could find "absolutely no grounds" for executive clemency. Peete had expressed confidence Warren would commute her sentence: "The Governor is a gentleman—and no gentleman could send a lady to her death."[24]

The *Times*'s execution story was lengthy and subjective. Sherman said Peete had died "alone and haughty." He noted that some had described her as "magnificent" at her execution. "If that she were, it was the macabre merciless magnificence that had marked a career of murder, thieving and duplicity. It was more defiance and coldness than 'magnificence.'" Sherman said Peete had a "cold and cunning charm" that attracted men, and she had learned early how to use her charm.

According to Sherman, during Peete's last moments in the gas chamber, she "sniffed for the almond perfume of destiny." She threw her head back and coughed. "A single white light over the chamber door flooded her face with pallor." Peete "fought to keep her head high, as if a proud tragedienne in a final curtain call." When she died, "Her face had changed no more than a mask."[25]

Elizabeth Duncan: *Times* Calls Case "Bizarre"

Why, in the late 1990s, would someone produce a made-for-television movie about Elizabeth Duncan, executed in California in 1962? Perhaps because she contracted for the murder of her daughter-in-law, who was five months pregnant when killed. Perhaps because Duncan posed as her daughter-in-law, hired a transient from a local Salvation Army center to pose as her daughter-in-law's husband, and obtained an annulment of their marriage. Perhaps because of allegations that Duncan was overly possessive of her son, Frank; one person described their relationship as "unnatural." Or perhaps because Duncan had married between eleven and sixteen times, including a marriage to her son's law school classmate.

The *Los Angeles Times* described Duncan's case as "bizarre," and it could not have chosen a more appropriate word. Duncan, fifty-eight years old when she died in California's gas chamber, was the last woman executed in the United States until 1984. Her case drew enormous attention in the *Times*, running every day from 16 December to 31 December 1958, and on the front page seven of those days. During the first four months of 1959, stories about Duncan ran in the *Times* on sixty days, and eleven of those days they were front-page stories. For much of March 1959, she was

24. "Louise Peete Dies Today in Gas Chamber," 11 April 1947.
25. "Meets Doom, Calm till End."

the news in Los Angeles, as the story ran twenty-two of the thirty-one days that month. As might be expected, such intense press coverage resulted in repeated claims of prejudice to Duncan's due-process and fair-trial rights, plus several futile motions for a change of venue.

The *Times* first published the story on 16 December 1958, reporting that police had arrested Duncan for impersonating her daughter-in-law, Olga Kupzyk Duncan, and obtaining an annulment of the marriage of Olga and Duncan's son, Frank, an attorney. The "annulment" was about a month after Frank and Olga had married despite his mother's vehement protests; the couple soon separated. Later, in November, Olga mysteriously disappeared from her Santa Barbara apartment. The story said Augustine Baldonado and Luis Moya had been arrested and questioned about Olga's disappearance.[26]

The next day's story, on page 1, said Duncan had threatened to kill Olga "if it's the last thing I do." Police were searching for Olga's body, and Duncan had paid someone sixty dollars to impersonate her son during the annulment proceeding. A later story said New Orleans police had arrested the man who had posed as Frank. Duncan reportedly called the Salvation Army and asked for someone to do an "odd job" for her and got him. A family friend told the *Times* that Olga was so afraid of Duncan that she moved from apartment to apartment. Olga "wasn't happy because her mother-in-law wouldn't let her be happy." Duncan was held on fifty thousand dollars bail, but Frank sought to have it reduced to five thousand dollars.[27]

Frank defended his mother, saying he believed Olga was alive: "At one time she threatened to cause me some unpleasant publicity but this would seem to be going to the extreme." He said he had "cross-examined" his mother about Olga's disappearance, and Duncan had said she knew nothing about it. "I know her and she would not lie." The *Times* said court attachés in Santa Barbara related that Frank and his mother often came into the courtroom "hand-in-hand." The *Times* termed Duncan "the oft-married mother of a Santa Barbara attorney," and stated in an early story she had been married at least five times, including once to a man from whom she separated hours after the wedding. According to the *Times*, when Duncan was fifty, she married Stephen Gillis, the "27-year-old handsome law school classmate of her son." Gillis sued for annulment two years later, saying the marriage was never consummated because Duncan told him she could not do so until after Frank graduated from law school because it would upset him.[28]

26. "Young Wife Vanishes in Bizarre Plot," ibid., 16 December 1958.

27. "Santa Barbara Police Seek Body of Lawyer's Wife in Bizarre Case," ibid., 17 December 1958; "FBI Captures Missing Duncan Case Figure," ibid., 19 January 1959.

28. "Mother Gets Bail Reduced in Weird Annulment Case," ibid., 18 December 1958.

Police, "after having guarded information from the press and public," asked the public to help find Olga's body. Lack of police cooperation did not keep the *Times* from publishing an enormous amount of information during the first four days. Police believed there likely was poison oak in the area where Olga was murdered because Moya had poison oak on him shortly after her disappearance.[29]

Duncan claimed Moya and Baldonado were trying to blackmail her, but when that failed, they tried to frame her by killing Olga. A grand jury hearing would soon begin, although the *Times* already had reported most of the prosecution's allegations and the details of the case. Ventura County district attorney Roy Gustafson told the *Times* he would present about a dozen witnesses and named some of them. He also said Duncan had offered four or five other people money to kill Olga, but Gustafson refused additional information, saying he "wanted to save it for the grand jury"; those names were "kept from the public."[30]

Gustafson might as well have talked because the *Times* reported grand jury testimony in detail. The newspaper claimed a witness testified that Duncan had offered him twenty-five hundred dollars to kill Olga, put her body in her bathtub, and pour concentrated lye solution on it. Another witness told reporters that Duncan had asked her to murder Olga. The *Times* named her, but the story said she refused to provide additional details, because "I can disappear, too, you know."[31]

Duncan "created a stir" when she was found in her jail cell moaning and saying she was having a heart attack. Taken to a hospital and reportedly found "in good health," she was then moved to the hospital's maximum security ward, which the *Times* said also served as "a psychopathic ward." When Duncan realized where she was, she said, "This is not for me. I'd rather be back in jail."[32]

The prosecutor released the grand jury transcript, and the *Times* published excerpts from the 249-page document, although little was revealed that the newspaper had not already published. Exceptions were statements about the intensity of Duncan's possessiveness, and Frank's defense of his mother. The transcript revealed "an almost unbelievable picture of a mother so agitated over losing her son's affections to another woman that she would stop at nothing to prevent it." The story also stated that testimony indicated something was amiss in Duncan and Frank's relationship.[33]

29. "Police Appeal for Help to Find Missing Bride's Body," ibid., 21 December 1958.

30. "Duncan Case Names Kept from Public," ibid., 25 December 1958.

31. "Mrs. Duncan and Two Men Indicted," ibid., 27 December 1958; "State Organizing Case against Mrs. Duncan," ibid., 28 December 1958.

32. "Grand Jury to Release Transcript," ibid., 30 December 1958.

33. "Duncan Plot Story to Jury Disclosed," ibid., 31 December 1958.

Duncan's attorney, Ward Sullivan, quickly filed for a change of venue. He said Gustafson had made statements to the press, and had "definitely attempted to influence the public in general against all the defendants." He most objected to Gustafson calling the crime "one of the most vicious and horrible crimes in the annals of modern justice." Gustafson countered that a "unique" case would get a lot of press coverage, and he defended the press's and his rights to comment publicly about the case.[34]

Duncan and Frank avoided the press at times, but played to the cameras at other times. During her arraignment, Duncan reportedly hung back from the other two defendants, not wanting to be photographed with them, throwing her hands over her face and running for the door to the jail, keeping her face covered while waiting for the elevator. When Frank visited her some days later, the *Los Angeles Times* reported he seemed "reserved" when he gave his mother "a brief peck on the cheek," but he repeated it for news photographers.[35]

Judge Charles F. Blackstock denied the change of venue. According to the newspaper, Blackstock, eighty-three, said the defendants would get a fair trial: "It is a sad commentary on the integrity, decency and humanity of Ventura County to say that defendants whose very lives may be at stake cannot receive a fair and impartial trial in this county." To further illustrate his belief, he reduced the first call for a jury panel from 250 to 150.[36] By the time Duncan's trial began in mid-February, much of what the jury heard had been published in the press.

The *Times* termed Duncan a "much-married but seemingly mild-mannered Santa Barbara matron." She was described as smiling and confident, even though a number of potential jurors said they already considered her guilty. This admission led Sullivan to again ask for a change of venue, which was denied. When the press interviewed Duncan, she denied a radio report that she had saved sleeping pills for a suicide attempt if she was found guilty.[37]

Duncan also told the press she had received between fifteen and twenty threatening letters while she was in jail, though Frank dismissed some letters that had drawings of her hanging from a tree as the work of "cranks." The court allowed the press to take natural-light photographs during the trial after Duncan, her attorney, and Gustafson all agreed. The *Times* noted each day what color dress Duncan wore.[38]

34. "Mrs. Duncan Plans to Ask Venue Shift," ibid., 3 January 1959.

35. "Release Transcript"; "2 Men Plead Insanity in Duncan Killing Case," ibid., 14 January 1959.

36. "Venue Change Refused in Duncan Slaying," ibid., 16 January 1959.

37. "Trial for Duncan Murder to Open," ibid., 16 February 1959; "Selection of Jury Starts in Duncan Murder Trial," ibid., 17 February 1959.

38. "Panel Selection in Murder Trial Proving Slow," ibid., 18 February 1959.

During jury selection, the American Civil Liberties Union of southern California supported another motion to move the trial, saying a fair trial was more likely in a community "in which the case has been discussed less in the press, over radio and on television than in Ventura County." Judge Blackstock again denied the motion, and Duncan told news reporters she did not believe she could get a fair trial. A jury of eight women and four men was seated. Duncan again revealed threatening letters to her, including one that said it was hoped she would hang and others that called her a "cutthroat," said "I could kill you," and termed Frank "Mamma's boy" and "apron strings." Even from as far away as San Francisco, she received hate mail, including one letter that said it was hoped she was executed.[39]

The trial became raucous once the jury was seated and testimony began. Duncan reportedly "ran the gamut of emotions" on the first day, including showing anger when one witness testified against her, and laughing when another claimed she had been plotting to "dope up" her son when Olga's murder was being carried out. Moya's testimony turned out to most disturb Frank, who reportedly left the courtroom in tears, sending a message back to his mother that he would continue to support her. Duncan "gazed stonily" at Moya as he testified, and Frank told the *Times:* "It is inconceivable my mother could associate with a man like that. What a cold-blooded man! I'd like to lay my hand on that ___."[40]

Although Moya's testimony damaged Duncan, it was not as harmful as testimony two days later by one of her friends, eighty-four-year-old Emma Short, who told the court that Duncan had told Olga, "If you don't leave him alone, I'll kill you." She also testified that Frank called his mother "doll," and had told her he would never leave her. Short testified she had seen Frank sleeping in the same bed with his mother before his marriage to Olga, and Duncan had come out of the bedroom and said, "Isn't he beautiful?" The testimony riled Duncan, who leaped to her feet and said, "You're a liar!" She said later, "This woman has my clothes on right now and she's a liar. I feel like tearing them right off of her."[41]

Duncan remained remarkably calm on the first day that she testified in her defense, save for "two brief interludes of quiet sobbing." She was not so composed when Gustafson asked her about eleven of her sixteen "known or purported marriages," and six children. It was the first mention that Duncan had six children; previously, only Frank and a daughter, Patsy, who died in 1948, had been mentioned in court, and the *Times* said

39. "Civil Liberties Union Enters Duncan Trial," ibid., 20 February 1959; "Eight Women, Four Men Chosen on Duncan Jury," ibid., 21 February 1959.
40. "Mrs. Duncan Tried to Hire Her to Kill, Carhop Says," ibid., 25 February 1959; "Attorney Leaves Room; Will Stick with Mother," ibid., 27 February 1959.
41. "Mrs. Duncan's Threat to Daughter-in-Law Told," ibid., 28 February 1959.

Gustafson had surprised and shocked Duncan and electrified the packed courtroom. During her last day on the stand, things got even testier when Gustafson was standing close to the witness stand, "directing slashing questions" at Duncan, who told him, "Don't you stand so close to me. You better get away." Gustafson moved and Duncan said, "That's the best place for you." The *Times* termed her reaction "an implied threat to strike" Gustafson. She also snapped at Judge Blackstock when he ordered her to answer one of Gustafson's questions, "How can I when you sit there and overrule everything?"[42]

In closing arguments, Gustafson was tough on Frank, asking whether he was "a man or a mouse." Gustafson said Frank certainly was "a spineless jellyfish." He termed Frank's testimony "an act," and said he and Duncan had preened for photographers. Gustafson attacked Duncan: "Have you ever seen anybody who showed less remorse, less regret, over the death of someone, with all her preening, smiling, laughing and giggling?" When Gustafson finished and walked past Duncan, she reportedly began to rise from her seat, but deputies restrained her. She then said something to Gustafson; the *Times* reported she had called him an "S.O.B.," but she said she had called him a liar.[43]

When the jury announced Duncan's guilty verdict, the *Los Angeles Times* said her expression "remained unchanged," and her later concern was for Frank, who "was ashen-faced and visibly disturbed." Duncan's sister told a *Times* reporter: "This was a terrible shock to all of us. I'm sure she must have been crazy to do this, if she did." She added, "She has always been a little bit overbearing and domineering. She had to have her own way."[44]

The case became even more bizarre during the sentencing phase when Gustafson recited a litany of Duncan's past marriages, and a past conviction for keeping a house of prostitution. The testimony of one of her exhusbands, George Satriano, had Duncan, Judge Blackstock, and almost everyone else in the courtroom laughing so much that Blackstock had to call a recess to restore order. According to the *Times*, "The bizarre spectacle of hilarity entering a proceeding with a woman's life at stake was matched by further revelations of Mrs. Duncan's amazing peccadilloes." Duncan had induced Satriano "to marry her on the spur of the moment." The *Times* described the scene: "Asked if she was attracted to Satriano, Mrs. Duncan smiled demurely at him (he remained seated in the front row

42. "Mrs. Duncan Admits She Plotted to Kidnap Her Son," ibid., 5 March 1959; "Hot Words Throw Trial into Uproar," ibid., 6 March 1959; "Duncan Takes Stand, Backs Mother's Story," ibid., 7 March 1959.

43. "Hurls Name at Him As He Ends Remarks; Defense Summing Up," ibid., 13 March 1959.

44. "Find Mrs. Duncan Guilty of Murder," ibid., 17 March 1959.

of spectators) and brought more laughter with the reply: 'I certainly was—and I still am.'"[45]

Days later, the hilarity turned deadly serious when Duncan was sentenced to die in the gas chamber. The *Times* stated that "the gray-haired matron stood impassive" as Blackstock read the sentence.[46]

Once Duncan was sentenced and an execution date was set, the political battles began for Gov. Edmund "Pat" Brown, who opposed the death penalty but did not commute death sentences because he said he was sworn to uphold the law. When he was lieutenant governor, Brown had criticized the process for Barbara Graham's execution, but now he found himself in a political dilemma with at least three parts. First, Duncan was a woman, and Brown had earlier said he did not like the idea of a woman being executed. Second, this execution was close to that of Caryl Chessman, executed in 1960. Brown, according to the *Times*, had become embroiled in a dispute when he granted Chessman a late reprieve and then asked the state legislature in 1960 to consider abolishing or modifying the death penalty, which the legislature refused. Third, the Republicans had nominated Richard Nixon to oppose Brown in the 1962 governor's race, and Nixon favored the death penalty, saying it was a "necessary deterrent" for murder. The *New York Times* said Duncan, "gray-haired and bespectacled, with at least a veneer of cultivation, fits the mother-image of American tradition."[47] Brown refused to grant clemency, and won re-election.

When Elizabeth Duncan died on 8 August 1962, the *Los Angeles Times* said she "died with impassive dignity." Baldonado and Moya, executed on the same day, died "in a blatant show of thigh-slapping bravado and elaborate farewells." Ironically, the three executions in one day were the first in California since Barbara Graham and her two accomplices were executed in 1955. The story said Duncan was "like a proud woman who had achieved the ultimate in poise and dignity." Her reaction reportedly puzzled two reporters, who asked if she was under heavy sedation and were told she was not, although she had requested to be "totally sedated" so that she would not have to see the witnesses. Frank, remarried to a San Francisco lawyer, claimed his mother's body. Four years later, Frank's wife, Elinor, sued him for divorce, charging cruelty.[48]

45. "Kept S. F. House of Ill Repute," ibid., 18 March 1959; "Jurors Told More of Her Peccadillos [sic]," ibid., 19 March 1959.

46. "Mrs. Duncan Gets Death Sentence," ibid., 4 April 1959.

47. "Duncan Case Decision Hard One for Brown," ibid., 15 July 1962; "Brown Faces Election Dilemma in Case of a Condemned Woman," *New York Times,* 29 July 1962.

48. "Duncan Dies with Conspirators"; "Wife Sues Frank Duncan for Divorce," *Los Angeles Times,* 4 January 1966.

Chapter 13

The Female "Tough Guy"

Irene Schroeder: The "Animal Woman"

Although all of the women who committed crimes for which they were executed violated the cultural norms about womanhood, some seemed to do so more than others, including Irene Schroeder. Schroeder was a West Virginian, not a westerner. However, in 1930, she eluded police across the United States and eventually became the subject of a major, ongoing news story in Arizona, Pennsylvania, and New York, but mainly in the West. She robbed and killed, she said, because it thrilled her, an eerie similarity to the more famous Leopold and Loeb of a few years earlier.

Her son, Donnie Schroeder, age five, was probably too young to understand when his mother told him: "I am going to die, my boy, but I am not afraid. Be a good boy and don't be afraid." As the youngster left the New Castle, Pennsylvania, jail, a newspaper reporter heard him say: "I'll bet mom would make an awful nice angel."[1]

Donnie might have considered his twenty-two-year-old mother, a waitress from Wheeling, West Virginia, an angel, but the newspaper press had other ideas. The *New York Times* called her a "blonde bandit," a "girl bandit," and the "diminutive waitress of 22 years who laid aside her apron to become a bandit." Although "diminutive" in New York, she was "chunky" in Phoenix. The *Philadelphia Evening Bulletin* referred to her as a "blonde bandit," a "gun girl," and a "blonde gun girl." She became so well known that the *Evening Bulletin* simply referred to her as "Irene." The Associated Press tagged her the "blonde tiger." The *Phoenix Gazette*, though, applied the most colorful monikers, calling her "trigger woman," "Iron Irene," "Irene of the six-shooters," "Irene of the glinting guns," and the "animal woman." The *Gazette* compared her to Belle Starr and Calamity Jane. Reporting the story of twentieth-century gun battles between po-

1. "Mrs. Schroeder Resigned," *New York Times,* 21 February 1931.

lice and a band of desperadoes on the run, one of them female, must have been like cowboys and Indians on wheels for the *Gazette.*

In 1931, Schroeder became the first woman executed by electrocution in Pennsylvania, and the fourth woman electrocuted in the United States. Her companion in crime and her lover, Walter Glenn Dague, thirty-four, a former Sunday-school superintendent and an insurance salesman from Sewellsville, Ohio, had deserted his wife and two children for Schroeder, and he died in the same chair within minutes of her execution. News stories described Dague as a "dapper individual, rather too smartly dressed, too carefully groomed . . . a middle-class family man making a modest living." Schroeder became so well known in Pennsylvania that a news article about her life, crimes, and death ran eleven years after her execution. Schroeder had a hard life. She was born Irene Crawford in Benwood, West Virginia, in 1909, one of a dozen children. At age fifteen, she married Homer Schroeder, and at sixteen gave birth to Donnie. Soon after, she left her husband and went to work in Wheeling, as a waitress. The *Philadelphia Inquirer* described her as "plump, blonde, uncultured, without charm or poise," but possessing "high spirits and a great stock of vitality." The *Inquirer* interpreted Schroeder and Dague's meeting as fatalistic, saying that two ordinary individuals joined to create a chemistry that destroyed them both.[2]

On 27 December 1929, near New Castle, state police received a call about a robbery at a grocery store in Butler, Pennsylvania. State police corporal Brady Paul and highway patrolman Ernest Moore stopped an auto fitting the description of the one used in the robbery and walked toward it, and Moore later testified that he had seen a pretty, well-dressed blonde in the car, along with a young boy and two men. One of the men got out of the car and pulled a gun, and the woman yelled, "Stick 'em up." Shots were fired, killing Paul and slightly wounding Moore.[3]

Schroeder and Dague fled to West Virginia and left Donnie with her father. Police found the boy and questioned him. "My mamma shot one cop and . . . Uncle Tom shot another one right in the head. He shot right through the windshield," the *New York Times* said the boy had told the police. "Uncle Tom" apparently was Tom Crawford, one of Schroeder's brothers, whom Donnie said had been in the auto. Crawford later was believed killed in Fort Worth, Texas, during a gun battle with police. Schroeder and Dague disappeared, aided by a heavy snowstorm that obliterated any traces of them around her father's home. The two surfaced

2. Winifred Van Duzer, "Trail of Crime Led Gun-Girl and Accomplice to the Death Chair," *Philadelphia Inquirer,* 1 February 1942.

3. "Girl Bandit Kills Highway Policeman," *New York Times,* 28 December 1929; "Confesses a Part in Police Killing," ibid., 20 January 1930.

briefly in St. Louis, where police nearly captured them, but they escaped after a gun battle.[4]

On 14 January 1930, an all-capitals banner headline in the *Phoenix Gazette* screamed: "Posse Expects Gun Battle." The newspaper published an extra edition that day, which featured a two-line banner headline that read: "Posse, Bandits Open Battle; Trio Surrounded on Hilltop." The news coverage was triggered when a car pulled into Florence, Arizona, on 13 January and cruised around town. Deputy Sheriff Joe Chapman said that at first he had assumed the young blonde driver was looking for gasoline and oil, but when she drove to a third station, Chapman became suspicious and asked her for the title to the car. She could not produce it, and Chapman told her she was under arrest. She burst into tears and slumped across the steering wheel, sobbing and repeatedly hitting the car's horn. Two nearby men walked toward the car, and suddenly the woman straightened up and pointed a pistol at Chapman. The men poked two more gun barrels into his ribs and forced him into the car. Other than Schroeder and Dague, the third man was later identified as Vernon Ackerman, an ex-convict. Schroeder's brother Tom had been killed by this time.

Seven hours later, the car drove into Chandler, Arizona, and deputy sheriffs almost immediately spotted it and forced it to the curb near the city's plaza. A gunman in the backseat opened fire. The *Gazette* described the scene:

> The roaring of shotguns, rifles and sixshooters filled Chandler as the battle progressed in front of the smart San Marcos hotel, turning back the pages of time to the days of Arizona gun battles and startling residents of the city.
> Cracking down with a six-gun in the battle was a bobbed-haired blond woman about 35 years old, who faced a booming shotgun and hurled lead in the fracas as calmly as her gun-fighting male companions and the daring officers rescuing Chapman.

Police called the woman "the most desperate feminine character ever to figure in police annals of Arizona." The *Gazette* reported that shots had been fired at "point blank" range, and shots from one officer's "belching shotgun were poured almost in the faces of the occupants of the kidnap car." The desperadoes slipped away during the confusion. Officer Chapman escaped during the shootout by grabbing Schroeder's hands, kicking open the door of the car, and sliding out onto the street, attempting to drag her out with him. The *Gazette* claimed Deputy Sheriff Lee Wright's

4. "Child Says Mother Killed Policeman," ibid., 1 January 1930; "Boy, 4, Accuses His Mother As Police Killer," *Philadelphia Inquirer,* 31 December 1929; "Mrs. Schroeder Condemned to Die," *Philadelphia Evening Bulletin,* 23 March 1930.

wounds in his left side and shoulder were not life threatening, but Wright died soon after.[5]

Schroeder, Dague, and Ackerman fled in the car, which was later found abandoned and riddled with bullets. The *Gazette* said the "most spectacular manhunt in Salt River valley's history" began as hundreds of police officers and volunteers searched. A short time later, officers surrounded the bandits on a peak known as Estrella Mountain. Officers expected a gun battle "to the finish," but that did not materialize because the three surrendered after a brief exchange of gunfire with an advance party. Officers slipped up close enough to yell, "Stick 'em up, Buddy," and the three surrendered without resistance.[6]

The *Gazette* reported that police strongly suspected the three to be Schroeder, Dague, and a third person whom police had not identified. Schroeder denied being wanted in Pennsylvania. A rifle bullet had slightly wounded her—a "crease" on her neck—during one of the exchanges of gunfire with Arizona police. Dague was wounded in the hip, but in another story the *Gazette* reported he had probably been wounded during an earlier shootout with Texas police.[7]

A front-page story the next day called Schroeder the "animal woman." Her nickname resulted from a statement she had made to a *Gazette* reporter after he said that her "iron nerve" and daring amazed people. She replied, "That woman angle stuff is all the bunk. I'm not a woman. I'm nothing but an animal. I'm full of nothing but animal instinct and self preservation." The first paragraph in the next day's lead story played on the folklore about previous Wild West women, while reaching far afield for literary effect. "The ghosts of Belle Starr, Calamity Jane and all the six-gun sisterhood of the old west stalked through the corridors of the Maricopa county jail today and placed shadowy, sympathetic arms about the shoulders of a modern counterpart—Irene Schroeder of the triggers." The story later called her "Irene of the six-shooters" and "the chunky little trigger girl." When Schroeder apparently fainted at the jail, the jailers dismissed it as being contrived. The assistant county health officer said Schroeder had suffered "from reaction to a canned heat jag," and she "showed all the signs of a canned heat addict."[8]

---

5. "Posse Expects Gun Battle"; "Posse, Bandits Open Battle."

6. "Plane and Hounds in Man-Hunt," *Phoenix Gazette*, 14 January 1930; "Posse, Bandits Open Battle"; "Tells Trigger Girl Capture," ibid., 15 January 1930; "Get Woman Outlaw in Arizona Siege," *New York Times*, 15 January 1930.

7. "'Animal Woman' Denies Being 'Trigger Girl' Wanted As Killer," *Phoenix Gazette*, 15 January 1930; "Link Bandits in Crime Net," ibid.

8. "Denies Being 'Trigger Girl'"; "Identify 'Trigger Woman,'" ibid., 16 January 1930. Compared with New York and Pennsylvania, Arizona was still very much the Old West, having gained statehood only eighteen years earlier, and in 1930 the population of the state was only slightly more than 435,500, with the most populous county being

Schroeder and Dague fought extradition to Pennsylvania, but Arizona officials said the pair would be charged with kidnapping for the purpose of robbery and assault with intent to murder unless they were charged with murder in Pennsylvania. Arizona did not charge them because Pennsylvania officials quickly extradited Schroeder and Dague. The *New York Times* reported that Dague had confessed to Arizona police that he and Schroeder had been in a gunfight with Pennsylvania state policemen, and that another man or Schroeder had shot Paul. Arizona police said Schroeder had shown no interest in Dague's confession.[9] The *Times*'s story ran before the pair were returned to Pennsylvania and indicted, and well before their trials.

Schroeder's trial began on 10 March 1930. The *Philadelphia Evening Bulletin* called her "Pennsylvania's most notorious woman criminal," and said she had a "shabbily colorful career." She appeared for trial wearing "a neat blue dress. Her hair was newly bobbed and her face was plentifully besprinkled with powder." She reportedly gave a scornful glance at the courtroom crowd. Early in the trial, when the court took jurors and Schroeder to where Paul had been shot, newspaper photographers asked her to "smile and look pretty." She replied in what the press described as a sharp, defiant manner, "How can you smile and look pretty when you are going to prison for life and are heart-broken?"[10]

The press closely covered the trial. Schroeder testified in her own defense, and said that if released she and Dague would preach the gospel. She denied shooting Paul. Schroeder testified that she had an irresistible impulse to steal and that the holdups she and Dague had committed thrilled her. She said the impulses began at age ten, when she fell and injured her head. She testified that she had attempted suicide on three or four occasions; the *New York Times* said the testimony was part of an insanity defense. The prosecution said the state did not recognize an impulse to rob as a form of insanity. Special Prosecutor Charles J. Margiotti told the jury in his closing arguments that Schroeder had masterminded a crime organization, and that she and her accomplices had been "carrion birds swooping into Pennsylvania to prey on fellow humans."[11]

Maricopa at almost 151,000 (1890 U.S. Census, http://www.ancestry.com/home/free/censtats/aznews.htm).

9. "Link Bandits"; "Identify 'Trigger Woman'"; "Confesses Part in Killing."

10. "Put Blonde Bandit on Trial As Killer," *Philadelphia Evening Bulletin,* 10 March 1930; "Jury Picked to Try Woman Accused of Slaying Trooper," *Philadelphia Inquirer,* 13 March 1930.

11. "Gungirl on Stand in Own Defense," *Philadelphia Inquirer,* 19 March 1930; "Mrs. Schroeder Condemned to Die," *Philadelphia Evening Bulletin,* 23 March 1930; "Crime Thrill Told by Mrs. Schroeder," *New York Times,* 21 March 1930; "Death Is Verdict for Mrs. Schroeder," ibid., 22 March 1930.

News reports said Schroeder laughed as she came into the court-room and remained calm when the guilty verdict was announced. She reportedly sneered when taken from the courtroom to her cell. Crowds followed, including newspapermen, with flashbulbs popping as they snapped pictures. An *Inquirer* story included a breezy dialogue between Schroeder and Dague that amplified her defiant, steely demeanor. She called to Dague, who was walking outside his cell on the floor below. Dague asked her, "How are you feeling Irene?"

"Come on up and see," she replied.

"I would if I could," he said.

"Why don't you?"

"Oh, just because."

"Go to bed, you old devil."

About a week later, Dague was sentenced to die. His defense was that Schroeder had dominated him.[12]

The *Phoenix Gazette* also closely followed Schroeder's trial, mostly relying on Associated Press coverage. However, the *Gazette* played heavily on a local angle when reporting Schroeder's death sentence, saying that Arizona had reached with "an arm of limitless length yesterday and wrote with vengeful fingers" the sentence. Playing on the vengeance theme, the story said more than one thousand miles "were spanned by the arm of retribution" of the state. The story claimed three Phoenix witnesses had sealed Schroeder's fate, and as a result, "Twenty-two thousand searing, jolting volts of electricity will avenge Lee Wright's death and the death of Brady Paul."[13]

On 18 February 1931, three attorneys pleaded with the Pennsylvania Board of Pardons for Schroeder's and Dague's lives. Schroeder's attorney said publicity had prevented his client from getting a fair and impartial trial. He also argued that women should not be subject to capital punishment because womanhood should be placed on a pedestal that would put them beyond the possibility of execution. Finally, he told the board that Schroeder and Dague said they had a vision in which they saw a burning cross and an ostrich, which they interpreted to mean that if they were released, Dague would go to Africa to preach the gospel. The prosecutor

---

12. "Gun-Girl Is Doomed to Electric Chair; Sneers at Jury," *Philadelphia Inquirer*, 22 March 1930; "Dague Found Guilty, with Death Verdict," *New York Times*, 1 April 1930.

13. "Implicate Two in Brady Death," *Phoenix Gazette*, 14 March 1930; "Gungirl Shot to Save Lover Witness Says," ibid., 17 March 1930; "Irene Insanity Plea Ruled Out," ibid., 18 March 1930; "Donnie Plays on Unconscious of Tragedy Facing His Mother," ibid., 19 March 1930; "Prosecution Wins in Irene Trial," ibid., 20 March 1930; "Dying Words of Paul Quoted in Attempt to Send Irene to Chair," ibid., 21 March 1930; "Death Penalty Given Gungirl," ibid., 22 March 1930.

ridiculed the vision as being "trumped up," and the board denied the pleas.[14]

In several stories during the last days before the executions, the newspaper press played on irony or used imagery to conjure the specter of death. For example, on the day before the execution, Dague's spiritual adviser, the Reverend H. O. Teagarden of Sewellsville, Ohio, visited. Dague had once been a Sunday-school superintendent in Teagarden's church. In addition, the *Philadelphia Inquirer* used angel-of-death imagery in a story about executioner Robert Elliott. It was not especially common to use an executioner's name and picture in a news story, and it would be unheard of today. However, Elliott was a celebrity because he had been the executioner for some famous executions, including Ruth Snyder in 1928 in New York. The *Inquirer*'s story painted Elliott as the angel of death, and had a melodramatic tone. "While these things were going forward within the prison walls, the presence of death loomed in concrete form with the appearance, and rapid disappearance, of the executioner who functions and has functioned, for several States, Robert Elliott." The article described Elliott as somber and unassuming, and called him the "lean instrument of the annihilation of the condemned." Passengers recognized him on the train to Pennsylvania, but Elliott shied away. The *Inquirer* said some passengers "stared their curiosity and awe," and Elliott was "whisked away" from the Milesburg train station and taken to a house to wait until called to perform the execution.[15]

Press reports about Schroeder's execution said she did not utter a word. The *Philadelphia Evening Bulletin* stated that the only voice heard was that of the chaplain praying. The story referred to Schroeder's physical appearance, noting she was obviously heavier than when arrested and had gained twenty-two pounds. She wore "a gray artificial-silk dress, loose and poorly fitting . . . beige stockings and black slippers." Officials had clipped hair from the back of her head for the electrode to be placed. Others were not as unemotional. Dague's wife, Theresa, was reported to be in a virtual state of collapse. Prior to the executions, Schroeder pleaded that she and Dague be given a joint funeral service and be buried in a common grave, but the request was denied. Dague's wife arranged for his body to

---

14. "Plea of Gungirl to Escape Chair Heard by Board," *Philadelphia Evening Bulletin,* 18 February 1931.

15. "Mrs. Schroeder Resigned"; "Irene Schroeder Goes to Place of Execution," *New York Times,* 22 February 1931; "Doomed Couple Calm As Death in Chair Nears," *Philadelphia Inquirer,* 23 February 1931. When sheriffs hanged defendants in the counties, there was no anonymity for the executioner. One U.S. president, Grover Cleveland, hanged two murderers when he was a sheriff in New York (H. Paul Jeffers, *An Honest President,* 34–35).

be shipped to her, and buried at Dallas, West Virginia, following a private funeral service. Schroeder's body was taken to Bellaire, Ohio.[16]

Elizabeth Potts: Wearing the Pants in the Family

The *Elko (Nev.) Weekly Independent* questioned Elizabeth Potts's role as a wife and her husband's role as the man of the family when it listed her name first and then her husband's in a story. "We say Elizabeth Potts and her husband because it is a notorious fact that she wears the pants."[17]

The *Phoenix Gazette*, in a later article about hangings of women in the West, erroneously said Potts and her husband, Josiah, were hanged in 1888; actually, the year was 1890. The *New York Times* did not mention the hangings, so they passed with little or no notice in the major media centers in the East, although they were news in the Midwest because the *Chicago Tribune* published a story. Newspapers in Denver and San Francisco covered the hangings, and in Elko, Nevada, it was big news, in both the *Independent* and the *Free Press.*

The *Elko (Nev.) Free Press* first reported on 26 January 1889 the crime for which the Pottses hanged, saying "a foul murder" had been unearthed in nearby Carlin, Nevada. The *Independent* followed one day later with "The Carlin Horror."[18] Police had found human remains in the cellar of a home; the *Independent* claimed it had refrained from publicizing the murder earlier at the police's request. The *Free Press*, which billed itself as the "County Official Newspaper," said little about the murder prior to the March 1889 trial. Its 26 January story was a bare-bones straight-news article, and a February story about a preliminary hearing ran only one paragraph.

The *Independent* had more detailed coverage; it said murder victim Miles Faucett apparently was the Pottses' relative. A couple living in the house had found the body, which had been burned. The newspaper speculated about a motive: "It is supposed that the murder was committed to get rid of a debt and also to get the old man's [Faucett's] property."[19]

Most of the details about the crime and the people involved ran in the execution stories in the *Free Press* and the *Independent*. Elko and surrounding-area readers could have put together a pretty good account of what had happened from those articles.

16. "Gungirl and Dague Calm As They Go to Death in Chair," *Philadelphia Evening Bulletin*, 23 February 1931; "Mrs. Schroeder Resigned"; "Gungirl and Dague Calm."
    17. "Should the Pottses Hang?" *Elko (Nev.) Weekly Independent*, 2 April 1890.
    18. "A Foul Murder Unearthed at Carlin," *Elko (Nev.) Free Press*, 26 January 1889; "The Carlin Horror," *Elko (Nev.) Weekly Independent*, 27 January 1889.
    19. "The Carlin Horror."

The *Independent* reported that on 1 January 1888, Faucett had told another man that the Pottses owed him money, that they could afford to repay it, and that he knew enough about Elizabeth Potts's past to force them to pay. The newspaper did not report what Faucett knew about her, but did say that Faucett and another man went to the Pottses' home on 1 January; the other man left, but Faucett stayed the night and was never seen alive again.

In its execution story, the *Free Press* recounted the events. About nine months after Faucett's disappearance, the Pottses moved to Rock Springs, Wyoming, and the George Brewer family moved into the house. Mrs. Brewer, who corresponded with the *Free Press* under the nom de plume "Busy Bee," said the home was haunted. The ghost sometimes tapped on the headboard of the Brewers' bed and other times walked across the kitchen floor and hammered at the door. "But the gayest capers of all are cut up in the cellar. There he holds high revels, and upsets the pickles and carries on generally." George Brewer investigated and found human remains "all cut to pieces." The newspaper described the scene: "[T]he head [was] charred and fleshless, having been chopped up and burned. The legs, arms and body were in small pieces and beyond recognition." The *Free Press* said Brewer had found a half-burned pants pocket with a knife inside; it was later identified as Faucett's. Police arrested the Pottses in Rock Springs and returned them to Elko. During the return trip, the couple claimed Faucett had committed suicide, a story they clung to until their deaths. A grand jury indicted them on 15 February 1889, and their trial began on 12 March. They pleaded not guilty. Both newspapers said the Pottses could not have been convicted if they had kept their mouths shut and had stuck with their original story about Faucett leaving Elko. In a retrospective portion of its story about the executions, the *Independent* said the coroner's inquest could not have identified the remains, and based its conclusion on the facts that Faucett was missing in January 1888, that human remains were found in January 1889, and that the remains were found in a cellar where the Pottses had lived.[20]

Both newspapers showed remarkable restraint about publishing information prior to the trial, especially if judged by today's standards. Of course, because the Elko County's population was only 4,794 in the 1890 census, most people probably knew the details of the case. Nonetheless, the *Independent* said it would not be proper to comment on preliminary court proceedings, because the case would be brought to trial and "we do not desire to publish anything that could be construed as influencing the public either for or against the defendants." The *Free Press* beat the *Inde-*

---

20. "Executed," *Elko (Nev.) Free Press*, 21 June 1890; "The Execution," *Elko (Nev.) Weekly Independent*, 22 June 1890.

pendent by a day in reporting on the preliminary hearing, but published only one paragraph at the bottom of page 3.[21]

The *Independent* had the more detailed trial coverage. Charley Potts, sixteen, said he had been in bed the night of the murder, heard loud noises, got up, and saw Faucett shoot himself. He said he had gone back to bed without saying anything. "His statement shows him to be quite shrewd for one of his age, but the most completely devoid of natural curiosity of any person we ever heard of." Elizabeth Potts testified that Faucett had killed himself after she discovered him "in an act of criminal assault" on the Pottses' four-year-old daughter. She claimed Faucett had shot himself to prevent exposure of his crime.[22]

The *Elko Weekly Independent* printed the judge's sentencing speech word-for-word. The newspaper was aghast that a woman had committed such a crime, noting that women seldom perpetrated murder. "To her we look for everything that is gentle and kind and tender; and we can scarcely conceive her capable of committing the highest crime known to the law."[23]

On 30 March, the *Elko Free Press* ran as its lead editorial "Let the Law Take Its Course." The newspaper lamented that many murders in the area had gone unpunished: "For years it has been the common talk all over the State that a conviction of murder in the first degree could not be had in Elko county." The newspaper argued that the law should take its course without interference, although hanging a woman was an awful punishment. Neither newspaper had much coverage for almost a year, until late May 1890. The *Independent* ran in late April an article that claimed Nevadans almost universally wished that the Pottses would not hang, but did not indicate how it divined the opinion of the state's residents.[24]

On 31 May, the *Free Press* ran a short item under the standing headline "This and That," with the subhead "Must Hang." The one-paragraph story was about the Nevada Board of Pardons's refusal to commute the sentences, but the newspaper added: "[The Pottses] will be launched into eternity from the same gallows and at the same moment." The *Independent* claimed that Elizabeth Potts would be the first woman hanged on the Pacific Coast, which was erroneous because a woman was hanged in California in 1851, as clarified in the *Los Angeles Times.* The *Independent* hinted that the hanging of a woman in Elko might amount to a festive occasion: "This fact will make the event one of unusual and exciting interest,

21. See Nevada census at http://www.ancestry.com/home/free/censtats/nvcens.htm. "The Carlin Murder," *Elko (Nev.) Weekly Independent,* 3 February 1889; "The Potts Case," *Elko (Nev.) Free Press,* 2 February 1889.
22. "The Potts Trial," *Elko (Nev.) Weekly Independent,* 17 March 1889.
23. "The Death Sentence," ibid., 24 March 1889.
24. "District Court," ibid., 27 April 1890.

and June 20, 1890, will be an eventful day in the history of Nevada." In the same edition, the paper first expressed its developing opposition to the death sentence: "Under all the circumstances we believe it would be but an act of justice to commute the sentence to imprisonment for life."[25]

The *Free Press* did not have a similar attitude about the death penalty. It briefly reported about the scaffold being built in California to be shipped to Nevada. In a story published after the execution, the *Free Press* said the gallows had been constructed at Placerville, California, and was made of seasoned lumber "made to work well." The cross beam was also made of seasoned timber "capable of sustaining a tremendous strain." The trap swung one way and was held in place by a bar. The paper noted that the gallows was tested prior to the hangings with bags of sand and "worked like a charm."[26]

The *Independent* launched an editorial attack on the death penalty after it visited the Pottses in jail. The newspaper questioned the fairness of the sentence, saying the Nevada Board of Pardons should commute the sentences because of "the feelings of the community," and because it was possible the Pottses had not committed the murder. The newspaper called the evidence circumstantial. It also attacked the death penalty in general, calling it a "relic of barbarism," and said no intelligent, enlightened people should have a death penalty because life imprisonment was an equally good punishment.[27]

The *Free Press* for the most part remained silent, but when it did comment, it favored the executions. It reprinted editorials from the *San Francisco Daily Report* and the *Reno Gazette* that supported the executions. The *Report* said it was dreadful for a woman to hang, but more dreadful for a woman to murder; the *Gazette* criticized Judge Bigelow for seeking commutation for the Pottses. The *Independent* defended Bigelow and said the people of Elko who understood the case—and the newspaper intimated those people understood it better than the *Gazette*—would honor Judge Bigelow. The newspaper said it was hoped there would never be another execution in Elko, and advised people to stay away from the town on 20 June because the executions were to be private.[28]

The Elko newspapers sharply differed in how they depicted the Pottses up to the time of the hangings, especially Elizabeth Potts. The *Free Press* described her as cool and collected at the trial, and it said when the ver-

25. "Girl's Hanging in 1851 Recalled," *Los Angeles Times,* 22 November 1941; "Commutation Denied," *Elko (Nev.) Weekly Independent,* 1 June 1890; "The Potts Case," ibid.

26. "This and That," *Elko (Nev.) Free Press,* 7 June 1890; "Executed."

27. "The Doomed Prisoners," *Elko (Nev.) Weekly Independent,* 8 June 1890.

28. "The Law Vindicated," *Elko (Nev.) Free Press,* 28 June 1890; "Hardly Probable," *Elko (Nev.) Weekly Independent,* 15 June 1890.

dicts were announced, her "face never changed color or expression. She looked straight ahead as unconcerned as if she was merely a spectator instead of the leading character in the terrible drama." Similarly, when the death sentences were announced: "A stranger to the case would have thought she was merely a defendant in a divorce suit." The *Free Press* said that while in jail, "Mrs. Potts put in her time swearing at everybody and everything." When the gallows was being erected and the Pottses could hear the hammering in the jail yard, the newspaper said the couple had cried, but added that later, Elizabeth Potts had "cussed the world and everybody in it." The *Free Press* claimed she "was the leader, he the tool." In contrast, on the rare occasion when the *Independent* described her, she was usually depicted as distraught. The *Chicago Tribune* stated that Elizabeth Potts's days were "marked by hysterical weeping and swearing at her husband, who spent his time in his own cell playing solitaire."[29]

Both the *Independent* and the *Free Press* ran lengthy and detailed stories about the hangings, although the former's was more detailed. Both newspapers said few people were in Elko on the day of the hangings, except for the press and law enforcement officers. Nonetheless, the *Independent* declared that "an air of feverish excitement seemed to prevail." The *Free Press* provided a detailed list of the law officers who had attended, almost like the attendance listed in social columns of newspapers for holiday parties, or the "country correspondent" reports in small newspapers.[30]

Elizabeth Potts's demeanor on execution day conflicted with descriptions of her earlier calm, almost disinterested attitude. The *Independent* also reported in its story about the hangings that the night before the executions, Potts was "in a high state of excitement and in great mental strain." A minister reportedly told her to say "Christ" to settle herself, and the newspaper said that when she did so, she calmed down.

On the morning of the hangings, officers "administered spirits," probably alcohol, to the Pottses. Elizabeth Potts stood erect, and Josiah leaned forward to hear when the sheriff read the death warrants. Both said they were innocent, and "another tonic was given." The press obviously witnessed the procedure because the *Denver Rocky Mountain News* said Elizabeth had shown emotion only once: when the word *hanged* was used in her husband's death warrant, the newspaper said she "gave a hysterical grasp [*sic*] and seemed to exhibit much feeling." During the emotional scene, it took the sheriff twenty minutes to read the warrants, and the *News* said a deputy had been emotionally overcome.[31]

29. "Executed"; "Husband and Wife on the Gallows," *Chicago Tribune*, 21 June 1890.
30. "The Execution"; "Executed."
31. "A Double Hanging," *Denver Rocky Mountain News*, 21 June 1890.

The Pottses walked calmly to the gallows, where they said, "We are innocent." They sat on chairs, had their shoes removed and their arms pinioned. They stood and Josiah told his wife, "Goodbye," and nudged her, the *News* reported. They then shook hands with one another with their wrists tied, leaned forward, and kissed affectionately, the *Independent* attested. As the hangman placed the rope around Elizabeth Potts's neck, she clasped her hands, looked up, and said, "God help me, as I am innocent."[32]

The trap was sprung, and the *Independent* recorded the reactions: "A second after a voice from below said distinctly breaking the deep silence, 'O.K.' A look from above saw the horror-stricken faces of the on-lookers, many being ghastly ashen. One man fainted away."

Elizabeth Potts was almost decapitated. She "died immediately," the *Independent* related, although, as with many newspapers that reported such facts, how was the reporter to know? The newspaper did not report the ghastly scene in too much detail, merely saying, "[T]he carotid artery [was] broken by the rope, as was shown by a stream of blood." The *Free Press* reported in more detail, saying that when hanged, "Her neck was broken, and the blood streamed down the front of her white dress. The head was almost severed from the body." The *Independent* had not reported Elizabeth Potts's weight before the execution, but the *Free Press* had, saying she had weighed about 190 pounds when jailed but had lost some weight since then. Despite the gory nature of the execution of Elizabeth Potts, and the excruciatingly slow death of Josiah, who apparently strangled, the *Free Press* claimed there was "not a hitch in the execution."[33] Out-of-town newspapers reported on the execution, including the *Denver Rocky Mountain News,* the *Cheyenne Daily Leader,* the *Arizona Weekly Journal Miner,* and the *Chicago Tribune.* Only the Denver newspaper gave a detailed report. The Arizona paper mentioned the near decapitation, but the others did not.

The *Free Press*'s description of the hanging was considerably more upbeat and much less detailed than the *Independent*'s. The latter newspaper said fifty-two people invited by Sheriff Barnard had gained admission, and that several women had tried to gain admittance "but were rightfully refused." The paper disapprovingly reported that two or three women, "overcome by a morbid curiosity," witnessed the execution by peeping through holes in the wooden fence.[34]

32. Ibid.; "The Execution."
33. "The Execution"; "Executed."
34. "Excerpts from the Daily *Independent*," *Elko (Nev.) Weekly Independent,* 29 June 1890.

Reporters who attended included, according to the *Free Press*'s execution story, a Miss Sweet, who wrote for the *San Francisco Examiner* under the nom de plume "Annie Laurie" (her actual name was Winifred Black). The *Independent*'s execution report said that the Pottses had requested that all reporters be excluded from the hangings, even "Annie Laurie, the lady representative of the Examiner, who came from San Francisco for the express purpose of interviewing Mrs. Potts."

The *Independent* reported that after the hangings, the bodies were cut down and placed on boards; the black caps were not removed. A funeral began at noon, and ten minutes later, the bodies were lowered into graves, side by side. Law enforcement officers provided bouquets of wildflowers. The newspaper said about twenty-five people attended, including one woman and several children. The Pottses were buried in a potter's field; Miles Faucett's remains were buried a short time later in the same field. According to the *Denver Rocky Mountain News*, Faucett's bones had been kept at the district attorney's office for "a long time."[35]

The story faded quickly from the *Elko Free Press*, but the *Elko Weekly Independent* continued to print news and opinions about the case until early July. One story claimed that one week before the hanging, Elizabeth Potts, in a suicide attempt, had cut an artery in her left wrist with a small sharp knife she kept hidden in her hair. She had put her hands under the covers of her bed to keep from being discovered, but a deputy sheriff had found her almost unconscious from loss of blood. He had applied pressure to stop the bleeding and called for a doctor who bandaged her. Potts had fought the deputy but was so weak that he was able to handle her, although he was "anything but a stout man." The *Independent* said the doctor's action had angered Potts, and also reported that "some persons," who were never named, regretted that her suicide attempt had not succeeded.[36]

The *Independent* printed slaps at its rival, some of which were letters. The Pottses' attorney said a *Free Press* story claiming there was not unanimous approval in Elko that the Pottses' sentences be commuted was true; of 141 people in Elko asked to sign a petition for commutation, 5 refused. The *Independent* also praised itself. It said only its reporter and reporters for the *San Francisco Examiner* and the Associated Press knew shorthand. Other newspapers were not named, but the *Independent* bragged that it "was strictly correct in every particular and without exaggeration. There were no drafts upon the imagination to fill up the report."[37]

---

35. "A Double Hanging."
36. "The Attempt at Suicide," *Elko (Nev.) Weekly Independent*, 29 June 1890.
37. "Not Unanimous," ibid., 22 June 1890; "Excerpts from the Daily *Independent*."

The Pottses' hangings were big news in the West, and the news reached as far east as Chicago. The story continued to be news well into the twentieth century. A 1970s recounting called the case "one of the most lurid and sensational murder cases in the history of Nevada."[38]

In 1924, Nevada ceased hanging and became the first state in the United States to use the gas chamber.

38. Nevada Historical Society, This Was Nevada series, Reno.

Chapter 14

Little Attention for "First" Executions

TWO CRITERIA OF NEWS ARE that it be new or that it be unusual. Women who were the first of their gender to be electrocuted, gassed, or lethally injected satisfy both criteria. These "firsts" are possible because, as "with so many other goods and services, America offers a greater variety of execution than any other country." Prior to 1890, most defendants were hanged. New York began electrocuting in 1890, and other states soon followed. In 1924, Nevada became the first state to use the gas chamber. Lethal injection, begun in the 1980s, is the most common method of execution. Even firing squads have been used, but I could find no instances of women executed in that way. More humane methods of execution have often been sought, especially for women. The *New York Times* said in an editorial in 1887 that executing women might not be so repulsive, or so infrequent, if an alternative to hanging could be found.[1]

One might expect more local or national press attention for a "first" execution. A study of news coverage and of executions led one researcher to conclude that unless the national media cover them, executions probably have little effect on public perceptions or homicide rates. Other scholars say national media publicity makes no difference. One thing is certain, though: if the press does not cover executions and publicize them, there is little chance for deterrence. The public and press quickly become uninterested as executions become more common. In 1987, Texas attorney general James Mattox said he believed executions were becoming so routine in that state that the deterrent effect was lost. In 1999, an Associated Press report said news reporters seldom competed to report on executions, and the news media ignored all but the most notorious killers.[2] In each of the

1. See, for example, Bruce D. Itule and Douglas A. Anderson, chap. 2 in *News Writing and Reporting for Today's Media;* and Weisberg, "This Is Your Death," 23–27. Editorial, *New York Times,* 1 March 1887.
2. Steven Sack, "Publicized Executions and Homicide, 1950–1980"; William C.

following cases, several men had been executed by the same methods in each state before the women were executed.

Martha Place: The First Woman Electrocuted

New York became the first state to electrocute inmates when it executed William Kemmler on 6 August 1890. It was a horribly botched job, and the method was controversial.[3] New York electrocuted Martha Place in 1899 for murdering her stepdaughter, but by then, forty-five men had died in its electric chair, and the press did not question the chair's use.

William W. Place arrived at his Brooklyn home on 7 February 1898 after a day's work to find the lower floor of his two-story apartment dark. He walked into the hallway and called to his wife, Martha. "Here I am," she said. Her skirts rustled as she came down the stairs. Place struck a match to light the hall gaslight and saw Martha standing on the stairs near him, holding above her head a large ax. She struck him twice, then stepped over him and walked into the parlor. Still conscious, Place opened a door and screamed for help. Two police officers came; one ran inside the home and smelled gas, which he traced to the second floor, where he found Martha Place lying on the floor. Gas flowed from two unlighted burners. The officer opened the windows and went to a back room to open more windows. He saw feet protruding from beneath bedding, and when he pulled it back, there lay Ida Place, Martha Place's stepdaughter. The *New York Times* described the scene: "There was a deep gash over the top of her head which reached down to the neck. She was in her working dress, which had been nearly torn from her body. . . . [H]er mouth was horribly burned, as if acid had been forced into it."[4] The *Times* later said Place had killed seventeen-year-old Ida because she was insanely jealous of her. On 20 March 1899, Place became the first woman electrocuted in the United States.

The *Times*'s first story was in parts confusing. One paragraph said William Place had been hospitalized but would probably recover, and that his wife was in critical condition. Five paragraphs later, a surgeon reported William Place had little chance of recovery because his skull had been

---

Bailey, "Murder, Capital Punishment, and Television: Execution Publicity and Homicide Rates"; "Top Official and Death Row Fear Texas Is Shrugging Off Executions," *New York Times,* 1 July 1987; "Sign of the Times: Reporters Seldom Compete to Witness Executions," *Jonesboro (Ark.) Sun,* 7 March 1999.

3. See Marlin Shipman, "'Killing Me Softly?' The Newspaper Press and the Reporting on the Search for a More Humane Execution Technology."

4. "A Woman's Triple Crime," *New York Times,* 8 February 1898.

cut through. The next day, the *Times* reported that Martha Place had left the hospital.[5]

The *Times* published detailed information about Martha's jealousy of Ida. William Place, a widower, had married Martha five years earlier because he believed Ida needed a mother; however, as Ida grew older, Martha Place's attitude toward her had "rapidly changed into hatred." Place had once threatened to kill Ida, and William had his wife arrested. She was arraigned, but the case was dismissed because her husband did not appear in court.[6]

The *Times* quoted Martha Place as telling police that on the morning of the murder, she had violently quarreled with her husband. Ida later sided with her father, which had so angered Place that she threw acid in Ida's face. Place said she had taken the ax upstairs because she believed the quarrel with her husband would resume when he came home and she wanted to be able to defend herself. "My husband came in afterward, and I struck him with it. That is all there is to it," she said. She denied murdering Ida. The *Times*'s article said when she refused to confess, police took her to the home and forced her to go into Ida's room. Then a detective "exposed to view the girl's body" and said to Place: "There is your daughter! She is dead." The *Times* said Place had closed her eyes and refused to look. Because the description of the scene was not attributed to police, a *Times* reporter might have witnessed it. The same news story might have explained Place's apparent violent behavior. Her brother, of New Brunswick, New Jersey, raised the possibility of a brain injury, claiming that she had been thrown from a sleigh and struck her head when she was twenty-three, and he did not believe she had ever fully recovered.[7]

Four months after the murder, but almost a month before Place went to trial, the *New York Times* published a story about an unusual circumstance in Place's unusual life. While in jail, she filed a complaint for grand larceny against Annie Simpson, the daughter of "Dutch Mary" Hanson, who was, the *Times* said, a notorious swindler. Place admitted attempting to bribe the district attorney and the police, but after being swindled, she was so outraged that she filed a complaint. Simpson had claimed she was Place's relative to gain entry to the jail. She had convinced Place that she had influence with the police and could "fix" things for her. Place said she had given Simpson a pair of diamond earrings valued at five thousand dollars to buy off the district attorney and police. When Place discovered the swindle, she reported it to police. Simpson was indicted for second-degree grand larceny.[8] The news story did not say if Place was indicted.

5. "The Place Murder Case," ibid., 9 February 1898.
6. "Mrs. Place Convicted," ibid., 9 July 1898; "A Woman's Triple Crime."
7. "The Place Murder Case."
8. "Mrs. Place Charges Theft," ibid., 12 June 1898.

The *Times* published no stories about Place's trial until a 9 July report of the jury's verdict. The lead of the story said Place would be the first woman ever electrocuted unless her verdict was overturned or her sentence was commuted. The 146-word lead was long and muddled by today's journalistic standards. It covered Place's reaction, the first-woman-electrocuted angle, a likely appeal, and a bit of trial testimony. The newspaper described Place in animalistic terms: "She is rather tall and spare, with a pale, sharp face. Her nose is long and pointed, her chin sharp and prominent, her lips thin and her forehead retreating. There is something about her face that reminds one of a rat's, and the bright, but changeless eyes somehow strengthen the impression." The newspaper said she looked as if she had "great strength of mind" and determination, but also described her as almost without emotion. The *Times* said Place's expression had changed only when her husband testified: "Then her thin lips parted in a sardonic grin, and she fixed her eyes upon him." The *Times*'s article contrasted William and Martha Place when he testified at her trial, calling him refined, quiet, pleasant, and calm; "on the other hand, it was impossible to make one's self believe that Mrs. Place was possessed of any other feeling than that of a mild curiosity." The newspaper also, for the first time, called Martha Place's suicide attempt at the time of the murder a sham.[9]

A story four days later at Place's sentencing could not have been more different about her reaction. The *Times* described her as pale, trembling, and weeping. "The indifferent, rather cynical look which was on her face throughout the trial had entirely disappeared." When she arrived at Sing Sing Prison, the newspaper reported, she wept convulsively, and when checked into the prison, she "broke down and wept in a hysterical manner." The newspaper said she later kissed her prison matrons. The lack of attribution and the inclusion of vivid detail in the story make it seem likely a reporter observed Place in the prison.[10]

The *Times* editorially supported Place's death sentence, and condemned the actions of "the sensational press," which the newspaper claimed had tried to save her. It said those who opposed her execution were "unreasoning sentimentalists" and called her a "particularly malignant and cruel murderer." The newspaper asserted that if the execution of a woman was horrible, then the law should be changed. The newspaper then added this seemingly ridiculous statement: "Mrs. Place had as many rights as men have and more, though not quite the same privileges." At the time, women had no right to vote and did not sit on criminal juries in New York. An ongoing argument for women's suffrage was that women had no voice in shaping the laws to which they were ac-

9. "Mrs. Place Convicted."
10. "Martha Place Sentenced," ibid., 13 July 1898.

countable. The *Times* said if a man committed the same sort of crime, then he would deserve death, and therefore so did Martha Place, although the newspaper admitted she would probably escape death because "sentimentality is a mighty power" and because "the sensational press considers her valuable."[11]

The *New York Times* did not run another story about Place for seven months, when it reported that the New York Court of Appeals had denied her appeal. After Sing Sing Prison warden O. W. Sage told Place about the court's decision, she cried hysterically and "was completely broken down."[12]

The *Times* did not report about Place again until a week before her execution. Although the stories were big news in the *Times*, they were not as big as might be expected. Place would be the first woman executed by electrocution, and New York had not executed a woman for more than ten years. There are at least two possible explanations why the story did not get more news play. One is that just two days before the execution, there was a deadly fire at the Windsor Hotel in New York City, and that event, plus U.S. troops fighting in the Philippines, dominated news coverage for several days. Second is that the *Times*'s editorials make it evident the newspaper was reacting to the New York tabloids' excesses of yellow journalism. For example, when New York governor Theodore Roosevelt ordered that press coverage of Place be restricted to prevent "hideous sensationalism," the *Times* praised him, saying the action helped prevent "sensational, revolting and yellow" reporting.[13]

Roosevelt instructed the prison warden to allow one member of the Associated Press and one representative of the *New York Sun* and other non–Associated Press newspapers to witness the execution. Just a few years earlier, the *Times* had vehemently objected to a New York law that prohibited the reporting of details of an execution, a law that had been winked at in the past. In an editorial, the *Times* had condemned the law as bad public policy, saying the public needed to know if the new use of electrocution was wise. However, now the *Times* praised Roosevelt's re-

11. "Personal," *New York Times*, 22 July 1898. I couch my criticism by using the word *seemingly* because the *Times* could have been using the word *privilege* as in the Privileges or Immunities Clause of the Constitution. The clause was still being debated during this time. See Akhil Reed Amar, *The Bill of Rights*, 227–28. Some months after the *Times*'s editorial, it ran a front-page letter to the editor that called for legal rights to be extended to eighteen-year-old men, with the rationale being that eighteen year olds were subject to execution by the state ("Legal Liabilities and Legal Rights," 16 March 1899). This issue was not new. More than one hundred years earlier, Abigail Adams, in a lighthearted letter to her husband, John, who was helping form the Declaration of Independence, said women in the new nation would not submit to laws if they could not help make them (David McCullough, *John Adams*, 104).

12. "Mrs. Place Must Die," *New York Times*, 5 February 1899.

13. "The Governor's Good Judgment," *New York Times*, 18 March 1899. Roxalana Druse, hanged in 1887, was the last woman executed before Place.

strictions for Place's execution, saying "respectable newspapers ceased to print the details of executions" after it became evident electrocution was an acceptable method of execution. The *Times* also noted that Roosevelt's rule did not restrict "the proper privilege of the press" because the Associated Press would provide a sufficient report. The *Times* asserted that its only lament was that Roosevelt did not have the power to "prevent the yellow journals from inventing the revolting stories and pictures which he forbids them to prepare from actual observation."[14]

Executing a woman was controversial in the legislature. The assembly considered but defeated by a vote of seventy-eight to forty-seven a bill to prevent future executions of women. The bill's sponsor, a Mr. Maher, said the execution of women was "an insult to womanhood." Maher erroneously speculated: "From what I know of Gov. Roosevelt, I know that he will commute the sentence of Mrs. Place." On 16 March, just days before the execution, the *New York Times* reported that Governor Roosevelt had said he would not interfere with the execution, because there were no grounds, there was no reasonable doubt of Place's guilt, and her crime was "of shocking atrocity."[15]

Some parts of the execution that differed slightly from executions of men drew press attention. The differences concerned the would-be attendants at the execution; how the electrode would be attached to Place's leg, given that she would be wearing a dress and not trousers; and when her hair would be cut so that an electrode could make contact with her head. Governor Roosevelt suggested that there be women attendants to slit the dress—a black dress Place had made in jail in anticipation of wearing it at a new trial—and attach the electrode to the ankle. Place's hair would not be cut until the last moments before the execution.[16]

A straightforward story on page 3 pointed out that Place was the first woman to die in the state's electric chair. The *Times* said the execution had gone marvelously well; a subordinate headline said Place had been "killed instantly," a dubious notion. The story, which claimed the electricity had "left scarcely a mark" on her, praised the women attendants and physicians. However, near its end, the story had a curious, almost social air: "The woman physician was bright looking and rapid in her movements. Her dress looked strange in that place. She wore a gray gown and a huge hat with pronounced crimson trimmings."[17]

14. "Governor Sends Instructions," *New York Times*, 17 March 1899; Shipman, "'Killing Me Softly?'"; "The Governor's Good Judgment." The argument sounded no better in 1899 than it did in 1798, when the Federalists restrained the "scandalous" Republican press. See, for example, Richard Rosenfeld, *American Aurora.*

15. "Capital Punishment Bill," *New York Times*, 14 March 1899; "No Mercy for Mrs. Place," ibid., 16 March 1899.

16. "Mrs. Place Seems Resigned," ibid., 18 March 1899.

17. "Mrs. Place Put to Death," ibid., 21 March 1899.

The *New York Times* noted that public interest in capital punishment was not especially keen: if true, that might explain why the newspaper did not give the execution more attention. In a later editorial, the *Times* said Place's execution had not given any special boost to the anti–capital punishment movement in New York. The newspaper claimed the general sentiment against executions seemed no stronger than before, and added, "We very much doubt if it is as strong." The newspaper argued that efforts by the yellow press to arouse public interest had fallen "very flat."[18]

Governor Roosevelt's decision to allow the execution drew praise from what seems an odd corner. The Reverend David Cole, Martha Place's spiritual adviser, said in a letter published in the *Times* that it was Roosevelt's duty to execute the law as written. Cole, the *Times* reported, had been the first person to question Place's sanity and to suggest that she should not be executed.[19]

Only ten people attended Place's burial at East Millstone, New Jersey, in the family plot. The *Times* said Cole, Place's brother and his three daughters, and the two prison matrons who had assisted at the execution attended, but there was no religious service.[20]

Place occupied a relatively prominent place in the *New York Times* during the story process, but not because she was the first woman to die by electrocution.

Ethel Spinelli: The First Woman to Die
in the Gas Chamber

Prosecutors described Ethel Spinelli in a *Los Angeles Times* news story as a "'scheming cold, cruel woman,' head of an underworld gang, an ex-wrestler and a knife-thrower who could pin a poker chip at 15 paces."[21] Spinelli, executed in California in 1941, was the first woman in the United States to die in the gas chamber, and therefore she should have been big news. She died for helping murder a nineteen-year-old member of her gang.

Despite the colorful descriptions of Spinelli, the press paid little attention to the facts that she was the first woman in the United States executed by lethal gas and that she reportedly was the first woman legally executed in California. There are several reasons. First, California, where she

---

18. "Capital Punishment," ibid.
19. "The Governor and Mrs. Place," ibid., 23 March 1899.
20. "Funeral of Mrs. Martha Place," ibid.
21. "Olson Hears Spinelli Son," *Los Angeles Times,* 10 July 1941.

died in 1941, had used the gas chamber since 1938 and executed twenty-two men before Spinelli. Second, threats of war dominated headlines. Two weeks after Spinelli's execution, the Japanese attacked Pearl Harbor. Finally, Spinelli was a less than sympathetic figure. A *Los Angeles Times* editorial about her execution carried this headline: "Good Riddance."

The press found Spinelli to be an enigma. Did she love her children and grandchildren and have a newly found religious faith? Or did she head a crime gang and ruthlessly order a murder?

The day Spinelli died, 21 November 1941, the *Times* described her as "tall," "lank," "homely," and a recent grandmother. The story said she had died with photographs of her three children and her grandson taped over her heart, and with "revitalized faith in the mercy of the maker whose Sixth Commandment, 'Thou shalt not kill,' she had flouted." In sum, the news story about her execution presented a somewhat touching portrait. The story said Spinelli had died ten and one-half minutes after the cyanide was dropped into the acid. Then, "the stethoscope had indicated that beyond doubt the Duchess' heart—the heart that the law said was too evil to live, yet only Tuesday had thrilled over the sight of a baby—had stopped."[22]

The news story and the "Good Riddance" editorial ran on the same day. The contrast between the two was almost as sharp as the contrast in Spinelli's life. She was known as the "Duchess" because of the iron hand with which she ruled a crime mob. She reportedly had earlier been affiliated with a Detroit gang. The *Times*'s editorial reflected more of this side of Spinelli. It said that other than "sentimentalists," no mourners could be found, not even the "squeamish Governor Olson." The newspaper asserted that Spinelli's execution showed that women were not exempt from the laws and might provide an overdue deterrent.[23]

According to a *Times* news story, Spinelli was among the first women legally or illegally executed in California. On 5 July 1851, a Mexican woman described only as "Juanita" hanged for stabbing a miner to death after he broke into her home and attacked her. The newspaper pointed out that during that time, if "a Mexican raised his hand against an Americano and killed him it was his death warrant." A jury of "frontiersmen" apparently disregarded Juanita's self-defense, and condemned her to be hanged from the highest girder of a bridge outside Downieville. She stood on a cross beam of the bridge, and a man placed the rope around her neck and prepared to push her off the beam; however, she smiled, said, "Adios, señores," and leaped off the beam.[24]

22. "'Duchess' Dies in Gas Chamber," ibid., 22 November 1941.
23. "Tehachapi Guards Added to Balk Plot to Free Doomed Woman," ibid., 1 April 1941; "Good Riddance," ibid., 22 November 1941.
24. "Girl's Hanging in 1851 Recalled," ibid., 22 November 1941.

California executed Spinelli for helping two members of her gang drug and murder fellow gang member Robert Sherrod. They feared he would talk to police about the murder of a San Francisco food-stand owner, the *Times* reported. Spinelli; her common-law husband, Mike Simeone, thirty-three; and Gordon Hawkins, twenty, died for the crime.

Spinelli ended up in California because her daughter, Lorraine, had run away from Detroit to California. Spinelli, Simeone, and sons Joseph and Vincent hitchhiked from Michigan, following Lorraine. The trip constituted one part of Spinelli's nomadic life, according to the *Times*. She was a washerwoman and a waitress in Texas's oil fields; she ran a gambling wheel at a Utah carnival, where daughter Lorraine was a "snake girl" in a sideshow; she was a sheepherder in Idaho; and she put children Joseph and Lorraine into a Texas home and left for Mexico. When she returned, she had baby Vincent. She and her children reportedly drifted to Detroit, where she met Simeone. When Spinelli and her family arrived in California, Lorraine reportedly introduced them to young men who would become members of Spinelli's gang.[25]

The day before Spinelli's execution, the press depicted her as resigned to her death, bitter, and in despair. Reporters said she cursed and also mumbled prayers and nervously plucked at her "threadbare" coat, and had a "lifeless" and "gaunt, bony frame." She told the newsmen it was not Christian to kill, and the Associated Press reported that she said of those who would execute her, "My blood will burn holes into their bodies. Before six months have passed they will be punished." She showed reporters a small picture of Christ and challenged them to read the inscription on it and to take pictures of it. She said to them, "I have asked God to forgive all of you."[26]

Times reporter Tom Cameron covered Spinelli's execution, and his story sharply differed in technique from the more straightforward wire-service stories. He said the execution's efficiency was "horrifying in its deadly technique." The story had the obligatory information about what Spinelli ate, and that she wore a short-sleeve green dress. Beneath a bold-faced subhead "Puppet in Play," Cameron's story played on the execution's drama. He wrote that Spinelli held a white handkerchief in her left hand, and when she arose to walk to the death chamber, she almost seemed "a puppet hoisted by concealed strings." Emphasizing the the-

25. "Olson Hears Spinelli Son."

26. "'Duchess' Goes to Doom Today," ibid., 21 November 1941. Her words are similar to those of Arkansas inmate Herbert Sease, who in 1923 seemingly believed God would protect him by causing the electricity to pass through his body and leave him unharmed. He said, "God delivered Daniel and he will deliver me." Sease also said the Arkansas governor would be smitten by God by contracting leprosy, and would die in a far-off land. See "Sease, Obviously Insane, Executed," *Little Rock Arkansas Gazette*, 28 July 1923.

atrical angle, he continued: "The cue had come for the desperate drama—a grim performance that almost everyone but the Duchess herself seemed to hope would somehow be prevented before the curtain could rise."[27] Cameron wrote his story in first person and took literary license that is seldom found in today's "straight" news stories. His use of imagery and vivid description might more effectively attract readers' attention.

Cameron's "puppet" reference might have described Spinelli's last moments. Sixty-seven witnesses jammed into the room. Just one minute before the scheduled execution, they were told to leave because a writ had been filed with the California Supreme Court. The court turned it down, but the delay was fourteen minutes. Cameron's description was vivid: The chairs in the death cell looked "not unlike an aerial bombardier's perch," an interesting analogy during the World War II years. When the cyanide pellets fell, they made "a muffled 'clunk' such as old plumbing sometimes makes." When Spinelli breathed the gas and coughed, "it sounded like that of an asthmatic sufferer," and she blew out breath "with a sound like that a horse sometimes makes with his lips." Cameron reported that a man described as a retired prison guard left, and someone whispered that the man had earlier said that "the gallows was more decent than this." Cameron described the last five minutes of the execution as "the longest 300 seconds I've ever watched go into eternity." To end his story, Cameron wrote: "Outside, after we had left the Duchess, the sun was warming the peninsula up, the bay mists were rising. Somewhere, a foghorn gave two deep-throated melancholy toots. That was the Duchess' only requiem."[28]

Although the *Los Angeles Times* did not report Spinelli's death as the first in the gas chamber, its execution story served as a commentary on lethal-gas executions. Spinelli reportedly was fifty-two years old when she died. Simeone and Hawkins died in the gas chamber a week later.

Margie Velma Barfield: The First Woman to Die by Lethal Injection

Margie Velma Barfield, almost always called Velma, spent her fifty-second birthday, 29 October 1984, at North Carolina's Central Prison in a death row holding cell, awaiting her 2 November execution for murdering her fiancé, Stuart Taylor. Barfield was the first woman executed in the United States after the Supreme Court ruled in 1976 that the death penal-

27. "'Duchess' Dies in Chamber."
28. "Woman Executed in Gas Chamber," *New York Times*, 22 November 1941; "'Duchess' Dies in Chamber."

ty was not inherently cruel-and-unusual punishment. No woman had been executed since Elizabeth Duncan of California, in 1962. Barfield's lethal injection came two years after Texas became the first state to execute to lethally inject, when it executed Charlie Brooks.[29] However, other controversies about her execution overshadowed her status as a "first."

The many issues surrounding Barfield's execution explain why national and international media covered her story. First, the United States had not executed a woman in twenty-two years. Second, her execution became intertwined with a closely contested United States Senate race pitting North Carolina governor James Hunt and Republican incumbent senator Jesse Helms. Barfield's execution was scheduled just days before the election. Third, North Carolina had executed only one person by lethal injection, and it was so new that Barfield had the choice of dying in the gas chamber or by lethal injection. Finally, well-known people, including evangelist Billy Graham's daughter, sought a gubernatorial commutation for Barfield because they said she had a religious rebirth while in prison. Concentration on these issues makes it unsurprising that the *Raleigh News and Observer* rarely mentioned that she was the first woman lethally injected.

About a month before her execution, the *News and Observer* published an Associated Press story that claimed lethal injection was not necessarily more humane than death by cyanide gas. A pathologist at the state medical examiner's office said both methods killed "rather rapidly," and the story said lethal injection "would appear to be more peaceful to observers than death by gas." The more humane "appearance" caused opponents of a lethal-injection bill to say the method could make juries more willing to impose the death sentence.[30]

29. "Barfield Transferred to Central Prison Cell," *Raleigh News and Observer*, 29 October 1984. Charles Brooks Jr. was executed on 8 December 1982 ("Technician Executes Murderer in Texas by Lethal Injection," *New York Times*, 8 December 1982).

30. A federal district court judge in California later ruled cyanide gas an unconstitutional "cruel and unusual punishment" ("Ruling Could Close Doors of San Quentin's Gas Chamber," *Jonesboro (Ark.) Sun*, 6 October 1994). When Mississippi executed Jimmy Lee Gray with lethal gas, a Jackson newspaper reported that witnesses said he convulsed for eight minutes and gasped eleven times, and his head jerked back and hit a steel pole on the back of the chair to which he was strapped ("Jimmy Lee Gray Executed," *Jackson Clarion-Ledger*, 2 September 1983). A national debate ensued in 1982, when Texas lethally injected Charles Brooks, and became the first state to use the method. Debate before and after the Brooks execution centered on using drugs meant to heal in executions, and on the ethics of medical doctors participating in state-sanctioned killings. A *New York Times* story said lethal injection "sharpened the debate over the moral validity of the death penalty" ("Execution by Injection Stirs Fear and Sharpens Debate," 8 December 1982). Henry Swartzchild, then director of the capital punishment project of the American Civil Liberties Union, later denounced lethal injection as a "high tech" execution. He said the killing of a person, not the method, should be emphasized. Swartzchild said that a woman who witnessed a 1989 lethal injection in Missouri said she did not find it traumatic or dramatic. "The shocking

The *Raleigh News and Observer* article described in some detail the three drugs used in lethal injection, including one "similar to curare, which is used by South American aborigines to paralyze their prey." Barfield's attorney said he saw little difference between execution by lethal gas or by lethal injection, but at least with lethal injection his client would not have to see the witnesses because she would be lying down. About a week before Barfield's execution, a North Carolina coordinator of a local Amnesty International chapter told the *News and Observer* that lethal injection constituted a form of torture, and that the death penalty and torture were closely related. "In Argentina, you can have an electric shock applied to your genitals until you pass out. Then if you're lucky, you get released. In the Commonwealth of Virginia, you can have electricity applied to your body until you're dead. They don't call that torture. They call that the death penalty."[31]

The press focused more on Barfield being the first woman executed in twenty-two years than on the lethal-injection angle, although even the "first-since" angle was not given prominent news play until the story about her execution.[32]

The Political Angle

The *New York Times* focused more on the political angle than did the *Raleigh News and Observer.* Governor Hunt, a popular Democrat, and Republican senator Helms were running nearly even shortly before the election, which Helms won. Barfield's execution would probably not have become a controversial "tough-on-crime" political issue if there had been no Hunt-Helms race. The *Wilson (N.C.) Daily Times,* in an editorial that ran in the *News and Observer* under the standing headline "Tar Heel Editors Speak," said politics should not play a part in commutation decisions. It said if Hunt had commuted, then he would have "overruled the courts of

---

thing about it was that it wasn't shocking," he said. "The notion of killing people efficiently is all too reminiscent of the [Nazi] execution camps." See Tom Uhlenbrock, "'Their Time Has Come,'" *St. Louis Post-Dispatch,* 8 January 1989.

31. "Desirability of Lethal Injection Questioned," *Raleigh News and Observer,* 1 October 1984; "Barfield Chooses Injection, to Study Avenues of Appeals," ibid., 26 October 1984; "Rights Group Asks Hunt to Spare Barfield's life," ibid., 27 October 1984.

32. Although mostly correct, the story erroneously said no women had been executed in Florida, Texas, or Nevada. Florida executed in 1848 a woman named Celia who was a freed slave and had murdered her former master, who was the father of her four children ("Woman on Death Row: Echoes of a Slave's Hanging in 1848," *Miami Herald,* 29 March 1998). Chipita Rodriguez was hanged in Texas in 1863, and two female slaves, Jane and Lucy, were hanged there in the 1850s ("Last Woman Executed Got a Raw Deal," *Dallas Morning News,* 25 January 1998). Elizabeth Potts was hanged in Nevada in 1890 (see Chapter 13).

the land." Hunt's press secretary claimed just six days before the execution that the Senate race had nothing to do with the governor's decision, although the *News and Observer* reported that "political observers" predicted Hunt could lose or gain crucial votes because of his decision.[33]

The *News and Observer* also noted in a story four days before the execution that four of seven state supreme court judges were Hunt appointees. Although the judges did not comment about the involvement of politics, the *News and Observer* did quote a University of North Carolina law professor who said he did not believe the supreme court would allow politics to influence its decision.[34]

The day before the execution, the *News and Observer* said former Watergate defendant Charles Colson, described as a born-again Christian, sent Hunt and Helms letters asking them "not to let Barfield be a pawn in their high-finance Senate campaign." Colson said the timing of the execution "inevitably creates the suspicion . . . she is being sent to her death so that one candidate cannot take political advantage of what might be perceived as the other's weakness."[35]

The *New York Times* stressed the political angle; two of the three front-page stories the *Times* published were about the politics surrounding the execution. According to the newspaper, polls showed most North Carolinians favored capital punishment, and noted that if Hunt commuted her sentence, then it would be particularly harmful to his campaign, but her execution and funeral just before the election might also cause some Hunt supporters to leave the fold. The *Times* also said Barfield's supporters had waged what the paper termed "an aggressive public relations campaign" on her behalf. One *Times* story pointed out that Helms held a narrow 4 percent lead in the latest poll, and, according to spokesmen in Hunt's office, North Carolinians sent Hunt three thousand letters, 77 percent of which favored Barfield's execution.[36]

The Religious Angle

The *Raleigh News and Observer* published a story that listed religious leaders from fourteen denominations who sent a joint letter to candidates for governor and lieutenant governor asking them to work to abolish cap-

---

33. "Hunt Made Right Decision in Velma Barfield Case," *Raleigh News and Observer*, 7 October 1984; "As Clock Ticks, Observers Await Barfield Decision on Stay," ibid., 28 October 1984.

34. "Barfield Tells Attorneys to Resume Appeals for Life," ibid., 30 October 1984.

35. "Execution Delay Urged by Colson," ibid., 1 November 1984.

36. "Decision on Execution Order a Key Issue in Carolina Race," *New York Times*, 27 September 1984; "Carolina Slayer Fails in Her Bid for a Reprieve," ibid., 28 September 1984.

ital punishment in North Carolina. The story noted that four of the candidates favored capital punishment. Religious opposition was nothing
new, although Barfield's execution occurred shortly after a major shift
in the Vatican's stand on capital punishment. Regardless, religious opinion within North Carolina's Roman Catholic Church was split. Bishop
Joseph Grossman of Raleigh opposed Barfield's execution, whereas Bishop Michael Begley of Charlotte, who said the execution in this case was
justified, reacted in what an author of a major work on religion and capital punishment describes as a "pre–Vatican II 'old school'" manner.[37]

The press often named Anne Graham Lotz, the daughter of evangelist
Billy Graham, as one who actively sought commutation for Barfield. Lotz
asked Hunt to spare Barfield's life because of her active prison ministry.
The *Times* reported that Ruth Graham—Billy Graham's wife—also asked
Hunt to commute Barfield's sentence. One day before Barfield's execution, the *News and Observer* published an editorial against capital punishment. The newspaper stated that fate determined the penalty, noting that
only thirty-nine persons had been sentenced to death for the more than
thirty-five hundred homicides committed in North Carolina since 1977.[38]

Late News Play

The *Raleigh News and Observer* mostly played Barfield's story inside until three days before the execution. Then the story ran on the front page
for five consecutive days, and was the lead four of those days. Coverage
was especially heavy 1–3 November, with an editorial and some fourteen
stories about or related to the execution.

One story detailed Barfield's decision to donate her body for organ
transplants. An official with the National Transplant Foundation said she
was the first executed prisoner ever to attempt to donate all her organs.
Perhaps Barfield was the first to donate all her organs, but she was not the
first executed donor. Foundation member Roger Whitfield said the transplant center's research showed only one other executed donor: Frank
Coppola, who died in 1982 in Virginia, donated his corneas. Some men in
the 1940s volunteered to have their corneas donated after their executions.[39]

37. "Religious Leaders Urge Opposition to Capital Punishment," *Raleigh News and
Observer,* 1 November 1984; Megivern, *Death Penalty,* 387–88.

38. "Clock Ticks." Lotz's argument is almost exactly the same made for Karla Faye
Tucker years later (see Chapter 18). "Decision on Execution Order"; "Mrs. Barfield's
Shadow," *Raleigh News and Observer,* 1 November 1984.

39. See, for example, the case of Vollie Bill Bates in 1947. The twenty-year-old
Arkansas youth donated his corneas for use ("Doomed Youth Glad His Eyes Will Be
Used," *Little Rock Arkansas Gazette,* 16 May 1947; "Feel Deeply Grateful to Vollie Bates,"
ibid., 17 May 1947).

A story on the day of Barfield's execution said her body would be rushed to a hospital after her execution, where a team of doctors would determine which organs were suitable for transplant. The next day's *News and Observer* reported that the transplant team had tried to restart Barfield's heart after the execution to try to save some of the organs. An official with the transplant foundation said there were no ethical or legal considerations; once doctors were assured of Barfield's "physical expiration," they considered restarting her heart an attempt to save someone else's life by keeping blood pumping to the organs. Governor Hunt agreed, saying the state's duty was to execute Barfield, and once doctors ruled her clinically dead, her body was turned over to the medical team. "A person cannot be revived because there is no coming back from clinical death." As it turned out, the time between Barfield being pronounced dead and the attempt to restart her heart interrupted blood flow for too long and made it impossible to retrieve some of her organs.[40]

Barfield's execution ran as the lead story in the *News and Observer,* under a banner headline that read: "Barfield Put to Death." The *New York Times* ran the execution story under a modest one-column headline at the bottom of page 1. Barfield dressed for her execution in pink floral-print pajamas, and the story described every meal and what she ate, including her last meal of Cheez Doodles and a Coca-Cola. Most of the story was a minute-by-minute account of Barfield's last hours. Also included were interviews with Barfield's son, Ronnie Burke, and with Alice Storms, the daughter of Stuart Taylor, Barfield's victim. Storms described Barfield as a "sadist who enjoyed . . . watching (her victims die) over and over again, watching them twist in agony and pain."[41] Barfield was executed for Taylor's murder, but had earlier confessed to murdering three other people, including her mother.

40. "Body, Organs Donated for Possible Transplant," *Raleigh News and Observer,* 2 November 1984; "Transplant Team Tried to Restart Barfield's Heart to Save Organs," ibid., 3 November 1984. In earlier years, requests by doctors to attempt to revive defendants executed by electricity were made in 1894 in New York and in 1908 in New Jersey. Both attempts were tied to Dr. P. J. Gibbons of Syracuse, who in 1894, the *New York Times* said, contended that strong currents of electricity did not produce death. In 1908, a *Times* article said Gibbons contended that defendants electrocuted were killed later "at the post-mortem examination or in quicklime" ("Death Chair to Be Tested," 7 December). In both instances, the state refused to allow attempts to revive the executed defendants. The *Times* reported in 1894 that a professor, William F. Z. Desant, would test on 22 November an invention for resuscitating persons and animals "apparently killed" by electric shock. Desant was to test his invention on "a large St. Bernard dog . . . a strong, healthy animal, weighing about 150 pounds." The *Times* did not report the results of the test. See "Wilson Must Remain Dead," *New York Times,* 22 November 1894.

41. "Barfield Put to Death," *Raleigh News and Observer,* 2 November 1984; "Woman Executed in North Carolina," *New York Times,* 2 November 1984.

The *News and Observer* also ran stories about Barfield's organ donation, a death penalty protest, women on U.S. death rows, and news coverage of the execution. The media story attested that news organizations from England, West Germany, and Sweden had covered the execution. News agencies gave different reasons for their interest: ABC News said it was gender, another cited the clemency campaign, and a third said it was the drama and human interest elements. Barfield's age and status as a grandmother also were story angles that others played up, calling her a "death row granny." A *News and Observer* story described some members of a raucous crowd outside the prison reportedly chanting, "Kill her, Kill her," and "Burn, bitch, burn."[42]

The *News and Observer* published a first-person account by *Raleigh Times* writer Ramona Jones, who had witnessed the execution. She said Barfield "seemed to slip peacefully into unconsciousness." Another story reinforced the clinical nature, quoting Anne Graham Lotz who said the execution chamber seemed "so small and so sterile." Jones wrote that a man in a white coat came into the death chamber, checked Barfield, and closed a curtain, blocking the witnesses' view. "Someone flipped a switch, and the room was flooded with sharp light, more like the end of a movie than the end of a life."[43]

42. "News Cameras Lurk at Prison, Waiting for Execution," *Raleigh News and Observer,* 2 November 1984; "Barfield Put to Death." Hendrik Hertzberg termed reactions such as "Burn, bitch, burn" as being "straight out of a sleazy teen exploitation movie" ("TRB from Washington," 4).

43. "Barfield Expressed Sorrow," *Raleigh News and Observer,* 3 November 1984; "'Then There Was Silence,' Witness Says of Barfield Death," ibid.

Chapter 15

Love Triangles

THE NEWS PLAY ON THE SEEMINGLY shocking *Atlanta Constitution* story did not indicate anything out of the ordinary. One paragraph on 9 May 1872, on page 2, which ran under "Georgia News Items," reported, "Ferdinand Spann, of Webster county, hung his wife, who had but one leg, with a plow-line, and eloped with a girl employed in his family—Sumter Republican."

Almost one year later, the story of Spann and his lover, Susan Eberhart, resulted in this statement in the *Constitution:* "There has been so much interest felt in the execution of Miss Eberhart, and such a demand for our special, lengthy and graphic account of the affair, covering over four columns, that we have been compelled to republish it in this morning's paper."[1]

When a young girl helped murder her lover's wife and then ran off with the husband in the 1870s, not only was it news, but it also gave the newspaper press the opportunity to serve up moral messages to readers and to expound upon the role of women in society.

Susan Eberhart of Georgia

The story contained love, sex, and murder, long a natural combination for novelists and playwrights, for television mysteries and soap operas, and a natural for the *Atlanta Constitution* because of the inherent elements of a tragic drama. The *Constitution* understood that point in 1873; its report about the hanging began: "To-day at this place has closed the saddest scene in the strangest real tragic drama that ever was enacted in the history of crime in America."[2]

1. "The Execution of Miss Eberhart," *Atlanta Constitution,* 4 May 1873.
2. "Miss Eberhart Hanged," ibid., 3 May 1873.

The love triangle continued to affect others fifteen years later. The *Constitution's* 13 October 1888 edition published news of former Webster County sheriff W. H. Matthews's death, reportedly of a drug overdose. The newspaper said, "Many insist it was suicide." Sheriff Matthews had to hang Susan Eberhart, a job the *Constitution* claimed he found especially disagreeable. "Sheriff Matthews, who was then a hale and hearty man, dreaded the task before, and though he had a strong sense of duty, yet he could never recover from the shock of having to hang a woman. The circumstances of his death, while claimed by some to be accidental, are looked upon by the superstitious as confirming the theory of suicide."[3]

Eberhart's hanging attracted enormous press and public interest. Georgia had hanged a white woman once, Polly Barclay in 1803. Estimates of Eberhart's age, according to press accounts, ranged from seventeen to nineteen. In a retrospective article, published in 1888 when Sheriff Matthews died, the *Constitution* said Eberhart was "a buxom country girl, aged 15," while working for Ferdinand and Sarah Spann.[4] At the time of the crime, the *Constitution* reported her age as seventeen.

The case began when Sarah Spann's husband reportedly strangled her with "a common plow-line tightly drawn about her neck." The story simply stated that Eberhart had aided or abetted the murder; however, the 1888 recounting of the crime said she had forced a handkerchief into Spann's throat, strangling her. Perhaps, in 1873, the newspaper considered the details too revolting to be published, because in a 3 May story, the *Constitution* did not reveal much of what it knew about the trial testimony, merely saying that the paper had examined the record. In addition, "there is a still more revolting revelation of testimony which does not bear recital, but which more than all else exhibits the loathsome criminality of the couple."[5] It was unclear whether the paper meant the gory details of the murder or the sexual escapades.

After the murder, Spann and Eberhart fled, but were captured six days later. The case soon drew public and press attention, although the first re-

3. "Susan Eberhart," ibid., 13 October 1888. The death penalty can have consequences far beyond the person executed. For an example, see Bledsoe, *Death Sentence.* It is the story of the execution of Velma Barfield, and the book tells in some detail how her execution affected many others, both in her family and in her victim's family.

4. "Susan Eberhart." The *Constitution* ran an editorial on 27 April 1873 that said Eberhart's hanging would be the second. It said that in about 1803, a Mrs. Bentley was hanged for murdering her husband. The newspaper said Mrs. "Bentley" (really, Barclay) was "a woman of wealth and personal attraction." Eberhart is the last white woman executed in Georgia, although others have been sentenced to death. Ida Hughes of Georgia was sentenced to death for murdering her mother-in-law. Her sentence was commuted by the governor in 1925. See "Woman Murderer Escapes Gallows," *Atlanta Constitution,* 12 April 1925.

5. "Miss Eberhart Hanged."

ports were brief. Two weeks after the first story, the *Constitution* reported under the "Georgia News Items" headline that Spann and Eberhart had been jailed. The newspaper later reported that "only through the most vigorous measures" were the two not lynched. The defendants were tried, convicted, and sentenced to hang less than one month after the murder.[6]

The *Atlanta Constitution,* through its reporting, played the role of the public's moral instructor. In an interview with Eberhart in her cell shortly before her execution, a reporter asked her if she was prepared to die and if she was "at peace with God." She said she was. The reporter then delivered a near monologue of Christian instruction:

> To be prepared for death is a privilege and a comfort which man cannot take from any one. To be prepared to die and have the consolation of religion in that hour, is a boon given us by our Creator, and no power on earth can take it away. And then again, it is a great truth, not fully appreciated by many, that to all whose hearts are truly right, whatever may befall them, however hard and trying may be their fate, it is really all for the best; and it is our duty to look upon all things that occur to us, no matter what they may be, as for the best. This a sincere Christian alone can do.[7]

Religion was important in helping shape legal codes, and religion, as evidenced in moral and cultural codes, also helped shape the news coverage of condemned defendants, more so in the early years, but even today to a degree. In some ways, the coverage reflected the standards of the propertied interests, showing condemned criminals as repentant. When they were not repentant, the newspapers often stepped in with instruction. Louis P. Masur contends that newspapers "redirected information pitched to the public" in execution stories and presented a more factual report as opposed to earlier reports about gallows speeches, in which "the criminal [was] usually shown as admitting guilt and [was] penitent." But that claim is only partly true. Execution reports until the late nineteenth century, and even the early twentieth century, were laced with moral instruction and opinion that passed for "news." The press instructed mostly in news stories, and not necessarily opinion articles. Late-nineteenth-century news content was, as Hazel Dicken-Garcia terms it, "an amalgam of event, idea and 'story' or drama." The notion of objectivity did not exist as it is thought of in today's press, although it slowly developed from the mid-nineteenth century until the mid-twentieth century.[8]

6. "Georgia News Items," ibid., 23 May 1872; "Miss Eberhart Hanged"; "Georgia News," ibid., 4 June 1872.

7. "Miss Eberhart Hanged."

8. Friedman, *Crime and Punishment;* Schiller, *Objectivity and the News,* 22–23; Masur, *Rites of Execution,* 114; Dicken-Garcia, *Journalistic Standards,* 63; Marion T. Marzolf, *Civilizing Voices: American Press Criticism, 1880–1950,* 119–21.

The *Constitution*, for a time, did not flatly say that Spann and Eberhart had had an adulterous affair. It came close in an editorial about three months before the execution, when the newspaper argued for the death sentence because good citizens' "lives and happiness demand preservation from the lust of adultery and the violence of murder." The *Constitution* reported that Eberhart had slept on a cot in the same room with the Spanns, but left Eberhart's role as seducer or seductress unclear.[9] Other than vague references, readers had to imagine why, other than an illicit love affair, Eberhart would so willingly participate in killing Sarah Spann.

Eberhart worked in the Spanns' home because her own family was poor. The *Constitution* described Sarah Spann as a good housewife, but disabled and "quite old." She was twelve years older than her husband. Most people called her a kind woman, but some said she "was high tempered and sometimes disagreeable and quarrelsome." Most people considered Ferdinand Spann a model husband, hardworking and religious.[10]

Eberhart denied any involvement in the murder. She said Sarah Spann had abused her husband, and that Ferdinand had once attempted to slit his own throat after a fight, but she and Sarah Spann had stopped him. Eberhart said Ferdinand Spann had awakened her on the night of the murder and asked her to help him kill his wife, but she refused.

The pressure was intense on Gov. James M. Smith to commute Eberhart's sentence. Some people doubted that her role in the murder was enough to justify the death penalty, some believed that a white woman should not hang, and Eberhart was young. Governor Smith made it clear that he did not want her hanged. In a retrospective article, the *Atlanta Constitution* reported that Smith had been "besieged by people all over the state" to commute the sentence because they said it would be a disgrace for Georgia to hang a woman. "Prominent ladies" urged Smith to commute the sentence, and letters asking for commutation came from as far away as New York. Smith received forty-five telegrams asking for commutation while the execution was in progress.[11] Eberhart's death sentence seemed especially distasteful to Preston County and Webster County residents. They petitioned Smith to commute, saying Eberhart was a victim of circumstances, had never been in trouble, was largely ignorant, and did not understand her "moral obligations." She could read, but had attended school for only three months.

A prominent Georgian, Judge Samson Bell, asked Smith to commute the sentence, as did all the members of the grand jury, and all but two of the trial jurors. Smith stood fast. In a letter to Judge Bell, the governor said the trial evidence showed Eberhart understood her moral and legal guilt,

9. "Susan Eberhart's Hanging," *Atlanta Constitution*, 8 February 1873.
10. "Miss Eberhart Hanged."
11. "Susan Eberhart."

and Smith said he should not second-guess the verdict unless given a legal reason to do so. "If allowed by my duty to the public to base my official action upon my feelings as a man, I would not hesitate to interpose Executive clemency to save a woman from the extreme penalty of the law."[12]

Two points should be made. One is that the governor and the *Constitution* saw the issue as one of morals as well as law. Morals have to do with personal character and behavior. Law has to do with rules or standards set by custom, agreement, or authority. A political authority enforces laws—not so with morals. The second point is that the *Constitution*'s strong support for the execution might have in part offset public pressure on the governor to commute. In an editorial that ran one week before the execution, the *Constitution* noted, "[I]t seems rather strange that because that human wears petticoats instead of breeches the crime is any less, or the penalty of hanging is less deserved."[13]

Concerning the moral issue, the governor said in his letter to Judge Bell that Eberhart understood her legal and her *moral* guilt. The *Constitution*, in an editorial, said mercy and gallantry were virtues, but were due good citizens and not *adulterers* and murderers. In a February editorial, the *Constitution* supported Governor Smith's decision not to commute the sentence, and berated those criticizing him, saying it was not Smith's fault the law allowed women to be hanged. The newspaper said that if the people did not like the law, then they should persuade the legislature to change it. In an editorial the day after the hanging, the newspaper argued there was no reason for sympathy for Eberhart. "Let us trust that this dark case will end the record of feminine criminality in Georgia." The newspaper so strongly stressed the moral issue of adultery that it seemed coequal with the murder. In its editorial a week before the hanging, the *Constitution* wrote: "The offense of Miss Eberhart is two-fold in its iniquity. It violated the sanctity of marriage besides spilling human blood. It involved adultery and murder. Certainly no more terrible combination of crimes could occur." The newspaper proclaimed that Sarah Spann was murdered "after the destruction of her wedded happiness by the same pernicious, deadly instrumentality." As the editorial progressed, its tone became more condemnatory. "Public justice less demands Miss Eberhart's hanging than that no more wedded homes shall be broken up and lawful wives remorselessly murdered in cold blood for the safe carnival of the devil's own hot and wicked lust."[14]

The account of Eberhart's hanging contained irony—intentionally or unintentionally—for readers who recognized it: Eberhart's neck did not

12. "Miss Eberhart Hanged."
13. "Ought a Woman to Be Hanged!" *Atlanta Constitution,* 27 April 1873.
14. "Susan Eberhart's Hanging"; "Ought a Woman to Be Hanged!"

break in the fall, so she died as Sarah Spann had died, by strangulation. The *Constitution* reported that a small crowd of about seven hundred attended the hanging. The newspaper gave a gender and racial break-down of the crowd, saying that about half were Negroes, and about a dozen were white women. The *Constitution* described Eberhart as neatly dressed, "at the expense of the Sheriff." She had braided hair and wore a calico sunbonnet. Eberhart said she did not mind dying because she would be better off. On the gallows, she forgave those who had wronged her and said she loved mankind. Eberhart's family was not at the execu-tion, and the *Constitution* reported that her mother had not seen her since the arrest because she was too overcome with grief. Eberhart's father claimed her body, and she was buried in Preston.[15]

Catharine Miller of Pennsylvania

Here's to my love! O true apothecary!
Thy drugs are quick—Thus with a kiss I die.

—Romeo

O happy dagger! This is thy sheath;
there rest, and let me die.

—Juliet

A play about two starry-eyed young lovers who preferred to kill
themselves rather than to live without each other.

• • •

She laid the plan. She often asked me to do it. When I had him killed
she gave me the rope to hang him up; she also gave me the apron to
wipe the blood up, and told me where to throw it—under the barn.

—George Smith, 3 February 1881

I never at any time urged George to kill my husband, and always
tried to prevent him from doing so, although he talked to me about
it; he [was] always introducing the subject; and if I had known that
George was to kill my husband that night I should have stopped it.

—Catharine Miller, 1 February 1881

15. "Miss Eberhart Hanged."

*A true drama about two young Pennsylvania lovers who most
decidedly were not willing to die for one another.*

At about twenty minutes past eleven on the morning of 3 February
1881, Catharine Miller and George Smith were hanged at Williamsport,
Pennsylvania, for murdering Miller's husband. The hangings were, as
hangings go, well-nigh perfect, said the *Williamsport (Pa.) Daily Banner.*
"The arrangements at the scaffold and the workings of the machinery of
execution were most perfect throughout."

The *Banner* said most of the witnesses intended not to watch, "but the
affair was accomplished so quickly when once all was in readiness that
many became unwilling witnesses to the fall which ushered these two
persons into eternity." Other than medical doctors and law enforcement
officers, all other people had passes and presumably chose to witness. For
those who could not attend, the *Banner* provided six columns of text that
jumped to an additional column on page 3. Detailed reporting of hangings in the late nineteenth century fostered debate. Those who favored the
reports argued the stories deterred potential criminals from committing
similar crimes; critics argued the stories taught others how to commit
crimes, or said the reports lessened people's natural abhorrence to crime,
and brought out the worst journalism.[16]

Catharine Miller was twenty-nine when she died. During her childhood, her poor family moved often and kept her home to help with the
household chores. She had only about one year of schooling and as an
adult could barely read or write. The *Banner* described her as a "rather prepossessing looking woman." In the summer of 1867, Andrew Miller "commenced paying attention" to her. Although Andrew was about thirty years
older than Catharine, they married with the blessing of Catharine's father
and mother, who were described as old and feeble.

---

16. "Hanged! George Smith and Catharine Miller Executed To-Day," *Williamsport
(Pa.) Daily Banner,* 4 February 1881. In the story, the *Banner* reported the murder date
as 13 March and 19 March. The correct date was 19 March. The idea that others mimic
or model what they see or read in mass media has long been argued. There was in
Germany the "Werther" effect, which held that young men had committed suicide
after reading about the lovelorn young man who did the same in Wolfgang von
Goethe's *Sorrows of Young Werther.* For some research on effects of publications, see
Melvin L. DeFleur and Sandra Ball-Rokeach, *Theories of Mass Communication,* 226; and
Melvin L. DeFleur and Everette E. Dennis, *Understanding Mass Communication,* 568–
70, for a description of modeling theory. See also Steven F. Messner, "Television
Violence and Violent Crime: An Aggregate Analysis"; J. Ronald Milavsky et al.,
Television and Aggression; and Marzolf, *Civilizing Voices,* 36–37. For a brief discussion
of how crime reporting resulted in the worst journalism, see Dicken-Garcia, *Journalistic Standards,* 203.

Banner news stories described Andrew as a kind and good man, "faithful and good" to his wife's parents, and "a hard and steady worker, kind and obliging to everybody." Poor but industrious, he seemed what scholars call a "pure" victim. Catharine Miller disputed her husband's reputation as a hard, steady worker, saying the family got along when her father was alive because he provided for it, but after her father's death, Miller "neglected to provide the necessities of life." In about 1877, Catharine left her husband and went to Williamsport to live with her sister. A few days later, Andrew brought his wife home, which the *Banner* said showed his "affection for his truant wife."[17]

By 1880, there was cause for rumors circulating about Catharine Miller's virtue. In her last statement, she said she "became intimate with George Smith" about two years before her husband's death. However, if she and Smith were lovers, then they did not show it during the months between their arrests and executions. After their arrests, they blamed each other for Andrew Miller's death, and Smith's account of how he and Catharine came to be lovers portrays her as a seductress who tempted him so he would kill her husband. Her story, however, portrayed Smith as the ever pursuing lover, jealous of the older man and bent on his destruction.

The *Banner* described Smith as about the same age as Catharine Miller, and as "a rather fine appearing man, fair complexion, curly hair, and about six feet high." He said Miller "ran after me wherever I would be at work." Smith said she first proposed that he kill Andrew; she said it was his idea. "I begged him not to do it; after [she and her husband] moved to Brown's house he commenced to talk to me again about destroying [Andrew]."[18]

Smith waited in the Millers' barn, and when Andrew investigated a noise, Smith struck him several times with a club and hanged him with a rope in the barn, trying to make the murder look like a suicide. Smith said Catharine did not help in the actual murder, but she "urged me on and planned the thing." He said he had never intended to marry Miller, adding that he and Andrew had gotten along reasonably well and always spoke to one another when they met. Miller claimed she had heard someone come into the house, and she went downstairs and found Smith, who asked her for a rope, but she said she had been too nervous to help him.[19]

Some people in the community knew about Miller's dislike for her husband, and perhaps her intention to kill him, and among them was John

17. "Hanged!" See Ericson, Baranek, and Chan, *Representing Order,* 8, 106, for a discussion of the "pure" victim.

18. "Murder or Suicide?" *Williamsport (Pa.) Daily Banner,* 22 March 1880; "Guilty! Mrs. Miller Makes a Confession," ibid., 24 March 1880; "George Smith Makes a Confession," ibid., 25 March 1880; "The Murder Trial," ibid., 9 May 1880.

19. "George Makes Confession"; "The Murder Trial"; "Guilty!"

Brown. In a confession shortly after the crime, Smith implicated Brown, saying he had helped kill Miller. Perhaps this accusation and Catharine Miller's statement that she had heard her husband yell, "You black son-of-a-bitch," led to Brown's arrest and indictment. However, evidence showed it unlikely that he was criminally involved, and Smith, in a last confession shortly before his execution, said Brown had played no role in the murder. The *Banner* reported that Smith and Miller had implicated Brown "thinking perhaps it would have some effect in mitigating their offense before the law." In 1880, as in Boston in the 1980s and in South Carolina in the 1990s, white criminals knew that accusing a black man of a crime might shift blame from themselves.[20]

The 19 March 1880 edition of the *Williamsport Daily Banner* proclaimed on page 4, "Murder!" A subordinate headline read: "Andrew Miller of Jersey Shore Found Murdered Last Night." The newspaper cited no source, but confidently reported that "an examination of the house and the yard leading to the barn" showed Miller was murdered in the house and dragged to the barn, "where his body was hung up to a beam to create the impression that he had committed suicide."

The next day, the *Banner* backed away from its murder theory. A headline on a lengthy story read: "Perhaps a Suicide." The newspaper said additional facts raised questions about "what at first was emphatically declared to have been an atrocious murder." To its credit, the newspaper later in the story noted that just the day before, it, too, had been convinced the death was a murder. The *Banner* called for "sober reflection," and said it was "loathe to publish anything that would tend to criminate two human beings . . . unless fully satisfied of their guilt." A coroner's inquest in the office of C. B. Seely of the *Jersey Shore Herald,* the local newspaper, ruled that Smith had murdered Miller and that Catharine was an accessory before and after the fact. Despite the findings, the *Banner* for the next three days strongly espoused the suicide theory. The newspaper noted that nothing indicated a struggle had taken place, and "Miller is known to have been quite despondent, and was even by some regarded as demented." Two days later, a *Banner* headline asked: "Murder or Suicide?" In a news story that began as more of an editorial, the *Banner* wrote that information it had gathered "has not only corroborated the views then taken, but has more than ever *convinced* us that Andrew Miller came to his death by his own hands" (emphasis added).

The *Banner* published information from two lengthy jailhouse interviews with Miller and Smith. Miller's began with a description of her, and she was variously termed "pleasant appearing," "mild-mannered,"

---

20. "Hanged!" For a brief discussion of the Boston and South Carolina cases, see Tom Wicker, *Tragic Failure: Racial Integration in America,* 186–87.

"modest looking," and "timid." "The whole expression of her countenance is rather prepossessing." The reporter said when he entered her cell, it was obvious Miller had been crying. Every description evoked sympathy for her. She sat on her cot with "a glimmer of tears coursing down her cheeks." She denied all aspects of the murder and said her husband had often threatened to kill himself. Moreover, the *Banner* described Smith as "a fine appearing young man and the very last person in the world" who would be suspected of committing such a crime. Evoking the theory that one can tell innate criminality by a person's physical features, the newspaper said of Smith: "There is nothing vicious-looking about his physiognomy, nor does his phrenological development indicate any traits you would look for in a hardened criminal." Instead, he was "a real fine looking fellow, with very pleasant countenance, fair complexion, bright blue eyes, pretty tall and hair inclined to curly." Smith, too, denied guilt. The *Banner* added that after Miller's body was found, "everything that could throw suspicion upon them was hunted up and hurled at them with a vindictiveness that does not argue well for the cause of justice." In addition, the two doctors who performed the postmortem said there was nothing inconsistent with the suicide theory.[21]

The next day's *Williamsport Daily Banner* published a letter from one of the doctors, T. W. Meckley, who said he had testified "*very decidedly* in favor of *suicide*" (emphasis added). He said that because his testimony so much favored suicide, it became necessary for authorities to "look for some other cause, or manufacture one."[22]

The *Banner*'s exhortation that Miller and Smith should not be judged before they had a legal hearing went out the window in the 24 March edition, one day after Dr. Meckley's letter was published. An all-capitals headline blared: "Guilty!" and deck headlines read: "Mrs. Miller Makes Confession" and "George Smith First Kills Then Hangs Andrew Miller." The *Banner* defended its earlier reporting, saying it had gotten all the information it could from reputable citizens, and from interviews with Miller and Smith. The newspaper declared that from the beginning of the case, it had striven for truth, and added, "No matter whether a suicide or a murder, that (truth) was the point with us." To further justify its earlier conclusions, the newspaper contended: "On the one hand was presented the spectacle of two human beings charged with that most fearful of all crimes, murder, and on the other hand there stood out the ghastly corpse of Andrew Miller, his gaping wounds crying out for justice. We were honestly mistaken in our theory of suicide, but we are glad to have erred on the side of humanity." The *Banner* again interviewed Miller and Smith.

---

21. "Murder or Suicide?"
22. "Suicide, and Not a Murder," *Williamsport (Pa.) Daily Banner*, 23 March 1880.

This time, it described Miller as "very much distressed," "nervous," and "trembling like an aspen," and said her eyes had "a sort of glassy look which at first made us doubt whether she really was in her right mind." She said she had confessed because authorities told her that her daughter Mary had confessed. The next day, Smith confessed.[23]

By the 5 May 1880 trial, the *Banner's* description of the defendants had changed. "The stories about Mrs. Miller being such an attractive woman and Smith such a giant of a man are just simply newspaper moonshine. They are a pair of very ordinary looking country people—neither very attractive nor very repulsive in physical form or dress." The *Banner* had initially portrayed Miller in glowing terms, and although it had not depicted Smith as a giant of a man, it did describe him as tall and better-than-average looking. The newspaper reported that ten of the twelve jurors said they had read newspaper accounts of the murder but had not formed an opinion in the case. Of those excused, according to the newspaper, seven had read news accounts; of those seven, some said they had not formed opinions, but were excused anyway.[24]

Once the trial began, the story moved from page 4, where it had been anchored since the first reports of the murder, to page 1. Near-verbatim accounts of testimony and questioning were published in morning and evening editions. Reports usually ran at least three full columns of text with no illustrations.

The jury was sequestered, which indicates that the court was concerned about information getting to the jurors, including press reports. A note under a standing headline "Local Laconics" said the jurors were "living as well as most of the people." In a plug for a local merchant, and perhaps a *Banner* advertiser, the newspaper commented: "Their meals are taken to them from the Henry House, which is a guarantee that they are prepared in good style, and from the best the market affords." The jurors were "allowed open air exercise in the Court House yard every morning, which attracts quite a gathering"; however, local constables made sure no one talked with the jurors.[25]

Suspense filled one item in "Local Laconics" near the end of the trial. "An exciting incident occurred at the close of the Commonwealth side of the murder trial yesterday afternoon, the particulars we suppress for reasons that will be apparent hereafter." One might have surmised the excitement concerned testimony about a jail turnkey who had arranged for Miller and Smith to spend a night together in her cell. The turnkey said he had hidden under the bed, at the insistence of the district attorney, and listened to determine if he could hear anything about the crime, but he

23. "George Makes Confession."
24. "The Courts Yesterday Afternoon," ibid., 6 May 1880.
25. "Local Laconics," ibid., 7 May 1880.

said he had heard nothing of the sort. However, the real "excitement" was that during an attorney-client conference at the defense table, a juror saw Smith's brother lean over the railing and hand something to Smith. Police found a skeleton key to Smith's jail cell in his pocket. By the time it was discovered, Smith's brother was gone.[26]

On Saturday, 8 May, at 9:55 P.M., the courthouse bell rang to signal that the jury had reached a verdict after deliberating almost seven hours. The *Banner* reported that Miller had caused the lengthy deliberation. On the first ballot, seven jurors voted for first-degree murder and five for second-degree murder for Miller. It was hours before a unanimous first-degree-murder verdict could be agreed upon. The bell ringing "drew together an immense number of people" who filled the courtroom "to the last inch of sitting and standing room," and enough people were in the corridors to fill the room again. The *Williamsport Daily Banner*'s reporter managed to get into the courtroom; "he hardly knows how himself—but he got in." Following the verdict, people jammed into the streets between the prison and the courthouse, "and to the shame of Williamsport a large proportion of the assemblage was females." The *Banner* reported: "None of these assemblages of people made any demonstration worth noting. Only idle, vulgar curiosity seems to have drawn them together at that time of night."[27]

On 2 February, Mary and Jennie Miller visited their mother for the last time. The newspaper described the meeting as "one of those tender, touching and harrowing scenes that make all natures akin." The description ran in the same story with the hangings, resulting in sharp contrast. Early in the lengthy story, the newspaper said that the parting of mother and children was "very affecting," and that Miller had shown great agony and grief. Toward the end of the story, though, the newspaper described the meeting in gut-wrenching terms and provided a moral lesson for readers. It said Miller's reaction to her children was proof that some good still was inside her. It also reinforced the stereotype of women: "With a mother's emotions, she gave vent to those holy instincts that belong to her nature." The *Banner* said the meeting had affected all who witnessed it. "When the last embrace, the last words of parting and the last kiss was given, every heart was full, and the very associations of the place were clothed in mourning, lamentation and woe. Few of those present ever witnessed a more impressive and tender interview." Before the children left, Miller gave them a doll dressed with clothing she had made in jail, and she gave them candies and fruit. That Miller's last meeting with her children was not private is a sad commentary, perhaps even more so because

26. Ibid.; ibid., 8 May 1880; "The Murder Trial."
27. "The Court," ibid., 10 May 1880.

news reporters witnessed and published information about such an intimate moment.[28]

Whether intended or not, there was strong biblical imagery in the *Banner*'s story about the executions. The story line concerned the condemned ascending the scaffold, sitting in the chairs, and descending through the trap into eternity, and their bodies then being covered in white cloth and laid in coffins. Miller was buried, per her request, beside her husband. Smith's body was taken to a Jersey Shore cemetery.[29]

A headline on the *Banner* editorial about the executions read: "The Wages of Sin Is Death." The day after the execution story, the paper ran short "Notes about the Execution," giving readers tidbits of information, such as the exact dimensions of the scaffold. The newspaper also ran a short story about people "of both sexes, prominent in religious affairs," offering prayers and spiritual ministering to Smith and Miller.[30]

Both Smith and Miller left wills, which the *Banner* published. Miller had little to bequeath: She left daughter Mary a silver watch, a black coat, and a Bible, and Jennie got Miller's heavy winter dress and a coat. Youngest daughter Eliza received two calico dresses, one of which Miller was wearing when hanged. She also directed that her pictures and other property be divided equally among the children. Her will's last wish was that her daughters "receive religious instruction, so that they will not go astray as their poor mother did."[31]

28. "Hanged!"; George Rider, "The Pretensions of Journalism," *North American Review* 135 (November 1882): 471–83, as reported in Dicken-Garcia, *Journalistic Standards,* 203.

29. "Hanged!"

30. "The Wages of Sin Is Death," *Williamsport (Pa.) Daily Banner,* 3 February 1881; "Notes about the Execution," ibid., 5 February 1881; "The Doomed Prisoners," ibid.

31. "Hanged!" Charlotte Jones and Henry Fife were hanged in Pittsburgh on 12 February 1858, although the Pittsburgh press did not moralize to a great extent ("The Execution," *Pittsburgh Gazette-Times,* 13 February 1858). Other Pennsylvania women were hanged, but I could find little press information about the executions. Lena Miller, a German woman who reportedly poisoned her husband, was hanged in Brookville, Pa., in November 1867. The *New York Times* reported the execution in a single paragraph ("Execution of Mrs. Lena Miller," 14 November 1867). The *Pittsburgh Post* gave the story only one paragraph ("Hanging of Mrs. Lena Miller," 14 November 1867). Mary Twiggs was hanged in October 1858 for the murder of her husband. The *New York Times* reported the hanging in a single paragraph, but did not say how she had murdered her husband ("Execution of Mrs. Twiggs at Danville, Pa," 23 October 1858). I found nothing in Pittsburgh or Philadelphia newspapers about this hanging.

Chapter 16

Little Support for Changes to Execution Laws

THE SCENE AT THE ARIZONA HANGING was horrible. Prison chaplain the Reverend Walter Hofmans said, "All those in favor of capital punishment, please take a good look down there." The *Phoenix Gazette* reported that Eva Dugan's headless body lay slumped in the pit, and there was "a black masked head lying about 10 feet from the pit, a pallid chin protruding from the black hood."[1]

Such grotesque execution stories were bound to make public officials squirm, and sometimes to react with bills to try to abolish capital punishment for women. The bills failed, and they differed from general opposition to capital punishment because they were only against the death penalty for women. Newspapers usually did not support the bills, although they at times said women should not be executed, especially by hanging. Governors, legislators, prison wardens, sheriffs, and editors grappled with the moral dilemmas about executing women.[2] Conversely, some women supported capital punishment for other women because they sought equality with men in society.

The *New York Times* questioned the hanging of women almost from the beginnings of the newspaper in 1851. In 1859, when a jury sentenced Mary Hartung to hang for poisoning her husband, a legislator introduced a bill that would legislatively commute her sentence. The *Times* opposed the bill as an unconstitutional assumption of executive powers. After the bill failed, the *Times* said it would support a law requiring life imprisonment

---

1. "Eva Dugan Dies on Gallows," *Phoenix Gazette,* 21 February 1930.
2. Famous New York editors Horace Greeley, William Cullen Bryant, and Parke Godwin opposed capital punishment during the 1800s. Philip English Mackey says about forty New York newspapers in 1846 urged death penalty reform. Many officers of the New York Society for the Abolition of Capital Punishment, founded on 5 January 1846, were editors or newspaper writers. See Mackey, ed., *Hanging in the Balance: The Anti–Capital Punishment Movement in New York State, 1776–1861,* 125, 177, 237.

for women convicted of murder. The governor later commuted Hartung's sentence. The *Times* said in an editorial that it did not consider hanging "a decent or proper punishment for a woman," and about two weeks later in another editorial, it called hanging "too ghastly and too horrid to be thought of when the victim is a woman."[3]

The *Times* consistently editorialized against executing women until at least 1909, when it spoke about public opposition to executing Mary Farmer. However, the *Times* did not favor any means of doing away with the death penalty for women. When Herkimer County hanged Roxalana Druse in 1887, the newspaper said: "It is very possible that executions of women would have been more frequent if the idea of choking a woman to death were less horrible or if some less brutal mode of giving effect to the law were provided, even as an alternative." Nonetheless, the *Times* defended the execution and Gov. David S. Hill's decision not to commute the sentence. In 1905, the newspaper followed similar editorial reasoning when Vermont hanged Mary Rogers, and called hanging a brutal execution method that shocked sensibilities. The paper said "some of us" might oppose executing women, but praised Vermont's governor, Charles J. Bell, for not commuting the sentence, saying that until the legislature changed the law, "women like Mrs. Rogers should be hanged by the neck until dead."[4]

In 1930, the hanging of Eva Dugan had something to do with Arizona changing its method of execution. Shortly after Dugan's decapitation, the Arizona legislature began considering another method of capital punishment and adopted the gas chamber.

Eva Dugan of Arizona: "All Those in Favor of Capital Punishment, Please Take a Good Look Down There"

The *Phoenix Gazette* staff hardly had time to catch its breath after the Irene Schroeder story before another female killer made headlines, this time an Arizonan. Eva Dugan was front-page news in the *Gazette* every day, save one, from 10 February until 21 February 1930, less than a month after the sensational coverage about Schroeder. The *Gazette* incorrectly said Dugan would be the first woman hanged under western law.[5] Regardless, there were many reasons Dugan interested the Phoenix newspaper press.

3. "Mrs. Hartung's Case," *New York Times,* 9 April 1859; "Mrs. Hartung's Case," ibid., 11 April 1859; "Capital Punishment of Women," ibid., 26 April 1859.
    4. Editorial, ibid., 1 March 1887; "Hanging a Woman," ibid., 9 December 1905.
    5. "Eva Holds Reception in Cell," *Phoenix Gazette,* 20 February 1930.

Dugan was convicted of murdering A. J. Mathis, a Tucson recluse, for whom she worked. After the murder, she disappeared but was later arrested in White Plains, New York. She claimed a man named Jack, who worked at Mathis's ranch, had murdered him and forced her to accompany him to Texas. On 11 February, just ten days before the scheduled execution, a letter signed "Jack" arrived from Agua Prieta, Mexico, at the jail, exonerating Dugan. Three days later, a letter from "Bob" came from Fort Worth and claimed "Bob" had seen Jack kill Mathis.[6] The *Gazette* published both letters.

Judging from the news coverage, Warden Lorenzo Wright did not want to hang Dugan because he requested a sanity hearing after Arizona governor John C. Phillips said state law did not give him the power to grant a reprieve or to commute the sentence. Dugan claimed she was insane. "Any body can look at me and see I'm bughouse," she said. Stories about the sanity hearing and the decision dominated the front page between 15 February and 20 February. The requested sanity hearing was denied. The day after the decision, the *Gazette* ran its only editorial about the hanging: "The hanging . . . marks a new chapter in the history of Arizona and the entire west. . . . It is regrettable that Arizona had to show the way. But . . . she has to pay."[7]

The execution divided the Phoenix community. On 13 February, the *Gazette* ran a front-page article with the headline: "Should Eva Dugan Be First Woman in Arizona to Hang?" A similar article the next day had the headline: "Expressions Show Opinions Divided in Eva Dugan Case." A "cowboy preacher," the Reverend J. C. Mulcay, said Arizona "old-timers" would have been ashamed at hanging a woman; however, the Reverend A. A. Kidd, pastor of the Bethel M. E. Church, South, in Phoenix, supported the death penalty for Dugan, and did so based on biblical teachings. He said the death penalty "is not a law passed nor a penalty fixed by barbaric tribes, but by Almighty God."[8]

Dugan's personality interested reporters. The day before her execution, she held what the *Gazette* termed a "reception" in her cell. "Eva played

6. "Woman Held for Murder," *New York Times*, 17 February 1927; "'Confesses' Mathis Murder," *Phoenix Gazette*, 11 February 1930; "Eva Holds Reception"; "'Eyewitness' Asserts Jack Killed Mathis," ibid., 14 February 1930.

7. "Warden to Ask Sanity Hearing for Eva Dugan," *Phoenix Gazette*, 15 February 1930; "'Eyewitness' Asserts"; "Sanity Hearing"; "Dugan Sanity Hearing Set for Tomorrow," ibid., 17 February 1930; "Pallor Grips Eva As Sanity Hearing Opens," ibid., 18 February 1930; "Eva's Fate in Hands of Jury," ibid., 19 February 1930; "Eva Dugan Must Pay Penalty," ibid., 20 February 1930.

8. Concerning the Bible and capital punishment, many of the main religions in the United States today are opposed to capital punishment. For an excellent discussion, primarily of the Roman Catholic position, see Megivern, *Death Penalty*.

hostess in her cell this morning to all who might want to chat with her. She was gracious as a society woman entertaining at a tea and she was just as clever with repartee." The tone contrasted with a description in the story about her reaction to the sanity hearing: "She had completely recovered from the hysteria she showed last night." The social-maven portrayal also clashed with other *Gazette* depictions. In the same story, the newspaper called her a "henna haired Magdalen" who rejected last-minute religious consolation. "I'm going to die as I've lived," she said. An earlier story called her a "condemned adventuress," and another article described how Dugan had lived: "Eva shows the effect of having led a hard life. Her face is lined and her dark eyes hold calculating glints. She knows men. She cast her lot with them a long time ago. And their treatment of her was cruel."[9]

Several stories described Dugan as being in good humor, contending she relished life and found it "mighty sweet." A story the day before her execution gave readers no reason to believe she was distraught. Even the alliteration the writer used communicated a playful tone: "The first feminine neck to feel the fatal pressure of the noose in the history of Western law will be that of smiling Eva Dugan, slayer of A.J. Mathis of Tucson." When asked by a reporter where she got her "iron will," Dugan replied, "The world loves a good sport and hates a bad loser."[10]

The newspaper's first lines about her execution told the story: "Eva Dugan, convicted on circumstantial evidence of the slaying of A.J. Mathis, Tucson recluse, was beheaded by the state of Arizona at 5:11 A.M. this morning. The prison death trap was converted into a guillotine when Eva's head was severed from her body by the noose in which she died."

A screamer headline on 21 February read: "Eva Dugan Dies on Gallows." Subordinate headlines read: "Head Severed from Body As Trap Is Sprung," and "Gruesome Scene Witnessed by 75." Prison physician L. A. Love pronounced that "tissues made flabby by disease in Eva's neck" had caused the decapitation. "Had her neck been of healthy sinews, the unfortunate spectacle would not have occurred."

Dugan was not the first woman involved in a botched, or nearly botched, hanging in the West. Elizabeth Potts was almost decapitated during her 1890 hanging in Nevada. Paula Angel, hanged in New Mexico on 26 April 1861, kicked and fought Sheriff Antonio Abad Herrera. The sheriff used a wagon bed for a scaffold, but failed to tie Angel's arms, and when she grabbed the rope and struggled, the sheriff grabbed her around her waist and tried to jerk her downward to her death. Herrera finally got Angel's hands and legs tied and began again to hang her. When some in

9. "Eva Holds Reception"; "'Life Mighty Sweet' Says Eva As She Waits Death in Prison Cell," *Phoenix Gazette*, 13 February 1930.

10. "'Life Mighty Sweet'"; "Eva Holds Reception."

the crowd protested, the sheriff said he would shoot the first man who tried to interfere.[11]

After Dugan's hanging, the story faded from the front page. Arizona's legislature began to question hanging as a method of capital punishment, and a bill to adopt the gas chamber passed the Arizona house fifty-eight to two in early March 1931, only about a year after Dugan's execution. In 1933, Arizona adopted the gas chamber as a more humane form of execution.[12]

Mary Ann Bilansky of Minnesota:
St. Paul's Newspaper Battle

Mary Ann Bilansky, known almost always as Ann, was the first person hanged after Minnesota joined the Union. She died on 23 March 1860, two years after Minnesota's statehood. Bilansky was hanged for killing her husband, Stanislaus, by lacing his food and drink with arsenic. St. Paul had two newspapers: the *Minnesotian and Times* supported the Republican Party, the *Pioneer and Democrat* the Democratic Party. The two newspapers, especially the *Times*, often and loudly said the other lied about anything pertaining to politics, and Bilansky's execution became embroiled in a political dispute.

The legislature considered a bill providing that no woman could ever be hanged in Minnesota, but those who opposed capital punishment for everyone amended the bill to that effect, and it failed. The *Times* speculated that the bill in its original form would have passed. The paper had no sympathy for the bill, and said "rabid anti-hanging members" attached the amendment. The *Democrat* said another bill to specifically reach Bilansky's case had passed the legislature, but the governor vetoed it, saying it unconstitutionally breached the separation of powers because it provided for legislative and not executive commutation.[13]

Both newspapers supported the governor's veto; the *Times* called it prompt and decisive, and the *Democrat* termed it "manly." The *Times* called the bill the product of "humane and honest feelings," but ill-advised and unconstitutional. An editorial said the "community owes the

11. There is little information about Angel's hanging. Peter Herzog attributes the lack of newspaper coverage to the fact that the New Mexico Territory's newspapers were covering the Civil War "and often overlooked happenings right under their noses" (*Legal Hangings*, 7–9). See also William A. Keleher, *Turmoil in New Mexico*, 397–99; and Kirby Benedict, *Frontier Federal Judge Aurora Hunt*, 76–77.

12. "Gas Execution Bill Passes," *Phoenix Gazette*, 4 March 1931; "Gallows Abolished As Moeur Signs Lethal Gas Measure," *New York Times*, 28 October 1933.

13. "Execution of Mrs. Bilansky, the Murderess," *St. Paul Minnesotian and Times*, 24 March 1860; "Mrs. Bilansky," *St. Paul Pioneer and Democrat*, 9 March 1860; "The Bilansky Murder," ibid., 24 March 1860.

meed of approbation" to Governor Ramsey for his firm stand against the legislature and against "well meaning but mistaken sympathizers with the criminal."[14]

News reports made Stanislaus Bilansky seem no prize catch. The *St. Paul Minnesotian and Times* claimed he regularly drank. He was described as possessive and jealous with "intemperate habits," a man who possessed a "singular disposition." The *St. Paul Pioneer and Democrat* said that "although he was intoxicated at times, [he] was regarded as a harmless, inoffensive man." The newspaper's assessment differed from an earlier story that declared Bilansky "was a man of violent disposition, and . . . abusive and jealous"; he had married three or four times, most recently to "a very estimable woman" who had left him because of his "constant abuse and ill-treatment."[15]

A news story said Bilansky's reputation for wealth had induced Ann Bilansky to marry him. An early settler in St. Paul, he had "made a claim of a part of the lower town site in 1848." In its execution story, the *Times* said Ann Bilansky had come to St. Paul because her "nephew" John Walker had written to ask her to come and care for him because he was sick. In an earlier story, the *Times* had refused to describe the relationship; however, the *Democrat* reported that Walker "is said to have been on very intimate terms with Mrs. B. before she was married to Mr. Belanskey [*sic*]."[16]

In its execution story, the *Democrat* concentrated on the sexual relationship. The newspaper said Walker and Bilansky had "criminal intercourse" prior to the murder. The newspaper recounted that one witness claimed to have seen Bilansky undress in front of Walker, and another said he saw her go in and out of Walker's room on several occasions. The *Democrat* attributed the murder to the relationship, saying evidence "leaves no doubt the murder was planned and consummated that she might marry, or have more unrestrained intercourse with her paramour." The *Times* said Stanislaus was jealous, "not without cause," and registered its own disapproval of Bilansky's behavior, saying that as soon as her husband died, "her paramour occupied the place of the dead husband in her bed!"[17]

Ann Bilansky showed little emotion when convicted, the newspapers reported. The *Democrat* said everyone in the courtroom seemed to trem-

14. "The Bilansky Murder"; "The Execution of Mrs. Bilansky—the Moral of It," *St. Paul Minnesotian and Times*, 24 March 1860.
15. "Execution of Bilansky, Murderess"; "The Bilansky Murder"; "Supposed Case of Poisoning," *St. Paul Pioneer and Democrat*, 17 March 1859.
16. "Death of an Old Resident," ibid., 17 March 1859; "Execution of Bilansky, Murderess"; "The Poisoning Case Concluded," *St. Paul Minnesotian and Times*, 26 March 1859; "Supposed Case of Poisoning."
17. "The Bilansky Murder"; "Execution of Bilansky, Murderess."

ble at the verdict "except the guilty woman whose fatal doom was involved in the word." She showed "no visible emotion, no blanching, no signs of betrayal were there. She preserved an immobile and hardened exterior, and not for a moment did a shadow of faltering or fear pass over the cold and stern features of the not handsome face of Ann Bilansky."[18]

In a highly opinionated article that morally condemned Bilansky's infidelity, the *Democrat* said the "female assassin" almost always chose poison, and that usually the husband was the victim and a paramour was involved. Bilansky's case was repeated "wherever a woman bad enough to be a harlot and bold enough to be a murderer" wanted to be rid of her husband. Infidelity made murder three times more horrible when it occurred "in the confidential intercourse of married life," because no innocent husband could guard "against the murderess, who lies with the interlocked caress of simulated love upon the bosom which she stabs, who plans the death of the husband in the domestic attentions of the wife." The *Democrat* could "scarcely recollect in the records of crime, a murder more coolly planned, executed with more cold blooded deliberation or calculated with a more cunning reference to circumstances, that would probably ward off suspicion." The newspaper displayed as much concern about her unfaithfulness as the murder. The lack of explanation for her crime "compels us to seek its explanation in the attributes of fiends."[19]

Both newspapers described Bilansky as cold, indifferent, and, for the most part, strong. The *St. Paul Minnesotian and Times* occasionally referred to her as unattractive or worse; it also said she was unfaithful to her husband. She was "defiant, hardened, and unmoved." The *St. Paul Pioneer and Democrat* called her heartless and "utterly devoid of all natural female modesty, and even of common decency." The newspaper maintained: "Probably no jail ever contained such a criminal, either male or female, under imprisonment for such a crime, who exhibited such a complete want of decency and propriety." Bilansky granted the press an interview on the day before her execution. The *Democrat* said she had appeared "pale and thin, with dark circles around her eyes, as if occasioned by incessant weeping." She denied her guilt and in her last statement proclaimed her innocence.[20]

The two newspapers' accounts ran on 24 March 1860, the day after the hanging. The *Democrat* focused more on the sexual element of the story, whereas the *Times* played more of a religious angle. The latter's story read like a morality play, although both newspapers played on the good-and-evil and repentance themes.

18. "Conviction of Anne Bilansky," *St. Paul Pioneer and Democrat*, 9 June 1859; "The Conviction of Mrs. Bilansky," *St. Paul Minnesotian and Times*, 11 June 1859.
19. "The Bilansky Poison Case," *St. Paul Pioneer and Democrat*, 9 June 1859.
20. "Execution of Bilansky, Murderess"; "The Bilansky Murder."

The hanging was private, although no state law prohibited public executions. The *Democrat* editorially supported the sheriff's decision to make "the execution as private as the means at his command permitted," and the *Times* had earlier said it hoped the governor would exercise his discretion and make the execution private. The enclosure that contained the gallows limited witnesses to only about 125 people, according to the *Democrat*. The newspaper estimated the crowd in town for the hanging at between 1,500 and 2,000. Because the gallows was enclosed, the crowds got to "every elevation which offered an opportunity of viewing within the enclosure." The *Democrat* said few persons from St. Paul, and "of American birth," were around the gallows, but there were many Germans and Irish. The newspaper also noticed a half-dozen Sioux women, with their children: "They were evidently interested in the manner the whites dealt out justice to murderers. We are doubtful if it impressed them with a very forcible idea of our superior civilization." The *Times* found it strange that women composed about one-fourth of all attending. The large number of women displeased the *Democrat*: "The most disgusting feature connected with it, was the eagerness and persistency with which females sought to obtain eligible places to view the dying agonies of one of their own sex."[21]

The *Times* had a more speculative and melodramatic story than the *Democrat*, and because the *Times* had expressed such certainty about Bilansky's guilt, one part of its report of the drop and her death seem odd. "The scaffold fell, and the body of Mary Ann Bilansky quietly dropped into the embrace of death, with scarcely a struggle or tremor, while her soul, either guilty or innocent of the terrible crime she died for, went to meet the Inscrutable Judge of all the living, at the bar of Heaven, where no mistakes are made." In an editorial that same day, the *Times* said Bilansky had gone to her death "in keeping with that of almost all the notorious and more monstrous of modern murderers; as though it were a fashion amongst them to go into eternity with a falsehood on their lips." The day after the execution, the *Democrat* tired of the story, saying it hoped "to have no occasion to allude to" the hanging again.[22]

Roxalana Druse of New York: Her "Sinister Eyes"

Roxalana Druse was the least likely of women executed to cause a legislature to consider ending the death penalty. She hanged in New York in 1887 for murdering her husband, William. She reportedly forced a

21. "Execution of Mrs. Bilansky," *St. Paul Pioneer and Democrat*, 24 March 1860; "Execution of Bilansky, Murderess"; "The Bilansky Murder."
22. "Execution of Bilansky, Murderess"; "Execution of Bilansky—Moral"; "Mrs. Bilansky—Correction," *St. Paul Pioneer and Democrat*, 25 March 1860.

fourteen-year-old nephew to shoot William, and when he was not dead, she struck him with an ax, severing his head. She and her daughter then cut up his body and burned it in a cookstove, and she threw her husband's severed head into a sack of buckwheat. That act eventually proved her undoing. The *New York Times* published the gory details of the murder in its 17 and 18 January 1885 editions.[23]

On 18 December 1884, "Roxie" Druse and her husband argued. A short time later, she stood pointing a pistol at her husband, who sat in a chair at the table, with a rope around his neck. Mary, eighteen, the Druses' daughter, held the rope. Roxie gave the pistol to fourteen-year-old Frank Gates, a nephew, and told him to shoot William. Gates fired twice, and William, still alive, lay on the floor. Roxie struck him on the head with an ax. "Oh, Roxie, don't," he moaned. She struck again, severing his head, which rolled away on the floor. She wrapped the head in her apron and laid it in a corner and sent her ten-year-old son, George, and Gates to gather shingles. Roxie Druse built a fire in both stoves, and then she and Mary chopped, carved, and sawed William Druse into pieces with an ax, jackknife, and razor, while Gates and George played checkers in an adjoining room. She burned the body parts—all except his head, which she threw into a sack of buckwheat. She and the boys disposed of the ashes, and threw the ax head, pistol, and a knife into the pond, and she threw a razor against a fencerow. Then she went home and painted and wallpapered the interior of her home.

Roxie Teftt met her husband-to-be in 1863; she was known for wearing brightly colored, gaudy ribbons, although the rest of her clothing was common and poorly made. William Druse lived alone on a large farm near Warren, New York. Roxie's calm demeanor, good figure, long black hair, and eyes attracted him. Her eyes "exercised over 'Bill Druse' . . . the fascination of a serpent." They gleamed and "had a snaky glitter that was repulsive, while it also had a measure of attraction." They were "sinister looking," and her face showed determination with a "large and sensuous" mouth; a "well-formed," straight nose that was too large; high cheekbones; a "broad, high forehead"; and "straight heavy eyebrows."[24]

William Druse, fifteen years older than Roxie, was slow in the courtship, and before he could propose, she asked him to marry her. Following the marriage, two children were born: Mary, the eldest, and George. Mary and her mother were close and were alike in a number of ways, including their propensity to wear clothing that cost far beyond the family's mod-

23. The first part of this story was reconstructed from "Roxie Druse's Last Sunday," *New York Times*, 28 February 1887; "Two Months More of Life," ibid., 23 December 1886; and "Georgie Druse's Story," ibid., 18 January 1885.

24. "Roxie Druse's Last Sunday"; "Mrs. Druse Facing Death," ibid., 27 February 1887.

est means. The *New York Times* also said they were "utterly heartless, their morality is of the lowest character, and they have impressed all who have come in close contact with them as lacking even in a desire to tell the truth where a lie will answer their purpose. Mother and daughter possess a spirit of vanity that, under less painful circumstances, would be ridiculous." The *Times* described Roxie Druse as "illiterate and of a low order of intelligence." When Mary was sixteen years old, men began visiting the Druse home. William Druse went to bed early, but laughter and "clinking glasses" often awakened him, and after a time he complained, angering his wife and daughter. Arguments became common. The neighbors talked about "nightly orgies in which [Druse] took no part, and in which Roxie Druse and her daughter were the ruling spirits, as well as the attraction to visitors who did not care to be seen entering or leaving the place."[25]

After the murder, William Druse's neighbors questioned his whereabouts, although the *Times* described him as an eccentric who "had at different times mysteriously disappeared, but always returned in due time." Gates's brother called him home shortly thereafter, and before Frank left, Roxie told him she would kill him if he talked. On the way home, young Gates's brother advised him to tell what he knew about William Druse.[26]

Soon after, the Herkimer County district attorney and two farmers questioned Frank Gates, and he confessed. Police arrested Roxie Druse at her home for her husband's murder. Mary and George would not talk; however, when Gates was telling his story in the presence of Druse and her children and said Druse had wrapped her husband's head in a newspaper, George blurted out, "That ain't so, she wrapped it in her apron." The next day, Gates told a coroner's jury about what the *Times* called "the most cold-blooded murder ever known in the annals of Herkimer County." The following day, George Druse testified. Roxalana and Mary sat, composed, and apparently neither was nervous.[27] Twelve days later, the jury ruled that Druse had shot and killed her husband.

The district attorney did not believe Druse had burned all of the body because no pieces of skull and no teeth were found in the ashes. In March 1885, a man working near the Druse home found in a buckwheat sack a human head with the hair cut off. Druse was convicted and appealed several times. The *Times* later pointed out that twelve jurors and eleven judges in different courts had eventually judged her.[28]

The prospect of hanging a woman did not appeal to New York's gov-

25. "Mrs. Druse Facing Death"; "Georgie Druse's Story"; "Roxie Druse's Last Sunday."

26. "A Wife's Terrible Crime," ibid., 17 January 1885; "Roxie Druse's Last Sunday."

27. "A Wife's Terrible Crime"; "Georgie Druse's Story"; "Roxie Druse's Last Sunday."

28. "Roxie Druse's Last Sunday."

ernor, David S. Hill, who on 22 December 1886 granted her a reprieve, although he refused to commute her sentence. Governor Hill did not believe it was his role to overrule jurors and judges, but he granted the reprieve so the New York legislature could act to save Druse, if it desired. In an editorial, the *Times* said the governor should not interfere with the execution, but stated that his decision to delay it so that the legislature could act, if it so chose, "may not be the most courageous, but it cannot be severely censored." The *Times* contended that arguments against Druse's execution, because of the nature of the crime, could be no less than arguments against capital punishment for anyone. Although the newspaper argued for reforms, it did not say capital punishment should be abolished; instead, it claimed the arguments being made for Druse were not good ones against her being executed. Even in its news columns, the *Times* opposed commutation: "The murder was deliberate, cold-blooded, and cruel, and a commutation would serve as an embarrassing precedent in other cases of female murderers which will undoubtedly be brought to the Governor's attention."[29] The legislature did not act.

The *New York Times* reported that some people tried to save Druse, although there was little public sympathy. Petitions circulated near her former hometown of Warren resulted in only five signatures. As the execution day approached, Druse reportedly had fits of temper or anxiety, such as when an Episcopalian priest visited her in her cell and prayed for her. When he handed her a prayer book, Druse apparently sat and listened quietly, then suddenly leaped to her feet, threw the book across the cell, and ordered the priest to leave. News reports said she was moody and refused to eat. The *Times* speculated that Druse would probably break down during the execution because "she will be incapable of bearing the awful ordeal with even a pretense of fortitude."[30]

Even the arrangements Druse made for after her death were not safe from publication. She directed the sheriff to give her body to the Reverend George W. Powell; deeded a cabinet organ to her daughter, Mary; and wrote a letter to the wife of a former sheriff, thanking the woman for her kindness. The *Times* obtained the letter and published it, and in what seems poor taste criticized it for being "extremely faulty in punctuation and spelling." Powell believed Druse to be a good woman and innocent. The *Times* criticized him, saying it "matters seemingly nothing to him that she has been adjudged guilty of an atrocious crime" by a jury, numerous judges, and a commission appointed to examine her sanity.[31]

Druse was the first person hanged among the forty murderers convict-

29. "May a Murderess Be Hanged?" ibid., 23 December 1886; "Two Months More."
30. "Mrs. Druse Facing Death"; "Roxie Druse's Last Sunday."
31. "Roxie Druse's Last Sunday."

ed in Herkimer County since 1783, the *Times* reported. New York prohibited public hangings, and an amendment to the penal code clearly spelled out who could witness the hanging. Although reporters were not listed to witness, they did.[32]

The day of the hanging, the temperature dipped near zero, and a brisk northwest wind blew. Some people braved the weather, the *New York Times* reported, including members of the Remington Rifles militia of Mohawk, who marched down the main street and expressed their feelings "in discordant and senseless howls." The *Times* derided the group, calling them "country yokels." "The privilege of parading around a jail in which a woman was to be hanged had induced several patriots to join the corps. They did not witness the execution, and may have been frostbitten, but they were at Herkimer on Feb. 28, 1887." Some people came as far as twenty miles in wagons, traveling over roads drifted with snow.

Druse slept only three hours during the three days before the execution, and only one hour on the night before her death, despite having taken sedatives. She spent her time writing poetry, a skill she had acquired in jail. On the night before she died, Powell stayed with her until late in the evening, and before he left, Druse cut a lock of her hair, tied a piece of black satin around it, and gave it to him, along with a poem, which the *Times* published:

> Who will care when I am gone,
> And the birds' music hushed,
> In the twilight dim and gloomy?
>
> Who my name will softly whisper,
> Who for me will kindly pray,
> When at last death has its sway?
>
> Lying on my narrow bed,
> Who will smooth dying pillow,
> Who will care when I am dead?

The next day, Druse dressed carefully for her execution, and the *Times* described her black satin dress in detail: "The skirt was narrow, made so for the occasion. The basque was tight fitting, and also of satin. At the bottom of the skirt it was ruffled. At her wrists she wore a white ruching, threaded with silver, and a deeper ruching of the same sort around the neck. In front and at the top of her bodice she wore a bunch of roses, taken from a large bouquet which her daughter had sent to her."

32. "Mrs. Druse Facing Death."

The twelve witnesses "and a large number of reporters" filled the parlor and dining room of the jail. Sheriff Delavan L. Cook read the death warrant to Druse, who wept, leaned heavily on Powell, looked nervous, and shook visibly when she saw the scaffold. It was just before noon, and the *Times* said sunlight flooded into the jail yard, making the snow glisten. The writer waxed eloquent about the bright sun: "[T]he sun poured its light from the southeast upon the solemn-faced 12 men who faced her, upon the Deputies who stood upon each side, upon Dr. Powell, who was on her right. Its beams fell upon the row of gilt buttons that fastened the front of her dress, and transformed them to globes of fire. The white snow glistened under its influence, and even the gloomy scaffold lost something of its sombre character."

Cook asked Druse if she had any last words, and Powell spoke for her, condemning capital punishment as being uncivilized and non-Christian. Powell turned to Druse and said, "Go to thy loving Father, God." As he said "Amen," two deputies stepped forward, and one placed a black cap over her head. She began to shriek, with a number of shrieks in quick succession, "each louder than the last." Cook gave the sign and the weight fell: "There was a rattle, a jar, and a strangled cry," the *Times* said, and Druse was dead moments later.

The *Times* said it would not be a surprise if someone took Druse's body from her grave. "It is known that more than one physician would like to examine the brain of such a woman, and there are spirits here who are not averse to rendering science all the assistance in their power in this particular case." Four days later, the *Times* reported that students at Albany Medical College had played a "joke." About a month earlier, a woman had died, and the college received her body for study. She remarkably resembled Druse. The students sent word to a reporter for the *Albany Argus* to come to the college at midnight for a good story. The next day, the *Argus* ran a sensational story that Druse's body had been exhumed and brought to the medical college. The *Times*, in an article titled "Hoaxing a Reporter," said doctors and others at the college denied the story, but the *Argus* and some members of the public insisted otherwise. The *Times* noted that people came daily to the college for mementos, some wanting locks of Druse's hair. "About 50 locks have been clipped from the head of the corpse and given to memento seekers, and the supply is now almost exhausted and was entirely inadequate to meet the demands of a curious public."[33]

33. "Roxalana Druse Hanged," ibid., 1 March 1887; "Hoaxing a Reporter," ibid., 5 March 1887.

Mary Rogers of Vermont: Not a "Spark of Womanliness"

An intense campaign to save Mary Rogers from hanging included petitions, pressure on the Vermont governor, and attempts to help her commit suicide. The governor said he did not want to hang her, and the sheriff who might be assigned the task wept at the thought.

Rogers wed at age fifteen, left her husband at nineteen, murdered him the same year, and hanged in Vermont's Windsor Prison at twenty-two. She wanted the finer things of life, although she neither was born into wealth nor married into it. During her short life, she relied on her wiles and on sex, although neither got her the riches and comfortable life she wanted. Instead, they proved her undoing because she hanged on 8 December 1905, two years after her 22 December 1903 conviction. The press loved the story because it involved passion, deceit, lust for money, love spurned, and prison sex scandals.

Rogers loved a man other than her husband, but the man did not love her, or even know that she loved him, according to press reports. Her husband loved her even after she rejected him, and a seventeen-year-old boy loved her and wanted to marry her, but she did not love him, although she did use him to try to achieve her ends.

Even behind bars, Rogers used sex to gain favors. She was at the center of a sex scandal and lengthy investigation at the famous Windsor Prison. Her execution was the first in Vermont since 1892, and she was the first person sentenced to death in the state between 1892 and 1905 to whom clemency was denied.

At times, it was hard to tell whether her crime or her lack of femininity most outraged the *Burlington Daily Free Press*. It said her crime "breathed of foul deceit, cunning and a viciousness inconceivable in a woman," and added she might have been spared "had there been one spark of womanliness" in her.[34]

The Crime

Rogers left her husband and fell in love with Maurice Knapp, "a well-known citizen of Bennington." The one-sided romance failed because Knapp reportedly did not know Rogers loved him.

News stories implied but did not flatly state that Rogers was a prostitute after she left her husband. Exercising discretion, the *Free Press* referred to her as "a woman of the street." A 1996 article in *American Heritage* said Rogers had worked as a maid for a family with two sons after

---

34. "Woman Hanged," *Burlington Daily Free Press,* 9 December 1905.

she left her husband, and that others reportedly saw her in bed with both, as well as with other men.[35]

Seventeen-year-old Leon Perham, described by the *Free Press* as "a half breed Indian" and by the *New York Times* as "a half-witted boy," fell in love with Rogers and wanted to marry her. She hatched a scheme to use Perham's infatuation to kill her husband. Rogers wrote to her husband and asked him to meet her one night near the Little Walloomsac River, where she induced him to let her tie him up with a piece of rope. The *Free Press* said she told him she had "learned a new trick" and wanted to try it on him. Once her husband was tied, Rogers put a chloroformed rag over his face and drugged him, and she and Perham rolled him into the river. Rogers left a suicide note from her husband, which she wrote. His body and the note were found the next day. The *Free Press* said Rogers's "unseemly haste" to collect her husband's insurance money and other "damaging circumstances" proved her undoing.[36]

Her 22 December 1903 conviction carried an automatic death penalty. The *Times*, in an unattributed statement, said Rogers did not fear the death sentence because she expected the legislature to commute it.[37]

Citizens Protest the Execution

The sentence brought public protest. A letter to the editor in the *New York Times* pleaded for mercy for Rogers, but did not flatter her. It said she was born with "poor brain stuff" and therefore could not resist the ways of the world, and "was degenerate and woefully ignorant of the ways of life." The writer said the state should provide Rogers with proper training and give her a second chance.[38]

Sheriff Henry H. Peck dreaded executing a woman. On 9 March, just hours before her scheduled execution, Gov. Charles J. Bell granted a four-month reprieve, which seemed more like a reprieve for Peck, who so dreaded the thought of hanging her that he "was on the verge of collapse." After the reprieve, Peck was so overcome that "tears filled his eyes and it was a few moments before he could speak." Another effort to keep Rogers from hanging involved a suicide plot. Harold Harpin, the son of Windsor's prison warden, received a $250 bribe in a letter, which offered him an additional $250 if he delivered poison to Rogers. Harpin gave the letter to his father, who gave it to the prison superintendent, who gave it to

35. Ibid.; Gene Smith, "In Windsor Prison," 100.

36. "Woman Hanged"; "Mrs. Rogers Hanged, Bell Upholding Law," *New York Times*, 9 December 1905.

37. "Woman Sentenced to Death," *New York Times*, 30 December 1903.

38. "Plea for Mary Rodgers," ibid., 19 November 1904.

the governor, who gave it to the postal authorities. It is unclear if any action resulted.[39]

Some prominent Vermonters, including Capt. Lloyd Clark of the U.S. Supply Station in Michigan, protested the hanging. Clark told Governor Bell that if the state hanged Rogers, then he wanted the picture of his brother, Admiral Clark, which hung in the state capitol, turned to the wall. Admiral Clark consented to his brother's action, and Lloyd Clark said every "real Vermonter would hang his head in shame before the world" if Rogers was hanged. Admiral Clark, the *Times* said, was a Spanish American War hero who had brought the ship the *Oregon* into Cuban waters, and the Vermont legislature had put a life-size portrait of him in the capitol.[40]

The controversy perhaps gave Governor Bell second thoughts because on the day Rogers was to be executed, the *Times* ran a story that said: "A reprieve until Dec. 8 for Mrs. Mary Rogers, who was to have been hanged at Windsor tomorrow, was signed this afternoon by Gov. Bell." It was her last reprieve.[41]

Press Outrage at Delays

The two years between Rogers's conviction and her execution outraged the *Burlington Daily Free Press*: "Every ingenious device, known in law, was used to save Mary Rogers from the gibbet." About two weeks earlier, when Rogers had pursued last-ditch legal efforts, and amid hearings about a sex scandal at the prison that involved her, the *Free Press* made it clear it was tired of her. The newspaper said in an editorial: "The public has heard so much concerning the case of Mary Rogers, the Bennington murderess, that the subject has become nauseating. . . . [I]t is certain that the experience of our State government with Mrs. Rogers has done more to retard the movement to abolish capital punishment than would all the champions of the death penalty could have said from now until the next Legislature meets." When it seemed Rogers's last chance to be saved had failed, the *Free Press* said: "Everything that the ingenuity of ambitious lawyers could devise or maudlin sympathizers suggest has been done, and if ever a murderess was given the benefit of every possible doubt, that woman is Mary Rogers."[42]

Rogers stayed in the news for another reason—a sex scandal at Windsor Prison. The *Free Press* termed conditions at the prison deplorable and

39. "Mrs. Rogers Unmoved by News of Reprieve," ibid., 3 March 1905.
40. "Says It's Vermont's Shame," ibid., 21 June 1905.
41. "Reprieve for Mrs. Rogers," ibid., 23 June 1905.
42. "Mary Rogers's Fate Sealed," *Burlington Daily Free Press*, 28 November 1905; "The Rogers Case," ibid., 22 November 1905; "Woman Hanged."

partly blamed "the baneful influence of the murderess Mary Rogers." Testimony about a sexual affair between Rogers and a prison trusty Vernon Rogers (they apparently were not related), said Mary Rogers had rapped on steam pipes to get his attention and then asked him if he wanted to be in the cell with her. Vernon said he had "visited" with Mary on four or five occasions before prison officials found out and moved her to an upstairs part of the prison. Mary Rogers could not come downstairs, and a woman prisoner was assigned to sleep in the cell with her. Surprisingly, Rogers did not testify during the hearings.[43]

The Gender Issue

A *Free Press* editorial said some people opposed executing a woman because one "instinctively thinks of the sex as the gentler in every sense." However, Rogers's crime had resulted in her "unsexing herself and making conspicuous her Lucretia [*sic*] Borgia character." The newspaper also criticized unnamed competitors: "When Mary Rogers's case is finally disposed of, the yellow journals may put on black borders."[44]

Others tried to use Rogers's femininity to prevent her execution, and one effort perhaps involved her lawyer E. B. Flinn, although that was speculated but never proved. Flinn's prediction that hope remained for Rogers left unsaid what the hope was. Two days later, and only a week before the scheduled execution, the *Free Press* said a story in Boston reported Rogers was "in a delicate condition," meaning she was pregnant; the prison physician said Rogers was not pregnant, and Flinn denied he had released the information to the Boston newspaper. If true, which apparently it was not, then obviously Rogers could not be hanged while pregnant, and just as obviously she would have had to conceive while in Windsor Prison. Prison officials were mad. Prison superintendent W. S. Lovell denied the truth of the story, and added, "This article is too ridiculous to be talked about and a person, who will report or print such an article, ought to be imprisoned for a long term of years."[45] The matter was not mentioned again in the *Free Press*.

A later story hinted that authorities still nursed their hurt feelings about press coverage, because the *Free Press* reported that no reporters would be allowed on the prison grounds or within the buildings until after the ex-

43. "Lest We Forget," ibid., 2 November 1905; "Prison Scandals," ibid., 1 November 1905; "Prison Hearing," ibid., 2 November 1905; "Finish at Prison," ibid., 9 November 1905; "Plan Execution," ibid., 22 November 1905.

44. "Mary Rogers's Fate Sealed."

45. "May Make Another Trial," ibid., 29 November 1905; "Sensational Story Denied," ibid., 1 December 1905.

ecution.[46] Just two days later, authorities relented and announced that four newsmen would be allowed as witnesses.

The Governor's Reaction

Commutation seemed out of the question when Governor Bell said, "If ever a woman should hang, Mary Rogers is that one." The *Burlington Daily Free Press* said the governor considered it his duty to uphold the law, although he personally opposed capital punishment. Efforts to prevent the execution reached national proportions. When Governor Bell attended the New England Society of Chicago banquet in Chicago, he received a petition that questioned his political motives for denying commutation. Bell was seated at the dinner table when given the petition. Before he reached the banquet, he received a set of resolutions from the Chicago Spiritualistic League asking that he show leniency for Rogers, and in Cleveland, Ohio, the United Women of the Republic sent a telegram asking him to grant clemency. The telegram said, in part, "It would be a shame and a disgrace in this enlightened day to execute a woman who for her actions was irresponsible at all times." In addition, Mrs. J. M. Partlon of Cincinnati traveled to Montpelier, Vermont, to present a petition with forty-three thousand names, asking clemency for Rogers.[47] None of the pleas changed Governor Bell's mind.

Despite the controversies and the national interest, the *Free Press* ran the execution story on page 2. The paper called Rogers "the calmest person in the chamber of death," stoical and indifferent. The newspaper attested the execution was enforced without incident, much to officials' relief. Her feet touched the floor after the drop, but deputies quickly tightened the rope, pulling "the lifeless form" upward. She "evidently suffered no pain," although she was not declared dead until fifteen minutes after the trap was sprung. In an article several days later, U.S. marshal H. W. Bailey said officials had not botched the hanging because Rogers's neck broke, and it did not take her an unusually long time to die.[48]

On the day after the execution, the *Free Press* ran an editorial titled "The Wages of Sin." The newspaper derided those who claimed the hanging would speed the abolition of capital punishment in Vermont, but also said

46. "Mother Visits Mrs. Rogers," ibid., 4 December 1905.
47. "Says She Should Hang," ibid., 7 December 1905; "Petitions for Mrs. Rogers," ibid.; "All Ready at Prison," ibid., 8 December 1905. Many governors have expressed personal opposition to the death penalty. Only a few have used the commutation power as an extension of personal beliefs, one of the most noteworthy being Arkansas governor Winthrop Rockefeller, who, just before leaving office in the 1960s, commuted the sentences of all fifteen death row inmates.
48. "Woman Hanged"; "Sensationalism Run Mad," *Burlington Daily Free Press,* 11 December 1905.

it did not believe the hanging would deter future murderers who were under the influence of liquor or drugs, or those who murdered in a blind rage. It would deter "any Vermont wife who may be tempted by illicit love to help her paramour bind her husband and apply chloroform to his nostrils and then roll his body into a stream or help murder her husband in any other way." A *New York Times* editorial stated that hanging "shocks even rude sensibilities and tortures those more delicate," which seems to oppose the hanging. However, the newspaper praised Governor Bell for "standing fast" and not commuting the sentence and said that until the legislature chose to change the law, it should be carried out equally for men and women.[49]

Often when a person is executed, news coverage quickly fades, but three days after the hanging, the *Free Press* lambasted "the metropolitan newspapers" for printing "everything discreditable about the State" they could conceive. The next day, the paper rebuked one of Rogers's attorneys for saying Governor Bell could have delayed her execution without violating his oath of office. The newspaper said the legislature had considered Rogers's case and did not act, and the delays "had become intolerable" concerning "one of the most cruel murderesses in the annals of American crime."[50]

On 13 December, the *Free Press* chastised the famous actress "the Divine Sarah" Bernhardt for criticizing capital punishment, especially when used for women. "[T]he reading public will not lose sight of the high moral ground taken by the divine Sarah in her opposition to capital punishment."[51]

Mary Rogers continued to make news even into the 1990s when a May–June 1996 article in *American Heritage* about the history of Windsor Prison prominently featured her.[52]

49. "The Wages of Sin," ibid., 9 December 1905; "Hanging a Woman."
50. "Sensationalism Run Mad"; "Begging the Rogers Question," ibid., 12 December 1905.
51. "Bernhardt on Mary Rogers," ibid., 13 December 1905.
52. G. Smith, "In Windsor Prison."

Chapter 17

Government Secrecy of Executions under Federal Authority

SOME PEOPLE, INCLUDING *ST. LOUIS POST-DISPATCH* writers, agreed there were two reasons for Bonnie Brown Heady's fall: money and booze. Heady only partly agreed: she said love and booze caused her demise; she "had not loved wisely" and drank heavily to cope with her marital problems.[1]

In a published confession that ran a full page in the *Post-Dispatch*, Heady said her infatuation with her male accomplice, Carl Austin Hall, caused her to consent to help with the kidnapping and murder of six-year-old Bobby Greenlease of Kansas City. The *Post-Dispatch* called Heady and Hall "victims of their own insatiable greed." Heady admitted, "I'd rather be dead than poor," and Hall once stated: "I hate little people. I like to be big."[2]

Heady was one of three women the federal government executed in the nineteenth and twentieth centuries, and all attracted a lot of press attention. Mary Surratt was hanged on 7 July 1865 for her role in the conspiracy to assassinate President Abraham Lincoln, and Ethel Rosenberg and her husband were electrocuted on 19 June 1953 in New York after being convicted of espionage.[3] Surratt's case will be briefly discussed. Rosenberg's case is well known and will not be discussed in detail in this book. Less well known is Heady, who died just six months after Rosenberg. Heady died in the gas chamber in Missouri on 18 December 1953 after pleading guilty to the kidnapping and murder of young Greenlease.

1. "U.S. Authorities Give Police Here Permission to Question Hall," *St. Louis Post-Dispatch,* 24 November 1953.
2. "Mrs. Heady's Signed Confession," ibid., 17 November 1953; "Hall and Mrs. Heady Victims of Their Own Insatiable Greed; Twisted Lives Smashed by Urge to Do Things in a Big Way," ibid., 18 October 1953.
3. "Rosenbergs Executed As Atom Spies after Supreme Court Vacates Stay; Last-Minute Plea to President Fails," *New York Times,* 20 June 1953.

272

John E. Neville's book about news coverage of the Rosenbergs' trial and executions contends they were "disembodied parts of a story" until shortly before their executions, when the press began to show them as a family.[4] The government used its restrictive dealings with the media in Ethel Rosenberg's case as a model for handling the media in Heady's case. Press restrictions for Surratt's trial also were tighter than was the norm for the time.

Bonnie Brown Heady: "I'd Rather Be Dead Than Poor"

There seemed little reason for Bonnie Brown Heady's involvement in the kidnapping and murder of Bobby Greenlease. When Heady was two years old, her mother died, but an aunt in Chicago reared her and later said Heady had a normal, happy childhood. She inherited a $44,000 estate in 1949 when her father died, and she married a "prosperous and reputable" man in St. Joseph, Missouri. She raised prize-winning dogs, was an excellent horsewoman, and was a respected citizen; neighbors described her as "a good looking woman" who always dressed exceptionally well. In 1951, she won third prize as the "best-dressed cowgirl" at the Pony Express Rodeo. The *St. Louis Post-Dispatch* said of Heady and her accomplice, Carl Austin Hall, "Compared with most people, they had the world on a string." However, after Heady and her husband were divorced, she began drinking heavily, about one- or two-fifths of whiskey per day. One year later, she was waiting to die in Missouri's gas chamber.

Stories about the kidnapping ran on the front page of the *Post-Dispatch* almost every day in October and November 1953, many times as the lead story. The case was big news outside St. Louis; the *New York Times* ran forty-two stories between 29 September and 18 December, four of which were on the front page. The story developed quickly and moved to a fast conclusion; Heady and Hall were executed seventy-three days after their arrests and eighty-one days after the kidnapping. They made almost no efforts to save themselves from the gas chamber.

The story began when Heady, posing as Bobby Greenlease's aunt, took him from his school, telling school officials his mother had a heart attack. Hall concocted the kidnapping, and Heady aided him. They made ransom demands of Robert Greenlease, a multimillionaire auto dealer from Kansas City, soon after the crime, and Greenlease paid them $600,000, which the *New York Times* said was "a record" amount at that time. The *Post-Dispatch* termed the crime one of seven "major" kidnappings in the

4. Neville, *The Press, the Rosenbergs, and the Cold War,* 124–25.

United States since 1900.[5] Hall assured the Greenleases their son was alive, although he and Heady had taken the child into Kansas where Hall shot him in the head. They wrapped the boy's body in a sheet of plastic, put him in the back of Heady's station wagon, covered him with a comforter, and returned to North Kansas City.

They stopped for a few drinks before going to St. Joseph, where they buried the boy behind Heady's home in a shallow grave and planted flowers on top of it. The kidnappers were caught because they went on a drunken spending spree in St. Louis and a taxi driver became suspicious and called police. Police recovered slightly less than $300,000 of the ransom, and the missing $303,720 resulted in indictments against some police officers and a scandal in the St. Louis Police Department.

The *Post-Dispatch* broke the murder story with a huge headline that read: "Kidnaped Boy Murdered, Body Found." The story said both defendants had admitted taking part in the kidnapping but said a third person had murdered the boy, which later proved untrue. The newspaper later called the murder "one of the worst crimes in American history." Not to be outdone, a U.S. prosecutor said it was "one of the outstanding kidnappings in the history of America—I might say in the world."[6]

The *St. Louis Post-Dispatch*, and especially the FBI, had egg on their faces a few days after the arrests because the paper's first story said the FBI had referred to Heady as the "widow of a gunman." The story detailed her record of six arrests and claimed prosecutors had once charged her with slipping a pistol to her husband, Dan Heady, who was in jail in Muskogee, Oklahoma. Police killed him in a shootout, and the story said when a reporter told Heady, she smiled at him and said, "That's too bad." The story turned out to be about another woman named Heady, who was unrelated to Bonnie Brown Heady. In an editorial, the *Post-Dispatch* blamed the FBI, saying the agency released the information too quickly and did so to prevent local police departments from getting the "glory."[7]

Police at first accommodated the press, allowing reporters to interview Heady and Hall on the day they were arrested. When police took Heady from St. Louis to Kansas City, reporters apparently rode in the vehicle because the *Post-Dispatch* described in detail her words and actions during

5. "Kidnapped Boy Found Slain; $600,000 Paid; Two Seized," *New York Times,* 8 October 1953; "List of Major Kidnapings since 1900," *St. Louis Post-Dispatch,* 7 October 1953.

6. "Kidnaped Boy Murdered, Body Found," *St. Louis Post-Dispatch,* 7 October 1953; "Hall, Mrs. Heady Appear Calm As Their Execution Draws Near," ibid., 16 December 1953; "U.S. Prosecutor Demands Boy's Kidnapers Die in Gas Chamber," ibid., 16 November 1953.

7. "Flower Garden Yields Body of Kidnaped Boy," ibid., 7 October 1953; "The Greenlease Case," ibid., 11 October 1953.

the trip and did not attribute the information to any source. Police wanted to avoid publicity when they went to Heady's home to dig for the boy's body, but a radio station got word and broadcast that police were digging a few minutes after they began. The *Post-Dispatch* stated that crowds of people "swarmed around the house," and motorists almost blocked streets. The curious came for days, even after there was nothing to see. A week later, the newspaper reported that sightseers came in a steady stream; many sat on the front lawn and had their pictures taken. A *Post-Dispatch* reporter went through Heady's home and described it in detail before police closed it.[8]

Heady's and Hall's cell mates gave the *Post-Dispatch* damning information, especially about her. The newspaper based a lead story on its interview with an unnamed source, and reported that Heady had told her cell mate about the murder "without a trace of remorse of the crime that has shocked the nation." An anonymous source, described as a police officer, attested in another story that Heady wanted to be executed, and her lack of effort to save herself made it probable the information was correct, but the story ran before a grand jury had considered indictments.[9]

Press access changed drastically when Heady and Hall were convicted and moved to the state prison in Jefferson City. The defendants were under federal jurisdiction, and U.S. Marshal William B. Tatman of the Kansas City office declared anyone connected with the case or with safeguarding the prisoners would be immediately fired for releasing information about them. Federal officials said representatives from the Associated Press, United Press International, and the International News Service could witness the executions but could not file their stories until other "accredited" newspaper, magazine, television, and radio journalists had interviewed them. The federal authorities also said reporters could not use prison telephones to inform the public of the executions, and photos before and during the executions were prohibited. In addition, no press interviews with the defendants were allowed. The *Post-Dispatch* said the federal government had used similar procedures for Julius and Ethel Rosenberg's executions six months earlier. The newspaper did not openly criticize the restrictions, but did run a front-page headline that read: "U.S. Clamps Lid on News about Hall, Mrs. Heady." The story noted the regulations were the strictest since the gas chamber was installed in 1937, and also said, "State officials have not been as iron-fisted as Tatman, who flatly turned

8. "Mrs. Heady Says Hall Beat and Shot Boy; He Indicates He May Enter Guilty Plea," ibid., 12 October 1953; "Flower Garden Yields Body"; "State Officials Pressing Hunt for Marsh in Kidnaping Case," ibid., 16 October 1953; "Aunt Who Reared Mrs. Heady Says She Got in 'Wrong Crowd,'" ibid., 10 October 1953.

9. "Beat and Shot Boy"; "Mrs. Heady Said to Be Resigned to Execution," ibid., 20 October 1953.

down a request for a daily press conference with Eidson [the prison warden] to learn details of the prisoners' reactions."[10]

As many newspapers have done when reporting about female defendants, the *Post-Dispatch* dwelled on what Heady wore and how she looked. The reports at times resembled a fashion-show story. When she and Hall waived a preliminary hearing, the *Post-Dispatch* said she "wore the same cheap gray dress she had on Tuesday, the night of her arrest." She wore a brown gabardine suit and platform shoes when she pleaded guilty, and a black dress trimmed with sequins and a black hat with black feathers on the first day of testimony. When the state rested its case two days later, the *Post-Dispatch* said Heady "dressed in a different outfit for the third straight day. She wore a dark gray suit, black gloves and a black, off-the-face hat." When taken to the state prison in Jefferson City to await execution, she changed from "her smart black dress, black short coat and hat" to a pale-green cotton dress, which she said "fits better than what I had in Kansas City."[11]

Although fashion was not an issue for her execution, her attire was. Only men had been executed in Missouri's gas chamber, and they wore only black shorts to prevent cyanide gas from accumulating in the clothing. However, because Heady and Hall were executed together, modesty required that both wear regular prison clothing; officials allowed extra time to let the gas out of the chamber and the clothing before they entered. Heady and Hall were executed together because it took too much time to execute one, clear the gas from the chamber, and execute the other. Missouri officials also did not know what to do about Heady's hair. The state director of corrections wrote California officials, where two women had been executed in the gas chamber, to determine if Heady's hair should be cut so gas would not accumulate in it.[12] Despite reporting the dilemma, the *Post-Dispatch* apparently did not report whether Heady's hair was shorn.

The *St. Louis Post-Dispatch* also frequently referred to Heady's size. The newspaper consistently described her as "plump" or "pudgy," and in one story said she had praised the food in jail and "was particularly pleased by the fried potatoes." At the time of her sentencing, the newspaper termed her "a pudgy, 41-year-old divorcee," and a later story called her the "plump Mrs. Heady, 41-year-old divorcee and alcoholic." Hall did not

10. "U.S. Clamps Lid," ibid., 22 November 1953.

11. "Kidnapers Waive Hearing; Search for Marsh, Lost Ransom Grows," ibid., 9 October 1953; "Hall, Mrs. Heady Plead Guilty; Court Calls Jury for Nov. 16 to Fix Penalty," ibid., 3 November 1953; "Prosecutor Demands"; "U.S. Rests Case in Kidnap Trial, Hall's Service in War Is Cited," ibid., 18 November 1953; "Hall, Mrs. Heady in 'Death Row' at State Prison to Await Gas Cell," ibid., 21 November 1953.

12. "Hall, Heady Appear Calm"; "Kidnapers Probably Will Die Together, State Official Says," ibid., 19 November 1953.

fare well, either: the newspaper called the pair the "ne'er-do-well Hall and plump Mrs. Heady, who lived together."[13]

During the court proceedings, Heady was described as almost cavalier. The *Post-Dispatch* said she seemed to almost laugh when the bailiff said, "God save the United States," and she smiled at the jurors when they announced the verdict. The newspaper seemed to doubt her relaxed attitude because when she was imprisoned and awaiting execution, it said she "continued her pretense of joviality." Whether pretending to be jovial or not, it does seem she wanted to die. She pleaded guilty and declined to appeal. Shortly before her trial, she told a tombstone dealer in Maryville, Missouri, to select a stone for her: "I might be needing it soon."[14]

The case attracted enormous public interest at every stage. Onlookers crowded the courtroom when Heady and Hall pleaded guilty, and during the sentencing hearing, the *Post-Dispatch* reported that a crowd of several hundred people, "mostly women, surged against a line of policemen and deputies," trying to get into the courtroom, which seated a maximum of two hundred. Many of those waiting brought their lunches and soft drinks. Shortly before the executions, prison officials said more than six hundred people had applied to witness; one man from Arizona made a collect call to the Missouri governor's office to "request a ticket" to the executions.[15]

Because of public outrage at the crime, security was strict. Shortly after they were arrested, Heady and Hall were put in solitary confinement in what the *New York Times* described as Kansas City's "penthouse" jail on the eleventh floor to protect them from mob violence and from other prisoners. Sheriff Arvid Owsley said a crowd had gathered outside Kansas City's Jackson County Courthouse on the day police brought Heady and Hall from St. Louis, and the sheriff said popular feeling against the defendants was "vicious." The *Times* used the word *lynch* in its headline describing security precautions. Owsley added that other prisoners had said they would kill Hall if he was jailed with them. Lights in the defendants' cells were always on, and three deputies reportedly stood by while Hall shaved with a safety razor. When the two were imprisoned in Jefferson City, their meals were brought from the officers' mess instead of from the

13. "Hall, Mrs. Heady Confess Killing Greenlease Boy," ibid., 12 October 1953; "Hall, Mrs. Heady Sentenced to Death," ibid., 19 November 1953; "Hall and Heady Are Taken to Jefferson City, Won't Appeal," ibid., 20 November 1953; "Hall, Heady in 'Death Row.'"

14. "Prosecutor Demands"; "Hall, Heady in 'Death Row'"; "Trial of Hall and Mrs. Heady Opens Tomorrow in Kansas City," ibid., 15 November 1953; "Costello Is Said to Be Quiet on Actions Night of Kidnap Arrests," ibid., 29 November 1953.

15. "Hall, Heady Plead Guilty"; "Prosecutor Demands"; "U.S. Clamps Lid"; "Dowd to Assist Chief O'Connell in Questioning Hall, Mrs. Heady," ibid., 27 November 1953.

prison kitchen because prison officials feared other inmates might try to poison the couple.[16]

Both defendants pleaded guilty, and there was no need for a trial; however, the *Post-Dispatch* said the proceedings were peculiar because the jury's only purpose was to determine the sentence. According to the newspaper, the Lindbergh kidnapping law said there could be no death penalty unless a jury recommended it; the maximum for a judge-imposed sentence was life in prison.[17]

A controversy arose during Judge Albert J. Reeves's instructions to the jury. The *Post-Dispatch* said Reeves told the jurors that it was their duty "to disregard any opinion or evaluation of testimony that I make." Then in his remarks, which the newspaper described as "extemporaneous," he told the jurors he could not find even one mitigating circumstance that "would justify taking this helpless lad out in a field and murdering him." He also said there was "no justification for this brutal, cold-blooded, first-degree murder of this helpless lad." He said that Congress, when it enacted the Lindbergh law, "could not have had in mind a more merciless, horrifying crime." He added that although the relationship between Heady and Hall was called a "common-law" marriage, Missouri did not recognize any such thing. The *Post-Dispatch* said: "His apparent point was to label the relationship of the defendants as unlawful." When a defense attorney said Judge Reeves's charge should be clarified so the jurors understood that the statute also permitted a prison sentence, Reeves reportedly replied, "The jury has been properly instructed." Furthermore, when the attorney said Reeves had not reviewed mitigating circumstances, the *Post-Dispatch* reported: "'The jury has been properly instructed,' Judge Reeves snapped."[18]

In the last days before the execution, the newspaper had little to report and ran trivia-laden stories. For example, Heady reportedly occupied her time solving crossword puzzles, and both defendants had "been eating

16. "Lynch Precautions Set for Abductors," *New York Times,* 10 October 1953; "Hall, Mrs. Heady Subdued, Quiet As Trial Draws Near," *St. Louis Post-Dispatch,* 13 November 1953; "Hall, Heady in 'Death Row.'"

17. "Jury to Decide Whether Hall, Mrs. Heady Die, Judge Asserts," *St. Louis Post-Dispatch,* 1 November 1953. In 1938, there had been a question about whether a defendant charged under the statute and who pleaded guilty could be sentenced to death. A famous kidnapping in Chicago answered that question, the *Post-Dispatch* said, explaining that John Henry Seadlund, sentenced to death in 1938 for the kidnap-murder of Charles S. Ross, had appealed the federal death sentence, claiming that his plea of guilty precluded imposition of the death penalty. The court turned down the appeal, saying the Lindbergh law authorized the use of the jury sentencing procedure. See "Precedent for Determining Fate of Boy's Kidnaper Set in 1938," ibid., 8 November 1953.

18. "Hall, Heady Sentenced."

heartily" and gained weight; Heady laughed when told Hall had gained twenty pounds.[19]

The story the day before the execution reinforced that Heady wanted to die because, according to her attorney, "If the gates of the prison were to open today and she could go free, I still think Mrs. Heady would choose to go to her death with Hall." The story pointed out that Heady had once rejected religion, but "as her whisky-dulled mind cleared with time," she began to show remorse. The writer injected irony into the story, noting that after the executions, Heady's and Hall's bodies would be wrapped in plastic sheeting, "similar to that in which Hall and Mrs. Heady wrapped Bobby Greenlease after shooting him."[20]

The execution story, as might be expected, ran as a shared lead in the *Post-Dispatch* on 18 December because a St. Louis policeman had been indicted for perjury for his testimony before a grand jury about the missing $303,720 of ransom money. The lengthy execution story jumped from page 1 and almost covered an entire inside page. The story focused on Heady and Hall's love for one another. It said that he "went to his death with lips red from Mrs. Heady's lipstick—the result of a final kiss in the death house before entering the chamber." Heady died slowly; the *Post-Dispatch* said a prison doctor had proclaimed her breathing lasted longer than any person he had seen die in the gas chamber. A minister told the *Post-Dispatch* that Heady was upset on the day before the execution when a police officer interviewed her about another murder "because she couldn't wear fine clothes . . . she had no fingernail polish and . . . her hair was not the way she would have liked to have it."[21]

In an editorial, the *Post-Dispatch* applauded the swiftness of the justice process, saying that for the death penalty to be a deterrent, it had to be applied "with such dispatch." The newspaper questioned why the defendants refused to appeal to prolong their lives and said perhaps they had "a small flicker of conscience" and "even they could perceive the essential wrongness of their act and the essential justice of the penalty they must pay for it."[22]

The federal government failed in its attempt to control the information about exactly when the execution occurred because reporters who were standing near a police car outside the prison overheard when information was radioed to state police.[23]

19. "Hall, Heady Appear Calm."
20. "Hall Still Says He Had All of Ransom Money till His Arrest," ibid., 17 December 1953.
21. "Dolan Indicted on Perjury Charge in Ransom Inquiry; Hall, Mrs. Heady Executed," ibid., 18 December 1953.
22. "81 Days Later."
23. "Dolan Indicted."

Heady was buried in the tiny town of Clearmont, Missouri, but one of her last wishes was not granted. Her request that Hall be buried beside her outraged Nodaway County residents. County prosecuting attorney Gene Thompson said burying Hall beside her was "unthinkable" because it would memorialize "a sordid, illicit relationship."[24]

Mary Surratt: "Damnable Deeds" and "Deep-Dyed Villains"

The press reported much differently in 1865 and 1953. The nineteenth-century news articles did not reflect as clear a line between news and opinion. For example, the *New York Times* called Mary Surratt "the female fiend incarnate, who figures as the *'mater familias'* of these criminals." The *Times* called her the "most prominent" of the four accused of conspiracy in President Lincoln's assassination and described her in intricate detail during her trial before a military commission. The paper said she was about fifty years old and was "a large Amazonian class of woman, square built, masculine hands, rather full face, dark gray, lifeless eye, hair not decidedly dark, complexion swarthy; altogether her face denotes more than ordinary intelligence. She seems too strong to be weighed down by the crushing testimony against her." The newspaper continued: "Her eye is rather soft in expression and strangely at variance with the general harshness of her other features. She seems a woman of undaunted metal, and fitted for Macbeth's injunction to 'bring forth men children only'; and yet she does not appear as Lady Macbeth prayed to be, 'from crown to toe-top full of direct cruelty.'"[25]

The *Times* made its boredom with the proceedings obvious, with headlines such as "Another Long, Dull, Dismal, Doleful Day's Doing"; "Protraction Protracted and Patience Tired Out"; and "The Old, Old Story, Over and Over Again." The paper devoted enormous space to the case; the 28 June story covered the entire front page and jumped inside to an additional half page.[26]

The press at first had difficulty covering the trial, which began 9 May, because it was closed; however, the 14 May edition of the *Times* reported the decision to open the courtroom to reporters, and coverage increased dramatically. The *Times* had criticized the closed doors in an editorial just

---

24. "Dolan Held in Jackson County Jail in Default of $25,000 Bail; Greenlease Kidnapers Buried," ibid., 19 December 1953.
25. "The Conspirators," *New York Times,* 12 May 1865; "The Trial of the Assassins," ibid., 15 May 1865.
26. "The Trial of the Assassins," ibid., 24 June 1865; ibid., 28 June 1865.

two days earlier, saying it would have been better for the case to be heard before a civil court and open to the public than before a military commission.[27]

When the death verdicts were announced, the *Times* speculated, "It is believed Mrs. Surratt's sentence will be commuted to imprisonment for life," but attached no source to the statement. The story said the death sentence weighed more heavily on her than the other defendants, and termed her the "general manager" of the assassination plot.[28]

The *Times* saved the most dramatic reporting for the story about the executions. Surratt, clearly the most interesting of the four defendants, received most of the coverage. The *Times*'s dramatic, opinionated, and speculative lead paragraph said:

> The conspirators have gone to their long home, the swift hand of justice has smitten them, and they stand before the judgment seat. Electrified—saddened as the country was by the terrible calamity brought upon it by the damnable deeds of these deep-dyed villains, astounded as it has been by the daily revelations of the trial of the criminals, it was doubtless unprepared, as were all here, for the quick flash of the sword of power, whose blade to-day fell upon the guilty heads of the assassins of our lamented President.

The *New York Times* said other newspapers had speculated that Surratt's sentence would be commuted, but the paper applauded its own good judgment: "Such a sentiment found no echo here." The *Times* devoted almost the first half of the execution story to Surratt, whom it termed a "remarkable woman," but "like most remarkable women [she] had an undertone of superstition which served her in place of true religion." The *Times* used Surratt's physical characteristics to explain her nature. "A cold eye, that would quail at no scene of torture; a close, shut mouth, whence no word of sympathy with suffering would pass; a firm chin, indicative of fixedness of resolve; a square, solid figure, whose proportions were never disfigured by remorse or marred by loss of sleep."

The *Times* recounted her behavior at her trial, saying that although indifferent at the trial, Surratt became so distraught when sentenced that some observers believed she would die. "Fainting, she cried aloud in the bitterness of her woe, wailing forth great waves of sorrow, she fell upon the floor and gave vent to a paroxysm of grief, partially hysterical, and wholly nervous."

Much of the execution story described Surratt's last-hour effort to avoid

27. Ibid., 12 May 1865.
28. "The Conspirators," ibid., 7 July 1865.

hanging. Her lawyers sought from the District of Columbia Supreme Court a writ of habeas corpus, claiming that a civil court and not a military commission should have tried her. Judge Andrew Wylie issued the writ, but the military came to the courtroom with a statement from President Andrew Johnson suspending the writ. Wylie said his court did not have the power to force the federal government to comply, and the matter was ended. The defendants hanged that day.

The *Times*'s reporter, who was allowed to look in on the prisoners while they were in their cells awaiting execution, said Surratt was in "physical prostration." When taken from her cell to the scaffold, "she had to be almost literally lifted and borne along by the officers." She looked in horror at the gallows. She was dressed in "a plain black alpacca [*sic*] dress, with black bonnet and thin veil." The Roman Catholic priest attending her made no last statement on her behalf. When the black cap was put over her head, she said, "Don't let me fall; hold on." Her words "Don't let me fall" are nearly identical to those Heady uttered eighty-eight years later.[29]

As might be expected, the hangings attracted thousands of curious onlookers. The *Times* said hotels were jammed and streets filled "with restless, impatient people." Many were "willing to spend hundreds of dollars" to see the hangings. Trains arrived all day loaded with people, and roads leading to Washington "were lined with pedestrians." Thousands assembled at the prison, and "streets and avenues were blocked up by hundreds of vehicles, and probably 2,000 lookers-on, whose only reward for their exposure and labor was a peep at the prison walls in the distance." The *Times* said rampant rumors all concerned Surratt. "Every one had his pet theory, but it concerned Mrs. Surratt alone—the fate of the others seemed certain." Some believed her sentence would be commuted because she was a woman, whereas others theorized she was shielding her son, John. The *New York Times* termed him a coward and said if he allowed his mother to die on the gallows when he was guilty, it would perhaps be better for him to commit suicide than to live with the shame.[30]

Mary Surratt is the only woman executed in the United States by a federal military commission.

29. See "Dolan Indicted."
30. "The Conspirators," *New York Times*, 8 July 1865.

PART V

The Late 1990s and Beyond

Chapter 18

The High-Tech Media at the End of the Twentieth Century

Karla Faye Tucker: "Pickax" Was Not Her Name

Picture this scene outside the prison at Huntsville, Texas, on 3 February 1998: More than two hundred reporters from newspapers, magazines, and television stations from the United States, Europe, South America, and Asia; a "sea" of television satellite trucks; live, continuous CNN coverage; and representatives from all the major networks. In addition, there was a person hawking his books; others dressed in Halloween-like costumes, parading about; protesters with signs, one of which read, "Forget Injection. Use a Pickax"; and a large-screen video production, with a girl singing a gospel tune and on the screen a condemned inmate using sign language to convey the words. It was a multimedia execution for the 1990s.

It would be hard to imagine a news event that began with so little fanfare and ended with so much as that of Karla Faye Tucker. The crime for which Tucker died attracted almost no interest in the Houston newspaper press, probably because murders are unremarkable in many cities, and in this case the man and woman murdered were not well known. The *Houston Chronicle* called the murders "just two of the 556 homicides in 1983" in Houston, and said the killings "were barely a blip on the media radar." A *Chronicle* reporter who had covered the crime in 1983 said in 1998 that he did not even remember the crime scene, and the murders "just sort of slipped through the cracks somehow." Regardless, in the weeks before Tucker's execution, the *Chronicle* referred to the case as "one of the most grisly murders in Houston history," and a *Chronicle* editorial after Tucker's execution said, "No, 'pickax murderer' was not part of her name, but it was what she was."[1]

1. "'Other Than the Pickax, It Wasn't That Unusual . . . ,'" *Houston Chronicle*, 1

Tucker's story did not make the *Chronicle*'s front page until the trial, which almost eliminates argument about prejudicial pretrial publicity. The story about her death sentence had a banner headline with letters that were one inch high.

A jury convicted her of murdering Jerry Lynn Dean; also murdered was Deborah Ruth Davis Thornton, who had met Dean earlier that evening and had gone home with him. They were killed with a pickax, which police found imbedded in Thornton's chest. Despite the crime's gruesome nature, the story ran far inside the *Chronicle*. The victims' names were not published in the first story. A month passed before police arrested Karla Faye Griffith and Daniel Ryan Garrett for the murders. (Griffith divorced her husband, Stephen, in 1983 and took back her maiden name, Tucker.) The story ran on the last page of the *Houston Post* under a standing-column headline "Courts / Police," and the story was not even the first item, instead running second under a tiny headline that read, "Trio Charged." Motives for the killings were said to be burglary and Griffith's "extreme dislike" for Dean, who had reportedly left a "leaky motorcycle" in her apartment.[2] The third person arrested was never tried. Garrett was convicted and sentenced to death, but died of liver disease.

Fifteen years later, when Tucker was executed, a banner headline on the *Chronicle*'s front page read, "Tucker Dies after Apologizing." A related story began: "Television's longest vigil for a condemned murderer ended with Tuesday's execution of Karla Faye Tucker." The press termed her a "household name" from Europe to parts of Asia and South America.[3] Her case attracted nationally known columnists such as Carl T. Rowan and William F. Buckley Jr.; celebrities such as actor Mike Farrell and Mick Jagger's former wife Bianca; and religious leaders such as television's *700 Club* host Pat Robertson, televangelist Jerry Falwell, and Pope John Paul II. The *Chronicle*'s opinion pages published scores of letters either opposing or approving of her execution, and Houston's religious community debated in the press whether she should be killed or spared.

The carnival-like scene at the prison on the night of the execution was bizarre. The *Chronicle* said the estimated five hundred people gathered were the largest crowd "ever to gather for a Texas execution." (Later press reports put the number at twelve hundred.) Tucker's supporters showed a big-screen video of her translating into sign language the lyrics of a

---

February 1998; "Court Rejects Tucker Plea," ibid., 29 January 1998; "Karla's Fate," ibid., 4 February 1998.

2. "Man, Woman Found Slain in Apartment," *Houston Chronicle,* 13 June 1983; "Trio Charged," *Houston Post,* 22 July 1983.

3. "Tucker Dies after Apologizing," *Houston Chronicle,* 4 February 1998; "TV Turns Last Day on Death Row into Media Marathon," ibid.; "The World Waits . . . and Watches," ibid., 1 February 1998.

gospel song, sung by the daughter of Tucker's minister. Local college students carried signs that read, "Hello Mom" and "Send Money," whereas others read, "Forget Injection. Use a Pickax" or similar messages. Supporters held candlelight prayer vigils; one man used the occasion to hawk copies of his book; another, the *Chronicle* said, "masqueraded as the grim reaper, complete with blood dripping from his mouth. His companion was dressed as a witch." Earlier that day, the area served as "a battleground of rhetoric, pitting an international cast of death penalty foes against a crew of largely home-grown capital punishment defenders."[4] More than two hundred reporters gathered from all over the world.

Why did this case attract so much international attention? For starters, Texas had not executed a woman since 1863 when Chipita Rodriguez was hanged for a crime she probably did not commit.[5] Moreover, no woman had been executed in the United States since 1984, and Tucker was only the third woman executed in this country since 1962. Third, the pickax murders were gruesome, and they were sensational because during the trial it was brought out that Tucker said she had gotten sexual gratification from killing Dean and Thornton. Fourth, well-known religious leaders or organizations such as the Reverend Pat Robertson, the Reverend Jerry Falwell, Pope John Paul II, and the National Council of Churches were involved. Finally, capital punishment cases in the United States often interest Western European media because the death penalty is no longer used there.

It also seems apparent the media were attracted because Texas would execute "a Bible-reading, angelic-looking woman," with "pink-tinged lips, lightly freckled face and cascading dark curls," who had "smiled her way into hundreds of thousands—if not millions—of homes across the country via coverage by every major television network and from newspaper and magazine pages." The *Houston Chronicle* said an attorney for an unnamed woman who was executed (surely, it was Velma Barfield) claimed his client had not gotten the same kind of media attention because "[s]he didn't look like the captain of the cheerleaders." Andy Kahan, the Houston mayor's crime victims' advocate, said people paid attention to Tucker's execution only because "she looks like one of the Brady Bunch girls and not Granny Clampett. In this case, she's being presented as a fuzzy-wuzzy bunny and everybody goes boo-hoo because the bunny is going to get stepped on. Well this fuzzy bunny stuck a pickax into two people 20 times and left it embedded in a woman's chest."[6]

4. "Tucker Dies after Apologizing."
5. The Texas legislature in 1985 granted Rodriguez "symbolic redress" ("Woman's Execution in 1863 Involved Ax Murder As Well," ibid., 1 February 1998).
6. "Should Tucker Be Executed?" ibid.; "Last Day Marathon"; "Tucker Dies After Apologizing."

The *Chronicle*'s coverage illustrated the enormous gap in perceptions about Tucker. Sister Helen Prejean termed Tucker a "gentle, beautiful Christian woman"; her former husband said she was "charismatic and beautiful"; and a foe of the death penalty remarked that Tucker could be "the Mother Teresa of the prison system." Her former husband said she was vindictive, and they had often fist-fought. He said she packed a wallop of a punch, and when they went to a bar, "I didn't have to worry because she had my back covered."[7] The *Chronicle,* at various times, said Tucker had been a heroin addict; "a drug-abusing, motorcycle-riding, hotheaded prostitute"; a "self-admitted ham who had always enjoyed mugging for a camera"; and "the prodigal daughter who finally found peace."

The Media

Although the story was big news in Houston for quite some time before the execution, and it was well known in death penalty circles, the coverage became most intense in the national and international media just before the execution. A *Chronicle*-sponsored statewide poll of Texans concerning their attitudes about Tucker's execution found more than one-fourth did not know enough about the case to form an opinion, even though Tucker had been "everywhere on TV . . . the subject of endless television debate, even on the daytime talk shows." A professor who helped conduct the study explained that the news play had not been as intense as it might have been because the scandal involving President Bill Clinton and Monica Lewinsky broke two days before the polling started and overwhelmed all other news.[8]

The *Chronicle* ran on 1 February two stories describing broadcast and print coverage. One story detailed plans of *Larry King Live,* CNN's *Burden of Proof,* NBC, CBS, ABC, Fox, the four Houston affiliates, and two Houston Spanish-language stations. The other story described coverage of Tucker by the *Mail* (London); Kyodo, a Japanese news service; and newspapers in Ireland, Singapore, Canada, Holland, Germany, and Italy. A German news agency, Deutsche Presse, and Agence–France Presse covered the case, as did Mexico's Telemundo, which also broadcast in Latin America. The *Chronicle* asserted that a New York company had completed the technical arrangements it needed for a broadcast satellite feed to all European television stations. A spokesman at the state prison in Huntsville, where Texas performs its executions, said about one hundred

7. "Ex-husband Loved Her Despite 'Wild Streak,'" ibid., 3 February 1998.
8. "Last Day Marathon"; "Court Rejects Tucker Plea."

reporters, fifty technicians and engineers, and twenty-five satellite trucks were expected. Fifty additional telephone lines were installed.[9]

All hotels in Huntsville were booked, and the *Chronicle* reported that parking around the prison was expected to be "virtually non-existent" and traffic "nightmarish." The estimate for the number of reporters was low; about two hundred reportedly were at the prison, and "a sea of television satellite trucks filled the block" between the prison and a local Dairy Queen. Ann Hodges, a *Chronicle* television critic, noted the fickle nature of television news: "TV was out of there so fast when it was over, that the announcement of Tucker's death had come almost as an anticlimax." She said that by seven that night, "it was sitcom business as usual" on Houston's network affiliates. Hodges remarked that Tucker had been "a bona fide media celebrity" for several months preceding the execution, adding that the question after the execution should be why Tucker "received such unprecedented media attention." She wondered: "Would she have received all that attention had she not been young, attractive and white?"[10]

Religion

Some Houston religious leaders appealed to Gov. George W. Bush and the Texas Board of Pardons and Paroles to commute the sentence. Not all Houston pastors opposed the execution: a letter to the editor attributed to "John A. Brooks, pastor," argued that Tucker should be executed, "even if she later became the most saintly and 'spirit-filled' Christian of history." The argument was based primarily on Mosaic law, but the writer claimed the New Testament endorsed that law.[11]

A *Chronicle* story attributed Tucker's religious conversion to an organization called the FamilyLife Training Center. The story said Tucker claimed to have started taking drugs when she was ten, and was a heroin addict who "danced in topless bars and sold heroin" to support her addiction. She dropped out of school in the seventh grade, shared drugs with her mother, and associated with "an even wilder biker group." Despite her background, the FamilyLife staffers said they were convinced

9. "Local, National TV Coverage of Execution to Be Extensive," ibid., 1 February 1998; "World Waits."

10. "World Waits"; "Tucker Dies After Apologizing"; "Last Day Marathon."

11. "Ministers, Groups Plead for Tucker's Life," ibid., 15 January 1998. The *Chronicle* said Texas law allowed Bush to commute the sentence only if the board recommended it; otherwise, he could grant only a one-time thirty-day reprieve. See "Murder Victim's Kin Get OK to Watch Tucker Die," ibid.; and "Execution Legal Penalty," ibid., 17 January 1998.

Tucker had changed. Also convinced was the Reverend Pat Robertson, who supported the death penalty but said Tucker should be spared "to continue preaching God's word to fellow convicts and be an example of what happens when someone turns to religion." Robertson's popular *700 Club* television show broadcast on her execution day the last interview she granted.[12]

Other religious leaders opposed Tucker's execution not because of her conversion, or because she was a woman, but because they opposed capital punishment. Sister Helen Prejean, a Roman Catholic nun who wrote the book *Dead Man Walking*, said Tucker's case helped death penalty abolitionists, but added that they must also fight against executing those who are "ugly, not particularly humanitarian and have done terrible things."[13]

Not everyone believed in Tucker's conversion. Richard Thornton, the husband of victim Deborah Ruth Thornton, argued: "As soon as she was apprehended, the cross popped out on her chest. If her religious conversion has any basis, then I'm very happy for her. She's going to need it when she meets her maker on Feb[ruary] 3." Even if Tucker was converted, according to the chairman of the Texas Board of Pardons and Paroles, that was no reason to commute her sentence.[14]

Politics

A press conference featuring Houston-area religious leaders and others stressed the international nature of the execution. David Atwood, a member of the Texas Coalition to Abolish the Death Penalty, said Governor Bush "should think about this if he has aspirations of becoming president." The European Union Parliament passed a resolution opposing Tucker's execution, as well as the use of the death penalty, and a delegation of European leaders asked to meet with the governor to try to persuade him to commute the sentence. Governor Bush declined to meet with them. The Parliament's resolution also recommended that European corporations do business only with the twelve states with no death penalty. Some European Parliament members asked to meet with Tucker, but prison officials denied the requests for security reasons and because it was

12. "Ups, Downs Mark Tucker's 'Church Home' Relationship," ibid., 25 January 1998; "'700 Club' Says It Will Air Tucker's Last Interview," ibid., 29 January 1998. The interview also was posted on the *700 Club*'s web site at http://www.cbn.org/living/christianwalk/interviews/Karla_chiero.asp.

13. "'Moment of Truth,'" ibid., 18 January 1998; "Execution Opposed by Pope, Report Says," ibid., 2 February 1998.

14. "Victim's Kin"; "Board Rejects Tucker's Plea for Clemency," ibid., 3 February 1998.

"not prudent to burden the inmate, the inmate's family or the (prison) unit with additional schedules."[15]

Sarilda Routier, the mother-in-law of Texas death row inmate Darlie Routier (who received the death penalty for murdering her children), said she believed Governor Bush would be politically vulnerable if he allowed the execution. "He may end up being governor, but we're going to work like everything to see that he's not our president." She believed people who had voted for Bush would reconsider their vote the next time he ran. However, the *Houston Chronicle* noted that "there was virtually no political pressure on Bush in Texas" where public-opinion polls showed much support for the death penalty. A Republican political consultant opined that any political fallout for Governor Bush would have come if he had *commuted* the sentence because that would have drawn the ire of conservatives. Tucker's execution did not politically damage Bush to the extent that it cost him the presidential election. However, capital punishment in Texas became a hot political issue in June 2000, after a *Chicago Tribune* series proclaimed there were serious problems in the state's system, and a Columbia University professor's study of death sentence appeals showed problems in every state system, including Texas.[16] However, Tucker was seldom, if ever, mentioned in this debate.

Gender

Gender became a prominent issue in press coverage and in editorials. A *Chronicle* editorial said, "[T]o exempt guilty women from equal punishment undermines their position as equals in society." Syndicated columnist Carl Rowan said the fact that Texas had not executed a woman since 1863 proved that the death penalty was biased. He said Tucker's case provided "a sickening example" that heinous crimes were tolerated "because of the sex, the wealth or the popularity of one felon," whereas crimes committed by "social outcasts" resulted in executions, "sometimes in total error." Rowan said Tucker herself had said her gender should not be an issue.[17]

Although Rowan declared he absolutely opposed capital punishment

15. "Ministers, Groups Plead"; "Tucker's Lawyers Plan to File Clemency Petition Next Week," ibid., 16 January 1998; "Condemned Killer Tucker Asks Parole Board for Clemency," ibid., 23 January 1998.

16. "'Moment of Truth'"; "Bush Prayed for Guidance before Denying Tucker's Appeal," ibid., 4 February 1998; "Flawed Trials Lead to Death Chamber," *Chicago Tribune*, 11 June 2000; "Gatekeeper Court Keeps Gates Shut," ibid., 12 June 2000, both as published in the *Tribune*'s Internet edition; "Researchers Saying Punishment System Is Full of Mistakes," *Jonesboro (Ark.) Sun*, 12 June 2000.

17. "Justice Demands," *Houston Chronicle*, 18 January 1998; Rowan, "Sickening Example of Death Penalty's Flaws," ibid., 16 January 1998.

because of its inherent bias, syndicated columnist William F. Buckley Jr. supported the execution because special protection for women "contends against the tidal wave of equality." He claimed people opposed to all executions introduced the gender issue because they "could in the case of Tucker profit from the ancient, not to say hoary, appeal to chivalry." Robyn Blumner, a columnist for the *St. Petersburg (Fla.) Times,* said the United States "has not overcome its faux Victorian notions that women are defenseless beings who need to be protected from harm and who lack the physical or mental capabilities to do harm themselves." Blumner used the gender issue in Tucker's case to argue for women's equality in other areas, such as the military. Although she said she opposed capital punishment, Blumner added that grouping women as defenseless creatures who needed men's protection "is probably the last vestige of institutionalized sexism that needs to be rubbed out. Ironically, as Texas will soon discover, gal murderers may be perfect for the task."[18]

"Black Widow" Killers

The press did not describe the next two women executed in the United States in the glowing terms used for Tucker, nor did the women capture the fancy of the press and public to the extent Tucker had. Judy Buenoano and Betty Lou Beets had several things in common: both committed murders years before being charged with the crimes; juries convicted both of killing former husbands for insurance money; both were older women; and the press called them both "Black Widow" killers. Buenoano, fifty-four, died in Florida's electric chair on 30 March 1998 for murdering her husband in 1971; she was charged in 1984 and convicted in 1985. Beets, sixty-three, was executed in Texas on 24 February 2000 for murdering her fifth husband in 1983; she was arrested and convicted in 1985 and also indicted for murdering her fourth husband, although she never stood trial for that murder. Beets's execution attracted more national media attention than did Buenoano's.

Judy Buenoano

Judy Buenoano died for murdering her husband with poison after he returned from Vietnam in 1971. Earlier, she was sentenced to life in prison for drowning her nineteen-year-old paraplegic son during a canoe trip.

18. Buckley, "Tucker's Death Redeems a Social Contract," ibid., 16 January 1998; Blumner, "Even in Death Chamber Sexism Is Alive and Well," reprinted in ibid., 18 January 1998.

Fifteen pounds of braces on his legs weighted him down. A court sentenced her to twelve years in prison for attempting to murder boyfriend John Gentry by bombing his automobile. He survived, but an investigation showed Buenoano had given him "vitamin pills" laced with poison. Police also suspected she had murdered a common-law husband in Colorado. Authorities exhumed his body, which showed traces of arsenic, but she never faced trial because of her Florida death sentence.

Despite the sensational aspects of the case, Buenoano never captured media attention, and they acknowledged as much. Both the *Atlanta Constitution* and the *Orlando Sentinel*, published in the Florida county in which Buenoano was convicted for murdering her husband, said "fanfare" and "outrage" were missing from the upcoming execution. "She isn't remorseful or repentant. She hasn't ministered to the spiritually needy. She doesn't have the support of the pope or televangelist Pat Robertson. In short, Buenoano, 54, is no Karla Faye Tucker."[19]

With Buenoano's execution coming just two months after Tucker's, comparison was inevitable. The *Sentinel* called Buenoano a less than sympathetic defendant, adding that her statements seemed self-serving, which probably made her execution "only of passing interest" to the public. Furthermore, whereas Tucker seemed to the public to be sincerely sorry for her crimes, Buenoano's national media appearances had little effect. "[S]he isn't winning many friends," the newspaper said. However, when Florida killed Buenoano, the *Sentinel* reported that the execution drew much press attention, and that there were almost as many lights from television cameras and satellite trucks as lights at the prison. "Reporters outnumbered protesters."[20]

A parallel between Buenoano's case and Tucker's is that at one point, Buenoano asked the state to spare her life so she could help other inmates through a prison ministry. The *Sentinel* reported that at her trial, she said she had found God and wanted to help other inmates. Unlike Tucker, famous religious leaders did not support her. Moreover, one victim was bitter. Just before her execution, her ex-boyfriend John Gentry told Fox News that if the state would let him, "I would pull the switch myself." He said Buenoano was so evil that she should not be among civilized people. "She preyed upon people that loved her."[21]

In her defense, Buenoano denied the murders and attempted murder. Just days before her execution, she denied killing her son, saying in an NBC television interview it was a terrible accident and she believed her-

19. "Black Widow Killer Executed in Florida," *Atlanta Constitution*, 31 March 1998; "Buenoano Execution Lacks Emotional Pull," *Orlando Sentinel*, 29 March 1998.

20. "Emotional Pull"; "Buenoano Goes to Chair Appearing Small, Scared," *Orlando Sentinel*, 31 March 1998.

21. "Buenoano Gets Death Sentence," ibid., 27 November 1985; "Emotional Pull."

self responsible. At her trial for murdering her husband James Goodyear, she told the jury she had not killed Goodyear and had not bombed Gentry's car. "That's the truth." However, a foster child who once lived with Buenoano expressed doubt. Debra Sims told the *Sentinel*, "She wanted all these finer things, but she didn't have the means or the education to get it." Sims said the murders were Buenoano's way of getting what she wanted.[22]

One day before Buenoano stood trial for poisoning her husband, a *Sentinel* story dramatically said: "When they pried open the coffin that held James Edgar Goodyear, they found his hands still clutching a withered flower, the gold wedding band on his finger shining even after 13 years in the grave. On Monday, the woman who put that ring on Goodyear's finger will stand trial."[23]

Following her conviction, at least two unusual legal appeals by Buenoano resulted in *Orlando Sentinel* stories. The first appeal contended her defense attorney, James Johnston, "cared more about negotiating film and book rights than saving his client from the electric chair." The appeal said, among other things, that Johnston deliberately misrepresented her to obtain a "lucrative film and book contract." The second appeal came after botched executions in Florida's electric chair, especially one where flames shot from the headpiece of Pedro Medina. About ten days before Buenoano's execution, attorneys filed for a stay, saying they believed she would be mutilated in the electric chair. They claimed electrocuting a woman was especially cruel "because research shows women have a lower pain threshold than men." In addition, Buenoano's female prison guards, who would prepare her for execution, had not been properly trained, and the result could be an error that could "cause Buenoano to be set afire," the attorneys said.[24]

The *Sentinel's* execution story opened with a contrast lead. "Gone were the painted, manicured fingernails and the fashionable dark hair. Gone was the tough-edged woman who drove around Pensacola in a Corvette and told bigger-than-life stories about her life, her businesses and her

---

22. "Buenoano Gets Death Sentence"; "Emotional Pull."

23. "Woman Going Back to Court in Murder Trial," ibid., 20 October 1985.

24. "New Trial Asked for Buenoano," ibid., 21 February 1990; "Lawyers: Old Sparky Too Painful for Women," ibid., 20 March 1998. The electric chair was discontinued in Florida, which now uses lethal injection. A controversy again arose in 1999 when Allen Lee Davis was electrocuted in a bloody execution. See "Electric Chair under Review," *Gainesville Sun*, 9 July 1999; and "Cruel and Unusual Punishment?" *Tampa Tribune*, 9 July 1999. The Georgia Supreme Court became the first such court to declare the electric chair unconstitutional "cruel and unusual punishment" ("Georgia Ruling a First: Chair Unconstitutional," *Atlanta Constitution*, 6 October 2001).

Chanel perfume." When Buenoano died, she was an "old, frightened woman."

Just as reporters have described condemned defendants for decades, the *Sentinel* said Buenoano faced her death with "stoic dignity." The story also told of a local man who had a day off from work and brought his seven-year-old grandson to the prison for the execution. "He needs to learn what is going on in this world. Maybe he won't get into a situation like this, himself, if he is exposed to it now."[25]

Betty Lou Beets

If Texas governor George W. Bush got himself in political hot water when he seemed to mock Karla Tucker during an interview with the magazine *Talk,* he did not make the same mistake in Beets's case. He stayed silent, and any short "official" statements came mainly from spokesmen in his office.

The *Athens (Tex.) Daily Review*—the largest newspaper in Henderson County, Texas, where the crime was committed—said Beets's upcoming execution was "fast becoming as big an event as the Karla Faye Tucker execution" and that the "media frenzy" was intensifying. However, about a week later, the *Daily Review* said of Beets's execution, "It didn't quite make for the circus that amassed before the 1989 [*sic*] execution of Karla Faye Tucker." About one hundred protesters and fifty journalists gathered at the Huntsville prison for Beets's execution, compared to an estimated twelve hundred onlookers and at least two hundred journalists at Tucker's execution.[26]

Beets's age attracted national and international media attention. The *Dallas Morning News* often referred to her as "the 62-year-old great-grandmother." The *Washington Post,* in an article just before the execution, played on that angle, saying, "After 14 years, Betty Lou Beets's days of sewing and embroidering on death row may soon be over." The *Post* then described her as a grandmother. The *Times* (London) said Beets was a "frail grey-haired great-grandmother" who would be taken to Texas's death chamber where witnesses would see her strapped to a gurney and injected with eighty-six dollars' "worth of lethal chemicals." *Time* said in its on-line version that Beets's case had not been noticed for fifteen years,

25. "Buenoano Small, Scared."
26. "Beets Supporters Rally As Execution Date Nears," *Athens (Tex.) Daily Review,* 25 February 2000; "Protesters Make Presence Known at Execution," ibid., 2 March 2000; "Beets Put to Death for Killing Husband," *Dallas Morning News,* 25 February 2000. All *Daily Review* articles can be found at http://www.athensreview.com/archives/index.

but it drew much interest just before her execution because she was a woman. It said the United States "still finds it difficult to execute females." She also was a great-grandmother, and "[i]mages of a seemingly nice old lady doomed to die always play well with the media."[27]

Beets became a grandmother at thirty, according to the *Times* (London). Married at fifteen, she became a mother at sixteen. She had her sixty-third birthday just days before she died. The *Dallas Morning News* said she was married seven times to five men.[28]

Her arrest made the *Fort Worth Star-Telegram*'s front page. Police said they had searched for Jimmy Don Beets's body because of "tips from the woman's relatives." Police quickly established collection of life insurance benefits as the motive for Beets's murder; she denied knowing anything about her husband's policies. Shortly after her arrest, the *Star-Telegram* published a front-page story that said Beets had shot another husband, Billy York Lane, in 1972. Beets pleaded guilty to misdemeanor aggravated assault after having first been charged with intent to commit murder. She and Lane later remarried but again soon divorced.[29]

Beets received sustained coverage in the *Star-Telegram* a second time during her murder trial. The newspaper ran stories every day from 7 October through 12 October 1985, and on 14 October announced her death sentence.[30] The *Star-Telegram* relied on the Associated Press coverage of the trial. The stories were short and the news play subdued.

News stories in the *Athens Daily Review* and other newspapers depicted Beets as a complex and sometimes mercurial person. The *Daily Review*'s articles were evenhanded but seemed less sympathetic than articles in other newspapers. The *Daily Review* refrained from playing the "grandmother" angle, instead terming Beets a "femme fatale," a "tiny middle-aged woman," a "murderer," and a "black widow," although the last term was in quotation marks. Most often, the newspaper simply referred to her as a "convicted murderer" or a "murderer." Shortly before her execution, Beets granted her first press interview in fourteen years, according to the *Daily Review.* The newspaper called her "a study in contradictions," not-

27. "State Board Denies Woman's Clemency Request," *Dallas Morning News,* 23 February 2000; "Judge Refuses to Halt Woman's Execution," ibid., 24 February 2000; "Texas-Sized Case of Injustice?" *Washington Post,* 22 February 2000; "Bush Refuses to Save Death-Row Grandmother," *Times* (London), 18 February 2000; Jessica Reaves, "Improbably, Betty Lou Beets's Death Is News," *Time Daily,* 24 February 2000, http://www.time.com/time/daily.html.

28. "Refuses Death-Row Grandmother"; "Death for Killing Husband."

29. "Woman Charged in Deaths of 2 Husbands," *Fort Worth Star-Telegram,* 10 June 1985; "Charges Called a Plot," ibid., 11 June 1985; "Bail Is Refused for Woman Accused of Killing Husbands," ibid., 16 June 1985; "Slaying Suspect Shot Husband in 1972," ibid., 13 June 1985.

30. "Beets Given Death in Spouse's Killing," *Fort Worth Star-Telegram,* 14 October 1985.

ing that some people described her as a "cold-blooded killer" and others called her "friendly, if temperamental." "Wrinkles from a hard-scrabble life etch her face like a road map of sorrow." In the interview, Beets claimed to be a Christian, and she denied killing Jimmy Don Beets, and her fourth husband, Doyle Wayne Barker. She claimed both men had physically abused her, although her attorney later said Jimmy Don Beets had not hit her. She said her attorney, E. Ray Andrews, did not represent her well at her trial, and did not even know she was hearing-impaired.[31]

The story drew a response. Jamie Beets denied his father's abusiveness, and Rodney Barker, Doyle Wayne Barker's son, called her allegations a "sob story about being the victim of domestic abuse." Rodney's wife called Beets "a very, very evil woman." One of Beets's friends claimed Beets had lied when she said she could not hear well. Jimmy Don Beets and Doyle Wayne Barker were found on her property in the trailer park where she lived. Beets was buried under a faux wishing well and Barker under a wooden storage building. Both had been shot in the back of the head.[32]

Betty Lou Beets claimed men had sexually and physically abused her since her childhood, and she said that as an adult she had suffered from battered-wife syndrome, which she did not know she had until after she was convicted and sentenced. The *Dallas Morning News* defined the syndrome as "a condition in which abused women feel such low self-esteem that they are unable to leave abusive relationships." The Texas Board of Pardons and Paroles rejected her clemency request, which was partly based on the abuse claims.[33]

The second major story theme, the incompetent representation at trial, was the subject of an *Athens Daily Review* feature story shortly before the execution. Attorney E. Ray Andrews defended his work. The *Daily Review*'s lead paragraph said Andrews's legend "reached near mythic proportions in Henderson County, a rare thing for a man not only still living but not yet 60." The story said he claimed to have won more criminal defense cases and to have tried more cases than any lawyer in the county. A group defending Beets, the Texas Council on Family Violence, called Andrews incompetent. The *Daily Review,* in an unattributed statement, attested, "Andrews is far from incompetent."[34]

31. "As Execution Approaches, Betty Beets Opens Up," *Athens (Tex.) Daily Review,* 4 February 2000. The reference to her as "middle-aged" was a stretch because dictionaries define that as between ages forty and sixty.
32. "Beets' Denial Angers Victims' Families," ibid., 18 February 2000; "Supreme Court Will Not Hear Beets' Appeal," ibid., 20 January 2000.
33. "State Board Denied Woman's Clemency Request," *Dallas Morning News,* 23 February 2000.
34. "E. Ray Andrews Defends His Performance As Beets' Attorney," *Athens (Tex.) Daily Review,* 25 February 2000.

Andrews later lost his law license for "soliciting a $300,000 payoff to drop a death penalty case against a businessman accused of killing his wife." The *Washington Post* said Andrews had resigned from the prosecutor's office, served nearly a year in a federal prison, and later spent three months in a federal detention center at El Reno, Oklahoma, for a parole violation after he was arrested for drunk driving. In the *Daily Review* story, Andrews denied being an alcoholic, although the *Post* said Andrews had cried at his sentencing and told the court he was a longtime alcoholic. The *Post* quoted a local VFW commander who claimed that Andrews drank "between one-half and three-quarters of a fifth of Wild Turkey per night."[35]

The *Post* concentrated on Andrews's representation in its article, which ran days before Beets's execution. The newspaper said he had a conflict of interest in the case because in 1984, Beets had him help her with her insurance after a fire at her trailer home. In a later affidavit, Andrews said Beets had not known if she was entitled to benefits because of her husband's disappearance. Police soon after arrested her, and at her trial the state had to prove she had killed Beets to get the $110,000 insurance money and pension benefits. Because that knowledge made Andrews a potential defense witness, the *Post* said, he should have given up representing her. Andrews's "fee" was "her signature on a contract surrendering all media rights to her story." Andrews later gave up his rights to the story.[36]

The *Dallas Morning News* ran the story about Beets's execution at the top of the front page. The straightforward account described the execution and the reactions of the protesters and those favoring her execution. The *Athens Daily Review* ran two stories, a main one about the execution and a sidebar about the protestors. The writer asserted that Beets had been "emotionless" just before her execution, and said Beets "appeared as though she fell into a sleep" when injected with the lethal drugs. The *Morning News* reported that of eleven hundred letters sent to Governor Bush, only two favored Beets's execution, and that about one thousand telephone calls were made to the governor, only fifty-five of which favored her execution.[37]

Christina Riggs: The "Volunteer"

Four of the five women executed since 1984 fought their executions in lengthy legal battles, and they spent years in prison. Christina Riggs, ex-

35. "Texas-Sized Case of Injustice?"; "Beets the Subject of True-Crime Novel," *Athens (Tex.) Daily Review,* 2 March 2000; "Texas-Sized Case of Injustice?"
36. "Texas-Sized Case of Injustice?"
37. "Death for Killing Husband"; "Protesters, Victims' Family Gather As Beets Meets Death," *Athens (Tex.) Daily Review,* 2 March 2000; "Protesters Make Presence Known"; "Death for Killing Husband."

ecuted in Arkansas on 3 May 2000, did neither. After her arrest, she said she wanted to die. She asked the jury to sentence her to death, refused almost all appeals, and refused to seek clemency from Republican governor Mike Huckabee. She died two and one-half years after murdering her two children, and after a failed suicide attempt. Her attorney said her Roman Catholic beliefs prevented her from attempting suicide because she could not go to heaven if she died by her own hand. Her attorney called her execution a state-assisted suicide.[38] She had "volunteered" to die, in death penalty parlance.

The *Little Rock Arkansas Democrat-Gazette* did not give Riggs's case especially prominent news coverage. On only three occasions did the paper give the story front-page coverage. The newspaper published front-page stories at the time of the crime, when she was sentenced to death, and shortly before she was executed, but her execution merited only a two-column headline below the fold on page B1. The *Memphis Commercial Appeal* ran the story on page 1, and the *Jonesboro (Ark.) Sun,* at that time the state's largest independently owned newspaper, gave the story prominent front-page coverage.

Riggs murdered her children in Sherwood, in the Little Rock metropolitan area. The *Democrat-Gazette*'s news play was not unusual for that newspaper. Since the early 1990s, the paper has seldom paid much attention to state executions; Riggs was no exception, even though she perhaps was the first woman executed in the state in more than 150 years.[39]

The most prominent coverage came at the time of the murders. The first story in the *Democrat-Gazette* named neither the victims nor their mother, and few government officials would comment, so the newspaper interviewed two neighbors. When one, Jimmie Birdsong, wound up on Riggs's jury, her participation became a matter of contention. However, her statements to the newspaper seemed innocent enough. She was not directly quoted and said only that she had seen a woman mowing the lawn but had never met her and did not know children lived there. The other neighbor interviewed said only that the residents were white; there was no indication in the story why race made a difference.[40]

The next day's newspaper said Riggs had been charged with capital murder and had left a suicide note. The newspaper reported speculation and used no named source when it said Riggs's occupation as a nurse, "coupled with her seemingly quick recovery from critical condition in less

38. "Sherwood Woman Accused of Killing Her 2 Children Wants Death," *Little Rock Arkansas Democrat-Gazette,* 24 June 1998.

39. Lavinia Burnett was hanged in Arkansas in 1845. See issues of the *Van Buren Arkansas Intelligencer,* 11 October, 8 November, and 13 December 1845, and 3 January 1846.

40. "Girl, 2, Brother, 5, Found Dead in Sherwood," *Little Rock Arkansas Democrat-Gazette,* 6 November 1997.

than a day, [has] led to speculation that the children's deaths and her suicide attempt could have reflected drug overdoses." Later, authorities claimed Riggs had injected herself with potassium chloride, but did not know the drug had to be diluted; it simply burned a hole in her arm without getting into her veins.[41]

Riggs's sanity when the crime was committed was a major issue in the stories. Before she entered a formal plea, her attorney said she was deeply depressed, in part because she worked as a nurse during the Oklahoma City bombing of the Alfred P. Murrah Building. The attorney claimed that Riggs went to the building to help victims, but the *Democrat-Gazette* reported that Veterans Administration officials said they did not send her to the hospital. Riggs used an insanity defense, but a state psychologist's evaluation in April 1998 said she was not mentally ill but "chronically unhappy" at the time of the murders. Her attorney, John Wesley Hall, said reports that the Oklahoma City bombing had caused her depression had "gotten too much display in the press" and said the bombing was "just a small part" of Riggs's mental problems. However, Hall had said in November 1997 that he was told that Riggs "was holding onto a woman's bra that had body parts splattered all over it" at the bomb scene.[42]

Perhaps the most damaging story for Riggs came just days before her trial; it said police had taped her confessing that she had thought about killing her children about three weeks before the murders. The *Democrat-Gazette* reported the confession, which was played at a pretrial hearing open to the public. The judge ruled the confession was admissible evidence. Just days later, when her trial began, the *Democrat-Gazette* reported that fifteen prospective jurors were excused, some because they said media coverage had prejudiced them.[43] However, the newspaper cannot be faulted for publishing information from a public hearing.

Jurors deliberated only fifty-five minutes before finding Riggs guilty, and the *Democrat-Gazette* reported that she said when sentenced to death: "I'm going home to be with my babies." After her conviction, during the penalty stage of the trial, Riggs told the jurors she should have protected her children and added, "Please let me go be with them." Earlier, she broke down when the jury announced its verdict and had to be carried to the defense table. When she sobbed uncontrollably, the judge called a re-

41. "Sherwood Mother of 2 Arrested in Tots' Deaths," ibid., 7 November 1997; "Mother Pleads Innocent in Kids' Deaths," ibid., 8 November 1997; "Mom's Note Near Slain Kids: 'Forgive Me,'" ibid., 11 November 1997.

42. "Sherwood Mother's Role Disputed in Oklahoma Bomb Rescue," ibid., 13 November 1997; "Sherwood Nurse Enters Insanity Plea in Children's Deaths," ibid., 14 November 1997; "Mother Relinquishes Competency Hearing in Children's Deaths," ibid., 24 April 1998.

43. "Mom Taped Saying She Plotted 2 Kids' Slayings 3 Weeks; Jury to Hear It," ibid., 16 June 1998; "Sherwood Woman Wants Death."

cess. One of Riggs's sisters screamed and collapsed in a hallway in the courthouse, the newspaper reported, and when "cameramen rushed toward her, the sisters' aunt ran over, crying out to photographers: 'Leave her alone!'"[44]

Later, in what seemed an odd decision because she had asked the jury to sentence her to death, Riggs filed a federal lawsuit. The *Little Rock Arkansas Democrat-Gazette* noted her seeming change of heart: "Christina Marie Riggs, the woman who last month asked for the death penalty so she could be with the children she killed, Tuesday filed a civil rights lawsuit claiming that she has been denied use of a telephone to contact her attorney."[45]

Even more unusual was the next day's story, which began: "In an unusual twist, a murder defendant and her attorney argued Wednesday that she should be put to death, and a prosecutor insisted that she be forced to appeal her death sentence." The judge ordered Hall to file an appeal on Riggs's behalf, seeking a hearing to determine if she was mentally competent to waive her right to appeal. This act led Riggs to say to the judge: "Three weeks ago, I was in court and was told I was competent to go to trial and that I was competent to understand the proceedings, and now someone's questioning my competency?" Riggs's sister told reporters, "If they were so interested in her damn rights, where were they three weeks ago?" The *Democrat-Gazette* explained that the Arkansas Supreme Court had ruled just days earlier in another death penalty case in which the defendant asked to be executed that the circuit court must ensure that the defendant is mentally evaluated and competent to make the decision to waive appeals.[46]

Riggs more or less dropped out of the *Democrat-Gazette*'s news columns until shortly before her execution. A weekly newspaper, the *Little Rock Arkansas Times*, ran an article in April 1999 titled "They Kill Women, Don't They?" The lengthy story was largely based on a prison interview with Riggs. It sympathized with her, pointing out her many problems with depression and family. The story had a surprising twist near the end when Riggs said that although she regularly heard from death penalty opponents, she had little in common with them. "I still believe in the death penalty, even though I'm sitting here on Death Row. In my case, I'm glad I have the option."[47] Riggs became one of three condemned inmates who

44. "Judge Decides Riggs Will Die for Killing Kids," ibid., 1 July 1998.
45. "Woman on Death Row Sues over Access to Attorney," ibid., 22 July 1998.
46. "Judge: Murdering Mom's Appeal a Must," ibid., 23 July 1998.
47. "They Kill Women, Don't They?" *Little Rock Arkansas Times,* 9 April 1999; "State Set to Comply Tonight with Riggs' Wish to Die," *Little Rock Arkansas Democrat-Gazette,* 2 May 2000.

did not request clemency from Governor Huckabee, who granted clemency in only one case.

Another unusual aspect of the case, when compared with past executions of women, was the governor's lack of comment or soul-searching. Another break from previous reporting about condemned women was that little was made of Riggs's weight. She weighed 270 pounds just before her execution; the *Democrat-Gazette* reported it, but did so in the context of prison officials putting her on a diet normally used for diabetics. "I'm about to die, and they're worried about my weight?" she told the *Democrat-Gazette*.[48]

Riggs made the front page of the *Democrat-Gazette* on the morning of 2 May; she was executed that night. The story concerned her repeated wish to die, and speculation from sources about whether she would go through with it. The newspaper pointed out that for Riggs to stop the execution, "all she has to do is ask for her attorney, request a phone call, raise her little finger, even—and she's pretty much guaranteed a stay." She did none of those things. The story in the state edition about her execution ran on page B1; it had no direct quotations from any sources, nor did it quote Riggs's last words. The Associated Press reported that her last words were: "There is no way no words can express how sorry I am for taking the lives of my babies. Now I can be with my babies, as I always intended. I love you, my babies."[49]

The *Democrat-Gazette* ran its most in-depth article about Riggs's case five days after her execution. The story was on the front page of the newspaper's Sunday edition, and carried the headline: "'I'm Sorry, Momma.'" The story jumped inside to two full pages of text and pictures and was based largely on a *Democrat-Gazette* interview with Riggs about a week before the execution. It also was a retrospective on the case. The text was broken in places with italic inserts of the text of letters Riggs had written to her mother, sister, and former husband, telling them that she intended to kill her children and herself. The story provided a much more sympathetic profile of Riggs than had previous stories, but it ran after her execution. The story quoted Riggs as saying, "I'll talk to you. But only if this is running afterward." The "volunteer" feared such coverage would cause people to intervene in her case.[50]

48. "'I'm Sorry, Momma,'" *Little Rock Arkansas Democrat-Gazette,* 7 May 2000.
49. "State Set to Comply"; "Riggs, Mother Who Killed Her 2 Children, Put to Death by State," ibid., 3 May 2000; "Woman Is Executed at State Prison," *Jonesboro (Ark.) Sun,* 3 May 2000.
50. "'I'm Sorry, Momma.'"

Epilogue

SOCIETAL CHANGES IN WOMEN'S STATUS HAVE changed how the press perceives women and reports on them, including those condemned to death.[1] Up to and including Velma Barfield's execution in North Carolina in 1984, most governors publicly lamented having to execute a member of the "fairer sex." Barfield's execution and Elizabeth Duncan's 1962 execution in California became political issues mostly because they were women; North Carolina had not executed a woman in about forty years.

However, even in the late twentieth century, some researchers said societal norms concerning women had not completely changed. A leading death penalty scholar, Victor Streib, believed there still was a degree of male chauvinism. An Oklahoma prosecutor agreed, saying a woman's crime had to be especially heinous for a jury to impose the death penalty. Two women who worked on death penalty cases and have written about the subject disagreed; they claimed the times had changed so juries, prosecutors, and politicians would not be so hesitant to impose and uphold death sentences for women.[2] The question for this book is whether the press's attitude toward women has changed, and it seems the answer is yes, although the press has probably followed society's changes instead of leading the way.

The cultural abhorrence at executing a woman played a major role— perhaps *the* major role—in the controversies until the 1990s. During the 1990s and early in 2000, Karla Faye Tucker and Betty Lou Beets were executed in Texas, where George W. Bush was governor; Judy Buenoano was executed in Florida, where Jeb Bush was governor; and Christina Riggs was executed in Arkansas, where Mike Huckabee was governor. None of the governors expressed the degree of consternation and soul-searching that marked the reactions of earlier governors who allowed ex-

1. For commentary on how the women's movement affected news coverage of women, see Gaye Tuchman, chap. 7 in *Making News.* The differences in press "theories" and how they might affect news coverage were first best outlined in Fred S. Siebert, Theodore Peterson, and Wilbur Schramm, *Four Theories of the Press.*
2. Robert Anthony Phillips, "No Gender Equality on Death Row," http://www.apdnews.com/cjsystem/findingjustice/2000/02/26/women0226_01.html, 25 February 2000.

ecutions of women. Governor Bush caused a stir by seemingly mocking Tucker's plea for mercy. His action, although probably not unknown, was rare. This might be the reaction of one man, or it might be that killing women does not now produce the indignation it once did. It probably is the latter. Governor Huckabee had little to say about Riggs's execution. His and Governor Bush's reactions perhaps reflect a change in culture in regard to women.

Neither the citizenry nor the press is as indignant as in earlier times about executions of women. Constitutional historian Leonard Levy contends in a book published at the end of the twentieth century that U.S. citizens have lost the sense of righteous indignation they once held about many issues. Included among that indignation are books portraying women's roles in society. For example, there is considerable difference in public reaction in 1899 to Kate Chopin's *Awakening,* which was removed from the shelves of one St. Louis library, and modern-day reaction to, for instance, the works of Florence King.[3]

The lack of public and press indignation about women's executions is perhaps illustrative of a lack of societal outrage about the death penalty. The indignation might be misplaced if society is offended only about executing women. Some people argue that subjecting women to the same ultimate punishment is a positive step toward equality. It is only recently that the outrage at executing women has diminished, and with it has gone the most blatant of the stereotypes in the press about women.

This book suggests that the press usually reported the popularly held viewpoints, which were usually those held by the powerful. When women began to gain power and status in society, the press shifted its view, and the more obvious stereotypes of women began to change.

Women defendants, and especially white women, were in a peculiar situation inasmuch as the social-caste system and capital punishment were concerned. On the one hand, women were expected to keep their "place" and not challenge a male-dominated society. That should have translated into executions of women who had violated social norms. However, white women were also placed on a pedestal; they were expected to be purer, more virtuous, than others. The societal norm that might have seemed to operate in favor of executing a woman who broke the mold clashed with the societal expectation of women as good and pure, and the latter won out; few women have been executed in the United States. Perhaps that is why in the nineteenth century, the press and society could characterize those women condemned to death for killing their husbands, children, or others only as "fiends." Such depictions of

3. Levy, *Blasphemy: Verbal Offense against the Sacred, from Moses to Salman Rushdie.* See, for example, King, *The Florence King Reader.*

women are rare in today's press, although there is the argument, and a seemingly good one, that a pretty, photogenic condemned female draws much more press attention than a not-so-pretty or not-so-charming female defendant.

Arguments about the collective, or society, and the individual are at the heart of many issues in the United States, and have been since the country's beginnings. When a mass press began in the United States in the 1830s, *New York Herald* editor James Gordon Bennett expressed collectivistic ideas about women and crime. One of the first sensational crime stories involved the killing of New York City prostitute Helen Jewett by a young dandy named Richard Robinson. As part of the case, Bennett wrote that society shared some of the blame for the crime for allowing such places to exist. However, when New York hanged Elizabeth Van Valkenburgh in 1846, Bennett's *Herald* paid little attention, and offered little or no moral instruction for the populace.[4]

The collective-responsibility argument is still used. Sister Helen Prejean, the author of *Dead Man Walking*, says that Europe and the United States approach the death penalty in different ways. She maintains that in the United States, the approach is more individualistic, with the focus placed on the need to punish a person. Conversely, in Europe, the approach is more collective or societal and emphasizes what the society or community did wrong that caused the person to commit a horrible crime.[5]

In 2000, Emma Bonino, a former European commissioner for humanitarian affairs, opined, "The institution of the state must be better than the individual." An important distinction made by Prejean refers to the difference in the ages of the societies, with Europe's much older societies having dealt with capital punishment longer. An Italian official with a Rome-based organization that opposes the death penalty made a similar point: "[The] U.S. is still a young country practicing the pioneer justice of an eye for an eye. . . . Europeans have evolved toward a more complex and compassionate justice." That view is not limited to Western Europe. The Canadian Catholic Conference in 1973 proclaimed, according to James J. Megivern, that the focus of Canadian Catholics should not be on the killer, but instead the "focus should be on us . . . as a community [to] try to break the escalating spiral of violence."[6]

The difference in attitude actually seems to be related more to philosophy in democratic societies than to the age of the culture. The formulation

4. Cohen, *Murder of Jewett*; "Case of Mrs. Van Valkenburgh," *New York Herald,* 23 January 1846; "Execution of Elizabeth Van Valkenburgh," ibid., 1 February 1846.

5. "Nun of 'Dead Man Walking' Brings Crusade for Life to ASU," *Jonesboro (Ark.) Sun,* 14 April 2000. Prejean made the remarks in a speech at Arkansas State University on 13 April 2000.

6. "Italians Fight U.S. Use of Death Penalty," *Philadelphia Inquirer,* 20 August 2000; Megivern, *Death Penalty,* 461.

of what "rights" mean seems to have developed seriously in the eighteenth century along with the development of what constitutes "democracy." Some societies were oriented more toward collective rights and others toward individual rights. Examples are the differing approaches of France and the United States toward "rights." Both countries fought eighteenth-century revolutions and had strong statements about the rights of the people. In France, however, the rights of the collective in many instances overrode the rights of the individual. The United States, on the other hand, stresses the rights of the individual over the rights of the collective or society. There is, to the minds of some scholars, a shift occurring within the Western legal tradition away from individualism and toward collectivism, although others have decried the decline of community and the loss of individual "social capital" in the United States.[7] The Bill of Rights for most of our national history has been couched in terms of individual rights, and it seems doubtful that Americans, or the U.S. press, will any time soon adopt the collective-rights ideas. How the press understands the Bill of Rights probably affects how it reports on individuals condemned to death.

The idea that expression (or the press) should perform a "public service" for society as a whole is nothing new, dating at least 140 years ago to philosopher John Stuart Mill. A century later, Harvard University legal scholar Zechariah Chafee noted Mills's contribution and amplified it.[8]

In general, though, U.S. mass media have not espoused the concept of societal guilt in respect to capital punishment. In some ways, this book has shown that the media focus on individual guilt or individual attributes, such as personality or characteristics. Although this concentration might be in some ways legitimate, it does ignore larger questions about the death penalty and crime, and a lack of focus on the social issues leaves those problems without debate and without solution.

Nineteenth- and twentieth-century news coverage of women condemned to death has been mixed. For the most part, the press did not do an especially admirable job of protecting defendants' rights. Although there were exceptions, press reports seemed more likely to produce unfairness than to guard against it, especially in the cases of minority defendants.

7. For a full discussion of how the French and U.S. differences evolved, see Susan Dunn, *Sister Revolutions: French Lightning, American Light.* Harold J. Berman also discusses the shifts in Western legal tradition, one of which is the shift away from the concepts of "natural" law, which were based on the individual, in large part (*Law and Revolution: The Formation of the Western Legal Tradition,* esp. 33–45). See also Robert N. Bellah et al., *Habits of the Heart,* for comment on collectivism and community; and Robert D. Putnam, *Bowling Alone,* for the decline of collective participation in the United States, and the individual loss of "social capital."

8. For a brief discussion, see Donald L. Smith, chap. 5 in *Zechariah Chafee, Jr.: Defender of Liberty and Law.*

In the 1960s, the Warren Court ruled in a series of cases that pervasive publicity before trial could violate criminal defendants' fair-trial rights. This decision put police and prosecutors on notice that parading defendants before the press or otherwise failing to protect defendants' rights might result in a new trial. The Court did not scold the press as much as it did the police, prosecutors, and judges, who were told it was their responsibility to ensure due process and a fair trial. This reprimand resulted in less press access to defendants before trial.[9] Those changes did not affect any of the female defendants until Velma Barfield, who was executed in 1984. However, the cases in this book show that the idea that press coverage could prejudice a trial did not spring forth in the 1960s. Defendants, judges, and attorneys have voiced concerns for years, dating almost to the beginnings of the country.

Increasingly in the late twentieth century, the press began to scrutinize the judicial system and capital punishment. Press reports had rarely focused on the process, but instead concentrated on the events: the murder, the arrest, the trial, and the execution. The *Chicago Tribune,* in 1999, published a series of articles that investigated the judiciary and the capital punishment system in Illinois. Two parts of the five-part series were about "how prosecutors turn to unreliable characters to put suspects on Death Row," and about police misconduct, including torture, during interrogations of suspects. The series showed that police or prosecutor errors probably put innocent people on death row. Shortly after publication of the series, Illinois governor George Ryan, a Republican, declared a moratorium on use of the death penalty in that state.[10]

In June 2000, the *Tribune* published a two-part investigation of Texas's death penalty process. The newspaper reported the following flaws: forty cases involving defense attorneys who had presented no evidence or only one witness during the trial's sentencing phase; forty-three cases involving defense attorneys sanctioned for misconduct before or after the cases; twenty-three cases involving jailhouse "snitches"; and twenty-three cases involving visual hair analysis, which the newspaper said has "consistently proved unreliable." At about the same time, a national study of the death penalty showed that in 68 percent of 4,578 death penalty cases, a state or federal court threw out the conviction or death sentence. The study's lead author, James Liebman, said: "You're creating a very high risk that some errors are going to get through the process." The newspaper press widely reported the study. A *Dallas Morning News* article on 4 June 2000 also examined the death penalty appeals process in Texas.[11] The

9. Ibid. See also Powe, *Warren Court,* esp. chap. 15 and pp. 415–20.
10. "Death Row Justice Derailed," *Chicago Tribune,* 14–18 November 1999; "Governor to Halt Executions," ibid., 20 January 2000, Internet edition.
11. "Flawed Trials Lead to Death Chamber," *Chicago Tribune,* 11 June 2000; "Gatekeeper Court Keeps Gates Shut," ibid., 12 June 2000; "Researchers Saying Punishment

move toward more process-centered reporting might be attributed in part to the reduction in press access to condemned prisoners. Whatever the reason, if the press continues to examine the process or system of capital punishment, errors are more likely to be exposed than with event-centered reporting.

Changes in the laws regarding press access have influenced the content of stories about condemned women, as they have the coverage of all defendants. The press has historically had no legal right of access to condemned defendants and still does not, but in practice the press had a great deal of access. Jailhouse interviews were common, even before the defendant was charged. The news reports in the stories in this book make it seem the press witnessed many, if not most, police actions, including sometimes sitting in on interrogations during which the defendant confessed. The press at times accompanied police to a crime scene with the defendant, then published information and pictures about the "reenactment" of the crime, usually with the defendant confessing.[12]

The Warren Court all but required that defendants have an attorney present before police obtain a confession. The due-process rights of criminal defendants were greatly strengthened, and police-obtained confessions, made in interrogations that were out of the view of anyone other than the police, were highly suspect. A point to be made is that at least in some areas of the country, the interrogations *were not* always out of view of others; the press sat in, as in the case of Marie Porter in the 1930s, and did not try to hide the fact. In some instances, newspaper reports indicated that reporters took part in asking defendants questions. If there were problems with police interrogations, as the Warren Court decisions implied, the press in those instances was not reporting them. It could be that press access prevented some abuses, or that the press overlooked problems, preferring not to challenge local norms. Regardless, the access reporters had to defendants began to change after attorneys routinely advised defendants of their rights before they were interrogated. In fact, in *Rideau v. Louisiana,* Justice Potter Stewart noted in his opinion that Elmer Rideau—whose taped confession was aired on television several times before his trial—had not had an attorney present to advise him that he did not have to talk.[13]

System Is Full of Mistakes," *Jonesboro (Ark.) Sun,* 12 June 2000; "Death Penalty Appeals Changes Are Criticized," *Dallas Morning News,* 4 June 2000. See also a series on death penalty abuses in the *Houston Chronicle,* 3–6 February 2001; and a similar series on Tennessee's death penalty in the *Nashville Tennessean,* 22–29 July 2001.

12. "Media Access to Prisoners," 28. For a description of early press access in one state, see Shipman, "Forgotten Men."

13. In December 2000, the Fifth U.S. Circuit Court of Appeals ruled that Louisiana must either release Rideau or reindict and reconvict him, ruling that his 1961 indictment was unconstitutional because blacks were systematically kept off his grand jury.

Decisions from the 1970s through the 1990s opened criminal trials and many pretrial proceedings and records to press and public scrutiny, but the access now is much more of an "official" nature. Federal court decisions in 2000 have made the "perp walk," which refers to parading a criminal defendant solely for the benefit of the cameras, constitutionally suspect as a Fourth Amendment violation.[14]

The question of how much press access is too much is difficult. First Amendment theory provides a potent argument for why the press and public should have more access to the process of capital punishment. Vincent Blasi, in the 1970s, argued that the press clause of the First Amendment to the Constitution was important because it encouraged the press to scrutinize government action. He asserted that because the state possesses the power and the resources to do great harm to individual citizens, the press should receive special protection under the First Amendment to monitor government actions.[15] This argument seems especially convincing when government has the power to take the life of an individual. On the other side, however, is access that damages a defendant's Fifth, Sixth, and Fourteenth Amendment rights. The question is whether press reports have really helped or hurt.

The message that has been presented might too often be that crime and the death penalty are more entertainment than news, and that should make the public shudder. Although the press might not bring home a moral message, and arguably should not do so except on the editorial pages, it seems unlikely that press reports have no effect. Inasmuch as the death penalty is concerned, people have few other ways to get information. Increasingly, the government is attempting to make information about executions more sanitized, and access to death row inmates has become more difficult.

The lack of access could cut two ways. It could result in more positive reporting on the system, such as that done by the *Chicago Tribune* and a few other newspapers, or it could result in the abandonment of reporting on death row inmates. It is the press's job to ensure that the whole story is told so that society can make informed decisions about whether the United States should continue to be the only Western nation that uses the death penalty.

14. See http://www.lanepowell.com/news/sbsummer99.htm for a discussion.
15. Blasi, "The Checking Value in First Amendment Theory."

Works Cited

Court Decisions

Houchins v. KQED, 438 US 1 (1978).
Richmond Newspapers, Inc. v. Virginia, 448 US 555 (1980).
Rideau v. Louisiana, 373 US 723 (1963).
United States v. Burr, 24 Fed. Cas. 49 No. 14692 (1807).

Newspapers

Aiken (S.C.) Standard and Review, 1943.
Athens (Tex.) Daily Review, 1999–2000.
Atlanta Constitution, 1872–1998.
Augusta Chronicle, 1941–1942.
Birmingham News, 1930–1953.
Burlington Daily Free Press, 1880–1905.
Centre (Pa.) Daily Times, 1996.
Charleston (S.C.) News and Courier, 1929.
Charlotte Chronicle, 1892.
Charlotte Observer, 1944.
Cheyenne Democratic Leader, 1884.
Chicago Defender, 1912.
Chicago Tribune, 1890–2000.
Cincinnati Enquirer, 1937–1954.
Cleveland Plain Dealer, 1938–1954.
Columbia (S.C.) State, 1943.
Columbus Dispatch, 1938–1954.
Dallas Morning News, 1998–2000.
Denver Rocky Mountain News, 1890.
Durham Morning Herald, 1943.
Elko (Nev.) Free Press, 1889–1890.
Elko (Nev.) Weekly Independent, 1889–1890.
Florence (S.C.) Morning News, 1947.
Forest (Miss.) News Register, 1922.
Fort Worth Star-Telegram, 1985.
Gainesville Sun, 1999.

Greene County (Miss.) Herald, 1922.
Houston Chronicle, 1983–2001.
Houston Post, 1983.
Jackson Clarion-Ledger, 1937–1983.
Jackson Daily News, 1860–1943.
Jonesboro (Ark.) Sun, 1994–2001.
Little Rock Arkansas Democrat-Gazette, 1997–2000.
Little Rock Arkansas Gazette, 1898–1947.
Little Rock Arkansas Times, 1999.
Los Angeles Times, 1941–1966.
Lynchburg Virginian, 1881.
Memphis Commercial Appeal, 1927–1942.
Miami Herald, 1929–1998.
Montgomery Advertiser, 1952–1957.
Nashville Tennessean, 2001.
Natchez Mississippi Free Trader, 1838.
New Brunswick Weekly Freedonian, 1867.
New Orleans Daily Picayune, 1888.
New Orleans Times-Picayune, 1888–1942.
New York Herald, 1846.
New York Times, 1859–1992.
Oklahoma City Daily Oklahoman, 1988–2001.
Orlando Sentinel, 1985–1998.
Oxford (Miss.) Eagle, 1902.
Petersburg (Va.) Index-Appeal, 1881.
Philadelphia Evening Bulletin, 1930–1931.
Philadelphia Inquirer, 1867–2000.
Philadelphia Pennsylvania Gazette, 1737.
Phoenix Gazette, 1930–1931.
Pittsburgh Gazette-Times, 1858–1866.
Pittsburgh Post, 1865–1867.
Raleigh News and Observer, 1892–1984.
Richmond Daily Dispatch, 1852.
Richmond Times-Dispatch, 1892–1912.
Roanoke Times, 1892.
Rolling Fork (Miss.) Deer Creek Pilot, 1937.
San Francisco Examiner, 1929.
Spokane Daily Chronicle, 1929.
St. Louis Post-Dispatch, 1937–1989.
St. Paul Minnesotian and Times, 1859–1860.
St. Paul Pioneer and Democrat, 1859–1860.
Tampa Tribune, 1999.
Times (London), 2000.
Tulsa World, 1929.

Van Buren Arkansas Intelligencer, 1845–1846.
Vicksburg (Miss.) Evening Post, 1944.
Virginian Pilot and Norfolk Landmark, 1912.
Washington Post, 1929–2000.
Williamsport (Pa.) Daily Banner, 1880–1881.
Wilmington (Del.) Morning News, 1935.
Woodville (Miss.) Republican, 1833.

Other Sources

Amar, Akhil Reed. *The Bill of Rights.* New Haven: Yale University Press, 1998.

Avrich, Paul. *The Haymarket Tragedy.* Princeton: Princeton University Press, 1984.

Bailey, William C. "Murder, Capital Punishment, and Television: Execution Publicity and Homicide Rates." *American Sociological Review* 55 (October 1990): 628–33.

Ball, Howard. *Hugo L. Black: Cold Steel Warrior.* New York: Oxford University Press, 1996.

Barry, John M. *Rising Tide: The Great Mississippi River Flood of 1927 and How It Changed America.* New York: Touchstone, 1997.

Bellah, Robert N., Richard Madsen, William M. Sullivan, Ann Swidler, and Steven M. Tipton. *Habits of the Heart.* Berkeley and Los Angeles: University of California Press, 1985; New York: Harper and Row, 1986.

Benedict, Kirby. *Frontier Federal Judge Aurora Hunt.* Glendale, Calif.: Arthur H. Clark, 1961.

Berman, Harold J. *Law and Revolution: The Formation of the Western Legal Tradition.* Cambridge: Harvard University Press, 1983.

Bierce, Ambrose. *The Best of Ambrose Bierce.* Secaucus, N.J.: Citadel Press, 1946.

Blasi, Vincent. "The Checking Value in First Amendment Theory." *American Bar Foundation Research Journal* 63 (1977): 521–649.

Bledsoe, Jerry. *Death Sentence.* New York: Dutton, 1998.

Böll, Heinrich. *The Lost Honour of Katharina Blum.* London: Secker and Warburg, 1975.

Bosco, Ronald A. "Lectures at the Pillory: The Early American Execution Sermon." *American Quarterly* 30 (summer 1978): 156–76.

Cahill, Thomas. *How the Irish Saved Civilization.* New York: Nan A. Talese, 1995.

Camus, Albert. *Resistance, Rebellion, and Death.* New York: Alfred A. Knopf, 1961.

Chopin, Kate. *The Awakening.* 1899. Reprint, New York: Avon Books, 1972.

Cohen, Patricia Cline. *The Murder of Helen Jewett: The Life and Death of a Prostitute in Nineteenth-Century New York.* New York: Alfred A. Knopf, 1998.

Copeland, David A. *Colonial American Newspapers.* Newark: University of Delaware Press, 1997.

Curran, Thomas J. *Xenophobia and Immigration, 1820–1930.* Boston: Twayne, 1975.

Curriden, Mark, and Leroy Phillips Jr. *Contempt of Court: The Turn-of-the-Century Lynching That Launched a Hundred Years of Federalism.* New York: Faber and Faber, 1999.

Dabney, Thomas Ewing. *One Hundred Great Years: The Story of the "Times-Picayune" from Its Founding to 1940.* New York: Greenwood Press, 1968.

Dallek, Robert. *Flawed Giant: Lyndon Johnson and His Times, 1961–1973.* New York: Oxford University Press, 1998.

DeFleur, Melvin L., and Sandra Ball-Rokeach. *Theories of Mass Communication.* 3d ed. New York: Longman, 1975.

DeFleur, Melvin L., and Everette E. Dennis. *Understanding Mass Communication.* 4th ed. Boston: Houghton Mifflin, 1991.

Dicken-Garcia, Hazel. *Journalistic Standards in Nineteenth-Century America.* Madison: University of Wisconsin Press, 1989.

Dicks, Shirley, ed. *Congregation of the Condemned.* Amherst, N.Y.: Prometheus, 1991.

Dunn, Susan. *Sister Revolutions: French Lightning, American Light.* New York: Faber and Faber, 1999.

Ellison, Ralph. *Invisible Man.* New York: Random House, 1952; New York: Vintage, 1972.

Emery, Michael, and Edwin Emery. *The Press and America.* 7th ed. Englewood Cliffs, N.J.: Prentice-Hall, 1992.

Ericson, Richard V., Patricia M. Baranek, and Janet B. L. Chan. *Representing Order: Crime, Law, and Justice in the News Media.* Toronto: University of Toronto Press, 1991.

Foster, R. F. *Modern Ireland, 1600–1972.* New York: Penguin, 1988.

Friedman, Lawrence. *Crime and Punishment in American History.* New York: Basic Books, 1993.

Gaines, Ernest. *A Lesson before Dying.* New York: Vintage, 1993.

Gould, Stephen J. *The Mismeasure of Man.* New York: W. W. Norton, 1981.

Graber, Doris. *Crime News and the Public.* New York: Praeger, 1980.

Hamburger, Philip. *Friends Talking in the Night.* New York: Alfred A. Knopf, 1999.

Hertzberg, Hendrik. "TRB from Washington." *New Republic* 200 (20 February 1989): 4, 49.

Herzog, Peter. *Legal Hangings.* Santa Fe: Press of the Territories, 1966.

Hofstetter, Richard, and David Dozier. "Useful News, Sensational News." *Journalism Quarterly* 63 (winter 1986): 815–20, 853.

Hohenberg, John, ed. *The Pulitzer Prize Story II.* New York: Columbia University Press, 1980.

Huie, William Bradford. "The South Kills Another Negro." In *The American Mercury Reader,* ed. Lawrence E. Spivak and Charles Angoff, 363–71. Philadelphia: Blakiston, 1944.

Itule, Bruce D., and Douglas A. Anderson. *News Writing and Reporting for Today's Media.* 4th ed. New York: McGraw-Hill, 1997.

Jeffers, H. Paul. *An Honest President.* New York: William Morrow, 2000.

Johnson, Robert. *Condemned to Die: Life under Sentence of Death.* Prospect Heights, Ill.: Waveland Press, 1981.

———. *Death Work.* Belmont, Calif.: Wadsworth, 1998.

Jones, Ann. *Women Who Kill.* New York: Holt, Rinehart, and Winston, 1980.

Keleher, William A. *Turmoil in New Mexico.* Albuquerque: University of New Mexico Press, 1982.

Kennedy, Roger G. *Burr, Hamilton, and Jefferson: A Study in Character.* New York: Dutton, 2000.

King, Florence. *The Florence King Reader.* New York: St. Martin's Press, 1995.

Kolchin, Peter. *American Slavery, 1619–1877.* New York: Hill and Wang, 1993.

Lesser, Wendy. *Pictures at an Execution: An Inquiry into the Subject of Murder.* Cambridge: Harvard University Press, 1993.

Levy, Leonard. *Blasphemy: Verbal Offense against the Sacred, from Moses to Salman Rushdie.* Chapel Hill: University of North Carolina Press, 1993.

Lippmann, Walter. *Public Opinion.* New York: Harcourt, Brace, 1922.

Lotz, Roy Edward. *Crime and the American Press.* New York: Praeger, 1991.

Mackey, Philip English, ed. *Hanging in the Balance: The Anti-Capital Punishment Movement in New York State, 1776–1861.* New York: Garland, 1982.

———. *Voices against Death: American Opposition to Capital Punishment, 1787–1975.* New York: Burt Franklin, 1976.

Marzolf, Marion T. *Civilizing Voices: American Press Criticism, 1880–1950.* New York: Longman, 1991.

Masur, Louis P. *Rites of Execution: Capital Punishment and the Transformation of American Culture, 1776–1865.* New York: Oxford University Press, 1989.

McCullough, David. *John Adams.* New York: Simon and Schuster, 2001.

McDonald, Forrest. *States' Rights and the Union.* Lawrence: University Press of Kansas, 2000.

"Media Access to Prisoners." *Quill* 85 (September 1997): 28.

Megivern, James J. *The Death Penalty: An Historical and Theological Survey.* New York: Paulist Press, 1997.

Menand, Louis. *The Metaphysical Club.* New York: Farrar, Straus, and Giroux, 2001.

Messner, Steven F. "Television Violence and Violent Crime: An Aggregate Analysis." *Social Problems* 33 (February 1986): 218–35.

Milavsky, J. Ronald, Ronald C. Kessler, Horst Stipp, and William S. Rubens. *Television and Aggression.* New York: Academic Press, 1982.

Miller, Kent S., and Michael L. Radelet. *Executing the Mentally Ill.* Newbury Park, Calif.: Sage Publications, 1993.

Miller, Kerby A. *Emigrants and Exiles: Ireland and the Irish Exodus to North America.* New York: Oxford University Press, 1985.

Morris, Willie. *North toward Home.* New York: Vintage, 2000.

Mott, Frank Luther. *American Journalism.* New York: Macmillan, 1962.

Neville, John E. *The Press, the Rosenbergs, and the Cold War.* Westport, Conn.: Praeger, 1995.

O'Shea, Kathleen A. *Women and the Death Penalty in the United States, 1900–1998.* Westport, Conn.: Praeger, 1999.

Oshinsky, David M. *"Worse Than Slavery": Parchman Farm and the Ordeal of Jim Crow Justice.* New York: Free Press, 1996.

Pember, Don R. *Mass Media Law.* New York: McGraw-Hill, 2000.

Phillips, Robert Anthony. "No Gender Equality on Death Row." http://www.APBnews.com.cjsystem/findingjustice/2000/02/26/women0226_01.html.

Powe, Lucas A., Jr. *The Warren Court and American Politics.* Cambridge: Harvard University Press, Belknap Press, 2000.

Prejean, Helen. *Dead Man Walking.* New York: Vintage, 1994.

Putnam, Robert D. *Bowling Alone.* New York: Simon and Schuster, 2000.

Rise, Eric W. *The Martinsville Seven: Race, Rape, and Capital Punishment.* Charlottesville: University Press of Virginia, 1995.

Rosenfeld, Richard. *American Aurora.* New York: St. Martin's Press, 1997.

Sack, Steven. "Publicized Executions and Homicide, 1950–1980." *American Sociological Review* 52 (August 1987): 532–40.

Schiller, Dan. *Objectivity and the News.* Philadelphia: University of Pennsylvania Press, 1981.

Sheleff, Leon S. *Ultimate Penalties: Capital Punishment, Life Imprisonment, Physical Torture.* Columbus: Ohio State University Press, 1987.

Shipman, Marlin. "Ethical Guidelines for Televising or Photographing Executions." *Journal of Mass Media Ethics* 10:2 (1995): 95–108.

———. "Forgotten Men and Media Celebrities." *Arkansas Review* 31 (August 2000): 110–24.

———. "'Killing Me Softly?' The Newspaper Press and the Reporting on the Search for a More Humane Execution Technology." *American Journalism* 13 (spring 1996): 176–205.

Siebert, Fred S., Theodore Peterson, and Wilbur Schramm. *Four Theories of the Press.* Urbana: University of Illinois Press, 1956.

Smith, Donald L. *Zechariah Chafee, Jr.: Defender of Liberty and Law.* Cambridge: Harvard University Press, 1986.

Smith, Gene. "In Windsor Prison." *American Heritage* 47 (May–June 1996): 100–109.

Smolla, Rodney. *Free Speech in an Open Society.* New York: Alfred A. Knopf, 1992.

Stevens, John D. *Sensationalism and the New York Press.* New York: Columbia University Press, 1991.

Surette, Ray. "Media Trials." *Journal of Criminal Justice* 17 (1989): 293–308.

Trombley, Stephen. *The Execution Protocol.* New York: Crown, 1992.

Tuchman, Gaye. *Making News.* New York: Free Press, 1978.

Weisberg, Jacob. "This Is Your Death." *New Republic* 205 (1 July 1991): 23–27.

Weisberger, Bernard A. *America Afire: Jefferson, Adams, and the Revolutionary Election of 1800.* New York: William Morrow, 2000.

Wicker, Tom. *Tragic Failure: Racial Integration in America.* New York: William Morrow, 1996.

Wright, George C. *Racial Violence in Kentucky, 1865–1940: Lynchings, Mob Rule, and "Legal Lynchings."* Baton Rouge: Louisiana State University Press, 1990.

Zimring, Franklin E., and Hawkins, Gordon. *Capital Punishment and the American Agenda.* Cambridge: Cambridge University Press, 1986.

Index

ish" attributes of, 9–10, 96–97, 125; grandmother label for, 7, 56, 57–58, 70, 201, 231, 239, 295–97; inaccurate newspaper reports on, 80, 274; labeling of women defendants generally, 6–8, 95, 111, 116, 171; lesbians as, 183–89; media trials and verbatim reports on, 16, 94n17, 118–20, 133–46; mob connections of, 195, 230–32; prejudicial press complaints concerning, 11–12; sensational stories of, as dramas, 13–16, 90, 128, 133–46, 133–34n1, 134n3, 232–33, 245–46; slave women as, 20–21, 149–54, 235n32; society's responsibility for, 19, 30, 160, 162, 197–98, 305, 306; from southern California, 193–208; statistics on, 1; suicide attempts and threats by, 43, 45, 76, 129, 197, 201, 205, 213, 222, 225, 227, 266, 267, 299–300; as "tough guys," 209–23; "unseemly interest" in, 18–19, 33, 113–14, 130, 221, 251, 260, 265, 275. *See also* Executions of women; Murders; Physical appearance of women criminals; Women prisoners; and specific women

Women prisoners: access to, by press, 11–12, 15, 47–48, 63, 103, 119, 134n4, 269–70, 274–76, 279–80, 308–9; artistic abilities of, 184–85; attempted bribery by, 226; calmness of, 31, 56–58, 69, 76, 80, 131–32, 176, 177, 179, 184–85, 201; and chaplains, 32; children of, in prison with, 138, 138n16; contacts by, with their children, 60, 112, 144–45; cost of incarceration of, 63, 197; eating habits of, 32, 36, 57, 62, 194, 198, 238, 276, 277–79, 302; "girl-

ish" attributes of, 9–10, 32, 96–97, 125; health of, 145, 146, 194–95, 197, 204, 212; and inability to cry, 53, 58, 59; mob connections of, 195; in pleasant surroundings in prison, 57; poetry by, 264; purported life story written by Coos, 80; security for, 197, 277–78; and sex scandals, 266, 268–69; sleeping habits of, 32, 36; social activities of, 9–10, 97, 100, 255–56; suicide attempts by, 45, 129, 197, 201, 205, 222, 266, 267, 299–300; threatening letters to, 205–6; violence by, 31, 195; visits of family to, 4, 12, 31, 60, 69, 124–25, 127, 145, 146, 180, 181, 184, 205, 209, 251–52; visits of lover to, 250–51; and walk of prisoner to execution, 40–41, 58, 131, 180, 194, 221. *See also* Clothing; Emotions of women criminals; Executions of women; Physical appearance of women criminals; Religion; Trials; and specific women

Women's movement. *See* Feminism

Women's suffrage, 227–28

Woodard, James C., 126

Woodville (Miss.) Republican, 153

World War II, 21, 21n45, 81, 82, 169–70, 199, 231, 233

Wright, Dora, 189

Wright, Harry, 77–79

Wright, Lee, 211–12, 214

Wright, Lorenzo, 255

Writ of habeas corpus, 282

Wylie, Andrew, 282

Yates, Andrea, 43n2

Yellow journalism, 228–30, 269. *See also* Sensationalism